T0183354

Lecture Notes in Computer Science　　12843

More information about this subseries at http://www.springer.com/series/7409

Ladjel Bellatreche · Marlon Dumas ·
Panagiotis Karras · Raimundas Matulevičius (Eds.)

Advances in Databases and Information Systems

25th European Conference, ADBIS 2021
Tartu, Estonia, August 24–26, 2021
Proceedings

 Springer

Editors
Ladjel Bellatreche (iD)
LIAS/ISAE-ENSMA
Futuroscope, Chasseneuil Cedex, France

Marlon Dumas (iD)
University of Tartu
Tartu, Estonia

Panagiotis Karras (iD)
Aarhus University
Aarhus, Denmark

Raimundas Matulevičius (iD)
University of Tartu
Tartu, Estonia

ISSN 0302-9743 ISSN 1611-3349 (electronic)
Lecture Notes in Computer Science
ISBN 978-3-030-82471-6 ISBN 978-3-030-82472-3 (eBook)
https://doi.org/10.1007/978-3-030-82472-3

LNCS Sublibrary: SL3 – Information Systems and Applications, incl. Internet/Web, and HCI

This Springer imprint is published by the registered company Springer Nature Switzerland AG
The registered company address is: Gewerbestrasse 11, 6330 Cham, Switzerland

Preface

This volume contains a selection of the papers presented at the 25th European Conference on Advances in Databases and Information Systems (ADBIS 2021), held during August 24–26, 2021, at Tartu, Estonia.

The ADBIS series of conferences aims at providing a forum for the presentation and dissemination of research on database and information systems, the development of advanced data storage and processing technologies, and designing data-enabled systems/software/applications. ADBIS 2021 in Tartu continues after St. Petersburg (1997), Poznań (1998), Maribor (1999), Prague (2000), Vilnius (2001), Bratislava (2002), Dresden (2003), Budapest (2004), Tallinn (2005), Thessaloniki (2006), Varna (20007), Pori (2008), Riga (2009), Novi Sad (2010), Vienna (2011), Poznań (2012), Genoa (2013), Ohrid (2014), Poitiers (2015), Prague (2016), Nicosia (2017), Budapest (2018), Bled (2019), and Lyon (2020). This edition has been totally managed during the COVID-19 pandemic.

The program of ADBIS 2021 includes keynotes, research papers, thematic workshops, and a doctoral consortium. The conference attracted 70 paper submissions from 261 authors in 39 countries from all continents. After rigorous reviewing by the Program Committee (73 reviewers from 28 countries), the 18 papers included in this LNCS proceedings volume were accepted as full contributions, making an acceptance rate of 26%.

Furthermore, the Program Committee selected 8 more papers as short contributions and 21 papers from the five workshops and doctoral consortium which are published in a companion volume entitled New Trends in Databases and Information Systems in Springer's Communications in Computer and Information Science (CCIS) series. All papers were evaluated by at least three reviewers and some by four reviewers. The selected papers span a wide spectrum of topics in databases and related technologies, tackling challenging problems and presenting inventive and efficient solutions. In this volume, these papers are organized in seven sections: (1) High-dimensional Data and Data Streams, (2) Social Media and Text Mining, (3) Advanced Query Processing, (4) Patterns and Events, (5) Data Integration, (6) Complex Data, and (7) Database Internals and Processes.

For this edition of ADBIS 2021, we had three keynote talks by experts from three continents: America, Asia, and Europe. The first keynote was given by Divesh Srivastava, Head of Database Research at AT&T, on *"Towards High-Quality Big Data: Lessons from FIT"*. The second one by Sanjay Chawla, Research Director of the Qatar Computing Research Institute (QCRI) Data Analytics department, on *"A perspective on prescriptive and reinforcement learning"*. The third keynote by Dirk Draheim, Head of the Information Systems Group at Tallinn University of Technology, Estonia, addressed *"Data exchange for Digital Government: Where are we heading?"*.

ADBIS 2021 strived to create conditions for more experienced researchers to share their knowledge and expertise with young researchers. In addition, the following five workshops and the doctoral consortium associated with ADBIS were co-allocated with the main conference:

- Intelligent Data - from data to knowledge (DOING 2021), organized by Mírian Halfeld Ferrari (Université d'Orléans, France) and Carmem H. Hara (Universidade Federal do Paraná, Curitiba, Brazil).
- Data-Driven Process Discovery and Analysis (SIMPDA 2021), organized by Paolo Ceravolo (Università degli Studi di Milano, Italy), Maurice van Keulen (University of Twente, The Netherlands), and Maria Teresa Gomez Lopez (University of Seville, Spain),
- Modern Approaches in Data Engineering and Information System Design (MADEISD 2021), organized by Ivan Luković (University of Novi Sad, Serbia), Slavica Kordić (University of Novi Sad, Serbia), and Sonja Ristić (University of Novi Sad, Serbia).
- Advances in Data Systems Management, Engineering, and Analytics (MegaData 2021), organized by Yaser Jararweh (Duquesne University, USA), Tomás F. Pena (University of Santiago de Compostela, Spain) and Feras M. Awaysheh (University of Tartu, Estonia).
- Computational Aspects of Network Science (CAoNS 2021), organized by Dimitrios Katsaros (University of Thessaly, Greece) and Yannis Manolopoulos (Open University of Cyprus and Aristotle University of Thessaloniki, Greece).
- Doctoral Consortium (DC), co-chaired by Mirjana Ivanović (University of Novi Sad, Serbia) and Olaf Hartig (Linköping University, Sweden).

Each workshop and the DC has its own international Program Committee. The accepted papers were published by Springer in CCIS.

The best papers from the main conference and workshops were invited for submission to special issues of the following journals: Information Systems (Elsevier), Information Systems Frontiers (Springer), and Computer Science and Information Systems (ComSIS Consortium).

We would like to express our gratitude to every individual who contributed to the success of ADBIS 2021. First, we thank all authors for submitting their research papers to the conference. We are also indebted to the members of the community who offered their precious time and expertise in performing various roles ranging from organizing to reviewing - their efforts, energy, and degree of professionalism deserve the highest commendations. Special thanks to the Program Committee members and the external reviewers for evaluating papers submitted to ADBIS 2021, ensuring the quality of the scientific program, despite the COVID-19 pandemic. A special thanks to our keynote speakers who honored us with their exciting talks at ADBIS 2021. Thanks also to all the colleagues, secretaries, and engineers involved in the conference organization, as well as the workshop organizers. Special thanks are due to the members of the Steering Committee, in particular, its chair, Yannis Manolopoulos, for all their help and guidance. A particular thank you to the University of Tartu's Institute of Computer Science for hosting and supporting the conference despite the uncertainties created by the ongoing pandemic.

Finally, we thank Springer for publishing the proceedings containing invited and research papers in the LNCS series. The Program Committee work relied on Easy-Chair, and we thank its development team for creating and maintaining it; it offered a great support throughout the different phases of the reviewing process.

Last but not least, we thank the participants of ADBIS 2021 for sharing their work and presenting their achievements, thus providing a lively, fruitful and constructive forum, and giving us the pleasure of knowing that our work was purposeful.

June 2021

Ladjel Bellatreche
Marlon Dumas
Panagiotis Karras
Raimundas Matulevičius

Organization

General Chairs

Marlon Dumas   University of Tartu, Estonia
Raimundas Matulevičius   University of Tartu, Estonia

Program Committee Co-chairs

Ladjel Bellatreche   ISAE-ENSMA Poitiers, France
Panagiotis Karras   Aarhus University, Denmark

Workshop Co-chairs

Ahmed Awad   University of Tartu, Estonia
Matthias Weidlich   Humboldt University of Berlin, Germany

Doctoral Consortium Co-chairs

Mirjana Ivanović   University of Novi Sad, Serbia
Olaf Hartig   Linköping University, Sweden

Webmaster

Mubashar Iqbal   University of Tartu, Estonia

Proceedings Technical Editor

Abasi-Amefon Obot Affia   University of Tartu, Estonia

Technical Arrangements

Orlenys Lopez-Pintado   University of Tartu, Estonia

Financial and Local Arrangements

Anneli Vainumae   University of Tartu, Estonia

Steering Committee

Yannis Manolopoulos   Open University of Cyprus, Cyprus
(Chair)
Ladjel Bellatreche   ISAE-ENSMA Poitiers, France

Maria Bielikova	Kempelen Institute of Intelligent Technologies, Slovakia
Barbara Catania	University of Genoa, Italy
Jérôme Darmont	University of Lyon 2, France
Johann Eder	Alpen Adria Universität Klagenfurt, Austria
Tomáš Horváth	Eötvös Loránd University, Hungary
Mirjana Ivanović	University of Novi Sad, Serbia
Marite Kirikova	Riga Technical University, Latvia
Rainer Manthey	University of Bonn, Germany
Manuk Manukyan	Yerevan State University, Armenia
Tadeusz Morzy	Poznan University of Technology, Poland
Kjetil Nørvåg	Norwegian University of Science and Technology, Norway
Boris Novikov	National Research University Higher School of Economics, Saint Petersburg, Russia
George Papadopoulos	University of Cyprus, Cyprus
Jaroslav Pokorny	Charles University in Prague, Czech Republic
Bernhard Thalheim	Christian Albrechts University, Kiel, Germany
Goce Trajcevski	Iowa State University, USA
Valentino Vranić	Slovak University of Technology in Bratislava, Slovakia
Tatjana Welzer	University of Maribor, Slovenia
Robert Wrembel	Poznan University of Technology, Poland
Ester Zumpano	University of Calabria, Italy

Program Committee

Alberto Abello	Universitat Politècnica de Catalunya, Barcelona, Spain
Reza Akbarinia	Inria, France
Bernd Amann	Sorbonne Université, Paris, France
Hassan Badir	ENSA Tanger, Morocco
Amin Beheshti	Macquarie University, Australia
Andreas Behrend	Technical University of Cologne, Germany
Sadok Ben Yahia	Tallinn University of Technology, Estonia
Soumia Benkrid	ESI Algiers, Algeria
Djamal Benslimane	University of Lyon 1, France
Fadila Bentayeb	University of Lyon 2, France
Miklos Biro	Software Competence Center Hagenberg, Austria
Kamel Boukhafa	USTHB, Algeria
Barbara Catania	University of Genoa, Italy
Tania Cerquitelli	Politecnico di Torino, Italy
Richard Chbeir	University of Pau and Pays de l'Adour, France
Isabelle Comyn-Wattiau	ESSEC Business School, France
Ajantha Dahanayake	Lappeenranta University of Technology, Finland
Jérôme Darmont	University of Lyon 2, France
Christos Doulkeridis	University of Piraeus, Greece

Cedric Du Mouza	CNAM, France
Markus Endres	University of Passau, Germany
Philippe Fournier-Viger	Harbin Institute of Technology, Shenzhen, China
Johann Gamper	Free University of Bozen-Bolzano, Italy
Gabriel Ghinita	University of Massachusetts at Boston, USA
Olga Gkountouna	George Mason University, USA
Giancarlo Guizzardi	Free University of Bozen-Bolzano, Italy, and University of Twente, The Netherlands
Hele-Mai Haav	Tallinn University of Technology, Estonia
Dirk Habich	TU Dresden, Germany
Mirian Halfeld-Ferrari	Université d'Orléans, France
Tomáš Horváth	Eötvös Loránd University, Hungary
Mirjana Ivanović	University of Novi Sad, Serbia
Stefan Jablonski	University of Bayreuth, Germany
Stéphane Jean	Poitiers University, France
Zoubida Kedad	University of Versailles, France
Marite Kirikova	Riga Technical University, Latvia
Attila Kiss	Eötvös Loránd University, Hungary
Sergio Lifschitz	Pontifícia Universidade Católica do Rio de Janeiro, Brazil
Sebastian Link	The University of Auckland, New Zealand
Ivan Luković	University of Novi Sad, Serbia
Zakaria Maamar	Zayed University, Dubai, United Arab Emirates
Wojciech Macyna	Wroclaw University of Technology, Poland
Federica Mandreoli	University of Modena, Italy
Yannis Manolopoulos	Open University of Cyprus, Cyprus
Patrick Marcel	Université de Tours, France
Pascal Molli	University of Nantes, France
Anirban Mondal	Ashaka University, India
Tadeusz Morzy	Poznan University of Technology, Poland
Kjetil Nørvåg	Norwegian University of Science and Technology, Norway
Boris Novikov	National Research University Higher School of Economics, Saint Petersburg, Russia
Andreas Oberweis	Karlsruhe Institute of Technology, Germany
Carlos Ordonez	University of Houston, USA
Oscar Pastor	Universidad Politécnica de Valencia, Spain
Jaroslav Pokorný	Charles University in Prague, Czech Republic
Franck Ravat	IRIT and Université Toulouse 1 Capitole, France
Stefano Rizzi	University of Bologna, Italy
Oscar Romero	Universitat Politècnica de Catalunya, Spain
Carmem S. Hara	Universidade Federal do Paraná, Curitiba, Brazil
Gunter Saake	University of Magdeburg, Germany
Kai-Uwe Sattler	Technical University Ilmenau, Germany
Milos Savic	University of Novi Sad, Serbia
Kostas Stefanidis	Tampere University, Finland

Sergey Stupnikov   Russian Academy of Sciences, Russia
Olivier Teste   Université de Toulouse, France
Maik Thiele   TU Dresden, Germany
Goce Trajcevski   Iowa State University, USA
Anton Tsitsulin   University of Bonn, Germany
Panos Vassiliadis   University of Ioannina, Greece
Thanasis Vergoulis   "Athena" Research Center, Greece
Tatjana Welzer   University of Maribor, Slovenia
Marek Wojciechowski   Poznan University of Technology, Poland
Robert Wrembel   Poznan University of Technology, Poland
Vladimir Zadorozhny   University of Pittsburgh, USA

Additional Reviewers

Petar Jovanovic   Universitat Politècnica de Catalunya, Spain
Elio Mansour   University of Pau and Pays de l'Adour, France
Sergi Nadal   Universitat Politècnica de Catalunya, Spain
Rediana Koçi   Universitat Politècnica de Catalunya, Spain
Nadia Yacoubi   Ayadi Institut Supérieur de Gestion de Tunis, Tunisia
Serafeim Chatzopoulos   "Athena" Research Center, Greece

ADBIS'2021 Keynotes

Towards High-Quality Big Data: A Focus on Time

Divesh Srivastava

AT&T Chief Data Office, USA

Abstract. Data are being generated, collected, and analyzed today at an unprecedented scale, and data-driven decision making is sweeping through all aspects of society. As the use of big data has grown, so too have concerns that poor-quality data, prevalent in large data sets, can have serious adverse consequences on data-driven decision making. Responsible data science thus requires a recognition of the importance of veracity, the fourth "V" of big data. In this talk, we first present a vision of high-quality big data, with a focus on time, and highlight the substantial challenges that the first three V's, volume, velocity, and variety, bring to dealing with veracity in long data. We present the FIT Family of adaptive, data-driven statistical tools that we have designed, developed, and deployed at AT&T for continuous data quality monitoring of a large and diverse collection of continuously evolving data. These tools monitor data movement to discover missing, partial, duplicated, and delayed data; identify changes in the content of spatiotemporal streams; and pinpoint anomaly hotspots based on persistence, pervasiveness, and priority. We conclude with lessons relevant to long data quality that are cause for optimism.

A Perspective on Prescriptive Learning

Sanjay Chawla

Qatar Computing Research Institute, Hamad Bin Khalifa University
schawla@hbku.edu.qa

Abstract. We provide a brief overview of the emerging area of prescriptive learning which combines supervised learning with optimization. Prescriptive Learning is most active in operations research but is now finding applications in diverse areas ranging from database optimization to chip design. Reinforcement Learning (RL) is the most developed form of PL for sequential and stochastic optimization problems. We will give an example of how RL can be applied to a traditional and well-studied join ordering problem for query optimization.

Data Exchange for Digital Government: Where Are We Heading?

Dirk Draheim

Information Systems Group, Tallinn University of Technology, Estonia
dirk.draheim@taltech.ee

Abstract. In all countries, we currently see major efforts in digital transformation initiatives. The United Nations e-Government Survey 2020 puts a strong emphasis on data, which makes sense, given the huge progress in big data and data science in the last decade. The UN survey distinguishes between data-informed, data-driven and data-centric approaches to digital government. Actually, Gartner defined the notion of data-centric government already in 2014. Still, today, we are far away from such data-centric government. How comes? How to shape the next generation of e-government technologies? In service of such and similar questions, we walk through a series of important data exchange technologies: the Estonian data exchange layer X-Road, the European federated data infrastructure GAIA-X, the European Blockchain Services Infrastructure (EBSI), and the IoT data management solution FIWARE. Finally, based on the notion of data governance architecture, we give an overview of our proposed digital government architecture framework that is intended to help in large-scale digital government design efforts.

Contents

Indexes, Queries and Constraints

High-Dimensional Data and Data Streams

Data Integration

Keynotes Talks

A Perspective on Prescriptive Learning ADBIS'2021 Keynote

Sanjay Chawla[✉]

Qatar Computing Research Institute, Hamad Bin Khalifa University,
Doha, Qatar
schawla@hbku.edu.qa

Abstract. We provide a brief overview of the emerging area of prescriptive learning which combines supervised learning with optimization. Prescriptive Learning is most active in operations research but is now finding applications in diverse areas ranging from database optimization to chip design. Reinforcement Learning (RL) is the most developed form of PL for sequential and stochastic optimization problems. We will give an example of how RL can be applied to a traditional and well-studied join ordering problem for query optimization.

Keywords: Prescriptive learning · Reinforcement learning · Database applications

1 Introduction

Data Science is an umbrella term to capture an array of methodologies centered around the concept of *data* as a first-class citizen [9]. This is in contrast to the traditional method of inquiry where data brackets the scientific process by first capturing observations of an underlying phenomenon and then as output of experiments to validate a theory proposed to explain the phenomenon. If $\mathbf{D}$ is data and $\mathbf{M}$ is a model, in the Sciences, the arrow of knowledge is $\mathbf{M} \rightarrow \mathbf{D}$, while in Data Science, the direction is reversed: $\mathbf{D} \rightarrow \mathbf{M}$. Prescriptive Learning (PL) goes beyond inferring a model from data, but uses the model to achieve an optimization objective denoted as $\mathbf{O}$. Thus PL can be codified as $\mathbf{D} \rightarrow \mathbf{M} \rightarrow \mathbf{O}$. To put succinctly:

$$\text{Prescription} = \text{Prediction} + \text{Optimization}$$

2 Prescriptive Learning

Prescriptive Learning (PL) thrives at the confluence of machine learning and operations research. For example, Bertismas and Kallus [1] show how traditional operation research problems can benefit from adding a prediction component to optimization problems. For example, consider the classical facility location

© Springer Nature Switzerland AG 2021
L. Bellatreche et al. (Eds.): ADBIS 2021, LNCS 12843, pp. 3–6, 2021.
https://doi.org/10.1007/978-3-030-82472-3_1

problem where the objective is to open a minimum number of facilities to service customers. Often the cost of facility is given as an input to the problem. However, if secondary data is available in the vicinity of potential facilities, then a supervised learning framework can be used to learn the facility cost followed by standard optimization. In our own work, we have combined supervised learning with reinforcement learning to optimize decision-making in air-cargo management [6]. However PL and RL are finding applications beyond traditional areas like operations research, robotics and games. Intractable combinatorial optimization problems, include those of interest to the database community are increasingly being looked at from the lens of PL [3].

3   Reinforcement Learning

Reinforcement Learning (RL) is the most well known example of PL and provides a general framework for modeling sequential problems where feedback and delayed rewards are an integral part of the problem formulation [8]. In a RL setting, an agent observes a state s of the environment and based on that takes an action a which results in a reward r and transitions to a new state s'. The interaction goes on until a terminal state is reached. The aim of the agent is to learn a policy π which is mapping from state to action which maximizes the expected cumulative reward over the space of policies. RL has several special cases which are studied independently. For example, when the system is stateless, it is referred to as a multi-armed bandit problem. When distinct states exists but the system does not transition to a new state after taking an action, it is referred to as a contextual bandit problem [2]. A famous and multi-billion dollar worth application of contextual bandit problem is in personalized online advertising. Here the state is a user (with features), the action is taken by the online system to show a personalized advertisement, the immediate reward is whether the user clicks or not.

4   Policy Gradient Optimization

Algorithms for RL come in three flavors: value-based, policy gradient and a combination known as actor-critic methods. We briefly describe a basic version of the policy gradient method as it is finding widespread usage outside traditional RL applications. In particular, policy gradient method can use the gradient descent approach for stochastic optimization problems even for a non-differentiable objective function by shifting the gradients to parameterized policies. This is known as the REINFORCE method.

Let $\mathcal{S}$ be a vectorized state space, $\mathcal{A}$ a discrete action space and $\pi_\theta : \mathcal{S} \to \mathcal{A}$ a parameterized policy distribution such that for a fixed $s, \sum_a \pi(a|s) = 1$. Let $\bar{s} = ((s_1, a_1), \ldots, (s_T, a_T))$ be a sequence of state action pairs known as the episode. Each pair (s_i, a_i) is associated with a reward r_i. Let $R(\bar{s}) = \sum \gamma^t r_t$ be the cumulative reward function. Note that we do not place any smoothness restrictions on R but expect it to be bounded. Then the RL problem can be abstracted as [7]:

$$\arg \max_{\theta} \; \mathbb{E}_{\bar{s} \sim P_{\theta}} [R(\bar{s})]$$

Note this is a very different problem from supervised learning and we are optimizing the space of policies which generates the sequential data. Thus data is not a sample from a fixed (but unknown) distribution as in supervised or unsupervised learning. The key insight that drives policy gradient is that we can express the gradient of the expectation in terms of the expectation over the gradient of the logarithm of the policy distribution. Thus, if we define $\hat{\nabla}(\bar{s}) = R(\bar{s}) \sum_t \log(\pi(a_t|s_t))$ then $\mathbb{E}_{\bar{s} \sim P_{\theta}} \hat{\nabla}(\bar{s}) = \nabla \mathbb{E}_{\bar{s} \sim P_{\theta}}[R(\bar{s})]$. Notice that gradients are not attached to $R(\bar{s})$ providing an opportunity to use an arbitrary function. However, the approach is not without limitations as it essentially becomes a zeroth-order optimization problem [5].

5   Join Ordering for Query Optimization

Given a collection of atomic relations $r_1, r_2, \ldots, r_n$ that need to be joined for a query, the join ordering problem is to recursively select pairs of atomic or intermediate relations that are most efficient from a query execution perspective. Marcus and Papaemmanouil apply the policy gradient method for obtaining an efficient ordering [3] that was shown to be superior than the default solution in PostgreSQL. In Table 1 we redefine the query optimization problem in an RL framework. Notice how the action space $\mathcal{A}_i$ is changing at each step and that there is no intermediate reward. Finally, the objective reward is just the reciprocal query cost and does not take any functional form.

Table 1. Elements of RL mapped for query optimization

RL	Query optimization
Episode	Query
Initial state (s_1)	Relations ($r_1, \ldots, r_n$)
Action space $\mathcal{A}_i$	$[1, |s_i|] \times [1, |s_i|]$
Action (x, y)	join the xth and yth element of s_i
s_{i+1}	$(s_i - \{s_i[x], s_i[y]\}) \cup (s_i[x] \bowtie s_i[y])$
Intermediate reward	Zero
Final reward	Reciprocal of join cost

6   Conclusion

Prescriptive Learning embeds the strengths of machine learning within optimization frameworks by combining elements of prediction with combinatorial or stochastic problems. PL is often contrasted with traditional supervised and unsupervised learning which are considered or reactive forms of inference. PL is a more active form of inference as it is driven by an optimization task. Reinforcement Learning which is the most prominent form of PL for sequential optimization problems is now finding applications beyond robotics, game playing, neuroscience into non-traditional applications like database query optimization and chip design [4].

References

1. Bertsimas, D., Kallus, N.: From predictive to prescriptive analytics. Manag. Sci. **66**(3), 1025–1044 (2020)
2. Li, L., Chu, W., Langford, J., Schapire, R.E.: A contextual-bandit approach to personalized news article recommendation. CoRR abs/1003.0146 (2010). http://arxiv.org/abs/1003.0146
3. Marcus, R., Papaemmanouil, O.: Deep reinforcement learning for join order enumeration. In: Proceedings of the First International Workshop on Exploiting Artificial Intelligence Techniques for Data Management, pp. 1–4 (2018)
4. Mirhoseini, A., et al.: A graph placement methodology for fast chip design. Nature **594**, 207–212 (2021)
5. Recht, B.: A tour of reinforcement learning: The view from continuous control (2018)
6. Rizzo, S.G., et al.: Prescriptive learning for air-cargo revenue management. In: 2020 IEEE International Conference on Data Mining (ICDM), pp. 462–471. IEEE (2020)
7. Shalev-Shwartz, S., Shammah, S., Shashua, A.: Safe, multi-agent, reinforcement learning for autonomous driving. CoRR abs/1610.03295 (2016). http://arxiv.org/abs/1610.03295
8. Sutton, R.S., Barto, A.G.: Reinforcement Learning: An Introduction. The MIT Press, second edn. (2018)
9. Zaki, M.J., Meira, W., Jr.: Data Mining and Machine Learning: Fundamental Concepts and Algorithms. Cambridge University Press, Cambridge (2020)

Data Exchange for Digital Government: Where Are We Heading? ADBIS2021 Keynote

Dirk Draheim[✉]

Information Systems Group, Tallinn University of Technology, Tallinn, Estonia
dirk.draheim@taltech.ee

Abstract. In all countries, we currently see major efforts in digital transformation initiatives. The United Nations e-Government Survey 2020 puts a strong emphasis on data, which makes sense, given the huge progress in big data and data science in the last decade. The UN survey distinguishes between data-informed, data-driven and data-centric approaches to digital government. Actually, Gartner defined the notion of data-centric government already in 2014. Still, today, we are far away from such data-centric government. How comes? How to shape the next generation of e-government technologies? In service of such and similar questions, we walk through a series of important data exchange technologies: the Estonian data exchange layer X-Road, the European federated data infrastructure GAIA-X, the European Blockchain Services Infrastructure (EBSI), and the IoT data management solution FIWARE. Finally, based on the notion of data governance architecture, we give an overview of our proposed digital government architecture framework that is intended to help in large-scale digital government design efforts.

Keywords: Digital government · e-government · Data governance · Consent management · Data exchange layers · X-Road · GAIA-X · European Blockchain Services Infrastructure · EBSI · FIWARE

In many countries, we currently see major investments into digital government. The so-called "digital transformation" of society is perceived as the key enabler for increasing wealth and well-being by many from politics, media and citizens alike. When it comes to concrete digital transformation initiatives, these are often simply about digital government implementations.

Data are a core asset of today's organizations supporting business processes [3, 8], decision making and knowledge management [20]. In digital government, data exchange between authorities makes administrative processes more efficient and effective. However, there is still a huge unused potential in exploiting data for decision making and leveraging innovations in the public sector. The United Nations e-Government Survey 2020 [26] puts a strong emphasis on data, which makes sense, given the immense progress in big data and data science in the last decade. The survey [26], p. 150, characterizes five different approaches to utilization of data by the several countries:

© Springer Nature Switzerland AG 2021
L. Bellatreche et al. (Eds.): ADBIS 2021, LNCS 12843, pp. 7–12, 2021.
https://doi.org/10.1007/978-3-030-82472-3_2

(i) *ICT-driven*: "Where Governments are highly influenced by the use of new and existing information and communications technology (ICT)" [26].

(ii) *Data-informed*: "Where Governments are guided by data; data play an inferential role in policymaking, [...]" [26].

(iii) *Data-driven*: "Where Governments use analytics and algorithms in decision-making [...]" [26].

(iv) *Evidence-based*: "Where policy approaches reflect the practical application of the findings of the best and most current research available [...]" [26].

(v) *Data-centric*: "Where Governments place data and data science at the core of public administration; data are seen as a key asset and central to government functions and are leveraged for the provision, evaluation and modification of people-centric services [7]" [26].

The chosen sequence of (i)–(v) is intended to express a ranking in regards of "how government data are increasingly leveraged for effective governance." [26], i.e., the data-centric approach can be considered as the ideal to be reached. Still, today, we are far away from such data-centric government. How comes? How to shape the next generation of e-government technologies? In this talk, we address such and similar questions. We start with walking through a series of important *established* and/or *emerging* data exchange technologies that are particularly relevant to digital government (actually and/or potentially):

– the Estonian data exchange layer X-Road: X-Road [1,2,16,17,21,28] is the backbone of what we call e-Estonia[1]. There are almost 3000 services on X-Road (June 2021) with a traffic of 1,57 billion answered queries in 2021[2]. The UN e-Government Survey 2018 uses X-Road to explain the concept of what they call "Government as an API" [25], p. 184. Dozens of countries have used X-Road to implement digital government data exchange[3]. We briefly answer some frequently asked questions about X-Road in Sect. 1.

– the European federated data infrastructure GAIA-X: In September 2020, GAIA-X [12] has been founded as a non-profit organization by 22 companies from Germany and France under the aegis of the German Federal Ministry for Economic Affairs and Energy (BMWi). GAIA-X aims "to create the next generation of data infrastructure for Europe, its states, its companies and its citizens."[4].

– the European Blockchain Services Infrastructure (EBSI): "[...] in 2018, 21 EU member states and Norway signed a declaration creating the European Blockchain Partnership (EBP) with the ambition to provide digital public services matching the required level of digital security and maturity of today's society." [15], p. 183.

– the IoT data management solution FIWARE: FIWARE is a European initiative of the Future Internet Public Private Partnership (FI-PPP)[5]. FIWARE

---

[1] https://e-estonia.com/.

[2] https://www.x-tee.ee/factsheets/EE/.

[3] https://x-road.global/xroad-world-map.

[4] https://www.data-infrastructure.eu/.

[5] https://www.fi-ppp.eu/.

has evolved into a community of more than 1000 startups and 150 cities (June 2021) with the mission "to build an open sustainable ecosystem around public, royalty-free and implementation-driven software platform standards that will ease the development of new Smart Applications in multiple sectors"[6]

Finally, we give an overview of a digital government architecture framework that we proposed in [10] with the intention to help in large-scale digital government design efforts. We give a brief overview of the key notions of the framework in Sect. 2.

1　The Data Exchange Platform X-Road

In 2020, X-Road[7] is mentioned in the UN e-Government Survey as follows [26]: "The data exchange platform in Estonia (X-Road) is administrated centrally to interconnect government information systems and databases and allow government authorities and citizens to securely send and receive information over the Internet within the limits of their authority." X-Road can be described best as a *peer-to-peer* data exchange system; X-Road teams together the following technological and organizational assets:

- a PKI (public key infrastructure),
- sophisticated software components for secure data exchange,
- a nomenclature of metadata items associated with each message,
- regulated organizational measures (Estonian Regulation no. 105).

What Is the X-Road Software About? The key software component of X-Road is the *security server*. An instance of the security server is installed by each X-Road member (authority or organization participating in X-Road). The security servers encrypt and decrypt messages, check identities of other servers, manage/enforce access rights and maintain message logs. Each X-Road member has to register its e-services in a centrally administered directory. Each member grants access to its e-services itself via its own instance of the security server, i.e., access right management remains with the member.

Is X-Road a Decentralized Platform? The technical basis of X-Road is decentralized. No middleware such as ESB (enterprise service bus) technology is involved. No man-in-the-middle is involved either, as we know it from the value-add networks (VAN) of the EDI (electronic data exchange) era. Messages are sent directly between members; however, streamlined by the joint X-Road protocol. This does not mean, that there is no *centralization* at all. First, there is a state-managed central organization plus a certification authority (CA) for establishing the PKI [24]. Then, each X-Road member must publish its information systems in central registry. Via this registration, different state authorities can monitor essential data principles: the *minimality principle, data quality* principles and

---

[6] https://www.fiware.org/about-us/.
[7] https://x-road.global/.

the *once-only* principle. Furthermore, X-Road does not prevent *centralized services*, which can be implemented on top of X-Road. The Estonian *Document Exchange Center* (DEC) [9,22], was a perfect example for this. Another example for a centralized service is the concept of X-Rooms, which is described in the architectural vision document of Estonia's Government CIO [27]. An X-Room is a publish-subscribe service, a standard pattern in message-oriented middleware.

Is X-Road a Blockchain Technology? Although X-Road has been often perceived as a blockchain technolgy by the media, it is not. The X-Road security server exploits cryptographic data structures and algorithms that are also used by blockchain technology (such as Merkle trees for implementing audit logs), but this alone does not make X-Road a blockchain [5,19]. X-Road makes no efforts to achieve consensus, except for authentication. What is true, however, is that many of the Estonian state registries are secured by a so-called KSI blockchain (keyless signature infrastructure) [4,6].

Is X-Road a Federated Platform? In 2014, Finland and Estonia decided to start joint efforts to realize cross-border, federated digital government services [14] on the basis of X-Road. The Nordic Institute for Interoperability Solutions NIIS[8] was founded as a joint agency of Finland and Estonia and was made the official product owner of the X-Road code base.

2   A Digital Government Archtitecture Framework

A key to successful architecture of digital government ecosystems is in understanding data governance (which aims at data principles: data protection [13], data quality [11,23], and the once-only-principle [18]). In the context of digital government, data governance is an ultra large-scale, cross-organizational challenge. In [10], we have elaborated a digital government architecture framework based on the following line of hypotheses:

- The form of state's institutions follows the state's functions. The entirety of the state's institutions (i.e., their shape, their interplay) makes the state's *institutional architecture*. The institutional architecture changes slowly: substantial changes, i.e., those that are the result of societal change, usually occur non-disruptively and take significant time.
- The state's institutional architecture determines the state's *data governance architecture*. The data governance architecture links data assets with accountable organizations along two dimensions: the *interoperability* dimension and the *provisioning* dimension.
- The data governance architecture limits the design space of the *digital government solution architecture*, which consists of all *digital administrative processes* and delivered *e-services*.The digital government solution architecture can show small, ad-hoc and fast changes.

---

[8] https://www.niis.org/.

– Changes in the institutional architecture are so severe, that they can trigger immediate changes in the digital government solution architecture, whereas changes in the digital government solution architecture can only have a long-term influence on changes in the institutional architecture (if at all).

We say that the data governance architecture and the digital government solutions architecture together form the *digital government architecture*. The data governance architecture forms the backbone, that deals with the necessary fulfilment of data governance; whereas the solutions architecture addresses all kinds of quality aspects of the offered solutions, i.e., usefulness, adherence to good service-design principles, maturity of processes etc.

References

1. Ansper, A.: E-State From a Data Security Perspective. Tallinn University of Technology, Faculty of Systems Engineering, Department of Automation, Tallinn (2001)
2. Ansper, A., Buldas, A., Freudenthal, M., Willemson, J.: High-performance qualified digital signatures for X-road. In: Riis Nielson, H., Gollmann, D. (eds.) NordSec 2013. LNCS, vol. 8208, pp. 123–138. Springer, Heidelberg (2013). https://doi.org/10.1007/978-3-642-41488-6_9
3. Atkinson, C., Draheim, D., Geist, V.: Typed business process specification. In: Proceedings of EDOC 2010 - the 14th IEEE International Enterprise Computing Conference, pp. 69–78. IEEE Press (2010)
4. Riis Nielson, H., Gollmann, D. (eds.): NordSec 2013. LNCS, vol. 8208. Springer, Heidelberg (2013). https://doi.org/10.1007/978-3-642-41488-6
5. Dang, T.K., Küng, J., Takizawa, M., Chung, T.M. (eds.): FDSE 2020. LNCS, vol. 12466. Springer, Cham (2020). https://doi.org/10.1007/978-3-030-63924-2
6. Buldas, A., Saarepera, M.: Document Verification with Distributed Calendar Infrastructure. US Patent Application Publication No.: US 2013/0276058 A1 (2013)
7. Di Maio, A.: Moving Toward Data-Centric Government. Gartner Group Report G00248186. Gartner (2014)
8. Draheim, D.: Business Process Technology - A Unified View on Business Processes. Workflows and Enterprise Applications. Springer, Berlin Heidelberg (2010)
9. Draheim, D., Koosapoeg, K., Lauk, M., Pappel, I., Pappel, I., Tepandi, J.: The design of the Estonian governmental document exchange classification framework. In: Electronic Government and the Information Systems Perspective, pp. 33–47. Springer (2016)
10. Draheim, D., Krimmer, R., Tammet, T.: Architecture of digital government ecosystems: from ICT-driven to data-centric. Transactions on Large-Scale Data- and Knowledge-Centered System, Special Issue In Memory of Univ. Prof. Dr. Roland Wagner XLVIII, pp. 165–195 (2021)
11. Draheim, D., Nathschläger, C.: A context-oriented synchronization approach. In: Electronic Proceedings of the 2nd International Workshop in Personalized Access, Profile Management, and Context Awareness: Databases (PersDB 2008) in Conjunction with the 34th VLDB Conference, pp. 20–27 (2008)
12. Eggers, G., et al.: GAIA-X: Technical Architecture. Federal Ministry for Economic Affairs and Energy (BMWi) Public Relations Division, Berlin (2020)

13. European Commission: Regulation 2016/679 of the European Parliament and of the Council of 27 April 2016 on the protection of natural persons with regard to the processing of personal data and on the free movement of such data, and repealing Directive 95/46/EC (General Data Protection Regulation). European Commission (2016)
14. Freudenthal, M., Willemson, J.: Challenges of federating national data access infrastructures. In: Farshim, P., Simion, E. (eds.) SecITC 2017. LNCS, vol. 10543, pp. 104–114. Springer, Cham (2017). https://doi.org/10.1007/978-3-319-69284-5_8
15. Giaglis, G., et al.: EU Blockchain Ecosystems Developments. The European Union Blockchain Observatory and Forum (2020)
16. Kalja, A.: The X-Road: a key interoperability component within the state information system. In: Information technology in public administration of Estonia - yearbook 2007, pp. 19–20. Ministry of Economic Affairs and Communications Estonia (2008)
17. Kalja, A.: The first ten years of X-Road. In: Kastehein, K. (ed.) Information technology in public administration of Estonia - yearbook 2011/2012, pp. 78–80. Ministry of Economic Affairs and Communications Estonia (2012)
18. Kalvet, T., Toots, M., Krimmer, R.: Contributing to a digital single market for Europe: barriers and drivers of an EU-wide once-only principle. In: Proceedings of DG.O 2018 - the 19th Annual International Conference on Digital Government Research, pp. 45:1–45:8. ACM (2018)
19. Nakamoto, S.: Bitcoin: A Peer-to-Peer Electronic Cash System (2008). https://bitcoin.org/bitcoin.pdf
20. Nonaka, I., Takeuchi, H.: The Knowledge-Creating Company: How Japanese Companies Create the Dynamics of Innovation. Oxford University Press (1995)
21. Paide, K., Pappel, I., Vainsalu, H., Draheim, D.: On the systematic exploitation of the Estonian data exchange layer X-Road for strengthening public private partnerships. In: Proceedings of ICEGOV 018 - the 11th International Conference on Theory and Practice of Electronic Governance, pp. 34–41. ACM (2018)
22. PricewaterhouseCoopers: Public Services Uniform Document Management - Final Report. PricewaterhouseCoopers (2014)
23. Tepandi, J., et al.: The data quality framework for the Estonian public sector and its evaluation. Trans. Large-Scale Data- Knowl.-Centered Syst. 35, 1–26 (2017)
24. Tsap, V., Pappel, I., Draheim, D.: Key success factors in introducing national e-identification systems. In: Dang, T.K., Wagner, R., Küng, J., Thoai, N., Takizawa, M., Neuhold, E.J. (eds.) FDSE 2017. LNCS, vol. 10646, pp. 455–471. Springer, Cham (2017). https://doi.org/10.1007/978-3-319-70004-5_33
25. UN Department of Economic and Social Affairs: United Nations E-Government Survey 2018 - Gearing e-Government to Support Transformation Towards Sustainable and Resilient Societies. United Nations, New York (2018)
26. UN Department of Economic and Social Affairs: E-Government Survey 2020 - Digital Government in the Decade of Action for Sustainable Development. United Nations, New York (2020)
27. Vaher, K.: Next Generation Digital Government Architecture. Republic of Estonia GCIO Office (2020)
28. Willemson, J., Ansper, A.: A secure and scalable infrastructure for inter-organizational data exchange and eGovernment applications. In: Proceedings of ARES 2008 - The 3rd International Conference on Availability, Reliability and Security 2008, pp. 572–577. IEEE (2008)

Patterns and Events

Maximal Mixed-Drove Co-Occurrence Patterns

Witold Andrzejewski$^{(\boxtimes)}$ and Paweł Boinski$^{(\boxtimes)}$

Poznan University of Technology, Institute of Computing Science,
Piotrowo 2, 60-965 Poznan, Poland
witold.andrzejewski@put.poznan.pl, pawel.boinski@put.poznan.pl

Abstract. Mining of Mixed-Drove Co-occurrence Patterns can be very costly. Widely used, Apriori-based methods consist in finding spatial co-location patterns in each considered timestamp and filtering out patterns that are not time prevalent. Such an approach can be inefficient, especially for datasets that contain co-locations with a high number of elements. To solve this problem we introduce the concept of Maximal Mixed-Drove Co-occurrence Patterns and present new algorithm MAXMDCOP-Miner for finding such patterns. Our experiments performed on synthetic and real world datasets show that MAXDCOP-Miner offers very high performance when discovering patterns both in dense data and for low values of spatial or time prevalence thresholds.

1 Introduction

One of the interesting types of patterns that can be found in spatio-temporal data is called Mixed-Drove Co-Occurrence Pattern (MDCOP) [5]. The idea of MDCOPs is based on the well-known co-location patterns [9]. MDCOP represents a set of spatial feature types (i.e. object types) whose instances are located close to each other in geographic space for a significant fraction of time. For example, MDCOP can represent a predator-prey relationship resulting from predator behavior, i.e. tracking his prey (not necessarily for the whole time and without interruptions). As time component exists in almost every dataset, co-occurrence patterns can provide useful knowledge in many domains, e.g. military - battlefield analysis, ecology/health - monitoring pollution and diseases etc.

Currently available methods for MDCOP discovery are based on iterative expansion of patterns using Apriori strategy known from frequent itemset mining [1]. In such an approach, the search space is traversed in breadth-first manner. In a result, to discover a particular pattern of size k, all of its 2^k subsets must be found in advance. This can be regarded as a main bottleneck in searching for patterns of greater sizes or in huge datasets, especially with fast evolving data. This problem has been considered in the context of standard co-location patterns discovery [15]. To eliminate costly Apriori-like generate and test methods, a concept of maximal spatial co-location has been introduced. In short, a co-location is maximal only if it has no superset co-location. A similar idea can be applied for MDCOP mining.

© Springer Nature Switzerland AG 2021
L. Bellatreche et al. (Eds.): ADBIS 2021, LNCS 12843, pp. 15–29, 2021.
https://doi.org/10.1007/978-3-030-82472-3_3

In this paper, we introduce and define the novel concept of Maximal Mixed-Drove Co-Occurrence Pattern. We propose to move away from Apriori-like strategy for candidate generation towards solutions based on maximal cliques discovery. In the proposed algorithm, we avoid costly computation of co-location pattern participation indices as much as possible by using multiple innovations: finding maximal candidates, estimating candidate time prevalence and caching partial results. We have implemented our new method and performed experiments on synthetic and real world datasets. The results show that we can achieve significant speedups in comparison to the Apriori-like approach.

2   Related Work

MDCOP mining is inspired by the idea of the Co-location Pattern Mining (CPM) introduced two decades ago [9]. CPM is dedicated for datasets where objects are stationary. A co-location pattern is defined as a set of features which instances are frequently located together in space. However, as more and more data is automatically and continuously collected, the time component can play a crucial role in various analysis. A trivial approach to cope with time is to calculate different sets of patterns for subsequent states of the data [2]. Such an approach might omit potentially useful and interesting patterns hidden in data changes between consecutive timestamps. Therefore, a new directions of research emerged to tackle this problem.

One of the very first attempts to incorporate the time component into a co-location pattern [14], focused more on associations among spatially extended objects than on the temporal aspects. The first type of pattern directly related to co-locations, called a co-location episode, was presented in [3]. The authors defined the co-location episode as a sequence of co-location patterns over consecutive time slots sharing the same feature (called a common feature). MDCOPs, which are the main topic of this paper, do not impose such constraints. For MDCOPs, time prevalence means that spatial features are spatially prevalent (i.e. instances are located close to each other) for the required, not necessarily consecutive, number of time moments. Moreover, there is no need to define a common feature. It is worth to mention that one can find other types spatio-temporal patterns inspired by the concept of co-locations, e.g. SPCOZs [8] or STCOPs [7].

MDCOPs can be discovered using a naive approach, i.e. by applying one of the algorithms for CPM to each analyzed time moment followed by computations to detect which co-locations are time-prevalent. Celik et al. [5] proposed non-naive algorithms MDCOP-Miner and FastMDCOP-Miner. Both algorithms discover all size k spatially prevalent patterns and then apply a time-prevalence based filtering to detect MDCOPs. These patterns are used to generate size $k + 1$ candidates for MDCOPs. FastMDCOP-Miner additionally utilizes more advanced filtering to prune candidates that cannot be prevalent. In [13], the authors tried to improve the efficiency of the MDCOP mining by applying a graph based data structure. Unfortunately, some parts of this solution are not explained, making them impossible to implement in a way intended by the authors. As the algorithm is also

Apriori-based and presented results show only a slight improvement in comparison to FastMDCOP-Miner, we will refer to FastMDCOP-Miner as that method is well defined and is the most popular approach to MDCOP mining.

Nonetheless, all Apriori-based methods can suffer from huge number of candidates when searching for long patterns (dense datasets, low thresholds for spatial and time prevalence). Similar problem has been addressed for CPM [10, 12, 15, 16], where researchers utilized the concept of maximal co-locations to reduce the number of computations. In this paper, we adopt the concept of maximal pattern and define a maximal MDCOP. We introduce a non-Apriori based algorithm, to efficiently calculate such patterns in spatio-temporal datasets.

3 Definitions

Let F be a set of *features*. We assume that a total order is defined on the set F. Each feature $f \in F$ has a set of *feature instances* I^f associated with it. We denote a set of all instances as $I = \bigcup_{f \in F} I^f$ and an instance of feature f as i^f. Let K be a set of coordinates. We do not make any assumptions about this set. A spatial dataset is a tuple $S^p = (S, p)$ where $S \subseteq I$ and p is a function $p : S \rightarrow K$ which assigns a coordinate to every feature instance from S.

Let $dist : K \times K \rightarrow \mathbb{R}^+ \cup \{0\}$ be a non-negative and symmetric function which computes a distance between two coordinates. Given *distance threshold* r and spatial dataset S^p we define a *neighborhood* relation $R(S^p, r)$. Any two spatial feature instances in a spatial dataset S^p are in relation $R(S^p, r)$ if the distance between their coordinates is less than or equal to the threshold r. Formally, $R(S^p, r) = \{(i_1, i_2) \in S \times S : dist(p(i_1), p(i_2)) < r\}$. In the subsequent text, we will denote the relation $R(S^p, r)$ as R if the arguments stem from the context.

A subset of a set of features $C \subseteq F$ is called a *spatial co-location pattern* (or *co-location* in short). A *spatial co-location instance* in a spatial dataset S^p is a subset $I^C \subseteq S$ such that $\forall_{i^{f_1}, i^{f_2} \in I^C}(i^{f_1}, i^{f_2}) \in R \wedge \{f : i^f \in I^C\} = C \wedge |I^C| = |C|$. To retrieve only potentially interesting co-location patterns, a spatial prevalence measure called a *participation index* has been proposed in [9]. To define the participation index, a *participation ratio* Pr must be introduced first. Given a spatial dataset S^p, a co-location pattern C, a set of all of its instances $\mathbb{I}^C_{S^p}$ in the spatial dataset and a feature $f \in C$, a participation ratio Pr is defined as $Pr(f, C, S^p) = \frac{|\{i^{f_1} : f_1 = f \wedge i^{f_1} \in I^C \in \mathbb{I}^C_{S^p}\}|}{|\{i^{f_1} : f_1 = f \wedge i^{f_1} \in S\}|}$. Participation index (also called *spatial prevalence* of spatial co-location pattern) $prev$ is defined as $prev(C, S^p) = min\{Pr(f, C, S^p) : f \in C\}$. Given a threshold $minprev$, we say that a spatial co-location C is *spatially prevalent* if $prev(C, S^p) \geq minprev$. Given a spatial dataset S^P, relation R and a threshold $minprev$, we denote the set of all spatially prevalent co-location patterns of size s as $\mathbb{C}_s(S^p, R)$.

Let T be a finite set of timestamps. A spatiotemporal ST dataset is set of pairs $S^p_t = (t, S^p)$ where $t \in T$ and t is a unique identifier of the S^p_t pair in the set, while S^p is some spatial dataset. Given a spatiotemporal dataset ST and a subset $C \subseteq F$ we define *spatial co-location time prevalence* $tprev(C)$ as a fraction of spatial datasets in ST in which C is a spatially prevalent co-location. Formally, $tprev(C) = \frac{|\{t:(t,S^p)\in ST \land prev(C,S^p)\geq minprev\}|}{|ST|}$. Given a threshold $mintprev$ we define a *Mixed Drove Co-occurence Pattern* as a subset $C \subseteq F$ such that $tprev(C) \geq mintprev$. Given a spatiotemporal dataset ST, relation R for every $S_t^p \in ST$, a threshold $minprev$ and a threshold $mintprev$, we denote the set of all size s MDCOPs as $\mathbb{C}_s^T(ST)$. A *maximal MDCOP* C is any MDCOP such that no proper MDCOP superset of C exists. A set of all maximal MDCOPs is denoted as $\mathbb{C}^T(ST)$.

The maximal MDCOP pattern mining problem can be defined as follows. Given a spatiotemporal dataset ST, a neighborhood relation R, minimum spatial prevalence threshold $minprev$ and minimum time prevalence threshold $mintprev$, find efficiently a complete set of maximal MDCOPs.

4   MAXMDCOP-Miner

In this section we present an algorithm, called MAXMDCOP-Miner, for mining maximal MDCOPs. Some parts of our solution are based on the approach presented in [15]. However, we use an iCPI-tree structure from [11] for spatial co-location instance identification since it allows for better optimizations. For ways on constructing such a tree we refer the reader to paper [11]. In the subsequent sections we assume that an iCPI-tree is constructed for every spatial dataset S^p in ST. Due to iCPI-tree properties, we assume that a set of neighbors of feature instance i^{f_1} which are instances of f_2 and $f_1 < f_2$, denoted: $N(i^{f_1}, f_2, S^p, R) = \{i^{f_2} \in S : (i^{f_1}, i^{f_2}) \in R \land f_1 < f_2\}$ can be found efficiently. We also assume that the number of instances $count(f, S_t^p) = |\{f : i^f \in S\}|$ of every feature f for every $S_t^p \in ST$ is known.

The MAXMDCOP-Miner algorithm is composed of five steps: (1) find prevalent size 2 co-location patterns, (2) find size 2 MDCOPs among them, (3) find candidates for maximal MDCOPs in each spatial dataset, (4) find global candidates for maximal MDCOPS and (5) mine MDCOPS. Step 5 also includes a highly optimized algorithm for finding spatial prevalence of the candidates. Below we give the description of each step.

Step 1. Find spatially prevalent size 2 co-location patterns $\mathbb{C}_2(S_t^p, R)$. This step is performed independently for every spatial dataset $S_t^p \in ST$. First, an iCPI-tree for S_t^p is scanned to get a list of all neighbor pairs (i^{f_1}, i^{f_2}) (where $f_1 < f_2$). Due to the index structure it is easy to obtain this list with entries grouped by (f_1, f_2). Based on each such group, we compute participation index of the spatial co-location $\{f_1, f_2\}$. If the computed participation index is greater or equal to $minprev$ then the co-location $\{f_1, f_2\}$ is added to the result set.

Step 2. Find size 2 MDCOPs $\mathbb{C}_2^T(ST)$. Only a size 2 spatially prevalent co-location from one of S_t^p can be an MDCOP. Therefore, as a first step we compute a sum of $\mathbb{C}_2(S_t^p, R)$ sets computed in Step 1 to obtain all unique, candidate MDCOPs. Next, for each candidate we compute its time prevalence based on the number of S_t^p it is spatially prevalent in. If the candidate's time prevalence is greater than $mintprev$, it is added to the result set.

Algorithm 1. Find global candidates for maximal MDCOPs

Require:

- a set of local candidates for maximal co-locations $K(S_t^p)$ for every $S_t^p \in ST$
- minimum frequency threshold $minfreq$

Ensure: a set of local candidates for maximal co-locations $K(ST)$
1: $K(ST) \leftarrow \{\}, Y \leftarrow \bigcup_{S_t^p \in ST} K(S_t^p)$
2: **while** $|Y| > 0$ **do**
3:     $maxlen \leftarrow max\{|X| : X \in Y\}$
4:     $M \leftarrow \{X : X \in Y \wedge |X| = maxlen\}, Y \leftarrow Y \backslash M$
5:     **for** $P \in M$ **do**
6:         **if** $\exists X \in K(ST) : P \subset X$ **then** skip to the next P
7:         $tprev \leftarrow |\{t : S_t^p \in ST \wedge \exists P' \in K(S_t^p) : P \subseteq P'\}|/|ST|$
8:         **if** $tprev \geq mintprev$ **then** $K(ST) \leftarrow K(ST) \cup \{P\}$
9:         **else if** $maxlen > 2$ **then** $Y \leftarrow Y \cup \{P' \subset P : |P'| = maxlen - 1\}$

Step 3. Build local candidates for maximal MDCOPs $K(S_t^p)$ **for** $S_t^p \in ST$.
In this step we find candidates for maximal MDCOPs separately in each $S_t^p \in ST$.
To find such candidates we use a method based on [15]. In [15] candidates for
maximal spatially prevalent co-location patterns are maximal cliques in a graph
$G(V, E)$ where each vertex corresponds to one feature ($V \subseteq F$) and edges represent size 2 spatially prevalent co-location patterns ($E = C_2(S_t^p)$). In our case,
we limit the set of spatially prevalent co-location patterns to only those that also
appear in the MDCOP set $C_2(ST)$ ($E = C_2(S_t^p) \cap C_2(ST)$), so that candidates
contain only spatially prevalent and time prevalent pairs of features.

Step 4. Build global candidates for maximal MDCOPs $K(ST)$ **(see
Algorithm 1).** Candidates found in Step 3 can contain co-locations that are:
(1) not time prevalent (they do not appear in enough of $K(S_t^p)$ sets) and (2)
can be subsets (a candidate in one of $K(S_t^p)$ sets is a subset of a candidate in
another $K(S_t^p)$ set). In this step we find a set of candidates $K(ST)$ free of these
flaws.

At first, a sum of all $K(S_t^p)$ sets Y is found to eliminate duplicates of candidates (line 1). Next, the candidates are processed in the order from the largest
to the smallest. We extract the largest sets from the set Y into set M (lines 3–4)
and for each of the candidates in the set M we check: (1) if the candidate is a
subset of some larger candidate found in previous iteration (line 6) and (2) if an
upper bound of the candidate's time prevalence computed based on how often it
appears in $K(S_t^p)$ sets (line 7) is greater than or equal to the threshold $mintprev$
(line 8). In the first case, the candidate is skipped as it is not maximal (line 6).
In the second case, the candidate is added to the result set $K(ST)$ (line 8).

In case when the candidate is not a subset of some other candidate but is not
time prevalent enough, we add all subsets (one item smaller) of the candidate
to the set Y for subsequent processing (line 9). We process the set Y until there
are no candidates of size 2 (line 2).

Step 5. Mine maximal MDCOPs $\mathbb{C}^T(ST)$ (see Algorithm 2, 3 and 4). Mining process is performed by Algorithm 2 At first, we initialize the results cache (line 2). This is a set of $cache[t]$ sets corresponding to all timestamps in T. Each such set will contain co-locations known to be spatially prevalent at S_t^p but not time prevalent. Next, we initialize a set Y with all of global candidates obtained in Step 4 (line 3). The candidates are processed in the order from the largest to the smallest. The largest candidates are extracted from the set Y into set M (line 10). Next, the set N, which will gather all new candidates generated during mining process, is initialized (line 11). In loop (lines 12–28) we process candidates P from the set M. We start by initializing the sets TP_e, TP_c, TN_e and TN_c (line 13) which will store timestamps t of S_t^p datasets at which the candidate P is spatially prevalent (TP sets) or not (TN sets). Subscript e means that the spatial prevalence of the candidate is determined based on previous results, while c means that it is based on participation index computations.

Next, in loop (lines 14–17), for each $S_t^p \in ST$ we determine whether the candidate P is spatially prevalent or not based on the information determined so far. If the candidate is not a subset of any local candidate in $K(S_t^p)$ then it cannot be spatially prevalent and consequently the timestamp t is added to TN_e set (line 15). However, if the candidate is a subset of any pattern known to be spatially prevalent in S_t^p then it must be spatially prevalent as well. In such a case, the corresponding timestamp t is added to TP_e set (line 16).

Sizes of TP_e and TN_e sets allow to determine lower ($|TP_E|/|ST|$) and upper $(1 - |TN_e|/|ST|)$ bound on the candidate's time prevalence. If the lower bound is greater or equal to $mintprev$ (candidate is time prevalent) or upper bound is smaller than $mintprev$ (candidate is not time prevalent) no subsequent computations are necessary (lines 17 and 18).

If the time prevalence of the candidate cannot be determined yet, then exact computations are needed. In loop (lines 19–23) for each $S_t^p \in ST$ (for which the candidate's spatial prevalence has not been determined yet) we compute the participation index (line 20) and based on the result, the corresponding timestamp is added either to TP_c or TN_c set (lines 21 and 22).

Based on the sizes of the TP and TN sets we compute lower ($\frac{|TP_e|+|TP_c|}{|ST|}$) and upper $(1 - \frac{|TN_e|+|TN_c|}{|ST|})$ bounds of candidate's time prevalence. Computations can be aborted based on these results, similarly as before (line 23).

Next we determine whether the candidate is time prevalent and update set $\mathbb{C}^T(ST)$ if required (line 24). Otherwise we add all of its subsets (one item smaller) to the set N (line 27). Additionally, we update the spatially prevalent patterns cache for timestamps at which the candidate is spatially prevalent.

After all of candidates in M are processed we check whether the newly generated candidates in the N set are subsets of the sets in the result set (line 29). If not, they are added to the set Y (line 29) for further processing (lines 12–28). The main loop terminates when the set Y is empty or size 2 patterns are processed. Since time prevalent size 2 MDCOPS were already found in Steps 1 and 2, it is sufficient to just find intersection $Y \cap \mathbb{C}_2^T(ST)$ to determine maximal size 2 MDCOPs (lines 6–8). This is also the cause for using cache for testing

---

Algorithm 2. Mining maximal MDCOPs

Require:

- a set of global candidates for maximal MDCOPs $K(ST)$
- sets of local candidates for maximal MDCOPs $K(S_t^p)$
- minimum spatial prevalence $minprev$ and time prevalence $mintprev$ thresholds

Ensure: a set of maximal MDCOPs $\mathbb{C}^T(ST)$
1: $\mathbb{C}^T(ST) \leftarrow \{\}$,
2: $\forall_{S_t^p \in ST} cache[t] = \{\}$
3: $Y \leftarrow K(ST)$
4: **while** $|Y| > 0$ **do**
5:     $maxlen \leftarrow max\{|X| : X \in Y\}$
6:     **if** $maxlen = 2$ **then**
7:       $\mathbb{C}^T(ST) \leftarrow \mathbb{C}^T(ST) \cup (Y \cap C_2(ST))$
8:       **break**
9:     **else**
10:       $M \leftarrow \{X : X \in Y \wedge |X| = maxlen\}, Y \leftarrow Y\backslash M$
11:       $N \leftarrow \{\}$
12:       **for** $P \in M$ **do**
13:         $TP_e \leftarrow \{\}, TN_e \leftarrow \{\}, TP_c \leftarrow \{\}, TN_c \leftarrow \{\}$
14:         **for** $S_t^p \in ST$ **do**
15:           **if** $\nexists X \in K(S_t^p) : P \subseteq X$ **then** $TN_e \leftarrow TN_e \cup \{t\}$
16:           **else if** $\exists X \in cache[t] : P \subset X$ **then** $TP_e \leftarrow TP_e \cup \{t\}$
17:           **if** $\frac{|TP_e|}{|ST|} \geq mintprev$ **or** $1 - \frac{|TN_e|}{|ST|} < mintprev$ **then break**
18:         **if** $\frac{|TP_e|}{|ST|} < mintprev$ **and** $1 - \frac{|TN_e|}{|ST|} \geq mintprev$ **then**
19:           **for** $S_t^p \in ST : t \notin (TP_e \cup TN_e)$ **do**
20:             $prev \leftarrow compute\_pi(S_t^p, P)$ {See Alg. 3}
21:             **if** $prev \geq minprev$ **then** $TP_c \leftarrow TP_c \cup \{t\}$
22:             **else** $TN_c \leftarrow TN_c \cup \{t\}$
23:             **if** $\frac{|TP_e|+|TP_c|}{|ST|} \geq mintprev$ **or** $1 - \frac{|TN_e|+|TN_c|}{|ST|} < mintprev$ **then break**
24:         **if** $\frac{|TP_e|+|TP_c|}{|ST|} \geq mintprev$ **then**
25:           $\mathbb{C}^T(ST) \leftarrow \mathbb{C}^T(ST) \cup \{P\}$
26:         **else**
27:           $N \leftarrow N \cup \{P' \subset P : |P'| = maxlen - 1\}$
28:           **if** $maxlen > 3$ **then: for** $t \in TP_c$ **do:** $cache[t] \leftarrow cache[t] \cup \{P\}$
29:       **for** $P \in N$ **do: if** $\nexists X \in \mathbb{C}^T(ST) : P \subset X$ **then** $Y \leftarrow Y \cup \{P\}$

---

candidates of size greater or equal to 3 (line 28). After the loop ends, the result set $\mathbb{C}^T(ST)$ contains all maximal MDCOPs.

Step 5a. Computing spatial prevalence. One of the most important parts of this algorithm, which was not described yet, is the spatial prevalence computation of a co-location. In [15], authors propose to compress instances of a single co-location in a spatial dataset using a trie structure [6]. We propose a method for storing such tries, which allows to: (1) improve the performance of participation index computations, (2) reuse results when finding instances of another

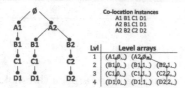

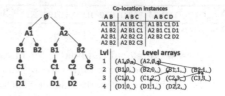

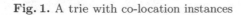

Fig. 1. A trie with co-location instances

Fig. 2. A trie with instances of co-location and its prefixes

co-location with a common prefix and (3) further improve compression ratio of co-location instances.

A trie is a tree structure which is used to store a set of sequences by representing them as paths from root to leaves. The set of sequences is compressed because sequences with common prefixes share the same paths in the trie. Assuming any total order on the feature set F, we can represent both co-locations and their instances as sequences and store them in a trie. For details please refer to [6,15]. An exemplary trie for a set of instances of a co-location $\{A, B, C, D\}$ is shown in Fig. 1. We propose to store levels of a trie as arrays of triples $(i^f, pos, visited)$ composed of feature instance i^f, an index in a higher level array to a parent entry pos and a boolean $visited$ flag which is used for participation index computations (we will ignore it for now). We call such arrays the *level arrays*.

Note, that the same trie can be used for storing instances of the co-location prefixes, e.g. for co-location $\{A, B, C, D\}$ instances of $\{A, B, C\}$ and $\{A, B\}$ can be stored as well. This is possible since prefixes of co-location instances are always instances of the corresponding co-location prefix. To retrieve instances of a specific co-location it is sufficient to follow paths from the nodes at level corresponding to the co-location length upwards toward the root. Hence, we use trie to store instances of a co-location and all of its prefixes. An exemplary trie for instances of co-location $\{A, B, C, D\}$ (and its prefixes) is shown in Fig. 2.

Let us consider two co-locations sharing the same prefix, e.g. $\{A, B, C, D\}$ and $\{A, B, E\}$. Note that the tries that store instances of those co-locations and their prefixes will have the same two first levels. Assuming the trie for the co-location $\{A, B, C, D\}$ has been computed first, we can reuse its first two levels and only compute the third level corresponding to the E feature. Moreover, since the first two trie levels are the same, we do not need to store them twice in memory. Hence, we propose the following data structure. We keep a collection (e.g. an array) of all level arrays. Additionally, we store co-locations (not co-location instances) in a trie. In further discussion to distinguish between two different trie structures we will refer to them as *instance tries* (which store co-location instances) and *co-location tries* (which store co-locations). In the co-location trie, each node represents a co-location composed of features stored on a path up to the root. With each node we associate a reference to a level array in the collection. Given a node corresponding to a co-location, by retrieving all references on a path to a root we can find all level arrays constituting the corresponding instance trie. Since co-locations need to have at least two features,

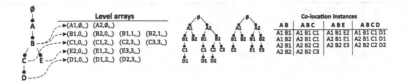

Fig. 3. A co-location tree with the corresponding collection of level arrays

---

Algorithm 3. Computing spatial prevalence (participation index)

Require:

- Spatial dataset S_t^p with iCPI-tree, co-location trie and relation R
- A candidate set of features P

Ensure: spatial prevalence *prev* of the candidate P
1: Identify instances of P if not available in the co-location trie {see Alg. 4}
2: $L \leftarrow$ an array of references to level arrays retrieved for P from the co-location trie
3: Set all *visited* flags in all level arrays in L (except last one) to *false*
4: $U \leftarrow$ an array of empty sets of size $|P|$
5: **for** $(i^f, pos, \_) \in L[|P| - 1]$ **do** {*visited* flag is ignored}
6: $\quad U[|P| - 1] \leftarrow U[|P| - 1] \cup \{i^f\}$
7: $\quad parent \leftarrow pos$
8: $\quad$ **for** $k \in |P| - 2, \ldots, 0$ **do**
9: $\quad\quad (i^g, new\_parent, visited) \leftarrow L[k][parent]$
10: $\quad\quad$ **if** *visited* **then break**
11: $\quad\quad U[k] \leftarrow U[k] \cup \{i^g\}$
12: $\quad\quad L[k][parent] \leftarrow (i^g, new\_parent, true)$
13: $\quad\quad parent \leftarrow new\_parent$
14: $prev \leftarrow min\{|U[k]|/count(P[k], S^p) : k \in 0, \ldots, |P| - 1\}$

---

the nodes at the first level of the co-location trie do not store any pointers, while nodes at the second level store two pointers for first and second level of the corresponding instance trie. Exemplary structures are shown in Fig. 3.

Given candidate P, participation index computation requires finding unique feature instances that are part of candidate P instances. The method utilizing the co-location trie structure is shown in Algorithm 3. As a first step, the co-location trie and the corresponding collection of level arrays is supplemented with candidate's instances if necessary (line 1). This step is detailed in Algorithm 4 and will be described later. Next, we retrieve consecutive references to level arrays from the co-location trie and store them in the array L (line 2). In order to obtain unique feature instances mentioned above, we will traverse the retrieved instance trie starting at each leaf and go up towards the root to retrieve all feature instances on the path. Since this is a tree, then paths starting at multiple different leaves might end up at some common node. To avoid traversing a once visited path, with each of the trie's node we associate a *visited* flag to mark whether the node has been visited or not. Since level arrays are shared, previous

---

Algorithm 4. Building co-location trie

Require:

    – Spatial dataset S_t^p with iCPI-tree, co-location trie and relation R
    – co-location P

Ensure: co-location trie for S_t^p is updated
  1: $V \leftarrow$ a sorted array with features from P
  2: $d \leftarrow$ length of P prefix already stored in co-location trie
  3: **if** $d = |P|$ **then** abort, all level arrays are computed
  4: **if** $d < 2$ **then**
  5:     $L0 \leftarrow$ empty level array, $L1 \leftarrow$ empty level array
  6:     **for** every $i^{V[0]}$ from first two levels of S^p iCPI-tree **do**
  7:       **if** $N(i^{V[0]}, V[1], S^p, R) = \emptyset$ **then continue**
  8:       append $(i^{V[0]}, \emptyset, false)$ to $L0$
  9:       $w \leftarrow |L[0]| - 1$
10:       **for** $i^{V[1]} \in N(i^{V[0]}, V[1], S^p, R)$ **do** append $(i^{V[1]}, w, false)$ to $L1$
11:     Store size 2 P prefix in colocation trie and add ref. to $L1$ and $L2$ to the leaf
12:     $d \leftarrow 2$
13: $L \leftarrow$ an array of references to level arrays retrieved for size d prefix of P
14: **for** $j \in d, \ldots, |P| - 1$ **do**
15:     Allocate new level array and store reference to it at $L[j]$
16:     **for** $parent\_pos \in 0, \ldots, |L[j-1]|$ **do**
17:       $CO \leftarrow \bigcap_{i^f \in \text{path to root starting at } L[j-1][parent\_pos]} N(i^f, V[j], S^p, R)$
18:       Append to $L[j]$ entries $(i^f, parent\_pos, false)$ where $i^f \in CO$
19:       Add node to co-location trie for size j P prefix and copy reference from $L[j]$

---

computations might have left the flags set to *true* at some nodes. Hence, we set them all to false (line 3). To find unique values among all retrieved feature instances we allocate $|P|$ sets in an array U (line 4), one for each candidate's feature. Next, the main loop (lines 5–13) iterates over all entries in the level array corresponding to the leaves of the instance trie. Retrieved feature instance is added the corresponding set in U (line 6). Next, we traverse up the instance trie (lines 8–13). Feature instances are retrieved (line 9) and added to the U sets (line 11). Each visited node is marked (line 12). If a node has already been visited, we abort the traversal (line 10). Finally, the participation index is computed (line 14).

The last algorithm we need to describe is Algorithm 4, which is used to update the co-location trie. As a first step we determine how much of the instance trie for the target co-location P has been computed previously. In case every level has already been built we abort further computations (line 3). Otherwise, we can have partially built instance trie (≥ 2 features from P are in the co-location tree) or no levels have been built yet (< 2 features from P are stored). In the first case, we continue with building remaining levels (lines 13–19). In the second case, we build the first two levels (lines 5–12) and then solve the first case.

Building the first two levels is easy, since they can be directly retrieved from the iCPI-tree structure. First, we allocate two new level arrays (line 5). Next, in loop (lines 6–10) we retrieve from the iCPI-tree all feature instances with feature $V[0]$ which is the first feature in the sorted co-location P. If the retrieved feature instance has neighbors with feature $V[1]$ (line 7) then new entries are added to level arrays $L1$ and $L2$ (lines 8–10). After level arrays have been built, the appropriate nodes are created in the co-location trie and the references to new level arrays are stored in the leaf node corresponding to feature $V[1]$.

To build remaining levels, we first retrieve levels that have already been built (line 13). Next, we build subsequent levels one by one in a loop (lines 14–19). To build a new level array, we iterate over entries in the previous level (lines 16–18). For each of these entries we retrieve feature instances from all nodes up to the root and find common neighbors with feature $V[j]$, which is a feature corresponding to the j-th level of the instance trie (line 17). For each of such common neighbors a new entry is appended to the new level array (line 18). After level array has been built, a new node is added to the co-location trie and the reference to the new level array is stored in it (line 19). Once all the level arrays have been built, the algorithm ends.

5 Experiments

To compare the performance we implemented both MAXMDCOP-Miner and FastMDCOP-Miner algorithms using Python3. All experiments have been conducted on a PC (Intel Core I7-6700 3.4 GHz CPU, 32 GB RAM). We examined processing times using synthetic and real world datasets. Synthetic data was generated using method based on [4]. First, size of each PAT_{ct} initial patterns (subsets of feature types potentially involved in MDCOPs) was randomly chosen using Poisson distribution (mean PAT_{avs}). Then, features were uniquely and randomly chosen (from F_{ct} initial features) and assigned to patterns. Next, initial patterns were divided into sets of persistent and transient patterns using RAT_p parameter - a ratio of persistent patterns over transient patterns. Instances of patterns were placed in spatial framework (a square with dim length side). Each pattern instance was placed in a square of size $dist$ randomly chosen from spatial framework. For each pattern, its instances were put in randomly chosen number of time frames from the set of TF_{ct} frames w.r.t. $mintprev$ parameter (persistent patterns had to occur in at least $mintprev$ fraction of frames). The number of instances of the particular pattern in a given time moment was randomly chosen from Poisson distribution (mean INS_{avc}). Finally, $NOISE_{ct}$ objects were placed in the framework. Each noise object was assigned a spatial feature randomly chosen (uniform distribution) from set of noise features. That set consisted of RAT_n percent of F_{ct} initial features (i.e. some of that features could take part in generated patterns).

We have prepared two datasets, namely SD1 (136K objects) and SD2 (29K objects), using following sets of values: (1) for SD1: $PAT_{ct} = 15$, $PAT_{avs} = 5$, $F_{ct} = 100$, $RAT_p = 0.4$, $dim = 10000$, $dist = 10$, $TF_{ct} = 100$, $minfreq =$

$0, 6$, $INS_{avc} = 25$, $NOISE_{ct} = 20000$, $RAT_n = 0.4$; (2) for SD2: $PAT_{ct} = 5$, $PAT_{avs} = 10$, $F_{ct} = 200$, $RAT_p = 0.3$, $dim = 10000$, $dist = 10$, $TF_{ct} = 50$, $minfreq = 0, 6$, $INS_{avc} = 15$, $NOISE_{ct} = 10000$, $RAT_n = 0.2$.

Real world dataset RD contains positions of pigeons from animal study [17]. We limited our analysis to a single day and we used linear interpolation to calculate pigeons positions for each of 1440 time moments (one per minute). There were 29192 objects and 29 spatial features in the RD dataset.

In the first experiment, we observed how the processing time for synthetic data (Fig. 4a and Fig. 4b for SD1 and SD2) is affected when changing the *minprev* threshold (constant *maxdist* = 10, *mintprev* = 0.3). In general, the lower the *minprev*, the higher probability that we will find a pattern in a particular frame. Thus, processing times should decrease with the decreasing values of *minprev*. Exactly such a behavior can be noticed for FastMDCOP-Miner. In the proposed algorithm, lower *minprev* results in a greater chance of generating long, prevalent patterns which eliminates the need to check their subsets. When we increase *minprev*, both algorithms start to behave similarly, although our proposal is still more efficient. For the largest values of *minprev* the number of candidates is very limited and both algorithms complete tasks very quickly.

In the second experiment, we examined the influence of *mintprev* on the processing time for synthetic data (Fig. 4c and Fig. 4d) while *maxdist* and *minprev* were set to 10 and 0.3 respectively. In MAXMDCOP-Miner, for low and high values of *mintprev* there is a higher chance that lower or upper bound time prevalence filtering will take place resulting in a reduced number of computations. For the lowest value of *mintprev*, MAXMDCOP-Miner is more than 4 times faster. For higher values of *mintprev*, the number of patterns decreases as well as the performance gap between algorithms.

In the third experiment, we checked how the maximum distance *maxdist* impacts the performance for synthetic data (Fig. 4e and Fig. 4f, *minprev* = 0.3, *minprev* = 0.3). It clearly observable that there is a significant increase in processing time when *maxdist* reaches 10. This is related to the parameters used for synthetic data generator ($dist = 10$). When *maxdist* is greater than 10, the number of instances (and candidates) increases very rapidly and Apriori-based approach is inefficient in comparison to the new method.

Finally, we examined the efficiency of the algorithms for the real world dataset. Due to the limited number of observed pigeons, we skip *minprev* threshold assuming that all candidates are spatially prevalent. We were varying *mintprev* (Fig. 4g, constant *maxdist* = 0.4) and *maxdist* (Fig. 4h, constant *mintprev* = 0.3). Gathered data confirm the results obtained for synthetic dataset. In all cases, the performance of the new method was better that in the compared algorithm, reaching approx. 7 times faster execution times for *mintprev* = 0.1.

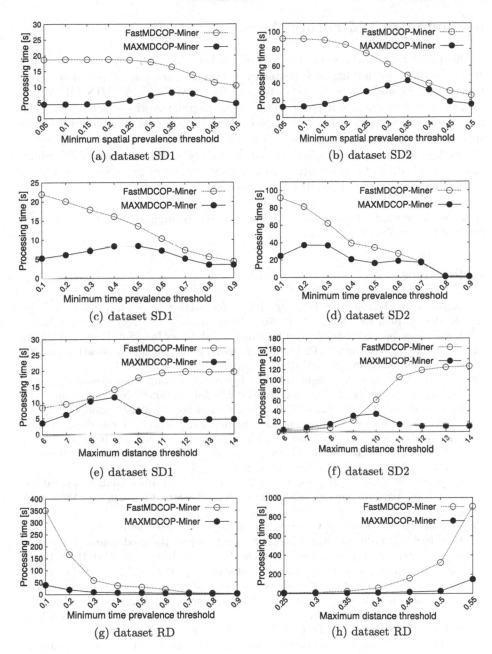

Fig. 4. Results of experiments

6   Summary and Future Work

In this paper we introduced the concept of maximal MDCOPs and proposed efficient algorithm for mining such patterns. We have tested the proposed solution using synthetic and real world datasets. Results show, that MAXMDCOP-Miner offers better performance in comparison to the popular Apriori-based approach. Moreover, we can notice that the more challenging parameter values (i.e. lower spatial or time prevalence thresholds or higher maximum distance thresholds), the higher performance gain is achieved. In future work, we plan to introduce more optimizations for eliminating even higher number of candidates as well as to parallelize maximal MDCOP mining process.

Acknowledgement. This research has been partially supported by the statutory funds of Poznan University of Technology.

References

1. Agrawal, R., Srikant, R.: Fast algorithms for mining association rules in large databases. In: Proceedings of the 20th International Conference on Very Large Data Bases, pp. 487–499. Morgan Kaufmann Publishers Inc., San Francisco (1994)
2. Andrzejewski, W., Boinski, P.: Parallel approach to incremental co-location pattern mining. Inf. Sci. **496**, 485–505 (2019)
3. Cao, H., Mamoulis, N., Cheung, D.W.: Discovery of collocation episodes in spatiotemporal data. In: Proceedings of the 6th International Conference on Data Mining, ICDM 2006, pp. 823–827. IEEE Computer Society, Washington, DC (2006)
4. Celik, M., Shekhar, S., Rogers, J.P., Shine, J.A.: Sustained emerging spatiotemporal co-occurrence pattern mining: a summary of results. In: Proceedings of the 18th IEEE International Conference on Tools with Artificial Intelligence (ICTAI 2006), pp. 106–115, November 2006
5. Celik, M., Shekhar, S., Rogers, J.P., Shine, J.A.: Mixed-drove spatiotemporal co-occurrence pattern mining. IEEE Trans. Knowl. Data Eng. **20**(10), 1322–1335 (2008)
6. Fredkin, E.: Trie memory. Commun. ACM **3**(9), 490–499 (1960)
7. Hamdi, S.M., Aydin, B., Angryk, R.A.: A pattern growth-based approach for mining spatiotemporal co-occurrence patterns. In: Proceedings of the 16th IEEE International Conference on Data Mining Workshops, pp. 1125–1132, December 2016
8. Qian, F., He, Q., He, J.: Mining spread patterns of spatio-temporal co-occurrences over zones. In: Gervasi, O., Taniar, D., Murgante, B., Laganà, A., Mun, Y., Gavrilova, M.L. (eds.) ICCSA 2009. LNCS, vol. 5593, pp. 677–692. Springer, Heidelberg (2009). https://doi.org/10.1007/978-3-642-02457-3_57
9. Shekhar, S., Huang, Y.: Discovering spatial co-location patterns: a summary of results. In: Jensen, C.S., Schneider, M., Seeger, B., Tsotras, V.J. (eds.) SSTD 2001. LNCS, vol. 2121, pp. 236–256. Springer, Heidelberg (2001). https://doi.org/10.1007/3-540-47724-1_13
10. Tran, V., Wang, L., Chen, H., Xiao, Q.: MCHT: a maximal clique and hash table-based maximal prevalent co-location pattern mining algorithm. Expert Syst. Appl. **175**, 114830 (2021)

11. Wang, L., Bao, Y., Lu, J.: Efficient discovery of spatial co-location patterns using the iCPI-tree. Open Inf. Syst. J. **3**(2), 69–80 (2009)
12. Wang, L., Zhou, L., Lu, J., Yip, J.: An order-clique-based approach for mining maximal co-locations. Inf. Sci. **179**(19), 3370–3382 (2009)
13. Wang, Z., Han, T., Yu, H.: Research of MDCOP mining based on time aggregated graph for large spatio-temproal data sets. Comput. Sci. Inf. Syst. **16**, 32–32 (2019)
14. Yang, H., Parthasarathy, S., Mehta, S.: A generalized framework for mining spatio-temporal patterns in scientific data. In: Proceedings of the 11th ACM SIGKDD International Conference on Knowledge Discovery in Data Mining, KDD 2005, pp. 716–721. ACM, New York (2005)
15. Yao, X., Peng, L., Yang, L., Chi, T.: A fast space-saving algorithm for maximal co-location pattern mining. Expert Syst. Appl. **63**(C), 310–323 (2016)
16. Yoo, J.S., Bow, M.: Mining maximal co-located event sets. In: Huang, J.Z., Cao, L., Srivastava, J. (eds.) PAKDD 2011. LNCS (LNAI), vol. 6634, pp. 351–362. Springer, Heidelberg (2011). https://doi.org/10.1007/978-3-642-20841-6_29
17. Zannoni, N., et al.: Identifying volatile organic compounds used for olfactory navigation by homing pigeons. Sci. Rep. **10**(15879), 1–16 (2020)

Efficiently Mining Large Gradual Patterns Using Chunked Storage Layout

Dickson Odhiambo Owuor[1]([✉])[iD] and Anne Laurent[2]([✉])[iD]

[1] SCES, Strathmore University, Nairobi, Kenya
dowuor@strathmore.edu
[2] LIRMM Univ Montpellier, CNRS, Montpellier, France
anne.laurent@umontpellier.fr

Abstract. Existing approaches for extracting gradual patterns become inefficient in terms of memory usage when applied on data sets with huge numbers of objects. This inefficiency is caused by the contiguous nature of loading binary matrices into main memory as single blocks when validating candidate gradual patterns. This paper proposes an efficient storage layout that allows these matrices to be split and loaded into/from memory in multiple smaller chunks. We show how HDF5 (Hierarchical Data Format version 5) may be used to implement this chunked layout and our experiments reveal a great improvement in memory usage efficiency especially on huge data sets.

Keywords: Binary matrices · Gradual patterns · HDF5 · Memory chunk · Zarr

1 Introduction

Gradual patterns may be described as linguistic rules that are applied on a data set to extract correlations among its attributes [7,10]. For instance, given a data set shown in Table 1 (which is a numeric data set with 3 attributes {age, games, goals}), a linguistic gradual correlation may take the form: *"the lower the age, the more the goals scored."*

Table 1. Sample data set $\mathcal{D}_1$.

id	age	games	goals
r1	30	100	2
r2	28	400	4
r3	26	200	5
r4	26	500	8

One major step in mining gradual patterns involves ranking tuples in the order that fulfill a specific pattern. For example, in Table 1 the pattern *"the*

© Springer Nature Switzerland AG 2021
L. Bellatreche et al. (Eds.): ADBIS 2021, LNCS 12843, pp. 30–42, 2021.
https://doi.org/10.1007/978-3-030-82472-3_4

lower the age, the more the goals scored." is fulfilled by at least 3 ordered tuples: $\{r1 \rightarrow r2 \rightarrow r3\}$. For the reason that computing processors are natively designed to operate on binary data, the approach of representing ordered rankings as binary matrices yields high computational efficiency for mining gradual patterns using the bitwise AND operator [2, 7, 10].

However, the same can not be said of these binary matrices in terms of main memory usage. For instance, given a data set with n tuples and m attributes:

- for every attribute a in m, there may exist at least 2 *frequent* gradual items - $(a, \uparrow)$ and $(a, \downarrow)$ and,
- for every gradual item, a binary matrix of size $(n \times n)$ must be loaded into memory.

Consequently, a single bitwise AND operation loads and holds multiple $n \times n$ binary matrices into memory. This problem becomes overpowering when dealing with data sets with huge number of tuples. Most often, algorithms implemented on this approach crash when applied on such data sets since they require to be assigned an overwhelming amount of main memory at once (when performing the bitwise AND operation).

In this paper, we propose an approach that advances the bitwise AND operation such that it operates on multiple smaller chunks of the binary matrices. This approach allows efficient use of main memory while performing this operation on huge binary matrices. In addition, we design GRAD-L algorithm that implements this proposed approach. Our experiment results show that our proposed approach by far outperforms existing approaches especially when dealing with huge data sets.

The remainder of this paper is organized as follows: we provide preliminary definitions in Sect. 2; we review related approaches in Sect. 3; in Sect. 4, we propose an approach that allows efficient use of main memory through chunking binary matrices for the bitwise AND operation; we analyze the performance of our proposed approach in Sect. 5; we conclude and give future directions regarding this work in Sect. 6.

2   Preliminary Definitions

For the purpose of putting forward our proposed approach for mining large gradual patterns; in this section, we recall some definitions about gradual patterns taken from existing literature [2, 10].

Definition 1. Gradual Item. *A gradual item g is a pair (a, v) where a is an attribute of a data set and v is a variation such that: $v \in \{\uparrow, \downarrow\}$, where $\uparrow$ denotes an increasing variation and, $\downarrow$ denotes a decreasing variation.*

Example 1. $(age, \downarrow)$ is a gradual item that may be interpreted as: *"the lower the age."*

Definition 2. Gradual Pattern. *A gradual pattern GP is a set of gradual items i.e.* $GP = \{(a_1, v_1), ..., (a_n, v_n)\}$.

Example 2. $\{(age, \downarrow), (goals, \uparrow)\}$ is a gradual pattern that may be interpreted as: *"the lower the age, the more the goals scored."*

The quality of a gradual pattern is measured by *frequency support* which may be described as: *"the proportion of objects/tuples/rows in a data set that fulfill that pattern."* For example, given the data set in Table 1, the pattern $GP = \{(age, \downarrow), (goals, \uparrow)\}$ is fulfilled by tuples $\{r1, r2, r3\}$ (which is 3 out of 4 tuples). Therefore, the frequency support, $sup(GP)$, of this pattern is 0.75.

On that account, given a minimum support threshold σ, a gradual pattern (GP) is said to be **frequent** only if: $sup(GP) \geq \sigma$.

In the case of designing algorithms for mining gradual patterns from data sets, many existing works apply 3 main steps [2,7,9,10]:

1. identify gradual item sets (or patterns) that become *frequent* if their frequency support exceed a user-defined threshold,
2. ranking tuple pairs that fulfill the individual gradual items (of a candidate item set) and representing the ranks as *binary matrices* and,
3. applying a *bitwise* AND operator on the binary matrices in order to identify which gradual items may be joined to form a *frequent* gradual pattern.

For instance, given the data set in Table 1, we may identify 2 gradual patterns: $gp_4 = \{(age, \downarrow), (games, \uparrow)\}$ and $gp_5 = \{(games, \uparrow), (goals, \uparrow)\}$. These 2 patterns require 3 gradual items $g_1 = (age, \downarrow)$, $g_2 = (games, \uparrow)$, $g_3 = (goals, \uparrow)$ whose binary matrices M_{G_1}, M_{G_2} and M_{G_3} (after ranking tuples of corresponding columns in Table 1) are shown in Table 2.

Table 2. Binary matrices M_{G_1}, M_{G_2} and M_{G_3} for gradual items: (a) $g_1 = (age, \downarrow)$, (b) $g_2 = (games, \uparrow)$, (c) $g_3 = (goals, \uparrow)$.

r*	r1	r2	r3	r4	r*	r1	r2	r3	r4	r*	r1	r2	r3	r4
r1	0	1	1	1	r1	0	1	1	1	r1	0	1	1	1
r2	0	0	1	1	r2	0	0	0	1	r2	0	0	1	1
r3	0	0	0	0	r3	0	1	0	1	r3	0	0	0	1
r4	0	0	0	0	r4	0	0	0	0	r4	0	0	0	0
(a)					(b)					(c)				

[2,7] propose the theorem that follows in order to join gradual items to form gradual patterns:

*"Let gp_{12} be a gradual pattern generated by joining two gradual items g_1 and g_2. The following matrix relation holds: $M_{GP_{12}} = M_{G_1}$ **AND** M_{G_2}".*

This theorem relies heavily on the bitwise AND operator which provides good computational performance. For instance, we can apply a bitwise AND operation

Table 3. Binary matrices $M_{GP_{12}}$ and $M_{GP_{23}}$ for gradual patterns: (a) $gp_{12} = \{(age, \downarrow),$ $(games, \uparrow)\}$, (b) $gp_{23} = \{(games, \uparrow), (goals, \uparrow)\}$.

r^*	r1	r2	r3	r4	r^*	r1	r2	r3	r4
r1	0	1	1	1	r1	0	1	1	1
r2	0	0	0	1	r2	0	0	0	1
r3	0	0	0	0	r3	0	0	0	1
r4	0	0	0	0	r4	0	0	0	0

(a)   (b)

on the binary matrices in Table 1 in order to find binary matrices $M_{GP_{12}}$ and $M_{GP_{23}}$ for patterns gp_{12} and gp_{23} as shown in Table 3.

As can be seen in Table 2 and Table 3, the total sum of ordered ranks in the binary matrices is given by $s = n(n-1)/2$ where n is the number of columns/attributes. Therefore, the support of a gradual pattern gp is the ratio of *concordant rank count in the binary matrix* to the sum s [7].

3   State of the Art

Scientific data is increasing rapidly every year, thanks to technological advances in computing and storage efficiency [11,12]. Technologies such as HDF5 (Hierarchical Data Format v5) and Zarr provide high performance software and file formats that efficiently manage these huge volumes of data. For instance, [6] and [14] describe two models whose efficiencies have been greatly improved by using the Zarr and HDF5 data formats respectively.

According to [4], HDF5[1] is a technology suite that comprises a model, a software library and a hierarchical file format for storing and managing data. This suite is designed: (1) to support a wide variety of datatypes, (2) for fast Input/Output processing and (3) for managing *BigData*. These similar features are offered by Zarr[2] technology suite.

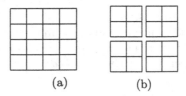

(a)   (b)

Fig. 1. (a) Contiguous storage layout and, (b) chunked storage layout.

---

[1] https://portal.hdfgroup.org/display/HDF5/HDF5.
[2] https://zarr.readthedocs.io/en/stable/index.html.

One particular feature (provided by HDF5 and Zarr) that may be useful in mining gradual patterns from huge data sets is the *chunked storage layout* shown in Fig. 1b. This feature allows for a huge data set to be split into multiple chunks which are stored separately in any order and any position within the HDF5/Zarr file. Additionally, chunks can be compressed, written and read individually, improving performance when dealing with such data sets [5].

Applying HDF5/Zarr chunked storage layout to binary matrices is one approach that may solve the problem (described in Sect. 1) of mining gradual patterns from huge data sets. The chunked storage layout may be exploited to allow the split of the bitwise AND operation (described in Sect. 1) on huge matrices (generated by reading and ranking all data set tuples in one attempt) into several repeated steps (where each step targets and loads manageable binary chunks into main memory).

However, using this approach implies chunking and storing binary matrices in secondary memory (i.e. HDF5/Zarr file) and, every repeated bitwise AND step includes the process of reading binary matrices from a secondary memory to main memory or/and writing updated binary matrices from the main memory to a secondary memory.

According to [4], chunked storage layout presents a higher overhead than contiguous storage layout when it comes to accessing and locating any element in the data set. The read/write overhead further increases when the chunked data set is compressed. Therefore, performance of the suggested approach of using a HDF5 chunked storage layout for gradual pattern mining may be greatly slowed down by the read/write overhead.

In the section that follows, we propose an approach that begins by chunking data set tuple reads in order to produce chunked binary matrices (getting rid of the need to store in HDF5/Zarr files).

4   Proposed Chunking Approach

In this section, we propose an approach for chunking binary matrices of gradual items into multiple small matrices that can be loaded and held into main memory piece-wisely in order to improve the memory usage efficiency. We modify the 3 main steps (described in Sect. 1) for mining gradual patterns as follows:

1. identify valid gradual patterns,
2. rank tuple pairs that fulfill the gradual items in the candidate gradual pattern in *chunks* and represent them in *multiple smaller* binary matrices and,
3. apply a bitwise AND operator on the *chunked* binary matrices in a *piecewise manner*.

4.1   Mapping Matrices into Chunked Layout

In the following, we use an example environment to expound on the steps of the proposed chunking approach. For the purpose of painting a clearer picture of this proposed approach, we use a sample data set (shown in Table 4a) to demonstrate the modified steps.

Example 3. Let $gp = \{(age, \downarrow), (games, \uparrow)\}$ be a candidate gradual pattern. Using a user-defined chunk size (in this case we set the chunk size to 2) as shown in Table 4b.

Table 4. (a) Sample data set $\mathcal{D}_2$, (b) data set $\mathcal{D}_2$ with its tuples chunked by a size of 2.

id	age	games	goals
r1	30	100	2
r2	28	400	4
r3	26	200	5
r4	25	500	8
r5	25	200	9
r6	24	500	1

(a)

id	age	games	goals	
r1	30	100	2	chunk 1
r2	28	400	4	
r3	26	200	5	chunk 2
r4	25	500	8	
r5	25	200	9	chunk 3
r6	24	500	1	

(b)

Firstly, we read and rank tuples fulfilling gradual items $g_1 = (age, \downarrow)$ and $g_2 = (games, \uparrow)$ using the chunks in a piecewise manner as shown in Table 5 and Table 6. Again in these two tables, we observe that the tuple rankings of gradual items $g_1 = (age, \downarrow)$ and $g_2 = (games, \uparrow)$ are represented by a total of 18 (2×2) binary matrices. In the classical approach, these rankings would be represented by 2 (6×6) binary matrices (see Table 1 and Table 2 in Sect. 1). Both approaches require the same size of memory to store all data in the binary matrices (which is 72 in total). However, the classical approach maps this data using a contiguous layout while, our proposed approach maps this data using a chunked layout.

Table 5. Chunked binary matrices for ranked tuples in Table 4b that fulfill gradual item $g_1 = (age, \downarrow)$.

Γ	r1	r2
r1	0	1
r2	0	0

(a)

Γ	r3	r4
r1	1	1
r2	1	1

(b)

Γ	r5	r6
r1	1	1
r2	1	1

(c)

Γ	r1	r2
r3	0	0
r4	0	0

(d)

Γ	r3	r4
r3	0	1
r4	0	0

(e)

Γ	r5	r6
r3	1	1
r4	0	1

(f)

Γ	r1	r2
r5	0	0
r6	0	0

(g)

Γ	r3	r4
r5	0	0
r6	0	0

(h)

Γ	r5	r6
r5	0	1
r6	0	0

(i)

Table 6. Chunked binary matrices for ranked tuples in Table 4b that fulfill gradual item $g_2 = (games, \uparrow)$.

↱	r1	r2
r1	0	1
r2	0	0

(a)

↱	r3	r4
r1	1	1
r2	0	1

(b)

↱	r5	r6
r1	1	1
r2	0	1

(c)

↱	r1	r2
r3	0	1
r4	0	0

(d)

↱	r3	r4
r3	0	1
r4	0	0

(e)

↱	r5	r6
r3	0	1
r4	0	0

(f)

↱	r1	r2
r5	0	1
r6	0	0

(g)

↱	r3	r4
r5	0	1
r6	0	0

(h)

↱	r5	r6
r5	0	1
r6	0	0

(i)

Secondly, we perform a bitwise AND operation on the corresponding chunked matrices of gradual items $g_1 = (age, \downarrow)$ and $g_2 = (games, \uparrow)$ in order to determine if by joining them, the gradual pattern $gp_{12} = \{(age, \downarrow), (games, \uparrow)\}$ is *frequent* (this is shown in Table 7). It should be underlined that gradual items (i.e. g_1 and g_2) should have binary matrices that match in number and size. Similarly, each matrix of one gradual item must be mapped to the corresponding matrix of the other gradual item during an AND operation. For instance, the matrix in Table 5(a) can only be mapped to the matrix in Table 6(a) during a bitwise AND operation to obtain the matrix in Table 7(a), and so on.

Table 7. Binary matrices for $gp_{12} = \{(age, \downarrow), (games, \uparrow)\}$ after performing bitwise AND operation on chunked matrices of g_1 and g_2.

↱	r1	r2
r1	0	1
r2	0	0

(a)

↱	r3	r4
r1	1	1
r2	0	1

(b)

↱	r5	r6
r1	1	1
r2	0	1

(c)

↱	r1	r2
r3	0	0
r4	0	0

(d)

↱	r3	r4
r3	0	1
r4	0	0

(e)

↱	r5	r6
r3	0	1
r4	0	0

(f)

↱	r1	r2
r5	0	0
r6	0	0

(g)

↱	r3	r4
r5	0	0
r6	0	0

(h)

↱	r5	r6
r5	0	1
r6	0	0

(i)

It is important to highlight that this chunked layout for binary matrices allows a bitwise AND operation to be broken down into multiple repetitions instead of a single operation as seen in the contiguous layout. This capability can be exploited to allow at least 2 chunked matching matrices to be loaded and held in main memory for every repeated AND operation. In this example, the bitwise AND operation is repeated at least 9 times for each twin of corresponding matrices.

Again in Table 7, we observe that binary matrices at (d), (g) and (h) sum up to 0; therefore, they are not significant in determining whether pattern gp_{12} is *frequent*. This phenomenon may be harnessed to increase the efficiency of this approach by skipping less significant binary matrices during the repetitive bitwise AND operation.

Lastly, let the user-defined support threshold be 0.5, then pattern $gp_{12} = \{(age, \downarrow), (games, \uparrow)\}$ is *frequent* since its support is 10/15 or 0.667 (see derivation for frequency support in Example 2 - Sect. 1).

4.2   GRAD-L Algorithm

In the following, we present GRAD-L (Gradual-Large) shown in Algorithm 1 which implements the approach described in Sect. 4.1.

Algorithm 1: GRAD-L (Gradual-Large)

    Input   : Data set $\mathcal{D}$, minimum support σ, chunk size C
    Output: gradual patterns GP

1   $GP \leftarrow \emptyset$;
2   $GP_c \leftarrow$ gen_gp_candidates();
3   **for** $gp \in GP_c$ **do**
      ; /* gp - gradual pattern   */
4      $M_{sum} \leftarrow 0$;
5   **for** $gi \in gp$ **do**
          ; /* gi - gradual item   */
6          $M_{bin} \leftarrow$ chunk_to_matrix($gi, \mathcal{D}, C$);
7   **if** calc_sum(M_{bin}) ≤ 0 **then**
8   Continue;
9   **else**
10   **if** gi is *firstElement* **then**
11               $M_{bin1} \leftarrow M_{bin}$;
12   Break;
13   **else**
14               $M_{bin2} \leftarrow M_{bin}$;
15               $M_{bin} \leftarrow M_{bin1}$ AND M_{bin2};
16               $M_{sum} \leftarrow M_{sum}+$ calc_sum(M_{bin});
17   **end for**
18      $sup \leftarrow$ calc_support(M_{sum});
19   **if** $sup \geq \sigma$ **then**
20   GP.append(gp);
21 **end for**
22 **return** GP;

In this algorithm, first we use existing techniques to identify gradual pattern candidates (*line* 2). Second, for each candidate we use its gradual items user-defined chunk-size to build chunked binary matrices and perform a bitwise

AND operation piece-wisely (*lines* $3 - 13$). Third, we determine if the candidate pattern is *frequent* by comparing its support to the user-defined threshold.

4.3   Computational Complexity

In the following, we use the big-O notation [1, 13] to analyze the computational complexity of GRAD-L algorithm. For every gradual pattern candidate that is generated: GRAD-L algorithm constructs multiple chunked binary matrices, performs a bitwise AND operation on the chunked binary matrices and calculates the frequency support of that candidate. We formulate the problem to and show the computational complexity of GRAD-L algorithm.

Problem Formulation. Given a dataset $\mathcal{D}$ with m attributes and n objects, we can generate numerous gradual pattern candidates each having k gradual items (where $2 \geq k \leq m$). For each candidate, the classical GRAANK algorithm (proposed in [7]) builds binary matrices for every gradual item as shown in Table 2 (see Sect. 2). Next, a bitwise AND operation is performed on these matrices and frequency support of the resulting matrix computed as shown in Table 3 (see Sect. 2). Using the big-O notation, constructing the binary matrices through GRAANK algorithm results in a complexity of $O(k \cdot n^2)$. The bitwise AND operation and support computation have small complexities in comparison to that of constructing binary matrices.

For the case of GRAD-L algorithm, a user-defined chunk-size $(q \times q)$ (where $q < n$) is used to construct y binary matrices for every gradual item. Therefore, the complexity of constructing binary matrices for every gradual pattern candidate is $O(k \cdot \sum_1^y q^2)$. Similarly, the bitwise AND operation and support computation have small and almost constant complexities.

Search Space Size. It is important to mention that for every generated candidate, the classical GRAANK algorithm and the proposed GRAD-L algorithm constructs binary matrices. Therefore, the complexity of x generated gradual pattern candidates is $O(x \cdot k \cdot n^2)$ for GRAANK algorithm and $O(x \cdot k \cdot \sum_1^y q^2)$ for GRAD-L algorithm.

5   Experiments

In this section, we present an experimental study of the computational and memory performance of our proposed algorithm. We implement the algorithm for GRAD-L approach described in Sect. 4 using `Python` Language. All the experiments were conducted on a High Performance Computing (HPC) **Meso@LR**[3] platform. We used one node comprising 14 cores of CPU and 128GB of RAM.

---

[3] https://meso-lr.umontpellier.fr.

5.1   Source Code

The `Python` source code of the proposed algorithm is available at our GitHub repository: https://github.com/owuordickson/large_gps.git.

5.2   Data Set Description

Table 8. Experiment data sets.

Data set	#tuples	#attributes	Domain
Cargo 2000 (C2K)	3,942	98	Transport
Power Consump. (UCI)	2,075,259	9	Electrical

The 'Cargo 2000' data set, obtained from `UCI Machine Learning Repository` (UCI-MLR) [8], describes 98 tracking and tracing events that span 5 months of transport logistics execution. The 'Power Consumption' data set, obtained from `UCI-MLR` [3], describes the electric power consumption in one household (located in Sceaux, France) in terms of active power, voltage and global intensity with a one-minute sampling rate between 2006 and 2010.

5.3   Experiement Resultts

In the following, we present our experimental results which show the computational and memory usage of our proposed algorithm (GRAD-L), HDF5-based algorithm (GRAD-H5) and classical algorithm (GRAD) for mining gradual patterns. Using these 3 algorithms, we perform test runs on C2K and UCI data sets with minimum support threshold (σ) set to 0.1.

We split the UCI data set into 5 data sets whose number of tuples range from 10,000 (10K), 116,203 (116K), 523,104 (523K), 1,000,000 (1M) and 2,075,259 (2M). All the test runs were repeated several times and the results are available at: https://github.com/owuordickson/meso-hpc-lr/tree/master/results/large_gps/.

Computational Performance Results. Table 9 shows a result summary for computational run-time performance, number of extracted patterns and memory utilization of algorithms GRAD, GRAD-H5 and GRAD-L. It is important to highlight that algorithms GRAD and GRAD-H5 yield *'Memory Error'* when executed on UCI data sets whose tuple size is greater than 100,000 and 500,000 respectively (represented as 'NaN' in Table 9). Figure 2 illustrates how run-time and memory usage breaks for GRAD (due to *'Memory Error'*) grows exponentially for GRAD-H5 (due to read/write overhead).

Computational run-time results show that GRAD-L (which implements our proposed chunked layout for loading binary matrices into memory) is the fastest of the 3 algorithms when executed in all the data sets. GRAD (which uses contiguous layout to load and hold binary matrices into memory) is relatively

Table 9. Summary of experiment results.

Data set	Size	Algorithm	Run-time (sec)		No. of patterns		Memory (KiB)	
			St.d.	Mean	St.d.	Mean	St.d.	Mean
C2K	3.9K	GRAD	24.125	702.536	0.000	2.000	2.044	**172.089**
		GRAD-H5	12.162	3786.30	0.000	2.000	4.313	497.450
		GRAD-L	0.653	**15.821**	0.894	1.400	38.643	501.200
UCI	10K	GRAD	1.448	51.682	0.408	1.833	0.564	**109.617**
		GRAD-H5	98.794	47.162	0.000	2.000	118.713	172.383
		GRAD-L	0.630	**5.017**	0.516	1.333	1.089	291.350
UCI	116K	GRAD	NaN	NaN	NaN	NaN	NaN	NaN
		GRAD-H5	143.543	33209.50	0.000	2.000	0.566	427.600
		GRAD-L	63.772	**524.787**	0.000	2.000	15.312	**276.367**
UCI	523K	GRAD	NaN	NaN	NaN	NaN	NaN	NaN
		GRAD-H5	NaN	NaN	NaN	NaN	NaN	NaN
		GRAD-L	1716.374	**10947.60**	1.000	**1.000**	22.228	**287.800**
UCI	1M	GRAD	NaN	NaN	NaN	NaN	NaN	NaN
		GRAD-H5	NaN	NaN	NaN	NaN	NaN	NaN
		GRAD-L	367.723	**39460.3**	0.577	**1.667**	1.386	**350.400**
UCI	2M	GRAD	NaN	NaN	NaN	NaN	NaN	NaN
		GRAD-H5	NaN	NaN	NaN	NaN	NaN	NaN
		GRAD-L	22113.287	**162616.7**	0.577	**1.333**	5.605	**367.333**

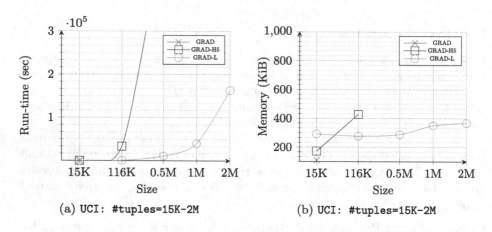

(a) UCI: #tuples=15K-2M   (b) UCI: #tuples=15K-2M

Fig. 2. Plot of run-time and memory usage against size of UCI data set.

fast (compared to GRAD-H5) when executed on data set C2K and UCI 10K. However, it yields *'Memory Error'* for UCI data sets greater than 100K since sizes of binary matrices in main memory increase exponentially within a very short time and this exceeds the available memory. GRAD-H5 (which implements HDF5-based approach for dealing with huge binary matrices) has the slowest run-times of all the 3 algorithms. This may be attributed to read-write overhead that occurs in all bitwise AND operations.

Memory usage results show that GRAD has better memory utilization on data sets C2K and UCI 10K. However, GRAD-L has the best overall memory utilization since it does not yield *'Memory Error'* on any of the 6 data sets. Number of patterns results show that almost all 3 algorithms extract similar number of gradual patterns.

Consistent Gradual Patterns. This experiment reveals the consistent gradual patterns extracted by the 3 algorithms from data sets C2K and UCI when minimum support threshold (σ) is set to 0.1. The results are shown in Table 10.

Table 10. Consistent gradual patterns.

Data set	Gradual patterns
C2K (3.9K)	$\{(i2\_rcs\_e, \downarrow), (o\_legid, \uparrow), (o\_dlv\_c, \downarrow)\}, sup = 0.23$
UCI (10K)	$\{(Sub\_metering\_3, \uparrow), (Global\_intensity, \downarrow)\}, sup = 0.172$
UCI (116K)	$\{(Voltage, \downarrow), (Sub\_metering\_1, \uparrow)\}, sup = 0.109$
UCI (523K)	$\{(Global\_intensity, \downarrow), (Sub\_metering\_2, \uparrow)\}, sup = 0.16$
UCI (1M)	$\{(Global\_reactive\_power, \downarrow), (Global\_intensity, \downarrow)\}, sup = 0.558$
UCI (2M)	$\{(Sub\_metering\_3, \uparrow), (Sub\_metering\_2, \downarrow)\}, sup = 0.159$

It is important to mention that for huge data sets, extracted gradual patterns are of relatively low quality. For this reason, we chose a low minimum support threshold ($\sigma = 0.1$) in order to extract gradual patterns from all the data sets.

6   Conclusion and Future Works

In this paper, we explore two different approaches to solve the problem of mining gradual patterns from huge data sets (see Sect. 3 and Sect. 4). From the experiment results (presented in Sect. 5), we conclude that GRAD-L algorithm is the best performing algorithm (relative to GRAD and GRAD-H5 algorithms) both in terms of computational run-time and memory utilization. This proves that our proposed chunking approach (described in Sect. 4) utilizes main memory more efficiently than the classical approach (proposed in [7]) HDF5-based chunking approach (discussed in Sect. 3).

Future work may involve extensive experimentation on the GRAD-L approach with the aim of improving its memory usage efficiency even further. In addition to this, other future work may entail integrating the GRAD-L approach into data lake environments that hold numerous huge data sets. A good example of such an environment is OREME[4] which is a scientific research observatory that holds a huge collection of large scientific data sets.

---

[4] https://data.oreme.org/.

Acknowledgements. This work has been realized with the support of the High Performance Computing Platform: **MESO@LR** https://meso-lr.umontpellier. fr, financed by the Occitanie / Pyrénées-Méditerranée Region, Montpellier Mediterranean Metropole and Montpellier University.

References

1. Cormen, T.H., Leiserson, C.E., Rivest, R.L., Stein, C.: Introduction to Algorithms. MIT Press (2009)
2. Di-Jorio, Lisa., Laurent, Anne, Teisseire, Maguelonne: Mining frequent gradual Itemsets from large databases. In: Adams, Niall M., Robardet, Céline, Siebes, Arno, Boulicaut, Jean-François (eds.) IDA 2009. LNCS, vol. 5772, pp. 297–308. Springer, Heidelberg (2009). https://doi.org/10.1007/978-3-642-03915-7_26
3. Dua, D., Graff, C.: UCI machine learning repository (2019). http://archive.ics.uci.edu/ml
4. Folk, M., Heber, G., Koziol, Q., Pourmal, E., Robinson, D.: An overview of the HDF5 technology suite and its applications. In: Proceedings of the EDBT/ICDT 2011 Workshop on Array Databases, pp. 36–47. AD 2011. Association for Computing Machinery, New York (2011). https://doi.org/10.1145/1966895.1966900
5. Howison, M., Koziol, Q., Knaak, D., Mainzer, J., Shalf, J.: Tuning HDF5 for lustre file systems. In: Workshop on Interfaces and Abstractions for Scientific Data Storage (IASDS10). Office of Scientific and Technical Information (U.S. Department of Energy), USA (2010). https://www.osti.gov/biblio/1050648
6. Krijnen, T., Beetz, J.: An efficient binary storage format for IFC building models using HDF5 hierarchical data format. Autom. Construc. **113**, 103–134 (2020). https://doi.org/10.1016/j.autcon.2020.103134
7. Laurent, Anne., Lesot, Marie-Jeanne, Rifqi, Maria: GRAANK: exploiting rank correlations for extracting gradual Itemsets. In: Andreasen, Troels, Yager, Ronald R., Bulskov, Henrik, Christiansen, Henning, Larsen, Henrik Legind (eds.) FQAS 2009. LNCS (LNAI), vol. 5822, pp. 382–393. Springer, Heidelberg (2009). https://doi.org/10.1007/978-3-642-04957-6_33
8. Metzger, A., et al.: Comparing and combining predictive business process monitoring techniques. IEEE Trans. Syst. Man Cybern. Syst. **45**(2), 276–290 (2015)
9. Negrevergne, Benjamin., Termier, Alexandre., Rousset, Marie-Christine, Méhaut, Jean-François: PARAMINER: a generic pattern mining algorithm for multi-core architectures. Data Min. Knowl. Disc. **28**(3), 593–633 (2013). https://doi.org/10.1007/s10618-013-0313-2
10. Owuor, D., Laurent, A., Orero, J.: Mining fuzzy-temporal gradual patterns. In: 2019 IEEE International Conference on Fuzzy Systems (FUZZ-IEEE), pp. 1–6. IEEE, New York, June 2019. https://doi.org/10.1109/FUZZ-IEEE.2019.8858883
11. Owuor, D., Laurent, A., Orero, J., Lobry, O.: Gradual pattern mining tool on cloud. In: Extraction et Gestion des Connaissances: Actes EGC'2021 (2021)
12. Owuor, Dickson Odhiambo., Laurent, Anne, Orero, Joseph Onderi: Exploiting IoT data crossings for gradual pattern mining through parallel processing. In: Bellatreche, L., et al. (eds.) TPDL/ADBIS/EDA -2020. CCIS, vol. 1260, pp. 110–121. Springer, Cham (2020). https://doi.org/10.1007/978-3-030-55814-7_9
13. Vaz, R., Shah, V., Sawhney, A., Deolekar, R.: Automated Big-O analysis of algorithms. In: 2017 International Conference on Nascent Technologies in Engineering (ICNTE), pp. 1–6, January 2017. https://doi.org/10.1109/ICNTE.2017.7947882
14. Xu, H., Wei, W., Dennis, J., Paul, K.: Using cloud-friendly data format in earth system models. In: AGU Fall Meeting Abstracts, pp. IN13C-0728, December 2019

A General Method for Event Detection on Social Media

Yihong Zhang$^{(\boxtimes)}$, Masumi Shirakawa, and Takahiro Hara

Multimedia Data Engineering Lab, Graduate School of Information Science
and Technology, Osaka University, Osaka, Japan
shirakawa@hapicom.jp, hara@ist.osaka-u.ac.jp

Abstract. Event detection on social media has attracted a number of researches, given the recent availability of large volumes of social media discussions. Previous works on social media event detection either assume a specific type of event, or assume certain behavior of observed variables. In this paper, we propose a general method for event detection on social media that makes few assumptions. The main assumption we make is that when an event occurs, affected semantic aspects will behave differently from its usual behavior. We generalize the representation of time units based on word embeddings of social media text, and propose an algorithm to detect events in time series in a general sense. In the experimental evaluation, we use a novel setting to test if our method and baseline methods can exhaustively catch all real-world news in the test period. The evaluation results show that when the event is quite unusual with regard to the base social media discussion, it can be captured more effectively with our method. Our method can be easily implemented and can be treated as a starting point for more specific applications.

1 Introduction

Event detection on social media in recent years has attracted a large number of researches. Given large volumes of social media data and the rich information contained in them, event detection on social media is both beneficial and challenging. With social media text as the base data, important previous works have proposed methods for detecting earthquakes [17], emerging topics for organizations [5], and influenza trends [8]. In these works and many others, however, it is required to have some prior knowledge or assumptions of the potential event. These assumptions include some known keywords or entity names that are associated with the event [4,5,13,14,17,22], and some manually created labels for events as the supervised training dataset [8,11]. Furthermore, the definition of event also differs in these works. Some consider an event as a temporal-spatial concentration of similar texts [7,8,11,22,26], while others consider it as an unusual burstiness in term frequency [5,15,24].

In this paper, in contrast, we attempt to provide a general solution to event detection in social media with minimum prior assumption of the event. First of all, we follow a general definition of event that is not restricted to social media

© Springer Nature Switzerland AG 2021
L. Bellatreche et al. (Eds.): ADBIS 2021, LNCS 12843, pp. 43–56, 2021.
https://doi.org/10.1007/978-3-030-82472-3_5

data. This definition was proposed by Jaegwon Kim, who considered that an event consists of three parts, a finite set of objects x, a property P, and a time interval t [10]. To better illustrate, let us consider a scenario of an amusement park. Normally, customers wander around the park, visiting different attractions in almost a random manner. When a show starts to perform in the central stage, those who are interested in the show will be moving towards the stage. In this scenario, the object x are the customers who interested in the show, the property P is the direction of the stage, and the time interval t is the duration of the show. Note that just as not all customers in the park are interested in the show, $x \in X$ in an event is a subset of all possible objects.

Putting it on the social media case, when an event creates an impact on people's lives, it is likely that it will be reflected on online discussions. Certain semantic aspects of posted text, which can be considered as the object set x, would suddenly have unusual trends together, whose deviation can be considered as the property P, for the duration of the event t. This is realistic, if we recall that when a critical political event happened, some aspects of social media discussion, such as the terms and sentiments involved in the event, would have a higher-than-usual visibility. The problem then is how to capture x, P and t in social media text through a computational method.

The principle of our design is to make as few assumptions about the event as possible. Here are two assumptions we make in our method. First, there is a finite set of components in the system, and a subset of components will be affected by the event. Second, for the duration of the event, affected components behave differently from their usual, normal behavior. We consider these are minimum assumptions that are within restrictions in Kim's definition of an event. Given these assumptions, our method takes two steps to achieve event detection. First, we convert unstructured social media text data into distributed representation, also called *word embeddings*, where each dimension represents a semantic aspect, and is considered as a component in the system. This can be done with existing distributed representation learning techniques such as *word2vec* [12]. Note that in this paper we consider only social media text. However, the images in social media can be studied in a similar way as they be turned into multi-dimension vector representations using models such as Inception [20]. Second, we design and use a multi-dimension anomaly detection algorithm to capture the unusual behavior, with a customizable normality test. The algorithm detects abnormal intervals in single time series and combines them to form affected components of an event by finding the intersections.

Our method is general in two ways. First, our method generalizes social media text into semantic aspects. With this generalization, we now look at the collective behavior of social media posts instead of tracking individual term frequency. This is useful in many scenarios. For example, during New Year holiday in Japan, many aspects of real-world phenomenon become visible, including New Year's meal (年越し), a specific TV program (紅白), New Year's greeting (挨拶), and the general happy mood. Individually, these terms may not have a significant frequency change, but collectively, they make the New Year event unusual.

Second, our method generalizes event detection as anomaly detection in time series. In contrast to previous works, we deal with durative events instead of punctual events. With a customizable normality test function, we can detect events with arbitrary lengths. Such generality allows our method to be applicable to a wider range of tasks than previous works. Since our method is straightforward to implement, future extension can be easily made for the need of specific tasks.

We organize the remainder of this paper as the following. In Sect. 2, we will discuss related works on event detection in social media. In Sect. 3 and 4, we will present our method to generalize social media text to temporal word embeddings, and to detect unusual behavior in them. In Sect. 5, we will present experimental evaluation, with a novel evaluation task of recommending newsworthy words. Finally Sect. 6 will conclude this paper.

2   Related Work

Previous surveys on social media event detection works have commonly divided works according to whether detected events are specific or non-specific [1,16]. Here we would like to provide a new aspect of events in existing works, that is whether events are considered as one-time events or events lasting for a period of multiple time units. In other words punctual and durative events. Essentially, punctual events are supposed to be the point of drastic change in the observed variables [9]. While this limits the phenomenon they can represent, events with this definition are indeed easier to capture, and many works followed this approach. For example, the Twitter-based earthquake detection system proposed by Sasaki et al. [18] raises an alarm at the moment when number of tweets classified as earthquake reports reaches a certain threshold. Similarly, the event detection system proposed by Zhang et al. raises an alarm at the moment when the number of incident reports within a geographical region reaches a threshold [25]. Weng and Lee proposed an event detection method based on wavelet transformation and word clustering [24]. An event flag is set for a time slot if frequency correlation of co-occurring words is larger than a threshold. The crime and disaster event detection system proposed by Li et al. aims to extract the time an event happened, by location estimation and geographical clustering [11]. The location-based event detection method by Unankard et al. also uses a threshold to decide if an event has happened, by comparing the frequency in the current and previous time unit [22]. The disaster monitor system by Rossi et al. decides if an event happened by determining if word frequency in the current time slot is an outlier [15].

While not uncommon in time series pattern mining [3], comparing to punctual events, social media event detection methods that follow a durative event definition are rather scarce. Relevant works include the emerging topic detection method proposed by Chen et al., which identifies two time points, the moment the topic starts and the moment the topic becomes hot [5]. The purpose of the method is to identify emerging topic before the topic becomes hot, and detected events thus last for periods of varied lengths. One requirement of the method, however, is that the tweets collected should be related to certain organizations, which makes the method less applicable. The multiscale event detection method proposed by Dong et al. [7] aims at discovering events with spatio-temporally concentrated tweets. Without a preset time length for the event, the method clusters tweets that have similar spatio-temporal context, and thus indirectly detects events that last for a period. However, the requirement of spatial information also limits the applicability of the method. In this paper, on the other hand, we aim at providing a general method for detecting durative events with less restrictions.

3   Generalized Representation of Temporal Social Media Text

We first deal with problem of representing temporal social media text in a general way. A simple way to represent social media text is through bag-of-words (BOW). BOW representation essentially considers that words in text are independent tokens, and each document is a collection of them. There are two problems with BOW representation. First, in a large text collection, the vocabulary is also large, usually includes thousands of words, and tracking temporal activity of each word is computationally expensive. Second, considering words as independent tokens ignores semantic information about words, which may be important for event detection. For example, Covid-19 and Corona are both names of the virus in current pandemic, and should be considered together in one event, but BOW representation would consider them separately.

To mitigate these problems, we propose to use *word embeddings* to represent temporal social media texts. First proposed by Mikolov et al., word embeddings are distributed representation of words learned from text contexts [12]. The learning technique extracts the surrounding words of a certain word and encode them in a neural network encoder, so that a vector, called an embedding, can be associated with the word, and each element in the vector represents a certain semantic aspect of the word. While the meaning of the semantic aspect of the embedding is difficult to be understood by human reader, it has been shown that words with similar embeddings would have a similar semantic meaning. For example, *apple* would have a more similar embedding to *orange* than to *bird*.

Using word embeddings thus mitigates the problems of BOW representation. First, it reduces dimensionality. Typical word embeddings would have between 50 and 300 dimensions. Second, it allows consideration of semantics, so that words of similar meanings can be considered together. By considering semantics, we actually generalize text into a more abstract level. For example, when detecting the pandemic event, we no longer deal with individual words such as Covid-19 and Corona, but the virus or disease these words refer to. Given it is effectiveness, previous works have already use word embedding to represent not only text documents, but also users and spatial units such as locations [19,23]. In this work, we utilize word embeddings to generate vector representations of time units.

To generate vector representation for a time unit, we take the following steps.

1. assigning collected text messages to time units.
2. tokenizing text messages so that words are also assigned to time units
3. obtaining word embeddings for assigned words
4. the vector representation for a time unit is taken as the average value of all embeddings of the words assigned to the time unit

We can use existing natural language processing libraries to segment and turn tweets into words. To obtain word embeddings, we can use existing implementations of *word2vec* and a general purpose training corpus such as Wikipedia[1]. Word embedding learned under such setting would represent words with their general meaning in daily usages. The final result of this process is a vector representing the totality of social media discussions for each time unit.

4   Generalized Multi-dimension Event Detection in Time Series

At this point we have a vector for each time unit representing social media discussions. The next task is to detect events from such representations. In a way this representation can be seen as multivariate time series data, with each dimension as one observed variable. While there are previous works that have proposed event detection for time series data, most of them are dealing with punctual event [6,9], or require the events to be repeating and predictable [3]. In this work, we accept the hypothesis that an event is something that cannot be predicted, thus the behavior of affected components cannot be pre-defined [21]. We aim to make minimum assumptions about the event, and the main assumption we make is that when affected by an event, the component will behave differently from its usual behavior.

Our method detects multi-dimension event from multivariate time series in two steps. First it detects unusual intervals of observations in a single dimension (Algorithm 1). Then given a list of abnormal intervals in each dimension, it finds basically the intersections of abnormal intervals, and outputs them as multi-dimension events (Algorithm 2).

Shown in Algorithm 1, we design an algorithm to find the largest interval with significant alternation to normality. It takes a univariate time series as input, as well as two parameters k_{min} and k_{max}, which are the minimum and maximum number of time units for the detected intervals. It also requires a customizable function f_n for the normality test, and a corresponding threshold δ. The algorithm starts from the beginning of the time series (line 2, 3). At each time point i, it tests all intervals that ends between $i+k_{min}$ and $i+k_{max}$ (line 5).

---

[1] An example online resource that provides an implementation under this setting: https://github.com/philipperemy/japanese-words-to-vectors.

Algorithm 1. Find largest intervals with significant alternation to normality

INPUT: TS, k_{min}, k_{max}, f_n, δ
OUTPUT: a list of intervals Is
1: $Is \leftarrow \{\}$
2: $i \leftarrow 1$
3: **while** $i < (|TS| - k_{min})$ **do**
4:     $largest\_interval \leftarrow \{\}$
5:     **for** j in $(i + k_{min})$ to $min(|TS|, i + k_{max})$ **do**
6:         **if** $f_n(TS \setminus TS(i,j)) - f_n(TS) > \delta$ **then**
7:             $largest\_interval \leftarrow (i,j)$
8:         **end if**
9:     **end for**
10:    **if** $largest\_interval$ is empty **then**
11:        $i \leftarrow i + 1$
12:    **else**
13:        $Is \leftarrow Is \cup largest\_interval$
14:        $i \leftarrow (b$ in $largest\_interval) + 1$
15:    **end if**
16: **end while**

With each interval, it performs normality test with the specified function f_n, and if the normality difference between the time series with and without the interval is larger than δ, then the interval is considered abnormal (line 6). The largest interval considered as abnormal will be taken as the abnormal interval starts at time i (line 7). If an abnormal interval is found, the algorithm will move to the end of the interval (line 13, 14), and continue until it reaches the end of the time series. Finally the algorithm returns all abnormal intervals found as Is.

It is worth noting that Algorithm 1 does not necessarily find intervals that deviate most from normality. For example, given a highly abnormal interval I, a few time units surrounding I may be normal by themselves, but when considered together with I, this larger interval may still be abnormal above the threshold. And our algorithm will pick the larger interval instead of the more deviating interval. Since our goal is to detect multi-dimension events, and the intervals are to be taken as the input of next step, it is rather desirable to have the largest possible abnormal intervals, instead of smaller, more deviating intervals.

The normality test function f_n can be defined by the user, as long as it outputs a score for data normality or randomness. There are many existing normality test functions available to use, including Box test and Shapiro Wilk test [2]. For the completion of the method, we use the rank version of von Neumann's ratio test [2] in our experimental analysis [2]. After some trying a few test functions, we found that this randomness test tests to capture unusual intervals in data more consistently.

---

[2] An implementation of this test is available as an R package: https://cran.r-project.org/web/packages/randtests/randtests.pdf.

Algorithm 2. Find multi-dimension events

INPUT: Is, k_{min}, c_{min}
OUTPUT: E

1: $E \leftarrow \{\}$
2: $E_{half} \leftarrow \{\}$
3: **for** i in 1 to $n - k_{min}$ **do**
4: $\quad D_{cur} \leftarrow \{d_j | i \in Is_j\}$
5: $\quad D_{old} \leftarrow \{\}$
6: $\quad$ **for each** $e_{half} \in E_{half}$ **do**
7: $\quad\quad D_{continuing} \leftarrow d(e_{half}) \cap D_{cur}$
8: $\quad\quad$ **if** $D_{continuing} = \{\}$ **then**
9: $\quad\quad\quad$ next
10: $\quad\quad$ **end if**
11: $\quad\quad$ remove e_{half} from E_{half}
12: $\quad\quad$ **if** $|D_{continuing}| > c_{min}$ **then**
13: $\quad\quad\quad e_{continuing} \leftarrow (start(e_{half}), i, D_{continuing})$
14: $\quad\quad\quad E_{half} \leftarrow E_{half} \cup e_{continuing}$
15: $\quad\quad\quad D_{old} \leftarrow D_{old} \cup D_{continuing}$
16: $\quad\quad$ **else**
17: $\quad\quad\quad D_{continuing} \leftarrow \{\}$
18: $\quad\quad$ **end if**
19: $\quad\quad e_{finished} \leftarrow (start(e_{half}), i, d(e_{half}) \setminus D_{continuing})$
20: $\quad\quad$ **if** $l(e_{finished}) > k_{min}$ & $|d(e_{finished})| > c_{min}$ **then**
21: $\quad\quad\quad E \leftarrow E \cup e_{finished}$
22: $\quad\quad\quad D_{old} \leftarrow D_{old} \cup (d(e_{finished}) \cap D_{cur})$
23: $\quad\quad$ **end if**
24: $\quad$ **end for**
25: $\quad D_{new} \leftarrow D_{cur} \setminus D_{old}$
26: $\quad$ **if** $|D_{new}| > c_{min}$ **then**
27: $\quad\quad E_{half} \leftarrow E_{half} \cup (i, i, D_{new})$
28: $\quad$ **end if**
29: **end for**

After processing the data with Algorithm 1, we now have a list of abnormal intervals Is for each of the word embedding dimension. The goal of next algorithm, shown as Algorithm 2, is to find the intersection of these intervals. It is an incremental algorithm that needs to go through the dataset only once. It takes the set of Is as inputs, as well as two parameters, k_{min} as the minimum length of an event period, and c_{min} as the minimum number of affected dimensions in an event.

At each time point i, the first thing to do is find the dimensions that behave unusually at i, based on the intervals detected (line 4). From there, these dimensions are either considered as a part of a continuing event, or put to form a new event. We always keep a list of events that are halfway through E_{half}, and at each time point, we check through all halfway events for continuity (line 2, 6). If affected dimensions at time i match halfway events, they are assigned to these events, and if enough dimensions are assigned ($> c_{min}$), the halfway event is considered as continuing (line 7 to 18). If a halfway event could not be matched with enough affected dimensions, the event is considered as finished (line 19 to 23). Those dimensions not matched with any halfway event are grouped to form a new halfway event, if there are enough of them (line 25 to 28). The final output is a list of events E, where each $e \in E$ has $e = \{\mathbf{x}, t\}$, with $\mathbf{x}$ as affected dimensions, and t as the event period.

5 Experimental Evaluation

We use real-world social media data to verify the effectiveness of our event detection method. We are unable to establish a way to directly evaluate the detected events, which consist of duration and affected dimensions in word embeddings, and are not human-readable. Therefore, we attempt to evaluate them indirectly. We extend our method to perform a task called recommending newsworthy words, which has been the evaluation task in other event detection works [7,22]. We will present the details of this task and the results in this section. It is worth noting here, though, that our event detection can potentially do more than recommending newsworthy words.

5.1 Evaluation Task

Our evaluation task is as follows. Given a set of time units $T = \{t_1, ..., t_c\}$, for each time unit, we apply the event detection method on a social media discussion dataset, and generate a ranked list of event words P from detected events. Also for each time unit, we generate from news sources a ranked list of news words G. The evaluation is done by comparing P and G. If $|G \cap P|$ is large, then the event detection method is considered as capable of capturing newsworthy words, which also shows that the news has an impact on the social media discussion.

Traditional evaluation of event detection is centered on detected events [22]. It verifies whether detected events is corresponding to real-world events, and does not do anything when a real-world event has not been detected (false negative). We on the other hand, attempt an exhaustive evaluation that concerns all real-world events happened. Specifically, we consider all news headlines from news source for each time unit, and evaluate to what degree corresponding information can be detected by the event detection method.

5.2 Social Media Discussion Dataset

Since it is not feasible to monitor all messages in a social media platform such as Twitter, we select a subset of all messages on Twitter as our social media discussion dataset. First we obtain a list of Japanese politician Twitter accounts[3]. Then we monitor all tweets mentioning these accounts using Twitter Stream

---

[3] Since politician are public, such a list can be found in many online sources, for example: https://meyou.jp/group/category/politician/.

API[4]. For period of six months between January and July, 2020, we collected about 6.9 million tweets, after removing retweets. We take this as the discussion dataset. We understand this dataset does not represent the overall discussion happening on Twitter, but rather has a focused theme that is Japanese politics. But such discussions and the community producing them may still be affected by general news, and it will be interesting to see what unusual events can be captured from these discussions and how they correspond to news sources. It is expected that if we can detect the events in this discussion dataset, we can also detect events in discussion of different themes in the same way.

We use the natural language processing package kuromoji[5] to process the Japanese text in social media discussion dataset. The package can effectively perform segmentation and part-of-speech (POS) tagging for Japanese text. After POS tagging, we select only nouns to represent the information in the text. We also filter out some less frequent words, and consider only 8,267 words that have appeared at least 500 times in the dataset.

5.3   Ground Truth Generation

We generate ground truth news words as follows. First we collect messages posted by a number of Japanese news Twitter accounts[6]. Among 916 news account considered, some are general news accounts reporting local and international news, some are specific news accounts reporting news for example in sports or entertainment. Messages sent from these accounts are usually news headlines. To make our target clearer, we select from collected messages three specific topics, namely, *politics*, *international*, and *Corona*. The selection is done by filtering collected messages with these three topic words as hashtags. During a one-month period between June and July, 2020, we collected 814 political news headlines, 503 international news headlines, and 602 Corona news headlines. These news headlines are assigned to time units of one hour length.

We turn these news headlines into nouns by the same kuromoji software described in the previous section, and count the frequencies. These words are then ranked using $tfidf$, which is calculated as:

$$tfidf(w) = tf(w) \cdot \log \frac{|D|}{|d \in D : w \in d|}$$

where $tf(w)$ is the frequency of word w, and D is a collection of documents, which in our case is messages assigned to $|D|$ time units. Finally, for each time unit, we pick top-20 words ranked by $tfidf$ as the ground truth news words.

---

[4] https://developer.twitter.com/en/docs/tutorials/consuming-streaming-data—.

[5] https://github.com/atilika/kuromoji.

[6] A list of popular Japanese news Twitter accounts can be found on the same source: https://meyou.jp/ranking/follower_media.

5.4   Recommending Newsworthy Words from Detected Events

Since our method does not generate ranked words directly, we need a method to convert the output of our method into words. The output of our method is a list of events $E = \{e_1, ..., e_m\}$, where for each event we have a set of affected dimensions $\mathbf{x}$ and duration t.

To convert this result back to words, we first calculate the deviation of a affected dimension in the event duration as the difference between mean value of the dimension in the event duration, and the mean value outside the duration:

$$dev_e(x) = mean\_freq(x, t) - mean\_freq(x, \neg t)$$

which can be considered as a part of event property P. Then for each word w with embedding $embedding_w$, an event score is calculated as the product of the embedding value and the deviation in the affected dimensions:

$$event\_score_e(w) = \sum_{x \in \mathbf{x}} embedding_w(x) \times dev_e(x)$$

In this way, words with the same deviation tendency as the affected dimensions will have a higher score. Finally, to calculate a word score in a time unit, we have

$$time\_score(w) = \sum_{e=1}^{m} event\_score_e(w)$$

which gives higher scores to words with higher event scores in multiple events. The time score is thus used to rank the words in each time unit.

5.5   Baseline Methods

We compare our method with two baseline methods in this evaluation task. The first is a $tfidf$-based method commonly used in previous works. In the same way we generate ground truth, we apply the method to the social media discussion dataset and obtain a $tfidf$ score for each word in each time unit. Essentially, with this method, we make a comparison of $tfidf$-ranked words between base source, which are social media discussion tweets, and the reference source, which are news tweets.

The second baseline method is based on the Shannon's Wavelet Entropy (SWE). This method is proposed in a Twitter event detection work by Weng and Lee [24], and can be adopted for news word recommendation. From the $tfidf$ time series of each word in the social media discussion dataset, the method first performs a wavelet transformation to learn a wavelet function ψ and a coefficient C. The coefficient C can be interpreted as the local residual errors. Then an energy value E is calculated as

$$E = \sum_{k} |C(k)|^2$$

where k indicates k-th coefficient. Then the Shannon's Wavelet Entropy is calculated as

$$SWE = -\sum_j \rho_j \cdot \log \rho_j$$

where $\rho_j = E_j/E_{total}$, j indicates the j-th time unit in the time slide. SWE measures how unpredictable of the time series in a time slide t, and it will be a higher value when residual errors are more even in the time slide. Once the SWE is obtained, a score can be assigned to a word for ranking.

$$s(w) = \begin{cases} \frac{SWE_t - SWE_{t-1}}{SWE_{t-1}}, & \text{if } SWE_t > SWE_{t-1} \\ 0, & \text{otherwise} \end{cases}$$

which means if SWE of a word is increasing, it will get a higher score. In our experiments, we use the R package *wavethresh*[7] to perform the wavelet transformation and obtain coefficient C.

5.6 Evaluation Results

Evaluation results measured as Recall@K are shown in Fig. 1, where K is the number of recommended words. We compare our method (event) with theoretic random, *tfidf*, and SWE methods. A number of Ks are taken between 20 and 200. The theoretical random Recall@K is calculated as $K/|W|$, where W is the set of candidate words. The higher the result means the more words in ground truth are recommended by the method.

At the first glance, we can see that generally, *tfidf* performs better for the political news, while event method performs better for the Corona news. SWE method performs better for the international news, although only slightly better than the event method. All three methods achieve better results than the theoretical random method.

We now attempt to explain the results. First thing to note is that recommended words from a method is the same for all three news categories. Since words from news categories are quite different, with limited space, a method better at recommending words for one news category will be worse for other categories. And we can see the results are showing different strength and weakness from different methods. The reason comes from different interpretation of what is news by different methods. For the *tfidf* method, news is considered as unusually rises of word usages, and thus words closer to the theme of the social media discussion will be more likely to be recommended. For the event method, news is considered as something quite different from the usual state of the discussion, and thus words different from the social media discussion will be more likely to be recommended. And indeed we understand that, since the social media discussion is generally related to politics, political news is more similar to the discussion, while Corona news is more different from the discussion. That is why we see *tfidf* performing better for political news, and event method performing better for Corona news.

---

[7] https://cran.r-project.org/web/packages/wavethresh/wavethresh.pdf.

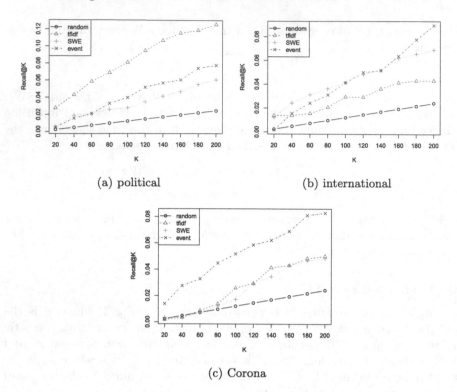

(a) political

(b) international

(c) Corona

Fig. 1. Recall@K results for three news categories

6   Conclusion

In this paper we propose a general method for event detection on social media. Two main steps of our method are generalizing social media text into word embeddings, and detecting multi-dimension event from time series. The detected events represent something unusual and affecting semantic aspects of social media discussions, over a finite period. Comparing to previous works on social media event detection, our method makes very few assumptions. We only assume that the event will be affecting a finite number of dimensions and, when affected, these dimensions behave differently from their usual, normal behavior. We evaluate detected events from social media discussions against three news categories, exhaustively collected over a testing period, and find that when the news is quite different from the base social media discussion, it can be better captured based on the detected events.

Despite some positive results from indirect evaluation, we consider that our method has some drawbacks. For example, our method demands test of normality, and requires a large portion of base data, which may not be always available. Furthermore, if it is a long period event, event-related semantics would become the norm and thus there would be problem detecting the event with our method. Nevertheless, our method has its merits. It can be easily implemented and applied to different, more specific datasets. One can, for example, pre-select a discussion dataset about finance or entertainment, and apply our method to detect events of certain type. The detected events can furthermore be used in various analysis, for example, for detecting associations between product sales and social media activities. Currently, our method detects events retrospectively. A future extension to our method would be making an incremental algorithm that can detect events in data streams.

Acknowledgement. This research is partially supported by JST CREST Grant Number JPMJCR21F2.

References

1. Atefeh, F., Khreich, W.: A survey of techniques for event detection in twitter. Comput. Intell. **31**(1), 132–164 (2015)
2. Bartels, R.: The rank version of von Neumann's ratio test for randomness. J. Am. Stat. Assoc. **77**(377), 40–46 (1982)
3. Batal, I., Fradkin, D., Harrison, J., Moerchen, F., Hauskrecht, M.: Mining recent temporal patterns for event detection in multivariate time series data. In: Proceedings of the 18th ACM SIGKDD International Conference on Knowledge Discovery and Data Mining, pp. 280–288 (2012)
4. Cataldi, M., Di Caro, L., Schifanella, C.: Emerging topic detection on twitter based on temporal and social terms evaluation. In: Proceedings of the Tenth International Workshop on Multimedia Data Mining, pp. 4:1–4:10 (2010)
5. Chen, Y., Amiri, H., Li, Z., Chua, T.-S.: Emerging topic detection for organizations from microblogs. In: Proceedings of the 36th International ACM SIGIR Conference on Research and Development in Information Retrieval, pp. 43–52. ACM (2013)
6. Cheng, H., Tan, P.-N., Potter, C., Klooster, S.: Detection and characterization of anomalies in multivariate time series. In: Proceedings of the 2009 SIAM International Conference on Data Mining, pp. 413–424. SIAM (2009)
7. Dong, X., Mavroeidis, D., Calabrese, F., Frossard, P.: Multiscale event detection in social media. Data Min. Knowl. Disc. **29**(5), 1374–1405 (2015)
8. Gao, Y., Wang, S., Padmanabhan, A., Yin, J., Cao, G.: Mapping spatiotemporal patterns of events using social media: a case study of influenza trends. Int. J. Geographical Inf. Sci. **32**(3), 425–449 (2018)
9. Guralnik, V., Srivastava, J.: Event detection from time series data. In: Proceedings of the Fifth ACM SIGKDD International Conference on Knowledge Discovery and Data Mining, pp. 33–42 (1999)
10. Kim, J.: Events as property exemplifications. In: Brand, M., Walton, D. (eds.) Action Theory, pp. 159–177. Springer, Dordrecht (1976). https://doi.org/10.1007/978-94-010-9074-2_9
11. Li, R., Lei, K.H., Khadiwala, R., Chang, K.-C.: TEDAS: a Twitter-based event detection and analysis system. In: Proceedings of 28th International Conference on Data Engineering, pp. 1273–1276 (2012)
12. Mikolov, T., Sutskever, I., Chen, K., Corrado, G.S., Dean, J.: Distributed representations of words and phrases and their compositionality. In: Advances in Neural Information Processing Systems, pp. 3111–3119 (2013)

13. Olteanu, A., Castillo, C., Diaz, F., Vieweg, S.: CrisisLex: a lexicon for collecting and filtering microblogged communications in crises. In: Proceedings of the 8th International AAAI Conference on Weblogs and Social Media, pp. 376–385 (2014)
14. Popescu, A.-M., Pennacchiotti, M.: Detecting controversial events from Twitter. In: Proceedings of the 19th ACM International Conference on Information and Knowledge Management, pp. 1873–1876 (2010)
15. Rossi, C., et al.: Early detection and information extraction for weather-induced floods using social media streams. Int. J. Disaster Risk Reduction **30**, 145–157 (2018)
16. Saeed, Z., et al.: What's happening around the world? a survey and framework on event detection techniques on twitter. J. Grid Comput. **17**(2), 279–312 (2019)
17. Sakaki, T., Okazaki, M., Matsuo, Y.: Earthquake shakes Twitter users: real-time event detection by social sensors. In: Proceedings of the 19th International World Wide Web Conference, pp. 851–860 (2010)
18. Sakaki, T., Okazaki, M., Matsuo, Y.: Tweet analysis for real-time event detection and earthquake reporting system development. IEEE Trans. Knowl. Data Eng. **25**(4), 919–931 (2013)
19. Shoji, Y., Takahashi, K., Dürst, M.J., Yamamoto, Y., Ohshima, H.: Location2Vec: generating distributed representation of location by using geo-tagged microblog posts. In: Staab, S., Koltsova, O., Ignatov, D.I. (eds.) SocInfo 2018. LNCS, vol. 11186, pp. 261–270. Springer, Cham (2018). https://doi.org/10.1007/978-3-030-01159-8_25
20. Szegedy, C., Vanhoucke, V., Ioffe, S., Shlens, J., Wojna, Z.: Rethinking the inception architecture for computer vision. In: Proceedings of the IEEE Conference on Computer Vision and Pattern Recognition, pp. 2818–2826 (2016)
21. Taylor, J.B., Williams, J.C.: A black swan in the money market. Am. Econ. J. Macroecon. **1**(1), 58–83 (2009)
22. Unankard, S., Li, X., Sharaf, M.A.: Emerging event detection in social networks with location sensitivity. World Wide Web **18**(5), 1393–1417 (2015)
23. Wang, Y., Jin, F., Su, H., Wang, J., Zhang, G.: Research on user profile based on User2vec. In: Meng, X., Li, R., Wang, K., Niu, B., Wang, X., Zhao, G. (eds.) WISA 2018. LNCS, vol. 11242, pp. 479–487. Springer, Cham (2018). https://doi.org/10.1007/978-3-030-02934-0_44
24. Weng, J., Lee, B.-S.: Event detection in twitter. In: Proceedings of the Fifth International Conference on Weblogs and Social Media, pp. 401–408 (2011)
25. Zhang, Y., Szabo, C., Sheng, Q.Z., Fang, X.S.: SNAF: observation filtering and location inference for event monitoring on Twitter. World Wide Web **21**(2), 311–343 (2018)
26. Zhou, X., Chen, L.: Event detection over twitter social media streams. VLDB J. **23**(3), 381–400 (2014)

5W1H Aware Framework for Representing and Detecting Real Events from Multimedia Digital Ecosystem

Siraj Mohammed[1]([⊠]) [iD], Fekade Getahun[1] [iD], and Richard Chbeir[2] [iD]

[1] Computer Science Department, Addis Ababa University, 1176 Addis Ababa, Ethiopia
{siraj.mohammed, fekade.getahun}@aau.edu.et
[2] Univ. Pau & Pays Adour, E2S UPPA, LIUPPA, 64600 Anglet, France
rchbeir@acm.org

Abstract. A digital media sharing platform (e.g., *YouTube, Twitter, Facebook, and Flickr)* is an advanced Digital Ecosystem that focuses on mobile device to share multimedia resources. Millions of users share different events (*e.g., sport, earthquake, concerts, etc.*) through social media platforms. As a result, the platforms host heterogeneous and a significant amount of user-generated multimedia documents (*e.g., image, voice, video, text, etc.*). In this paper, we introduce a general framework for representing events while keeping expressivity and capability to recognize events from Multimedia-based Digital Ecosystem. It takes as input: a collection of multimedia objects from heterogeneous sources, and then produces as output clustered real-world events. The proposed framework consists of two main components for: *(i)* defining and representing each dimension of multimedia objects (*such as, participant (who), temporal (when), spatial (where), sematic (what) and causal (why)*); *(ii)* detecting real events using scalable clustering algorithm in an unsupervised manner. To improve our clustering framework, we developed clustering comparison strategies using combination of dimensions (contextual features) of multimedia objects. We also showed how clustering comparison strategies can be used to detect real-world events and measured the quality of our clustering algorithm using *F-score*. The experimental results exhibited promising result.

Keywords: Multimedia documents · Event detection · Multimedia Digital Ecosystem · Event Representation

1 Introduction

In modern society, digital technologies and digital innovations are bringing various forms of specialized Digital Ecosystems, such as Bank-based Digital Ecosystem [1], Healthcare Digital Ecosystem [2], Industry-based Digital Ecosystem [3], and Social Media-based Digital Ecosystem [4]. A Digital Ecosystem can provide a standardized way to design heterogeneous and adaptive systems that are digitally connected, enabled

© Springer Nature Switzerland AG 2021
L. Bellatreche et al. (Eds.): ADBIS 2021, LNCS 12843, pp. 57–70, 2021.
https://doi.org/10.1007/978-3-030-82472-3_6

by modularity, and exchange information in a mutually beneficial manner [5]. Furthermore, Digital Ecosystem can be viewed as a framework that can provide a general reference/guideline to a particular approach, having high-level phases to design, develop, and interact with digital platforms in an open, heterogeneous, loosely coupled, independent and distributed manner [6, 7]. It also includes characteristics like scalability, compatibility, sustainability, self-organizing, self-management, and much more. More specifically, Social Media-based Digital Ecosystem aims at creating a digital environment for agents (*e.g., machine or human*) to easily publish and share multimedia resources (*i.e., texts, images, movies, etc.,*) for a mutually beneficial purpose [7]. Digital media sharing platforms (*e.g., YouTube, Twitter, Facebook, and Flickr*) are primarily internet/mobile-based systems for creating, sharing, and using massive heterogeneous data. Currently, many of us freely and spontaneously generate and share various types of multimedia data using Digital media sharing platform [8]. As a result, the digital ecosystem has a huge amount of real-time, machine/user-generated multimedia content with diversified representations [7]. Due to this, several issues and challenges are exhibited [7, 8], such as: *(i)* absence of common description technique that facilitate creating, sharing, collecting, and representing heterogeneous multimedia content; *(ii)* existing platforms do not provide generic services for representing events, detecting events stated in the multimedia content, and searching relevant events that fits to the request of users; and *(iii)* identifying real-world events and model relationship among them remain one of the challenging tasks.

Moreover, a large number of multimedia data are produced and shared every day in unstructured format in heterogeneous content type (*e.g., texts, images, videos, etc.*), having different standard formats (*e.g., svg, mpeg, x3d, etc.*), created by various users using different digital platforms (*e.g., YouTube, Twitter, Facebook, and Flickr*). Due to these data handling technique becomes more and more complicated. To mitigate these complexities, the concept of "*Multimedia –Oriented Digital Ecosystem*" has been introduced and applied in digital platforms (e.g., [6, 7]). Multimedia-Oriented Digital Ecosystem (MMDES) is a comprehensive form of Digital Ecosystem (DES) which consists of Web applications, physical objects (devices) and actors (*i.e., users/software agents*) as components within the Ecosystem with predefined usage rules for sharing and processing multimedia resources [6]. It serves as a bridge between different digital platforms and users with characteristics of scalability, compatibility, sustainability, self-organization, self-management, and much more. The goal of MMDES [7] is to provide a shared digital environment and effective multimedia data handling technique in an open, loosely coupled, independent, adaptive and distributed manner [6]. MMDES allows actors (*i.e., users/software agents*) to collaborate and share their multimedia data to build collective knowledge (CK) [7]. From this heterogeneous multimedia-based collective knowledge, extracting, representing, and detecting meaningful events are important. Thus, a new approach that effectively (*i*) extracts multimedia contents from Multimedia Digital Ecosystem; (*ii*) identifies context features (5W1H) for event only (e.g., *capture time/location)* to distinguish multimedia objects that are potentially indicative of an event from non-events; and (*iii*) detects real-world events based on the 5W1H aspect of an event is needed. In this paper, we proposed a novel framework that keeps expressivity and capability to identify real events from Multimedia-based Digital Ecosystem. It takes as input a collection of multimedia objects from heterogeneous sources, and then produces as output clustered real-world events. In summary, the main contributions of this study are as follows:

- We introduced a unified 5W1H aware framework which handles representation of real event from multimedia documents (cf. Sect. 6).
- We presented an incremental/scalable clustering algorithm for detecting real-world event from different social media platforms.
- We provided a new cluster comparison strategy based on hierarchical clustering and expressed in incremental clustering algorithm (cf. Sect. 7.2).
- We demonstrated the effectiveness of our proposed approach using different similarity-based clustering comparison strategies using participant, temporal, spatial, and semantic dimensions/features of multimedia objects.

2 Motivation

A person is looking for relevant information about earthquake event in Hawassa, Ethiopia. This person could search the web for relevant information using single source search engines (*e.g., Google*). Unfortunately, web search results are a list of information resources (or ranked lists of URLs) containing the search query terms, the result may not be necessarily about the requested event, and user involvement is necessary to browse, interpret and combine results. Overall, such web search results do not consider basic event related features/dimensions of multimedia objects (*e.g., time (when), location (where), sematic (what), etc.*). Moreover, vast amount of user/machine generated event-related multimedia documents are published, shared, and distributed every day on social media platforms. However, multimedia contents from these sources having different representations pose several issues and challenges, such as: *(i)* harmonizing the different multimedia representation models and providing a unified framework for representing events and *(ii)* detecting real-world events from multimedia contents considering different dimensions of event. Thus, there is a need of designing unified framework to address these issues and challenges. In this study, we proposed a unified 5W1H aware framework for representing and detecting real-world events from different social media sites.

3 Event Characteristics, Challenges, Opportunities and Approaches

Real-world events can be characterized using five W's (*i.e., Where, When, What, Who, and Why*) and one H (*i.e., How*) dimensions/features [9]. Specifically, these features of events have been well explored and studied in rich textual narrative texts, such as news articles. From such texts, extracting event expressive features set (i.e., 5W1H) to decide a given text as an event and non-event is not difficult [9]. In contrast, multimedia objects published on social media sites contain little textual description, usually in the form of a short textual description, title, or keyword tags [7]. Importantly, this text often heterogeneous (*in terms of contents and formats*) and noisy (*containing spelling error, abbreviation, non-standard words, etc.*) which makes existing event detection approaches less efficient from multimedia-based social media documents [10]. Although the nature of multimedia contents published on social media sites present challenges for event detection, they also present opportunities not found in news articles, among them, *"context features/dimensions"* is one of them. Some of these context features are: *(i)* semantic (what) (*e.g., title/tags/content description*); *(ii)* spatial (where) (*e.g., longitude-latitude pairs values*); *(iii)* temporal (when) (*content capture time*); and *(iv)* participant-related information (who) (*e.g., who created it and who participated in it*). Often these features can be used to determine whether a given multimedia object is event-related or not. Following this intuition, numerous recent approaches have been proposed for event detection from multimedia-based digital ecosystem (*cf. Sect. 4, for more details*).

4 Related Work

Recently, several related works focusing on event detection especially from digital media sharing platforms are available. Existing event detection approaches from multimedia digital ecosystem can be grouped into three main categories: cluster-based [6, 14] and hybrid-based [10, 11], and classification-based [12, 13]. The hybrid approaches combine classification-based (or supervised) and clustering-based (or unsupervised) techniques. As an example, the authors in [10] introduced a hybrid-based event detection approach for grouping event and non-event contents. They use multi-features similarity learning techniques to measure social media document similarity, considering textual features, date/time, and location information. However, this approach does not take into account the semantic meaning of textual features and only focuses on *TF-IDF* weight analysis. Moreover, participant-related dimension (*e.g., Who*) and additional semantic dimensions (*e.g., Why and How*) are not considered.

Classification-based approaches have been used to detect events from multimedia-based social media documents. The goal is to classify events into pre-defined categorical class labels based on their similarity by learning from labeled data sets. The authors in [12] propose a classification-based approach using only location (*Where*) and time (*When*) dimensions. The approach is inefficient as it ignores semantically information (*i.e., What*) associated to the multimedia objects. The authors in [13] present a method that classify social media documents based on multi-features (*e.g., textual, temporal and geographical*) similarity learning techniques. The task is however does not consider the semantic meaning of textual features (*e.g., content titles, descriptions, and tags*) and additional semantic dimensions (*e.g., Why and How*).

Take a cluster-based event detection approach as an example, in which consider only temporal features might be insufficient to detect events and identify which multimedia objects correspond to the same events. This is mainly because, different events (*e.g., sport events, music festivals, etc.*) can occur at the same time or different events can occur at the same location. Therefore, using a clustering approach based on individual feature (*e.g., only spatial/temporal feature*) for clustering events is not effective as context features are ignored; and *(ii)* considering the combination of spatial and temporal event descriptive features in the event detection process can cause missing semantically related information (*i.e., What*) associated with multimedia contents. To address the above two research gaps, Abebe, M.A. *et al.*, [6] proposed a novel approach based on an aggregate of three event descriptive features (*i.e., Spatial (Where), Temporal (When), and Sematic (What)*). This study effectively addressed the issue of how to use semantic features (*what*) of multimedia objects in cluster-based event detection process. However, scalability, participant-related information (*i.e., Who*) and additional semantics (*i.e., Why and Wow dimensions*) were not considered in this study.

To summarize, most prior event-detection approaches are either: (*i*) only focus on two/three of 5W1H aspect of event descriptor and focus on homogenous event (*sport only, criminal only, etc.*); (*ii*) Do not incorporate participant (Who) dimension of event in event detection process; or (*iii*) do not consider scalability while detecting events. To address the above listed research gaps, we proposed scalable event detection approach. Our event detection approach is inspired by Abebe, M.A. et *al.* works [6, 14] to include participant-related information (*i.e., Who*) in scalable manner from Multimedia Digital Ecosystem.

5   Preliminaries and Problem Definition

5.1   Basic Definition

Let us define formal concepts used in this paper.

Definition 1 (Multimedia Objects (*O*)). A multimedia object *O* is any uniquely identifiable media type such as *image, video, audio, text, etc.*, having Name/title, location, temporal information related to when it was taken or uploaded/shared time, who appears or take part in the object and specific category of the object. It is formalized as follows:

$$O = (oid, N, L, T, S, P, C). \tag{1}$$

where:

- *Oid: a unique id;*
- *N: name(title);*
- *L: a spatial information (i.e., location);*
- *T: temporal information;*
- *S: textual description;*
- *P: participants within multimedia object; and* **C**: *category of multimedia object.*

Although these features can be used to characterize/describe a multimedia object, we cannot use them directly to determine whether a given multimedia object is event-related or not. For example, the availability of *textual description, upload time/location and uploader information, i.e., organization/social media user* for a multimedia object is not sufficient to determine to claim that multimedia object is event-related or not, except for live events (*e.g., football live match*). This is the case as the event's occurrence location and time may differ from the Uploaded/Shared time and location. Therefore, there is a need for further research that can (*i*) identify common features for both event and non-event multimedia objects (e.g., a *textual description of multimedia objects (i.e., title/tag/content description)*); (*ii*) extract unique features for event only (e.g., *capture time/location (When/Where), participates (Who) during the course of the event)* and define the characteristics of an event to distinguish multimedia objects that are indicative of an event from non-events. Following this intuition, we define an event as follows:

Definition 2 (Event ε). An event ε is concept that describes an occurrence of social, political, natural, etc. phenomena in a certain time T_ε and location L_ε involving one or more participants P_ε with semantic textual descriptions S_ε, discussing the cause C_ε and the used method M_ε. It is represented as follows:

$$\varepsilon = (T_\varepsilon, L_\varepsilon, S_\varepsilon, P_\varepsilon, C_\varepsilon, M_\varepsilon). \tag{2}$$

where:

- T_ε: *temporal information (e.g., content creation time) describing **when** the event occurs,*
- L_ε: *spatial information (e.g., longitude-latitude pairs) describing **where** the event is taking place,*
- S_ε : *textual semantic description (e.g., name/title/tags/content description) describing **what** happened,*
- P_ε : *participants (e.g., person/organization) describing **who** take part during the event,*
- C_ε: *causal description describing **why** the event occurred (or which event is causing this event and hence shows the causal relationship between two events where event 1 is identified as the cause and event 2 as the effect),*
- M_ε : *textual information related to **how** an event was performed.*

5.2   Multimedia Object Dimensions Definition and Representation

Structure of multimedia documents, especially from social media sites, consists of two essential parts [15]: *(i)* contents, *e.g., image, voice, video, text, etc.*, and *(ii)* contextual features, e.g., *participant (who), semantic (what), spatial (where), temporal (when), etc.* These dimensions together provide a means for detecting events from Multimedia Digital Ecosystem. Each dimension attached to multimedia objects is defined as follows:

Definition 3 (Participant Dimension (P_ε)). Event participant dimension P_ε refers to an actor (*e.g., person/organization*) who participated during the event. The participant-related information is usually stated in the content description. Extracting such information can be done by knowing Entities (*e.g., person/organization*) applying Named Entity recognition.

Definition 4 (Temporal Dimension (T_ε)). It indicates the date/time of an event (or object) when occurred, shared, uploaded, or modified. A single multimedia object posted on social media platforms may contain several timestamps; it may be the past, the present, or the future. Such timestamps could be capture time, content uploaded time, content modification time, and streaming time (*e.g., football live match*). In this study, we use only content creation and streaming timestamp since they accurately express event occurrences. Following temporal dimension definition, we represent the temporal coverage representative point (*i.e., midpoint values*) as a secondary descriptor.

Definition 5 (Spatial Dimension (S_ε)). Multimedia object spatial dimension S_ε defines where the multimedia object was created using latitude ($\emptyset$), longitude (λ) and altitude (λ) [14]. Formally, it is represented as follows:

$$L = < \emptyset, \lambda, h > \tag{3}$$

Definition 6 (Semantic Dimension (S_ε)). The semantic dimension is represented using concepts from a knowledge base (KB). The KB contains three types of information, namely: *(i)* a set of concepts *(e.g., words/phrases* extracted from the *title/description/tag of multimedia objects); (ii)* concept description (or gloss) including sentences to describe the meaning of concept for a better understanding of its semantic; and *(iii)* relationship to see meanings as relations between concepts *(e.g., "hyponymy", "cause-effect", "part of", etc.)* [16]. It is represented as a graph having three main attributes, *i.e.,* G = (N, E, R), where N is the set of nodes representing concepts, E is a set of edges linking nodes and R symbolizes the set of semantic relationships. Note that representing of multimedia textual feature terms as graph do not capture the meaning (semantic) of synonymous terms, which means that the relationships among concepts are disregarded. To address this problem, we used WordNet [17] as knowledge based to identify synonymous concepts so that similar concepts *(e.g., car, auto-care, automobile, etc.)* are viewed as one concept.

Definition 7 (Causal/Reason Dimension (C_ε)). A causal dimension C_ε is defined as a set of causal knowledge representing the causes of the effect. The causal dimension deals with determining how various events relate in terms of cause and effect; it can be represented as below:

$$C_\varepsilon = < O_i, O_j, R_n > \tag{4}$$

Where: C_ε represents causal dimension; O_i represents causal objects; O_j represents the effect of the causal object, i.e., O_i; and R_n represents relationship among objects/events.

Definition 8 (Method Dimension (M_ε)). A method dimension M_ε is defined as a set of textual information representing how an event O_i was performed using the method *(or How)* M_i and represented as follows:

$$M_\varepsilon = < O_i, M_i > \tag{5}$$

6 Proposed Framework

In this study, we propose a novel framework, shown in Fig. 1, to represent and detect event. The proposed approach adopts existing approach with *(i)* include one additional dimension of multimedia object/events *(i.e., participant)*, and *(ii)* scalable event detection approach to handle the high amount and continuously growing nature of multimedia contents. It consists of two main components: (*I*) multimedia documents (objects) extraction and representation and (*II*) real event detection and event type determination.

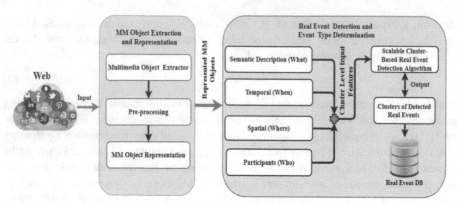

Fig. 1. Proposed framework for representing and detecting real events.

6.1   Multimedia Object Extraction and Representation

In this component, first, we extract multimedia objects via the APIs provided by Twitter, YouTube and Flicker. Then, the objects are preprocessed to transform into a unified format without changing their forms to handle the structure and format heterogeneity problem [6]. To do this, we begin by examining the nature of multimedia objects and its context features. One of the basic context features of multimedia object is textual description attached to a multimedia object. Multimedia object textual description is incomplete, inaccurate (contain noise contents) and often consists of concatenations of keywords and short sentences [6, 10, 14]. Therefore, several acceptable linguistic pre-processing tasks are essential to identify semantically meaningful words. In our study, the pre-processing phase involves activities like, smoothing noise data, tokenization, stop word removal, part of speech tagging, word sense disambiguation, named entity recognition and stemming. Similarly, HTML tags and special characters are removed and multimedia objects describing by less than 3 features are also removed, as these multimedia objects are less likely to have 5W1H elements. Moreover, indexing and feature selection (e.g., *spatial, temporal, semantic, etc.*) are performed for detecting events. Location distance value transformed into geospatial midpoint value (*or center of gravity*) and metric unit. On the other hand, any kind of temporal value is transformed into second(s) unit.

6.2   Cluster-Based Real Event Detection

In this study, the problem of detecting real events is done as a clustering problem. To do so, we begin with the task of selecting an appropriate and scalable clustering approach from previous works. For our multimedia document scenario, the selected clustering algorithm considering features: (*i*) scalable (*to handle the continuously growing nature of multimedia contents*); (*ii*) ability to handle noise data as well as data variety (*e.g., video, text, photo, etc.*); (*iii*) incremental (*automatically assigning new object to a cluster, when it arrives*); and *(iv)* absence of a-prior knowledge about the number of clusters. Thus, clustering approaches that require knowledge about the number of clusters, such as Expectation-Maximization (EM), K-mean, and Fuzzy C-means (FCM) are not suitable for our problem. Graph Partitioning Algorithm (SGPA) is also not appropriate as it is difficult, cost-ineffective, and memory-intensive when the graph/data size is becoming too large. Moreover, Agglomerative Hierarchical Clustering Algorithm [14] is also not suitable as it does not work well for heterogeneous and large datasets. On the basis of the above observation, we adopt a scalable clustering approach called "*Incremental Clustering Algorithm*". The *incremental clustering algorithm* is preferred compared to conventional static clustering algorithms, as the approach is simple, scalable and effective. In the following subsection, we describe the algorithm in detail.

Algorithm 1: Event Detection based on 5W1H aspect of events

Input:
1   Multimedia Objects: Collection   // Represented Multimedia Objects. these representations includes Semantic (e.g. title, description and tag), Spatial(geographical mid-point values), Temporal (time/date) and participants (person/organizations).

Variables:
2   Sim(): Decimal //similarity function
3   Threshold Values(Δ): Decimal //a pre-defined threshold Value
4   Clusters: Collection   // Cluster of Objects

Output:
5   Cluster of Events   //contain Detected Events

Begin:
6   Initialize empty set Ω of cluster
7   Initialize empty set decision score value of cluster Z
8   If O_1 be the first multimedia object Then
9   Putting object O_1 into the first cluster $C_i = \{O_1\}$
10   Else
11   for each object o $\in$ O , do: // one by one
12   Lookup the decision score value Z_i of each cluster $C_i, ..., C_n$ // Decision score value computing using single-link, group average-link and complete-link techniques
13   Sim(o, z_i) //Computing the similarity between the current object and decision score value for each cluster
14   If Sim(o, z_i)$\geq \Delta, do$:
15   assigned a given object o to C_i
16   Recomputed/Update the decision score value of z_i
17   Go to Step 8 and Continue processing the input objects.
18   End If
19   Next
20   End If
21   Next
22   If a given object o not assigned to any existing clusters Then
23   Create a new cluster $C_{new} = \{o\}$ put C_{new} into Ω
24   Set its decision score value $z_{new} = o$ and put z_{new} into Z
25   Return Events // Cluster of Detected Events
26   End

Fig. 2. Pseudo code of real event detection algorithm

Algorithm Description: The algorithm pseudo-code is shown in Fig. 2. Given multimedia objects $O_1, \ldots, O_n$, a similarity threshold Δ, a similarity function, the algorithm starts by producing an empty set, Ω, of clusters and an empty set Z of decision score. The algorithm has two parts initialization and iteration. In the iteration step, the first object O_1 be added as the element of the first cluster i.e., C_1 consisting of $O_1 \cdot C_1 = \{O_1\}$. The iteration steps make sure that all objects are clustered. It picks a multimedia object O_i, add it to the most relevant cluster otherwise add it to a new cluster. The relevance of a cluster to an object O_i is computed as similarity between the object and the cluster using cluster decision score (O_i, C_j), cluster decision score is either the average score per dimensions (*i.e., semantic, location, time and participant*) across all objects in the cluster, multimedia object with maximum decision score in a cluster or multimedia object with the highest minimum score in each cluster. If the similarity of O_i to the cluster decision score (or object-cluster pairs) is $\geq \Delta$, then O_i is assigned to the corresponding cluster C_j and the decision score is recomputed/updated. Otherwise, it generates a new cluster that contains only O_i. In Sect. 6, we describe the similarity measures used in our clustering approach.

7 Similarity Measures and Cluster Comparison Strategies

The process to construct clusters can be summarized into three main steps: *(i)* define similarity measure to compare the similarity of two events, *(ii)* threshold estimation to yield high-quality clustering result and *(iii)* cluster comparison strategies to compare the quality of clusters. We discuss similarity measure and cluster comparison strategy in more detail hereunder.

7.1 Similarity Measures

Clustering algorithms use the notion of similarity function to place similar events into the same cluster, while dissimilar events are located into the different cluster. Typically, event similarity is computed using contextual features of multimedia objects. The rest of this section describes similarity measure functions used in our clustering algorithm.

Participant (Who) Similarity. To compute the similarity between two participants P_i and P_j, first represent values as a list of participants. Then, we used a Jaccard Coefficient similarity measure as defined in (6):

$$Sim_P(P_i, P_j) = \frac{|p_i \cap p_j|}{|p_i \cup p_j|} \tag{6}$$

The similarity value is between 0 and 1; a value close to 1 implies that p_i and p_j are relating to one another otherwise are relatively dissimilar.

Temporal (When) Similarity. For temporal (*i.e., time/date*) similarity, first, we represent values as second units (*cf. Definition 4*). Then, Euclidian distance is utilized to compare the temporal similarity ($Sim_T(O_i, O_j)$) [6, 10, 14]. The similarity decision scores close to 1 imply that object O_i and O_j are relating to one another temporally otherwise they are relatively dissimilar temporally.

Spatial (Where) Similarity. The spatial similarity measure considers the distance between two events on the surface of a sphere. We compute the similarity between two points of event locations ($Sim_L(\mathcal{L}_1, \mathcal{L}_2)$) using the Haversine distance [18] as follows:

$$Dist_L((O_i, O_j) = 2 * r * \arcsin(\sqrt{sin^2\left(\frac{\emptyset_j - \emptyset_i}{2}\right) + \cos\emptyset_i \cos\emptyset_j \, sin^2\left(\frac{\lambda_j - \lambda_i}{2}\right)} \tag{7}$$

where:

- r is radius of Earth in kilo meters i.e., 6,371 km;
- $\emptyset_j$, $\emptyset_i$: represent latitude values of the two multimedia objects;
- λ_j, λ_i: represent longitude values of the two multimedia objects;
- arcsin is the invers of sine function.

Semantic (What) Similarity. Semantic similarity measures play an important role in the event detection processes. The semantic (meaning) similarity between words can be computed by involving a lexical knowledge base, such as WordNet [17]. The measurement determines how similar the meanings of the two concepts are.

Events (ε) Similarity. The similarity between pairs of events can be computed by combining the above aforesaid individual dimensional similarity measures, such as, average, weighted, maximum, or minimum sum. In this study, we consider the average. The average function is computed as follows

$$Sim(\varepsilon_i, \varepsilon_j) = \frac{Sim_P(\varepsilon_i, \varepsilon_j) + Sim_T(\varepsilon_i, \varepsilon_j) + Sim_L(\varepsilon_i, \varepsilon_j) + Sim_S(\varepsilon_i, \varepsilon_j)}{N} \in [0, 1] \quad (8)$$

Where, N is number of dimensions in a single event. The similarity value is between 0 and 1; a value close to 1 implies that ε_i and ε_j are relating to one another otherwise they are relatively dissimilar.

7.2 Cluster Comparison Strategies

This section explains how to measure the efficiency of our clustering algorithm. For efficiency, we represent each cluster using cluster comparison strategies, namely: *single-link, average-link, and complete-link strategies*. We summarize these strategies as follows:

- In single-link strategy, we define the similarity between two objects/events as the maximum similarity score between the current object O_i and any single object in each cluster. At each stage, if there is no cluster with the maximum optimistic similarity score (*or if no similarity score exceeds the user-defined maximum threshold value*), it creates a new cluster for the object O_i. Otherwise, object O_i is assigned to the cluster that has the highest similarity score.
- In the average-link strategy, we define the similarity between two events/objects as the average similarity between the members of their clusters. Accordingly, the algorithm assigns O_i to a cluster that has the nearest cluster average decision score. Otherwise, it creates a new cluster for object O_i .
- In complete-link strategy, similarity is computed taking the minimum similarity score of members of pairs of clusters. The cluster containing the highest minimum similarity score will be used for assigning the current multimedia object O_i . Otherwise, it initiates a new cluster for object O_i .

8 Experimental Settings and Results

To demonstrate the efficiency of the proposed framework and its algorithm, we carried out experiments using single, average and complete linkage clustering strategies to measure the influence of participant (*Who*), spatial (*Where*), temporal (*When*), and semantic (*What*) dimensions in detecting real-world events. In the following subsection, dataset, cluster quality metrics, and experimental results are described.

Experimental Dataset. We evaluate our real event detection method using MediaEval 2013 dataset [19], which has been used in the Social Event Detection (SED) task. The dataset consists of more than 400,000 Flickr images assigned to 21, 000 unique events. The dataset also includes context features (or dimensions) such as *location, time, tags, title, description, username, image_id, etc.* in an XML format. Statistics for each dimension are given as follows, on average, 100% of the images include temporal information, 98.3% of the images include capture time information, 45.9% of them include geographic information, 95.6% of them include tags, 97.6% of them include titles, 37.8% of the images include description information, and 100% of them include uploader information. Based on our dimension definitions, we only extract and process images with semantic (*i.e., title, tags and descriptions*), temporal (*i.e., capture time*), spatial (*i.e., capture location specified by Latitude-Longitude Pairs*), and participant dimension (*i.e., person/organization*).

Cluster Quality Metrics. To evaluate the quality of our algorithm, we use *F-score* quality metric, which is a widely used metric in information extraction, particularly in event detection. F-score considers both precision (PR) and recall (R) into a single measure and measures how good the resulting of the clustering solution and computed as:

$$F - score = \frac{2 \times PR \times R}{PR + R} \tag{9}$$

Evaluation Results. We ran our experiments using different similarity-based clustering comparison strategies based on participant, temporal, spatial, and semantic dimensions of multimedia objects for detecting real events. The effectiveness of our incremental clustering algorithm depends on the used comparison strategies. We measured F-score for clusters having size of 25, 50, 10, 200, and 400. Figure 3 summarizes the results of the three clustering comparison strategies applied on MediaEval 2013 dataset [19]. These results indicate three main observations: *(i)* the average-link strategy does perform better than the single and complete-link strategy as it pays too much attention to the entire structure of the cluster; *(ii)* in single-link strategy, the entire structure of the cluster are not taken into account to assign an object to a cluster, since it is preoccupied on the maximum-similarity between two objects; *(iii)* the complete-link is not effective in comparing to other strategies or is sensitive to noise, since it focuses too much on the longest distance (or the minimum-similarity) between two objects.

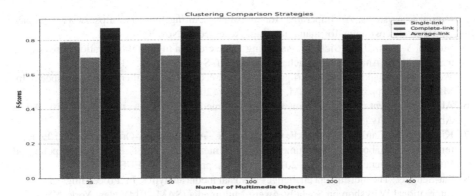

Fig. 3. Visualizing F-Scores results on the three clustering comparison strategies.

Figure 3 illustrates F-score measurement results for each clustering comparison strategies. For example, on MediaEval 2013 corpus using 100 features, the experimental result exhibited 0.85, 0.77 and 0.70 average F-score value using average-link, single-link and complete-link strategies, respectively. In terms of processor time, single-link is better than average-link approach. For example, the average-link approach required a few hours, whereas the single-link approach ran in a few minutes for clustering events.

9 Conclusion and Further Research

This paper introduced a general event representation and extraction framework along with its algorithms. The framework has two main components for representing each dimension of a multimedia objects, and real event extraction using a scalable clustering algorithm. To evaluate our clustering approach, we employed clustering comparison strategies using dimensions of multimedia object. We showed how clustering comparison strategies detect events. Finally, we measured the quality of our clustering algorithm using cluster quality metric (i.e., F-score). The experimental results show the quality and potential of our clustering algorithm.

We are currently conducting further experiments using dimension weighting approach for improving quality of event detection. In future work, we are planning to develop dedicative event relationship inference rules to identify semantic relationships among pairs of objects. We also plan to (i) include additional semantic dimensions (*e.g., causal (Why) and method (How)*) and (ii) represent events and relationships among them using graph model.

References

1. Digital Banking Ecosystem: strategies, investments, and digital transformation in 2020, https://www.businessinsider.com/digital-banking-ecosystem-report?IR=T. Accessed 01 Nov 2020
2. Serbanati, L.D., Ricci, F.L., Mercurio, G., Vasilateanu, A.: Steps towards a digital health ecosystem. J. Biomed. Inform. **44**, 621–636 (2011)

3. Digital Ecosystems: An Imperative for the Manufacturing Industry. https://www.logicbay.com/digital-ecosystems-for-manufacturing. Accessed 02 Nov 2020
4. Suseno, Y., Laurell, C., Sick, N.: Assessing value creation in digital innovation ecosystems: a Social Media Analytics approach. J. Strateg. Inf. Syst. **27**(4), 335–349 (2018)
5. Wenbin, L., Youakim, B., Frédérique, B.: Digital ecosystems: challenges and prospects. In: MEDES 2012, pp. 117–122. ACM, Addis Ababa (2012)
6. Abebe, M.: Event extraction framework in multimedia digital ecosystem. Ph.D, diss, Addis Ababa University (2018)
7. Kidanu, S.A., Cardinale, Y., Tekli, G., Chbeir, R.: A Multimedia-Oriented Digital Ecosystem: a new collaborative environment. In: 14th International Conference on Computer and Information Science (ICIS), vol. 2015, Las Vegas, pp. 411–416. IEEE (2015)
8. Tat-Seng, C.: The multimedia challenges in social media analytics. In: Proceedings of the 3rd International Workshop on Socially-Aware Multimedia (SAM 2014), New York, NY, USA, pp. 17–18. Association for Computing Machinery (2014)
9. Wang, W.: Chinese news event 5W1H semantic elements extraction for event ontology population. In: 21st International Conference Proceedings on World Wide Web, New York, pp. 197–202. ACM (2012)
10. Becker, H., Naaman, M., Gravano, L.: Learning similarity metrics for event identification in social media. In: Proceedings of the Third ACM International Conference on Web Search and Data Mining, New York, USA, no. 10, pp. 291–300. ACM (2010)
11. Nguyen, T., Dao, M., Mattivi, R., Sansone, E., De Natale, F., Boato, G.: Event clustering and classification from social media: watershed-based and kernel methods. In: MediaEval 2013 Multimedia benchmark Workshop, Barcelona (2013)
12. Becker, H., Iter, D., Naaman, M., Gravano, L.: Identifying content for planned events across social media sites. In: Proceedings of the Fifth ACM International Conference on Web Search and Data Mining, Seattle, Washington, USA, pp. 533–542. ACM (2012)
13. Timo, R., Philipp, C.: Event-based classification of social media streams. In: Proceedings of the 2nd ACM International Conference on Multimedia Retrieval (ICMR12), New York, NY, USA, pp.1–8. ACM (2012)
14. Abebe, M.A., Tekli, J., Getahun, F., Chbeir, R., Tekli, G.: Generic metadata representation framework for social-based event detection, description, and linkage. Knowledge-Based Syst. **188**(2020), 104817 (2020)
15. Liu, X., Troncy, R., Huet, B.: Using social media to identify events. In: SIGMM International Workshop on Social Media, Scottsdale, Arizona, USA, pp. 3–8. ACM (2011)
16. Mylonas, P., Athanasiadis, T., Wallace, M., et al.: Semantic representation of multimedia content: knowledge representation and semantic indexing. Multimed Tools Appl. **39**, 293–327 (2008)
17. Miller, G.A.: WordNet: a lexical database for English. Commun. ACM **38**(11), 39–41 (1995)
18. Chopde, N.R., Nichat, M.: Landmark based shortest path detection by using a* and Haversine formula. Int. J. Innov. Res. Comput. Commun. Eng. **1**(2), 298–302 (2013)
19. MediaEval-2013 dataset. http://www.multimediaeval.org/mediaeval2013/sed2013/index.html. Accessed 13 Oct 2020

Social Media and Text Mining

MONITOR: A Multimodal Fusion Framework to Assess Message Veracity in Social Networks

Abderrazek Azri[1](✉), Cécile Favre[1](✉), Nouria Harbi[1](✉),
Jérôme Darmont[1](✉), and Camille Noûs[2](✉)

[1] Université de Lyon, Lyon 2, UR ERIC, 5 avenue Pierre Mendès France,
69676 Bron Cedex, France
{a.azri,cecile.favre,nouria.harbi,jerome.darmont}@univ-lyon2.fr
[2] Université de Lyon, Lyon 2, Laboratoire Cogitamus, Lyon, France
camille.nous@cogitamus.fr

Abstract. Users of social networks tend to post and share content with little restraint. Hence, rumors and fake news can quickly spread on a huge scale. This may pose a threat to the credibility of social media and can cause serious consequences in real life. Therefore, the task of rumor detection and verification has become extremely important. Assessing the veracity of a social media message (e.g., by fact checkers) is a very time-consuming task that can be much helped by machine learning. In the literature, most message veracity verification methods only exploit textual contents and metadata. Very few take both textual and visual contents, and more particularly images, into account. In this paper, we second the hypothesis that exploiting all of the components of a social media post enhances the accuracy of veracity detection. To further the state of the art, we first propose using a set of advanced image features that are inspired from the field of image quality assessment, Then, we introduce the Multimodal fusiON framework to assess message veracIty in social neTwORks (MONITOR), which exploits all message features (i.e., text, social context, and image features) by supervised machine learning. Extensive experiments are conducted on two multimedia datasets. The experimental results show that MONITOR can outperform the state-of-the-art machine learning baselines.

Keywords: Social networks · Rumor verification · Image features · Machine learning

1 Introduction

After more than two decades of existence, social media platforms has attracted a large number of users. They enable the rapid diffusion of information in real-time, regardless of its credibility, for two main reasons: first, there is a lack of a means to verify the veracity of the content transiting on social media; and second,

© Springer Nature Switzerland AG 2021
L. Bellatreche et al. (Eds.): ADBIS 2021, LNCS 12843, pp. 73–87, 2021.
https://doi.org/10.1007/978-3-030-82472-3_7

(a) Black clouds in New York
City before Sandy!!!

(b) NepalEarthquake
4Years old boy pro-
tect his little sister.
make me feel so sad

Fig. 1. Two sample rumors posted on Twitter

users often publish messages without verifying the validity and reliability of the information. Consequently, social networks, and particularly microblogging platforms, are a fertile ground for rumors to spread.

Widespread rumors can pose a threat to the credibility of social media and cause harmful consequences in real life. Thus, the automatic assessment of information credibility on microblogs that we focus on is crucial to provide decision support to, e.g., fact checkers. This task requires to verify the truthfulness of messages related to a particular event and return a binary decision stating whether the message is true.

In the literature, most automatic rumor detection approaches address the task as a classification problem. They extract features from various aspects of messages, which are then used to train a wide range of machine learning [26] or deep learning [27] methods. Features are generally extracted from the textual content of messages [20] and the social context [29]. However, the multimedia content of messages, particularly images that present a significant set of features, are little exploited.

In this paper, we second the hypothesis that the use of image properties is important in rumor verification. Images play a crucial role in the news diffusion process. For example, in the dataset collected by [8], the average number of messages with an attached image is more than 11 times that of plain text ones.

Figure 1 shows two sample rumors posted on Twitter. In Fig. 1(a), it is hard to assess veracity from the text, but the likely-manipulated image hints at a rumor. In Fig. 1(b), it is hard to assess veracity from both the text or the image because the image has been taken out of its original context.

Based on the above observations, we aim to leverage all the modalities of microblog messages for verifying rumors; that is, features extracted from textual and social context content of messages, and up to now unused visual and statistical features derived from images. Then, all types of features must be fused to allow a supervised machine learning classifier to evaluate the credibility of messages.

Our contribution is twofold. First, we propose the use of a set of image features inspired from the field of image quality assessment (IQA) and we prove that they contribute very effectively to the verification of message veracity. These metrics estimate the rate of noise and quantify the amount of visual degradation of any type in an image. They are proven to be good indicators for detecting fake images, even those generated by advanced techniques such as generative adversarial networks (GANs) [5]. To the best of our knowledge, we are the first to systematically exploit this type of image features to check the veracity of microblog posts.

Our second contribution is the Multimodal fusiON framework to assess message veracIty in social neTwORks (MONITOR), which exploits all types of message features by supervised machine learning. This choice is motivated by two factors. First, these techniques provide explainability and interpretability about the decisions taken. Second, we do also want to explore the performance of deep machine learning methods in the near future, especially to study the tradeoff between classification accuracy, computing complexity, and explainability.

Eventually, extensive experiments conducted on two real-world datasets demonstrate the effectiveness of our rumor detection approach. MONITOR indeed outperforms all state-of-the-art machine learning baselines with an accuracy and F1-score of up to 96% and 89% on the MediaEval benchmark [2] and the FakeNewsNet dataset [22], respectively.

The rest of this paper is organized as follows. In Sect. 2, we first review and discuss related works. In Sect. 3, we detail MONITOR and especially feature extraction and selection. In Sect. 4, we present and comment on the experimental results that we achieve with respect to state-of-the-art methods. Finally, in Sect. 5, we conclude this paper and outline future research.

2 Related Works

2.1 Non-image Features

Studies in the literature present a wide range of non-image features. These features may be divided into two subcategories, textual features and social context features. To classify a message as fake or real, Castillo *et al.* [4] capture prominent statistics in tweets, such as count of words, capitalized characters and punctuation. Beyond these features, lexical words expressing specific semantics or sentiments are also counted. Many sentimental lexical features are proposed in [12], who utilize a sentiment tool called the Linguistic Inquiry and Word Count (LIWC) to count words in meaningful categories.

Other works exploit syntactic features, such as the number of keywords, the sentiment score or polarity of the sentence. Features based on topic models are used to understand messages and their underlying relations within a corpus. Wu *et al.* [28] train a Latent Dirichlet Allocation model [1] with a defined set of topic features to summarize semantics for detecting rumors.

The social context describes the propagating process of a rumor [23]. Social network features are extracted by constructing specific networks, such as diffusion [12] or co-occurrence networks [21].

Recent approaches detect fake news based on temporal-structure features. Kwon *et al.* [11] studied the stability of features over time and found that, for rumor detection, linguistic and user features are suitable for early-stage, while structural and temporal features tend to have good performance in the long-term stage.

2.2   Image Features

Although images are widely shared on social networks, their potential for verifying the veracity of messages in microblogs is not sufficiently explored. Morris *et al.* [18] assume that the user profile image has an important impact on information credibility published by this user. For images attached in messages, very basic features are proposed by [28], who define a feature called "has multimedia" to mark whether the tweet has any picture, video or audio attached. Gupta *et al.* [6] propose a classification model to identify fake images on Twitter during Hurricane Sandy. However, their work is still based on textual content features.

To automatically predict whether a tweet that shares multimedia content is fake or real, Boididou *et al.* [2] propose the Verifying Multimedia Use (VMU) task. Textual and image forensics [13] features are used as baseline features for this task. They conclude that Twitter media content is not amenable to image forensics and that forensics features do not lead to consistent VMU improvement [3].

3   MONITOR

Microblog messages contain rich multimodal resources, such as text contents, surrounding social context, and attached image. Our focus is to leverage this multimodal information to determine whether a message is true or false. Based on this idea, we propose a framework for verifying the veracity of messages. MONITOR's detailed description is presented in this section.

3.1   Multimodal Fusion Overview

Figure 2 shows a general overview of MONITOR. It has two main stages: 1) Features extraction and selection. We extract several features from the message text and the social context, we then perform a feature selection algorithm to identify the relevant features, which form a first set of textual features. From the attached image, we drive statistics and efficient visual features inspired from the IQA field, which form a second set of image features; 2) Model learning. Textual and image features sets are then concatenated and normalized to form the fusion vector. Several machine learning classifiers may learn from the fusion vector to distinguish the veracity of the message (i.e., real or fake).

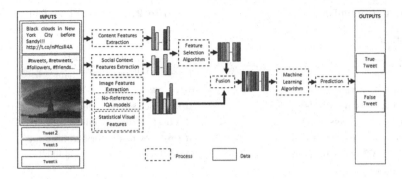

Fig. 2. Overview of MONITOR

3.2   Feature Extraction and Selection

To better extract features, we reviewed the best practices followed by information professionals (e.g., journalists) in verifying content generated by social network users. We based our thinking on relevant data from journalistic studies [15] and the verification handbook [24]. We define a set of features that are important to extract discriminating characteristics of rumors. These features are mainly derived from three principal aspects of news information: content, social context, and visual content. As for the feature selection process, it will only be applied to content and social context features sets to remove the irrelevant features that can negatively impact performance. Because our focus is the visual features set, we keep all these features in the learning process.

Message Content Features. Content features are extracted from the message's text. We extract characteristics such as the length of a tweet text and the number of its words. It also include statistics such as the number of exclamation and question marks, as well as binary features indicating the existence or not of emoticons. Furthermore, other features are extracted from the linguistics of a text, including the number of positive and negative sentiment words. Additional binary features indicate whether the text contains personal pronouns.

We calculate also a readability score for each message using the Flesch Reading Ease method [10], the higher this score is, the easier the text is to read. Other features are extracted from the informative content provided by the specific communication style of the Twitter platform, such as the number of retweets, mentions(@), hashtags(#), and URLs.

Social Context Features. The social context reflects the relationship between the different users, therefore the social context features are extracted from the behavior of the users and the propagation network. We capture several features from the users' profiles, such as number of followers and friends, number of tweets the user has authored, the number of tweets the user has liked, whether the user

Table 1. Content features

Description
chars, words
(?), (!) mark
uppercase chars
positive, negative words
mentions, hashtags, URLs
happy, sad mood emoticon
1st, 2nd, 3rd order pronoun
The readability score

Table 2. Social context features

Description
followers, friends, posts
Friends/followers ratio, times listed
re-tweets, likes
If the user shares a homepage URL
If The user has profile image
If the user has a verified account
# of Tweets the user has liked

is verified by the social media. We extract, also, features from the propagation tree that can be built from tweets and re-tweets of a message, such as the depth of the re-tweet tree. Tables 1 and 2 depicts a description of a sets of content feature, and social context features extracted for each message.

To improve the performance of MONITOR, we perform a feature selection algorithm on the features sets listed in Tables 1 and 2. The details of the feature selection process are discussed in Sect. 4.

Image Features. To differentiate between false and real images in messages, we propose to exploit visual content features and visual statistical features that are extracted from the joined images.

Visual Content Features. Usually, a news consumer decides the image veracity based on his subjective perception, but how do we quantitatively represent the human perception of the quality of an image?. The quality of an image means the amount of visual degradations of all types present in an image, such as noise, blocking artifacts, blurring, fading, and so on.

The IQA field aims to quantify human perception of image quality by providing an objective score of image degradations based on computational models [14]. These degradations are introduced during different processing stages, such as image acquisition, compression, storage, transmission, decompression. Inspired by the potential relevance of IQA metrics for our context, we use these metrics in an original way for a purpose different from what they were created for. More precisely, we think that the quantitative evaluation of the quality of an image could be useful for veracity detection.

IQA is mainly divided into two areas of research: first, full-reference evaluation; and second, no-reference evaluation. Full-reference algorithms compare the input image against a pristine reference image with no distortion. In no-reference algorithms, the only input is the image whose quality we want to measure. In our case, we do not have the original version of the posted image; therefore, the approach that is fitting for our context is the no-reference IQA metric. For this purpose, we use three no-reference algorithms that have been demonstrated to be highly efficient: The Blind/Referenceless Image Spatial Quality Evaluator (BRISQUE) [16], the Naturalness Image Quality Evaluator (NIQE) [17], and the Perception based Image Quality Evaluator (PIQE) [25].

For example, Fig. 3 displays the BRISQUE score computed for a natural image and its distorted versions (compression, noise and blurring distortions). The BRISQUE score is a non-negative scalar in the range [1, 100]. Lower values of score reflect better perceptual quality of image.

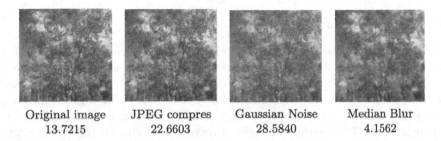

| Original image | JPEG compres | Gaussian Noise | Median Blur |
| 13.7215 | 22.6603 | 28.5840 | 4.1562 |

Fig. 3. BRISQUE score computed for a natural image and its distorted versions

No-reference IQA metrics are also good indicators for other types of image modifications, such as GAN-generated images. These techniques allow modifying the context and semantics of images in a very realistic way. Unlike many image analysis tasks, where both reference and reconstructed images are available, images generated by GANs may not have any reference image. This is the main reason for using no-reference IQA for evaluating this type of fake images. Figure 4 displays the BRISQUE score computed for real and fake images generated by image-to-image translation based on GANs [30].

| Real image | Fake image | Real image | Fake image |
| 17.7778 | 22.0260 | 12.5000 | 22.5279 |

Fig. 4. Distribution of true and false classes for top-15 important features

Statistical Features. From attached images, we define four statistical features from two aspects.

Number of Images: A user can post one, several, or no images. To denote this feature, we count the total number of images in a rumor event and the ratio of posts containing more then one image.

Spreading of Images: During an event, some images are very replied and generate more comments than others. The ratio of such images is calculated to indicate this feature. Table 3 illustrates the description of proposed visual and statistical features. We use the whole set of these features in the learning process.

3.3   Model Training

So far, we have obtained a first set of relevant textual features through a feature selection process. We have also a second set of image features composed of statistical and visual features. These two sets of features are scaled, normalized, and concatenated to form the multimodal representation for a given message, which is fed to learn a supervised classifier. Several learning algorithms can be implemented for the classification task of message veracity. In the experimental part, we investigate the algorithms that provide the best performance.

Table 3. Description of image features

Type	Feature	Description
Visual features	BRISQUE	The BRISQUE score of a given image
	PIQE	The PIQE score of a given image
	NIQE	The NIQE score of a given image
Statistical features	Count_Img	The number of all images in a news event
	Ratio_Img1	The ratio of the multi-image tweets in all tweets
	Ratio_Img2	The ratio of image number to tweet number
	Ratio_Img3	The ratio of the most widespread image in all distinct images

4   Experiments

In this section, we conduct extensive experiments on two public datasets. First, we present statistics about the datasets we used. Then, we describe the experimental settings: a brief review of state-of-the-art features for news verification and a selection of the best of these textual features as baselines. Finally, we present experimental results and analyze the features to achieve insights into MONITOR.

4.1   Datasets

To evaluate MONITOR's performance, we conduct experiments on two well-established public benchmark datasets for rumor detection. Next, we provide the details of both datasets.

MediaEval [2] is collected from Twitter and includes all three characteristics: text, social context and images. It is designed for message-level verification. The dataset has two parts: a development set containing about 9,000 rumor and 6,000 non-rumor tweets from 17 rumor-related events; a test set containing about 2,000 tweets from another batch of 35 rumor-related events. We remove tweets without any text or image, thus obtaining a final dataset including 411 distinct images associated with 6,225 real and 7,558 fake tweets, respectively.

FakeNewsNet [22] is one of the most comprehensive fake news detection benchmark. Fake and real news articles are collected from the fact-checking websites PolitiFact and GossipCop. Since we are particularly interested in images in this work, we extract and exploit the image information of all tweets. To keep the dataset balanced, we randomly choose 2,566 real and 2,587 fake news events. After removing tweets without images, we obtain 56,369 tweets and 59,838 images. The detailed statistics of these two datasets are listed in Table 4.

Table 4. MediaEval and FakeNewsNet statistics

Dataset	Set	Tweets		Images
		Real	Fake	
MediaEval	Training set	5,008	6,841	361
	Testing set	1,217	717	50
FakeNewsNet	Training set	25,673	19,422	47,870
	Testing set	6,466	4,808	11,968

4.2 Experimental Settings

Baseline Features. We compare the effectiveness of our feature set with the best textual features from the literature. First, we adopt the 15 best features extracted by Castillo et al. to analyze the information credibility of news propagated through Twitter [4]. We also collect a total of 40 additional textual features proposed in the literature [6,7,12,28], which are extracted from text content, user information and propagation properties (Table 5).

Feature Sets. The features labeled *Textual* are the best features selected among message content and social context features (Tables 1 and 2). We select them with the information gain ratio method [9]. It helps select a subset of 15 relevant textual features with an information gain larger than zero (Table 6).

The features labeled *Image* are all the image features listed in Table 3. The features labeled *MONITOR* are the feature set that we propose, consisting of the fusion of textual and image feature sets. The features labeled *Castillo* are the above-mentioned best 15 textual features. Eventually, the features labeled *Wu* are the 40 textual features identified in literature.

Table 5. 40 features from the literature

Feature
Fraction of (?), (!) Mark,# messages
Average Word, Char Length,
Fraction of 1st, 2nd, 3rd Pronouns,
Fraction of URL,@, #,
Count of Distinct URL, @, #,
Fraction of Popular URL, @, #,
If the Tweet includes pictures,
Average Sentiment Score,
Fraction of Positive, Negative Tweets,
Distinct People, Loc, Org,
Fraction of People, Loc, Org,
Fraction of Popular People, Loc, Org,
Users, Fraction of Popular Users,
Followers, Followees, Posted Tweets,
If the User has Facebook Link,
Fraction of Verified User, Org,
comments on the original message
Time between original message and repost

Table 6. Best textual features selected

MediaEval	FakeNewsNet
Tweet_Length	Tweet_Length
Num_Negwords	Num_Words
Num_Mentions	Num_Questmark
Num_URLs	Num_Upperchars
Num_Words	Num_Exclmark
Num_Upperchars	Num_Hashtags
Num_Hashtags	Num_Negwords
Num_Exclmark	Num_Poswords
Num_Thirdpron	Num_Followers
Times_Listed	Num_Friends
Num_Tweets	Num_Favorites
Num_Friends	Times_Listed
Num_Retweets	Num_Likes
Has_Url	Num_Retweets
Num_Followers	Num_Tweets

Classification Model. We execute various learning algorithms for each feature set. The best results are achieved by four supervised classification models: decision trees, KNNs, SVMs and random forests. We use Scikit-learn library for Python [19] implementation. Training and validation is performed for each model through a 5-fold cross validation. Note that, for MediaEval, we retain the same data split scheme. For FakeNewsNet, we randomly divide data into training and testing subsets with the ratio 0.8:0.2. Table 7 present the results of our experiments.

4.3   Classification Results

From the classification results recorded in Tables 7, we can make the following observations.

Performance Comparison. With MONITOR, using both image and textual feature allows all classification algorithms to achieve better performance than baselines. Among the four classification models, the random forest generates the best accuracy: 96.2% on MediaEval and 88.9% on FakeNewsNet. They indeed perform 26% and 18% better than Castillo and 24% and 15% than Wu, still on MediaEval and FakeNewsNet, respectively.

Compared to the 15 "best" textual feature set, the random forest improves the accuracy by more than 22% and 10% with image features only. Similarly, the

Table 7. Classification results

Model	Feature sets	MediaEval				FakeNewsNet			
		Acc	Prec	Rec	F_1	Acc	Prec	Rec	F_1
Decision trees	Textual	0.673	0.672	0.771	0.718	0.699	**0.647**	0.652	0.65
	Image	0.632	0.701	0.639	0.668	0.647	0.595	0.533	0.563
	MONITOR	**0.746**	**0.715**	**0.897**	**0.796**	**0.704**	0.623	**0.716**	**0.667**
	Castillo	0.643	0.711	0.648	0.678	0.683	0.674	0.491	0.569
	Wu	0.65	0.709	0.715	0.711	0.694	0.663	0.593	0.627
KNN	Textual	0.707	0.704	0.777	0.739	0.698	0.67	0.599	0.633
	Image	0.608	0.607	0.734	0.665	0.647	0.595	0.533	0.563
	MONITOR	**0.791**	**0.792**	**0.843**	**0.817**	**0.758**	**0.734**	**0.746**	**0.740**
	Castillo	0.652	0.698	0.665	0.681	0.681	0.651	0.566	0.606
	Wu	0.668	0.71	0.678	0.693	0.694	0.663	0.593	0.627
SVM	Textual	0.74	0.729	0.834	0.779	0.658	**0.657**	0.44	0.528
	Image	0.693	0.69	0.775	0.73	0.595	0.618	0.125	0.208
	MONITOR	**0.794**	**0.767**	**0.881**	**0.82**	**0.704**	0.623	**0.716**	**0.667**
	Castillo	0.702	0.761	0.716	0.737	0.629	**0.687**	0.259	0.377
	Wu	0.725	0.763	0.73	0.746	0.642	0.625	0.394	0.484
Random forest	Textual	0.747	0.717	0.879	0.789	0.778	0.726	0.768	0.747
	Image	0.652	0.646	0.771	0.703	0.652	0.646	0.771	0.703
	MONITOR	**0.962**	**0.965**	**0.966**	**0.965**	**0.889**	**0.914**	**0.864**	**0.889**
	Castillo	0.702	0.727	0.723	0.725	0.714	0.669	0.67	0.67
	Wu	0.728	0.752	0.748	0.75	0.736	0.699	0.682	0.691

other three algorithms achieve an accuracy gain between 5% and 9% on MediaEval and between 5% and 6% on FakeNewsNet. Compared to the 40 additional textual features, all classification algorithms generate a lower accuracy when using image features only.

While image features play a crucial role in rumor verification, we must not ignore the effectiveness of textual features. The role of image and textual features is complementary. When the two sets of features are combined, performance is significantly boosted.

Illustration by Example. To more clearly show this complementarity, we compare the results reported by MONITOR and single modality approaches (textual and image). The fake rumor messages from Fig. 1 are correctly detected as false by MONITOR, while using either only textual or only image modalities yields a true result.

In the tweet from Fig. 1(a), the text content solely describes the attached image without giving any signs about the veracity of the tweet. This is how the textual modality identified this tweet as real. It is the attached image that looks quite suspicious. By merging the textual and image contents, MONITOR can identify the veracity of the tweet with a high score, exploiting some clues from the image to get the right classification.

The tweet from Fig. 1(b) is an example of a rumor correctly classified by MONITOR, but incorrectly classified when only using the visual modality. The image seems normal and the complex semantic content of the image is very difficult to capture by the image modality. However, the words with strong emotions in the text indicate that it might be a suspicious message. By combining the textual and image modalities, MONITOR can classify the tweet with a high confidence score.

4.4   Feature Analysis

The advantage of our approach is that we can achieve some elements of interpretability. Thus, we conduct an analysis to illustrate the importance of each feature set. We depict the first most 15 important features achieved by the random forest. Figure 5 shows that, for both datasets, visual characteristics are in the top five features. The remaining features are a mix of text content and social context features. These results validate the effectiveness of the IQA image features issued, as well as the importance of fusing several modalities in the process of rumor verification.

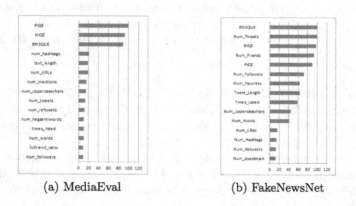

(a) MediaEval   (b) FakeNewsNet

Fig. 5. Distribution of true and false classes for top-15 important features

To illustrate the discriminating capacity of these features, we deploy box plots for each of the 15 top variables on both datasets. Figure 6 shows that several features exhibit a significant difference between the fake and real classes, which explains our good results.

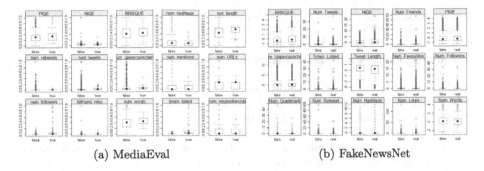

(a) MediaEval

(b) FakeNewsNet

Fig. 6. Distribution of true and false classes for top-15 important features

5 Conclusion and Perspectives

To assess the veracity of messages posted on social networks, most machine learning techniques ignore the visual content. In this paper, to improve the performance of the message verification, we propose a multimodal fusion framework called MONITOR that uses features extracted from the textual content of the message, the social context, and also image features have not been considered until now. Extensive experiments conducted on the MediaEval benchmark and FakeNewsNet dataset demonstrated that: 1) the image features that we introduce play a key role in message veracity assessment; and 2) no single homogeneous feature set can generate the best results alone.

Our future research includes two directions. First, we currently fuse modalities into a single vector, which is called early fusion. By combining classifiers instead, we also plan to investigate so-called late fusion. Second, we plan to use deep learning models capable to learn latent representations of both text and images. However, we would like to compare their performance with MONITOR's to study the tradeoff between classification accuracy, computing complexity, and explainability.

References

1. Blei, D.M., Ng, A.Y., Jordan, M.I.: Latent Dirichlet allocation. JMLR **3**(Jan), 993–1022 (2003)
2. Boididou, C., et al.: Verifying multimedia use at mediaeval 2015. In: MediaEval (2015)
3. Boididou, C., Papadopoulos, S., Zampoglou, M., Apostolidis, L., Papadopoulou, O., Kompatsiaris, Y.: Detection and visualization of misleading content on twitter. IJMIR **7**(1), 71–86 (2018)
4. Castillo, C., Mendoza, M., Poblete, B.: Information credibility on Twitter. In: 20th WWW, pp. 675–684. ACM (2011)
5. Goodfellow, I., et al.: Generative adversarial nets. In: ANIPS, pp. 2672–2680 (2014)
6. Gupta, A., Lamba, H., Kumaraguru, P., Joshi, A.: Faking sandy: characterizing and identifying fake images on Twitter during hurricane sandy. In: WWW 2013, pp. 729–736. ACM (2013)

7. Gupta, M., Zhao, P., Han, J.: Evaluating event credibility on Twitter. In: Proceedings of the 2012 SIAM DM, pp. 153–164. SIAM (2012)
8. Jin, Z., Cao, J., Zhang, Y., Zhou, J., Tian, Q.: Novel visual and statistical image features for microblogs news verification. IEEE Trans. Multimedia **19**(3), 598–608 (2017)
9. Karegowda, A.G., Manjunath, A., Jayaram, M.: Comparative study of attribute selection using gain ratio and correlation based feature selection. Int. J. Inf. Technol. Knowl. Manage. **2**(2), 271–277 (2010)
10. Kincaid, J.P., Fishburne Jr., R.P., Rogers, R.L., Chissom, B.S.: Derivation of new readability formulas (automated readability index, fog count and flesch reading ease formula) for navy enlisted personnel (1975)
11. Kwon, S., Cha, M., Jung, K.: Rumor detection over varying time windows. PloS ONE **12**(1), e0168344 (2017)
12. Kwon, S., Cha, M., Jung, K., Chen, W., Wang, Y.: Prominent features of rumor propagation in online social media. In: 2013 IEEE 13th DM, pp. 1103–1108. IEEE (2013)
13. Li, J., Li, X., Yang, B., Sun, X.: Segmentation-based image copy-move forgery detection scheme. IEEE Trans. IFS **10**(3), 507–518 (2014)
14. Maître, H.: From Photon to Pixel: The Digital Camera Handbook. Wiley (2017)
15. Martin, N., Comm, B.: Information verification in the age of digital journalism. In: SLAA Conference, pp. 8–10 (2014)
16. Mittal, A., Moorthy, A.K., Bovik, A.C.: Blind/referenceless image spatial quality evaluator. In: 2011 ASILOMAR, pp. 723–727. IEEE (2011)
17. Mittal, A., Soundararajan, R., Bovik, A.C.: Making a "completely blind" image quality analyzer. IEEE SPL **20**(3), 209–212 (2012)
18. Morris, M.R., Counts, S., Roseway, A., Hoff, A., Schwarz, J.: Tweeting is believing?: understanding microblog credibility perceptions. In: ACM 2012 CSCW, pp. 441–450. ACM (2012)
19. Pedregosa, F., et al.: Scikit-learn: machine learning in Python. JMLR **12**, 2825–2830 (2011)
20. Pérez-Rosas, V., Kleinberg, B., Lefevre, A., Mihalcea, R.: Automatic detection of fake news. In: Proceedings of the 27th ICCL. pp. 3391–3401. ACL, Santa Fe, New Mexico, USA, August 2018. https://www.aclweb.org/anthology/C18-1287
21. Ruchansky, N., Seo, S., Liu, Y.: CSI: a hybrid deep model for fake news detection. In: ACM on CIKM, pp. 797–806. ACM (2017)
22. Shu, K., Mahudeswaran, D., Wang, S., Lee, D., Liu, H.: FakeNewsNet: a data repository with news content, social context and dynamic information for studying fake news on social media. arXiv preprint arXiv:1809.01286 (2018)
23. Shu, K., Wang, S., Liu, H.: Understanding user profiles on social media for fake news detection. In: 2018 IEEE MIPR, pp. 430–435. IEEE (2018)
24. Silverman, C.: Verification Handbook: An Ultimate Guideline on Digital Age Sourcing for Emergency Coverage. EJC (2014)
25. Venkatanath, N., Praneeth, D., Bh, M.C., Channappayya, S.S., Medasani, S.S.: Blind image quality evaluation using perception based features. In: 2015 NCC, pp. 1–6. IEEE (2015)
26. Volkova, S., Jang, J.Y.: Misleading or falsification: inferring deceptive strategies and types in online news and social media. In: Proceedings WC2018, pp. 575–583. IWWWeb CSC (2018)
27. Wang, Y., et al.: EANN: event adversarial neural networks for multi-modal fake news detection. In: 24th ACM SIGKDD, pp. 849–857. ACM (2018)

28. Wu, K., Yang, S., Zhu, K.Q.: False rumors detection on Sina Weibo by propagation structures. In: 2015 IEEE 31st DE, pp. 651–662. IEEE (2015)
29. Wu, L., Liu, H.: Tracing fake-news footprints: characterizing social media messages by how they propagate. In: 11th ACM WSDM, pp. 637–645. ACM (2018)
30. Zhu, J.Y., Park, T., Isola, P., Efros, A.A.: Unpaired image-to-image translation using cycle-consistent adversarial networks. In: 2017 IEEE ICCV (2017)

Joint Management and Analysis of Textual Documents and Tabular Data Within the AUDAL Data Lake

Pegdwendé N. Sawadogo[1(✉)], Jérôme Darmont[1], and Camille Noûs[2]

[1] Université de Lyon, Lyon 2, UR ERIC 5 avenue Pierre Mendès France,
69676 Bron Cedex, France
{pegdwende.sawadogo,jerome.darmont}@univ-lyon2.fr
[2] Université de Lyon, Lyon 2, Laboratoire Cogitamus, Bron, France
camille.nous@cogitamus.fr

Abstract. In 2010, the concept of data lake emerged as an alternative to data warehouses for big data management. Data lakes follow a schema-on-read approach to provide rich and flexible analyses. However, although trendy in both the industry and academia, the concept of data lake is still maturing, and there are still few methodological approaches to data lake design. Thus, we introduce a new approach to design a data lake and propose an extensive metadata system to activate richer features than those usually supported in data lake approaches. We implement our approach in the AUDAL data lake, where we jointly exploit both textual documents and tabular data, in contrast with structured and/or semi-structured data typically processed in data lakes from the literature. Furthermore, we also innovate by leveraging metadata to activate both data retrieval and content analysis, including Text-OLAP and SQL querying. Finally, we show the feasibility of our approach using a real-word use case on the one hand, and a benchmark on the other hand.

Keywords: Data lakes · Data lake architectures · Metadata management · Textual documents · Tabular data

1 Introduction

Over the past two decades, we have witnessed a tremendous growth of the amount of data produced in the world. These so-called big data come from diverse sources and in various formats, from social media, open data, sensor data, the Internet of things, etc. Big data induce great opportunities for organizations to get valuable insights through analytics. However, this presupposes storing and organizing data in an effective manner, which involves great challenges.

Thus, the concept of data lake was proposed to tackle the challenges related to the variety and velocity characteristics of big data [10]. A data lake can be defined as a very large data storage, management and analysis system that handles any data format. Data lakes use a schema-on-read approach, i.e., no schema is fixed

© Springer Nature Switzerland AG 2021
L. Bellatreche et al. (Eds.): ADBIS 2021, LNCS 12843, pp. 88–101, 2021.
https://doi.org/10.1007/978-3-030-82472-3_8

until data are analyzed [12], which provides more flexibility and richer analyses than traditional storage systems such as data warehouses, which are based on a schema-on-write approach [20]. Yet, in the absence of a fixed schema, analyses in a data lake heavily depend on metadata [16]. Thus, metadata management plays a vital role.

Although quite popular in both the industry and academia, the concept of data lake is still maturing. Thence, there is a lack of methodological proposals for data lakes implementations for certain use cases. Existing works on data lakes indeed mostly focus on structured and/or semi-structured data [15,17, 23,26], with little research on managing unstructured data. Yet, unstructured data represent up to 80% of the data available to organizations [9]. Therefore, managing texts, images or videos in a data lake is an open research issue.

Furthermore, most of data lake proposals (about 75%) refer to Apache Hadoop for data storage [31]. However, using Hadoop requires technical human resources that small and medium-sized enterprises (SMEs) may not have. Thence, alternatives are needed. Last but not least, data lake usage is commonly reserved to data scientists [12,20,24]. Yet, business users represent a valuable expertise while analyzing data. Consequently, opening data lakes to such users is also a challenge to address.

To meet these issues, we contribute to the literature on data lakes through a new approach to build and exploit a data lake. We implement our approach in AUDAL (the AURA-PMI[1] Data Lake). AUDAL exploits an extensive metadata system to activate richer features than common data lake proposals. More concretely, our contribution is threefold. First, we introduce a new methodological approach to integrate both structured (tabular) and unstructured (textual) data in a lake. Our proposal opens a wider range of analyses than common data lake proposals, which goes from data retrieval to data content analysis. Second, AUDAL also innovates through an architecture leading to an "inclusive data lake", i.e., usable by data scientists as well as business users. Third, we propose an alternative to Hadoop for data and metadata storage in data lakes.

The remainder of this paper is organized as follows. In Sect. 2, we focus on our metadata management approach. In Sect. 3, we detail AUDAL's architecture and the analyses it allows. In Sect. 4, we demonstrate the feasibility of our approach through performance measures. In Sect. 5, we review and discuss the related works from the literature. Finally, in Sect. 6, we conclude the paper and hint at future research.

2   Metadata Management in AUDAL

The most critical component in a data lake is presumably the metadata management system. In the absence of a fixed schema, accessing and analyzing the lake's data indeed depend on metadata [15,23,35]. Thence, we particularly focus in this section on how metadata are managed in AUDAL.

---

[1] AURA-PMI is a multidisciplinary project in Management and Computer Sciences, aiming at studying the digital transformation, servicization and business model mutation of industrial SMEs in the French Auvergne-Rhône-Alpes (AURA) Region.

First and foremost, let us precise what we consider as metadata. We adopt the definition: "structured information that describes, explains, locates, or otherwise makes it easier to retrieve, use, or manage information resources" [37]. This definition highlights that metadata are not limited to simple atomic data descriptions, but may be more complex.

AUDAL's metadata management system is based on MEDAL [33], a metadata model for data lakes. We adopt MEDAL because it is extensive enough to allow both data exploration and data content analysis by business users. In line with MEDAL, our metadata system implements data polymorphism, i.e., the simultaneous management of multiple raw and/or preprocessed representations of the same data [33]. Our motivation is that different analyses may require the same data, but in various, specific formats. Thus, pregenerating several formats for data would lead to readily available and faster analyses [2, 22].

Still in line with MEDAL, we use the term "object" as our lower-granularity data item, i.e., either a tabular or textual document. We also exploit three types of metadata that are detailed in the following sections. Section 2.1 is dedicated to *intra-object metadata* management; Sect. 2.2 focuses on *inter-object metadata* management; and Sect. 2.3 details *global metadata* management.

2.1   Intra-object Metadata

Definition and Generation. Intra-object metadata are atomic or more complex information associated with a specific object. We classify them in two categories.

Metadata properties are information that describe an object. They often take the form of simple key-value pairs, e.g., author name, file path, creation date, etc. However, they may sometimes be more complex. Particularly, the description of the columns of a table can be viewed as a complex form of metadata properties.

Metadata properties are mostly provided by the file system. However, especially when dealing with textual documents, we use Apache Tika [36] to automatically extract metadata such as the author, language, creation timestamp, mime-type and even the program used to edit the document.

Refined representations are more complex. When an object is transformed, the result may be considered as both data and metadata. This is in line with the definition we adopt for metadata, since such transformed data make easier the use of the original object. In AUDAL, refined representations of textual documents are either bag-of-word vectors [30] or document embedding vectors [21]. Bag-of-words can easily be aggregated to extract top keywords from a set of documents. However, they do not suit distance calculation, due to their high dimensionality. By contrast, embedding vectors do not bear this disadvantage, while allowing the extraction of top keywords. Refined representations of tabular data are plain and simply relational tables. Eventually, let us note that AUDAL's metadata system may be extended with additional types of refined representations, if needed.

To generate bag-of-word representations, we perform for each document a classical process: tokenizing, stopword removal, lemmatization and finally word count. To generate embedding representations, we project documents in an embedding space with the help of the Doc2Vec model [21]. Each document is thus transformed into a reduced vector of only a few tens of coordinates. Eventually, we use a custom process to generate refined representations from tables. Each tabular document is read in a Python dataframe and then transformed into a relational table.

Modeling and Storage. Still using MEDAL [33], we follow a graph approach to model the interactions between data and metadata. Therefore, AUDAL's metadata system is centered on Neo4J [29]. We exploit four types of nodes to manage intra-object metadata.

Object nodes represent raw objects. They contain atomic metadata, i.e., metadata properties, in particular the path to the raw file. As Neo4J does not support non-atomic data inside nodes, we define *Column* nodes to store column descriptions. *Column* nodes are thus associated to *Object* nodes only in the case of tabular documents.

Each *Object* node is also associated with *Refined* nodes that reference refined representations stored in other DBMSs. Refined representations of textual documents, i.e., embedding and bag-of-word vectors, are indeed stored in MongoDB [27]. Similarly, refined representations of tabular documents are stored in the form of SQLite tables [34]. *Refined* nodes stored in Neo4J actually contain references to their storage location.

Figure 1 illustrates the organization of intra-object metadata.

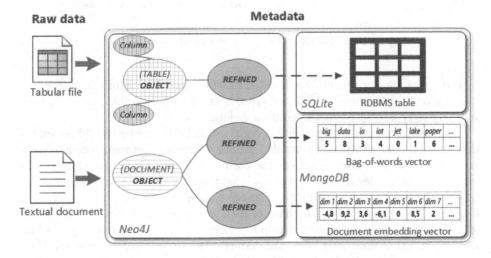

Fig. 1. Organization of intra-object metadata in AUDAL

2.2   Inter-object Metadata

Definition and Generation. Inter-object metadata are information that reflect relationships between objects. We manage two types of inter-object metadata.

Data groupings are organized tag systems that allow to categorize objects into groups, i.e., collections. Each data grouping induces several groups, i.e., collections. Then, data retrieval can be achieved through simple intersections and/or unions of groups. Data groupings are particularly interesting as they are not data type-dependent. For example, a grouping based on data source can serve to retrieve tabular data as well as textual documents, indistinctly (Fig. 2A).

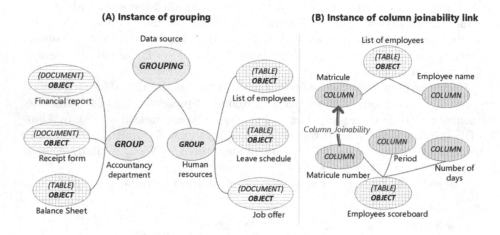

Fig. 2. Organization of inter-object metadata in AUDAL

Data groupings are usually generated on the basis of categorical properties. Starting from the property of interest, we first identify possible groups. Then, each object is associated to the group it belongs to.

Similarity links are information on relatedness between objects. These metadata are obtained applying a suitable similarity measure between couple of textual documents. In our case, we use the cosine similarity that is classically used in information retrieval to compare document vector-space representations [1]. As the number of potential links increases exponentially with the number of documents, we simply retain the links of each document to its ten closest. When dealing with tabular data, we use primary key/foreign key relationships to link columns and thus connect tables. We deduce primary key/foreign key relationships from raw data with the help of the PowerPivot method [7], which is casually used in structured data lakes [14].

Modeling and Storage. To set up data groupings, we introduce two types of nodes in AUDAL's metadata catalogue: *Grouping* and *Group*. A *Grouping* node represents the root of a partition of objects. Each *Grouping* node is associated with several *Group* nodes that represent the resulting parts of such a partition. For example, a partition on data source could lead to a *Group* node for "accounting department", another for "human resources" and so on (Figure 2A). *Object* nodes are then associated with *Group* nodes with respect to the group they belong to. A data grouping organization may thus be seen as a three-layer tree graph where the root node represents the grouping instance, intermediate nodes groups, and leaf nodes objects.

More simply, similarity measures in AUDAL are edges linking nodes. Such edges potentially carry information that indicates the strength of the link, how it was measured, its orientation, etc. More concretely, textual similarity is represented by edges of type *Document_Similarity* between Neo4J *Object* nodes. We model tabular data similarity with *Coulumn_Joinability* edges between *Column* nodes to connect primary key/foreign key column pairs that appear to be joinable. Figure 2B depicts an instance of *Column_Joinability* edge that connects two tables through columns.

2.3 Global Metadata

Definition and Generation. Global metadata are data structures that are built and continuously enriched to facilitate and optimize analyses in the lake. AUDAL includes two types of global metadata.

Semantic resources are knowledge bases (thesauri, dictionaries, etc.) that help improve both metadata generation and data retrieval. Dictionaries allow filtering on specific terms and building vector representations of documents. Similarly, AUDAL uses a thesaurus to automatically expand term-based queries with synonyms. Such semantic resources are ingested and enriched by lake users.

Indexes are also exploited in AUDAL. An inverted index is notably a data structure that establishes a correspondence between keywords and objects from the lake. Such an index is particularly needed to support and, above all, speedup term-based queries. There are two indexes in AUDAL: *document_index* and *table_index*. The first handles the entire content of each textual document, while the latter collects all string values in tabular documents

Modeling and Storage. As global metadata are not directly linked to objects, we do not focus on their modeling, but on their storage, instead. In AUDAL, we manage indexes with ElasticSearch [11], an open-source indexing service that enforces scalability. We define in ElasticSearch an alias to allow simultaneous querying on the two indexes. Eventually, we store semantic resources, i.e., thesauri and dictionaries, in a MongoDB collection. Each is thus a MongoDB document that can be updated and queried.

3 AUDAL's Architecture and Analysis Features

In this section, we highlight how AUDAL's components are organized (Sect. 3.1) and the range of possible analyses (Sect. 3.2).

3.1   AUDAL Architecture

AUDAL's functional architecture is made of three main layers: a storage layer, a metadata management layer and a data querying layer (Fig. 3).

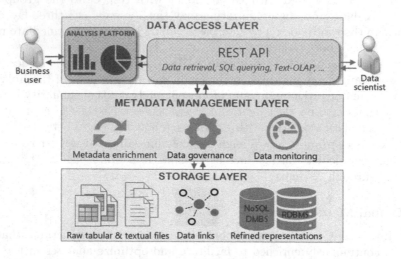

Fig. 3. Architecture of AUDAL

The **storage layer** is in charge of storing raw and processed data, as well as metadata, through a combination of storage systems, each adapted to a specific storage need. In AUDAL, we use a simple file system for raw data storage, a graph DBMS to store links across data entities, a document-oriented DBMS to store refined representations and a relational DBMS for table storage.

The **metadata management layer** is made of a set of processes dedicated to data polymorphism management. More concretely, this layer is in charge of generating metadata, notably refined representations from raw data, as well as links. It allows future analyses and avoids a data swamp, i.e., a data lake whose data cannot be accessed [35]. The data swamp syndrome is indeed often caused by a lack of efficient metadata management system.

Finally, the **data querying layer** is an interface that consumes data from the lake. Its main component is a representational state transfer application programming interface (REST API) from which raw data and some ready-to-use analyses are accessible to data scientists. However, a REST API is not accessible to business users who, unlike data scientists, do not have enough skills to transform raw data into useful information on their own. In addition, business users are not familiar with API querying. Thence, we also provide a graphical analysis platform for them in AUDAL. This platform features the same functions as the REST API, but in a graphical way. Thus, each type of user can access the lake with respect to its needs, which makes AUDAL "inclusive", unlike the common vision of data lakes that excludes business users [12,20,24].

Overall, AUDAL's architecture looks a lot like a multistore system, i.e., a collection of heterogeneous storage systems with a uniform query language [22]. AUDAL indeed offers a single REST API to query data and metadata across different systems (Neo4J, MongoDB, ElasticSearch, and SQLite). However, AUDAL also features an extensive metadata management layer that goes beyond what multistore systems do, i.e., multistores handle only intra-object metadata.

3.2   AUDAL's Analysis Features

Data Retrieval. Data retrieval consists in filtering data from the lake. The techniques we propose for data retrieval are suitable for both textual and tabular documents.

Term-based querying allows to filter data with respect to a set of keywords It includes a fuzzy search feature that allows to expand queries with syntactically similar terms.

Navigation exploits groupings, i.e., organized sets of tags that allow data filtering by intersecting several groups. For example, we can retrieve documents edited by a given author on a specific year, who is associated with a department via the intersection of three groups, e.g., "Scott", 2010 and "Human resources".

Finding related data consists retrieving the objects that are the closest of a given object. Closeness is obtained from similarity links. For example, in the case of tabular data, we use *Column_Joinability* links.

Document Content Analysis. Content analyses provide insights from one or several objects, while taking their intrinsic characteristics into account. The techniques we propose are specific to each data type. In the case of textual documents, AUDAL allows OLAP-like analyses [8]. Groupings may indeed serve as dimensions and thus allow data filtering in multiple manners. Thus, the lake's data can quickly and intuitively be reduced to a subset by intersecting groups, which is comparable to OLAP Slice & Dice operations.

Once documents are filtered, they can be aggregated to obtain valuable insights. Aggregated results can be compared across different subsets of documents using suitable visualizations.

Top keywords summarize documents through a list of most frequent keywords, by aggregating a bag-of-word representation of documents. Thanks to the principle of data polymorphism, different top keyword extraction strategies can coexist. For instance, one can be based on a predefined vocabulary, while another is based on a free vocabulary. We graphically display top keywords using bar charts or word clouds.

Scoring numerically evaluates the relatedness of a set of documents to a set of query terms with the help of a scoring algorithm that takes into account, amongst others, the appearances of query terms in each document. Due to the wide number of documents, the scores per document may not be readable. Thence, we propose instead an aggregated score per group.

Highlights display text snippets where a set of terms appear. In other words, it can be viewed as a document summary centered on given terms. This is also commonly called a concordance.

Group comparison exploits embedding representations to show together groups of documents using a similar vocabulary. This is done in two steps. First, we average the embedding vectors of all documents per group. Then, we exploit the resulting mean embedding vectors to extract group likeness using KMeans clustering [19] or principal component analysis (PCA) [38]. KMeans analysis identifies strongly similar groups into a user-defined number of clusters, while PCA provides a simple two-dimensional visualization where the proximity between groups reflects their similarity.

Tabular Content Analysis. We propose several ways to analyze tabular data.

SQL querying helps users extract or join tabular data. SQL queries actually run on the refined representations of tabular data. As such refined representations are in the form of classical relational tables, all SQL features are supported, including joins and aggregations.

Column correlation evaluates the links between a couple of table columns. We use a suitable statistical measure with respect to columns types. For example, a Jaccard similarity measure can serve to compare categorical columns, while the Kolmogorov-Smirnov statistic is suitable for numerical columns [5].

Tuple comparison consists in running a KMeans clustering or a PCA on a set of tuples, by taking only numeric values into account. Tuples to compare are extracted through a SQL query, potentially including joins and/or aggregations.

4   Quantitative Assessment of AUDAL

The goal of the experiments we propose in this section is to show the feasibility and adaptability of our approach. For this purpose, we implement AUDAL with two different datasets. AUDAL's source code is available online[2].

4.1   Datasets and Query Workload

The first dataset we use comes from the AURA-PMI project. It is composed of 8,122 textual documents and 6 tabular documents, for a total size of 6.2 GB. As the AURA-PMI dataset is quite small, we also create an artificial dataset by extracting 50,000 scientific articles from the French open archive HAL. To these textual documents, we add 5,000 tabular documents coming from an existing benchmark [28], for a total volume of 62.7 GB.

To compare how AUDAL works on our two datasets, we define a set of 15 queries that reflect AUDAL's main features (Table 1). Then, we measure the response time of our workload to assess whether our approach is realistic. In Table 1, the terms document, table and object refer to textual document, relational table and one or the other indistinctly, respectively.

---

[2] https://github.com/Pegdwende44/AUDAL

Table 1. Query workload

Data retrieval queries	
1	Retrieve documents written in English and edited in December
2	Retrieve objects (tables or documents) containing the terms "big" and "data"
3	Retrieve objects with terms "big", "data", "document" and "article"
4	Retrieve 3 tables, joinable to any table.
5	Retrieve 5 most similar documents to a given document
Textual content analysis	
6	Calculate document scores w.r.t. the terms "big", "data", "article" and "document"
7	Extract a concordance from documents using the terms "data" and "ai"
8	Extract a concordance from documents using the terms "data", "ai" "article" and "paper"
9	Find top 10 keywords from all documents
10	Run a 3-cluster KMeans clustering on documents grouped by month
11	Run a PCA analysis on documents grouped by month.
Tabular content analysis	
12	Run a join query between two tables
13	Run a join query between two tables while averaging all numerical values and aggregating by any categorical column.
14	Run a 3-cluster KMeans clustering on the result of *query 12*
15	Run a PCA on the result of *query 12*

4.2 Experimental Setup and Results

Both instances of AUDAL are implemented on a cluster of three VMware virtual machines (VMs). The first VM has a 7-core Intel-Xeon 2.20 GHz processor and 24 GB of RAM. It runs the API. Both other VMs have a mono-core Intel-Xeon 2.20 GHz processor and 24 GB of RAM. Each hosts a Neo4J instance, an ElasticSearch instance and a MongoDB instance to store AUDAL's metadata. The execution times we report in Table 2 are the average of ten runs of each query, expressed in milliseconds.

Our experimental results show that AUDAL does support almost all its query and analysis features in a reasonable time. We also see that AUDAL scales quite well with respect to data volume. All data retrieval and tabular content analyses indeed run very fast on both the AURA-PMI dataset (174 ms on average) and the larger, artificial dataset (183 ms on average). Admittedly, half of textual content queries, i.e., queries #9, #10 and #11, take longer to complete: 5, 2 and 2 s on average, respectively, on the AURA-PMI dataset; and 188, 27 and 27 s on average, respectively, on the artificial dataset. However, we note that without our approach, such tasks would be definitely impossible for business users. Moreover, the situation can certainly be improved by increasing CPU resources. Thus, we consider our results promising.

However, AUDAL's features are achieved at the cost of an extensive metadata system. Table 3 indeed shows that the size of metadata represents up to half

Table 2. Query response time (ms)

Query	AURA-PMI dataset	Artificial dataset
Data retrieval queries		
Query 1	194	653
Query 2	108	207
Query 3	143	305
Query 4	59	81
Query 5	51	79
Textual content analysis		
Query 6	85	117
Query 7	169	198
Query 8	62	92
Query 9	4,629	188,199
Query 10	1,930	26,969
Query 11	1,961	26,871
Tabular content analysis		
Query 12	71	37
Query 13	61	12
Query 14	174	144
Query 15	670	520

Table 3. Raw data vs. metadata size (GB)

System	AURA-PMI dataset	Artificial dataset
Raw data		
–	**6.2**	**62.7**
Metadata		
Neo4J	0.9	2.0
SQLite	0.003	1.7
MongoDB	0.28	3.4
ElasticSearch	1.6	27.6
Total	**2.8**	**34.7**

of raw data. Yet we deem this acceptable given the benefits. Moreover, it is acknowledged that metadata can be larger than the original data, especially in the context of data lakes, where metadata are so important [18].

5 Related Works

The research we present in this paper relates to many systems from the data lake literature. Some of them address data retrieval issues, while others mostly focus on data content analysis. We discuss them with respect of our structured and unstructured data context.

5.1 Data Retrieval from Data Lakes

A great part of the literature considers data lakes as a playground dedicated to data scientists. Related research focuses on data retrieval, since content analyses are assigned to expert users. We identify three main approaches for data retrieval in data lakes, namely navigation, finding related data and term-based search. A first retrieval-by-navigation model exploits tags to easily and quickly find the target object [28]. A similar approach is implemented in several data lakes [3,17,26]. However, all these models are set in the context of structured data only.

A second data retrieval approach exploits data relatedness, i.e., finding a significant similarity between objects or their components [5]. Several techniques help detect relatedness between tabular data through column joinability and unionability [5,13,14,23]. To the best of our knowledge, only one proposal [9] is relevant to unstructured data.

Finally, term-based querying is particularly useful for textual data. Thus, in previous work, we used an indexing system to allow textual documents data retrieval [32]. This technique, i.e., inverted indexes, is also implemented with structured data in Google's data lake [17] and CoreKG [4].

5.2   Data Content Analysis from Data Lakes

An alternative vision of data lakes considers that business users, i.e., not data scientists, can also consume data from a lake. Thus, content querying is required and methods must be used to ease the users' work. In the structured data world, fuzzy SQL querying can be used in data lakes [25]. Similarly, a custom query rewriting system is exploited to analyse data from the Constance lake [16]. There is also a way to personalize table querying by taking user profile into account [3]. Although very few, some approaches propose content analysis for semi-structured [15] and unstructured data [32]. The latter exploits text and graph mining techniques to enable document aggregation.

5.3   Discussion

As stated above, most data lake approaches focus either on data retrieval or data content analyses. Therefore, they present a partial vision of data lakes, in our opinion. In contrast, there exists a system that frees itself from this cleavage [3]. However, it does not support unstructured data. More generally, unstructured data are very rarely supported in data lakes. Our own CODAL data lake [32] does manage textual documents management, but only textual documents. It is therefore limited. In contrast, AUDAL goes beyond these limitations by featuring both data retrieval as well as content analyses. In addition, AUDAL supports both tabular documents and, above all, textual documents whose inclusion in data lakes still challenging.

6   Conclusion and Future Works

In this paper, we present AUDAL, presumably the first methodological approach to manage both textual and tabular documents in a data lake. AUDAL includes an extensive metadata system to allow querying and analyzing the data lake and supports more features than state-of-the-art data lake implementations. In terms of queries, AUDAL indeed supports both data retrieval and data content analyses, including Text-OLAP and SQL querying. Moreover, AUDAL also allows the exploitation of a data lake not only by data scientists, but also by business users. All these makes AUDAL an "inclusive" data lake.

In our near-future research, we plan a deeper validation of AUDAL on two aspects. First, we will work on that complexity and time cost of metadata generation algorithms. Second, we will study how AUDAL's analysis interface is useful to and usable by business users, e.g., using the widely used SUS (System Usability Scale) protocol [6]. Another perspective is data lineage tracking to allow AUDAL support version management. This is particularly important for tabular documents that are often merged or altered. Such a lineage could be implemented by extending AUDAL's refined representations. Finally, we envisage to include more unstructured data types into a lake, i.e., images, videos and/or sounds, and manage their particular metadata for retrieval and analysis.

Acknowledgments. P. N. Sawadogo's Ph.D. is funded by the Auvergne-Rhône-Alpes Region through the AURA-PMI project.

References

1. Allan, J., Lavrenko, V., Malin, D., Swan, R.: Detections, bounds, and timelines: UMass and TDT-3. In: Proceedings of TDT-3, pp. 167–174 (2000)
2. Armbrust, M., Ghodsi, A., Xin, R., Zaharia, M.: Lakehouse: a new generation of open platforms that unify data warehousing and advanced analytics. In: Proceedings of CIDR (2021)
3. Bagozi, A., Bianchini, D., Antonellis, V.D., Garda, M., Melchiori, M.: Personalised exploration graphs on semantic data lakes. In: Proceedings of OTM, pp. 22–39 (2019)
4. Beheshti, A., Benatallah, B., Nouri, R., Tabebordbar, A.: CoreKG: a knowledge lake service. In: PVLDB, vol. 11, no. 12, pp. 1942–1945 (2018)
5. Bogatu, A., Fernandes, A., Paton, N., Konstantinou, N.: Dataset discovery in data lakes. In: Proceedings of ICDE (2020)
6. Brooke, J.: SUS: a quick and dirty usability scale. Usability Eval. Ind. **189**, 4–7 (1996)
7. Chen, Z., Narasayya, V., Chaudhuri, S.: Fast foreign-key detection in Microsoft SQL server PowerPivot for excel. In: PVLDB, vol. 7, no. 13, pp. 1417–1428 (2014)
8. Codd, E., Codd, S., Salley, C.: Providing OLAP (on-line analytical processing) to user-analysts, an IT mandate. E. F. Codd and Associates (1993)
9. Diamantini, C., Giudice, P.L., Musarella, L., Potena, D., Storti, E., Ursino, D.: A new metadata model to uniformly handle heterogeneous data lake sources. In: Benczúr, A., et al. (eds.) ADBIS 2018. CCIS, vol. 909, pp. 165–177. Springer, Cham (2018). https://doi.org/10.1007/978-3-030-00063-9_17
10. Dixon, J.: Pentaho, hadoop, and data lakes (2010). https://jamesdixon.wordpress.com/2010/10/14/pentaho-hadoop-and-data-lakes/
11. Elastic: Elasticsearch (2020). https://www.elastic.co
12. Fang, H.: Managing data lakes in big data era. In: Proceedings of CYBER, pp. 820–824 (2015)
13. Farrugia, A., Claxton, R., Thompson, S.: Towards social network analytics for understanding and managing enterprise data lakes. In: Proceedings of ASONAM, pp. 1213–1220 (2016)
14. Fernandez, R.C., Abedjan, Z., Koko, F., Yuan, G., Madden, S., Stonebraker, M.: Aurum: a data discovery system. In: Proceedings of ICDE, pp. 1001–1012 (2018)

15. Hai, R., Geisler, S., Quix, C.: Constance: an intelligent data lake system. In: Proceedings of SIGMOD, pp. 2097–2100 (2016)
16. Hai, R., Quix, C., Zhou, C.: Query rewriting for heterogeneous data lakes. In: Benczúr, A., Thalheim, B., Horváth, T. (eds.) ADBIS 2018. LNCS, vol. 11019, pp. 35–49. Springer, Cham (2018). https://doi.org/10.1007/978-3-319-98398-1_3
17. Halevy, A., et al.: Managing google's data lake: an overview of the GOODS system. In: Proceedings of SIGMOD, pp. 795–806 (2016)
18. Hellerstein, J.M., et al.: Ground: a data context service. In: Proceedings of CIDR (2017)
19. Jain, A.K.: Data clustering: 50 years beyond K-means. Pattern Recogn. Lett. **31**(8), 651–666 (2010)
20. Khine, P.P., Wang, Z.S.: Data lake: a new ideology in big data era. In: Proceedings of WCSN. ITM Web of Conferences, vol. 17, pp. 1–6 (2017)
21. Le, Q., Mikolov, T.: Distributed representations of sentences and documents. In: Proceedings of ICML, pp. 1188–1196 (2014)
22. Leclercq, E., Savonnet, M.: A tensor based data model for polystore: an application to social networks data. In: Proceedings of IDEAS, pp. 110–118 (2018)
23. Maccioni, A., Torlone, R.: KAYAK: a framework for just-in-time data preparation in a data lake. In: Proceedings of CAiSE, pp. 474–489 (2018)
24. Madera, C., Laurent, A.: The next information architecture evolution: the data lake wave. In: Proceedings of MEDES, pp. 174–180 (2016)
25. Malysiak-Mrozek, B., Stabla, M., Mrozek, D.: Soft and declarative fishing of information in big data lake. IEEE Trans. Fuzzy Syst. **26**(5), 2732–2747 (2018)
26. Mehmood, H., et al.: Implementing big data lake for heterogeneous data sources. In: Proceedings of ICDEW, pp. 37–44 (2019)
27. MongoDB-Inc.: The database for modern applications (2020). https://www.mongodb.com/
28. Nargesian, F., Zhu, E., Pu, K.Q., Miller, R.J.: Table union search on open data. In: PVLDB, vol. 11, pp. 813–825 (2018)
29. Neo4J Inc.: The Neo4j graph platform (2018). https://neo4j.com
30. Pu, W., Liu, N., Yan, S., Yan, J., Xie, K., Chen, Z.: Local word bag model for text categorization. In: Proceedings of ICDM, pp. 625–630 (2007)
31. Russom, P.: Data lakes purposes. Patterns, and platforms. TDWI Research, Practices (2017)
32. Sawadogo, P.N., Kibata, T., Darmont, J.: Metadata management for textual documents in data lakes. In: Proceedings of ICEIS, pp. 72–83 (2019)
33. Sawadogo, P.N., Scholly, É., Favre, C., Ferey, É., Loudcher, S., Darmont, J.: Metadata systems for data lakes: models and features. In: Welzer, T., et al. (eds.) ADBIS 2019. CCIS, vol. 1064, pp. 440–451. Springer, Cham (2019). https://doi.org/10.1007/978-3-030-30278-8_43
34. SQLite-Consortium: What is SQLite? (2020). https://www.sqlite.org/
35. Suriarachchi, I., Plale, B.: Crossing analytics systems: a case for integrated provenance in data lakes. In: Proceedings of e-Science, pp. 349–354 (2016)
36. The Apache Software Foundation: Apache Tika - a content analysis toolkit (2018). https://tika.apache.org/
37. Visengeriyeva, L., Abedjan, Z.: Anatomy of metadata for data curation. J. Data Inf. Qual. **12**(3), 1–3 (2020)
38. Wold, S., Esbensen, K., Geladi, P.: Principal component analysis. Chemometr. Intell. Lab. Syst. **2**(1), 37–52 (1987)

Aggregation and Summarization of Thematically Similar Twitter Microblog Messages

Markus Endres[1]([✉]), Lena Rudenko[2], and Dominik Gröninger[2]

[1] University of Passau, Innstr. 43, 94032 Passau, Germany
markus.endres@uni-passau.de
[2] University of Augsburg, Universitätsstr. 6a, 86159 Augsburg, Germany
lena.rudenko@informatik.uni-augsburg.de, dominik.groeninger@t-online.de
http://fim.uni-passau.de/dke/

Abstract. Information is one of the most important resources in our modern lifestyle and society. Users on social network platforms, like Twitter, produce thousands of tweets every second in a continuous stream. However, not all written data are important for a follower, i.e., not necessary relevant information. That means, trawling through uncountable tweets is a time-consuming and depressing task, even if most of the messages are useless and do not contain news. This paper describes an approach for aggregation and summarization of short messages like tweets. Useless messages will be filtered out, whereas the most important information will be aggregated into a summarized output. Our experiments show the advantages of our promising approach, which can also be applied for similar problems.

Keywords: Twitter · Microblog · Summarization · Aggregation

1 Introduction

Twitter[1] is a micro-blogging and social networking service where users post and interact with messages known as *tweets* (280 Unicode character short messages). Individuals, organizations, companies and mass media use Twitter as a platform for distributing their content on the web.

To *follow* a particular user's account makes sense if you have a constant interest in the content published there and want to be up-to-date. But there exist millions of other tweets, and not all of them are valuable. Twitter allows to browse posted tweets using *keywords* or *hashtags* (topics on Twitter written with a # symbol, e.g., #WorldCup2018). Users can also use search terms, term combinations or more complex queries to get tweets related to these terms.

---

[1] Twitter: https://twitter.com.

© Springer Nature Switzerland AG 2021
L. Bellatreche et al. (Eds.): ADBIS 2021, LNCS 12843, pp. 102–117, 2021.
https://doi.org/10.1007/978-3-030-82472-3_9

However, Twitter reports about 330 million monthly active users, who send over 500 million tweets daily, which means 6 thousand messages per second[2]. Therefore, it is very difficult to navigate through this data, which, moreover, is constantly increasing. Processing big data and searching for interesting and relevant information in large data sets is a highly important topic in both, academia and business. In general, users want to get *personalized results*, which are filtered out from the ever-growing amount of data according to *user's preferences*, cp. [8]. However, due to the nature of Twitter, even the reduced information could be too large on the one hand and have a lot of duplicates and incomplete information snippets on the other hand. Thus, it is extremely important to present the result in a way that it can be easily consumed. Hardly anyone enjoys skimming through reams of tweets in order to find the most valuable information. The objective of this paper is to *aggregate* a thread of text messages in order to provide a *short summarization* of the most important information content.

Example 1. Assume we want to find some facts about the soccer team Germany at the World Cup 2018 in Russia. The search on Twitter may contain the hashtags *#Germany* and *#WorldCup2018* and yields to the following set of tweets.

```
1. It's a sad day for all of #Germany and the World Cup ⋆.
2. After a loss against South Korea, team Germany leaves the World Cup.
3. 0:2 defeat in the last group match and team Germany leaves the World
   Cup in Russia.
4. RT @UserXyz It's a sad day for all of #Germany and the World Cup ⋆.
```

Each of these tweets reports about the same event: *"soccer team Germany leaves the World Cup after group stage"*. The first message describes some user's emotions and is less important for someone looking for factual information. The following two posts provide (incomplete) facts. The last one is a *retweet* (a Twitter form of quoting) of the first message with no additional information at all. An aggregated form and summarization of this set of tweets could be:

```
''Team Germany loses its last group match against South Korea 0:2
and leaves the World Cup in Russia.''
```

A summarization of micro-blog posts, such as tweets, has different challenges, goals, and tasks in comparison to large text documents, which must be considered, e.g., emojies, abbreviations, grammar, spelling mistakes, etc. A *summary* should *not contain duplicates* and should *provide as complete information as possible*. Some aggregation methods apply Neural Networks to solve this task. However, this requires a huge amount of (reliable) training data. Our approach does not rely on training data, is easy to understand and to implement, suitable for (near) real-time analytics, and based on the following steps: (1) *data preprocessing*, (2) *data clustering* and (3) *data aggregation*, which will be described in detail below.

---

[2] Tweets per second, last visited 2021/03/01: www.internetlivestats.com/twitter-statistics/.

The rest of this paper is organized as follows: Sect. 2 discusses *related work*. Afterwards we introduce the *general concept* of our approach in Sect. 3. Section 4 contains details about *data preprocessing*. The *clustering task* is discussed in Sect. 5, and the *aggregation and summarization process* in Sect. 6. A comprehensive *evaluation* can be found in Sect. 7, and a *conclusion* in Sect. 8.

2   Related Work

The most related papers to ours are [4] and [12]. In the first approach, the summary is a kind of label or keyword sequence for a cluster of terms, which titles the topic of every message in the group. Such kind of summary is very short and does not provide much information. The second approach is to choose only one text message as representative. This search is called "budgeted median problem" and considers the summary as good if every message in the document cluster is assigned to a selected one and can be inferred from the latter. This approach gives the user more details, but some information is still lost.

Related to Twitter, content analysis is also often in the focus, cp. [1,2,11]. In [9] the authors try to build a news processing system based on Twitter. Tweets are analyzed to determine if it is news or not, and thereafter clustered into news topics. In [5] the authors describe an event notification system that monitors and delivers semantically relevant tweets if these meet the user's information needs. As an example they construct an earthquake prediction system targeting Japanese tweets. For their system they use keywords, the number of words, and the context of an event. The problem addressing in [7] is to determine the popularity of social events (concerts, festivals, sport events, conferences, etc.) based on their presence in Twitter in order to improve infrastructure organization. In [6] the authors describe a system to detect events from tweets. This is based on the textual and temporal characteristics.

We want to provide a solution for tweet summarization producing a short aggregated message, rather than a general meaningless headline. The objective was not to get involved with Neural Networks, because they require a huge amount of training data, which is often not available for real-time analytics.

3   Background and General Concept

The aim of this paper is to provide an automatically created summary of Twitter posts related to a certain topic. The idea of our approach is based on [10], where the *Phrase Reinforcement* (PR) algorithm was developed to display words from text messages as nodes in a graph structure to handle the problem of summarizing microblogs. Walking through the paths of this graph, it is possible to restore text messages. Some of these paths are selected, converted back into a human readable format and presented to the user. However, this approach only relies on the original phrases and does not apply further processing of the data.

As an extension, we perform a comprehensive *data preprocessing* (1) step to clean the data from unwanted characters and phrases. Afterwards, in order to gather as much information from the posts as possible, we apply a *data clustering* (2) step to find the most common phrases and terms. Using a clustering approach, we also overcome the disadvantages of previous methods, cp. [4,12]. Finally, our *data aggregation* (3) approach can generate a summarized message. In contrast to [10], we use *more than one path* to generate the final message. The main idea of the algorithm is to find the most commonly used phrases in a graph. These phrases can then be used as a summarization of tweets.

The algorithm was inspired from the observations that users often use the same words when describing a key idea. Furthermore, users often retweet the most relevant content for a topic. These two patterns create highly overlapping sequences of words when considering a large number of posts for a single topic.

In our preprocessing step, we remove irrelevant sources (e.g., stop words, hyperlinks, duplicates) from the tweets. This is important to focus the algorithm on the most relevant content. Afterwards we cluster all terms in order to find the most common sequences of words. Based on this clustering result our algorithm builds a tweet graph representing the common sequences of words (i.e., phrases). The main idea behind that is to represent words from phrases as nodes in a graph. These nodes have certain weights, depending on how often they appear in the text collection. The paths with the highest weights can then be used as a summarization.

Fig. 1. Example Phrase Reinforcement graph.

Example 2. Using the sample sentences from the introductory Example 1, our algorithm would generate a graph similar to the one in Fig. 1 (after preprocessing and clustering). The nodes are weighted according to their occurrence in the text collection.

The most common word (or word sequence) serves as *root node*, here *Germany*. *World Cup* also can be found 3 times, but it follows after the word *leaves* twice and comes right after *Germany* once. Together with the word *team* that is located directly before *Germany*, the most important key information from our collection is: *team Germany leaves World Cup*. The path *after loss against South Korea team Germany leaves World Cup Russia* has a weight of 14, *0:2 defeat last group match team Germany leaves World Cup Russia* comes up to 15, and so on.

In the original *Phrase Reinforcement* algorithm the authors only consider the highest weight, which obviously is not enough for summarizing complex tweet posts. Our first idea was to consider all paths having a weight above a given threshold. However, this leads to very similar sentences and therefore we decided to use another approach: We start with the path having the highest weight and then continue using the paths that differ the most from the used paths so far. This leads to a great diversity among the selected information and serves as a summarization at the end.

4   Data Preprocessing

Tweets often include abbreviations, errors (intentional or accidental), internet slang, emojis, URLs, etc. Therefore, *preprocessing* of tweets is a very important step in order to get a reliable summarization of text messages. The main goal of our preprocessing step is to transform the tweets into a *normalized, generalized* form and therefore are mainly aimed to eliminate "unwanted" components. This takes into account special characters (e.g., *links* and *emojis, user references* and *hashtags*). In this section we describe our preprocessing steps:

Algorithm: Data Preprocessing

Input: A set of tweets
Step 1: *Substitute retweets by its original message.*
Step 2: *Transformation of upper case letters to lower case.*
Step 3: *Translation of any existing HTML entities*[3] *into "standard" entities.*
Step 4: *Normalization with compatible decomposition:* Special characters are separated into their components.[4] This prevents misunderstanding of unformatted HTML remnants as words and treatment of special characters different from their normal counterparts. E.g., Señor will be normalized to sen˜or.
Step 5: *Removal of URLs and e-mail addresses:* URLs and email addresses that are less common in tweets, are removed, otherwise they will appear as annoying elements in the clustering step.
Step 6: *Removal of "unwanted" characters (e.g., ⋆ ' ' , . ! ˜ ' '):* All special characters that may negatively affect the clustering process and are not important for the content of a tweet are removed. Characters that have an added value with regard to the information content remain in the text. This includes *arabic numerals, spaces* and *apostrophes*, as well as $+, -, ., :, ,,$ if they appear in connection with numbers (e.g., in $-2.100, 55$). The *glyphs* for ampersand (&), paragraph (§), percent (%) and for common currencies (dollar, euro, pound, etc.) are also preserved. *hash* (#) and *at* (@) also play a special role. They serve as a marker for *hashtags* (#...) and *references* to user accounts (@...).
Step 7: *Lemmatization of the remaining text elements:* Words are reduced to their stems. Lemmatization provides linguistically correct expressions. This is done by using linguistic analyses and a large vocabulary, cp. [3]. *Hashtags* and *user references* remain unchanged, but their identifiers (# or @) are separated. This way it is ensured that the "simple" hashtags (e.g., *#usa*) are matched with the same terms not marked as hashtags during the clustering process.

---

[3] HTML entities: https://en.wikipedia.org/?title=HTML_entity.
[4] Unicode normalization: https://en.wikipedia.org/wiki/Unicode_equivalence.

Step 8: *Tokenisation of lemmatized messages:* All lemmatized tweets are tokenized: each term forms a separate token.

Step 9: *Removal of stop words (e.g., "of, the, in, by, and, its, be, a"):* Stop words are not relevant w.r.t. the content. Therefore, they are removed from the token sequences. However, they are important for the comprehensibility of a sentence, hence stored in background in order to produce a human readable summarization.

Step 10: *Building of N-grams:* The final preprocessing step is the generation of N-grams. These consist of N successive tokens each and are used to compare the tweets. As default value $N = 3$ is recommended. In addition, lexicographic sorting of the tokens within an N-gram is performed. N-grams, which are similar in content, but differ due to the sequence of tokens, are considered identical in the clustering process.

Output: A set of N-grams describing the posts

Example 3. Consider the first Twitter message from Example 1 as input: After the first steps, e.g., upper case to lower case, URL and special character removal, lemmatization, our post is as follows after Step 7:

$$it's \ a \ sad \ day \ for \ all \ of \ \# \ germany \ and \ the \ world \ cup$$

Finally, we end up with the following N-grams after tokenization and stop word removal: { *(germany day sad), (day germany world) (cup germany world)*}.

5   Data Clustering

Our goal is to summarize short messages that fit together in terms of content. Therefore, we perform a clustering and collect the tweets describing the same topic or event in the same group. Afterwards, the messages in each group can be summarized using our approach described in the next section.

Our clustering approach is based on the *k most common N-grams* as cluster centroids. Phrases having the same N-grams are simply assigned to the same cluster. That means that we have a large set of clusters after the first round, some of them are *exactly the same* (but with different N-grams as centroids), others *overlap to a certain degree*. This will be resolved by *merging clusters* that are "similar" w.r.t. a threshold (certain percentage).

Using this kind of *clustering*, only *one data iteration* is necessary. No similarity between the tweets is calculated, because the affiliation to a cluster is determined with the help of the N-gram centroids. This makes this cluster approach quite efficient, e.g., for real-time Twitter stream processing, which still was an open issue in [10]. Our approach is as follows:

Algorithm: Data Clustering

Input: A set of N-grams for each tweet after data preprocessing (cp. Sect. 4)

Step 1: *Build a cluster for each N-gram, sort the tweets and eliminate duplicates.* All N-grams generated during the preprocessing step are used as cluster *centroids.* N-grams (and their text phrase, resp.), for which a cluster already exists, are assigned to existing clusters. This approach allows us a clustering process in linear time. Since each cluster is a *set*, they are duplicate free. At the end, each cluster contains only phrases and their corresponding centroid (or one of the unsorted permutations of the $N-$gram).

Step 2: *Combining of overlapping clusters:* Clusters overlapping to a certain percentage p are merged. For the parameter p we suggest a value between 0.6 and 0.7 (or 60% − 70%), based on our experience. Two clusters C_1 and C_2 are merged if the following condition holds: $\frac{|C_1 \cap C_2|}{\min(|C_1|,|C_2|)} \geq p$

Step 3: *Discarding small clusters.* The resulting clusters are now either larger clusters, which were constructed by merging, or smaller clusters, which could not be merged. Based on a given minimum cluster size s, some clusters can be classified as negligible.

Output: The k largest clusters.

Example 4. Table 1 represents our sample input tokens (abbrv. with letters) and the set of $N = 3$-grams (after the preprocessing step). For example, *(a b c d e f g e)* represents input tokens and *(a b c), (b c d), (c d e), ... (e f g)* the N-grams. We want to determine the $k = 2$ largest clusters.

Table 1. Input tweets with the corresponding 3-grams.

ID	Text (tokens)	Set of N-gramms
11	*(a b c d e f g e)*	*(a b c), (b c d), (c d e), (d e f), (e f g),* ~~*(e f g)*~~
12	*(a b c d e f h g)*	*(a b c), (b c d), (c d e), (d e f), (e f h), (f g h)*
13	*(a b c d e f g h)*	*(a b c), (b c d), (c d e), (d e f), (e f g), (f g h)*
14	*(b c d e f g h)*	*(b c d), (c d e), (d e f), (e f g), (f g h)*
15	*(l m n o p q r s)*	*(l m n), (m n o), (n o p), (o p q), (p q r), (q r s)*
16	*(u v w x y z a b)*	*(u v w), (v w x), (w x y), (x y z), (a y z), (a b z)*
17	*(u v w x y z a)*	*(u v w), (v w x), (w x y), (x y z), (a y z)*
18	*(w x y z a x y z)*	*(w x y), (x y z), (a y z), (a x z), (a x y),* ~~*(x y z)*~~

For each 3-gram we build a cluster having the N-gram as centroid (blue), cp. Table 2. For example, for *(a b c)* we have the tweets with ID 11, 12, and 13 as cluster objects. Clusters are duplicate free, hence we remove ID 11 in *(e f g)*.

Table 2. Cluster centroids and 3−grams.

Centroid (size)	ID	Text (tokens)
	11	(a b c d e f g e)
a b c (3)	12	(a b c d e f g h)
	13	(a b c d e f g h)
	11	(a b c d e f g e)
b c d (4)	12	(a b c d e f h g)
	13	(a b c d e f g h)
	14	(b c d e f g h)
	11	(a b c d e f g e)
c d e (4)	12	(a b c d e f h g)
	13	(a b c d e f g h)
	14	(b c d e f g h)
	11	(a b c d e f g e)
d e f (4)	12	(u b c d e f h g)
	13	(a b c d e f g h)
	14	(b c d e f g h)
	11	(a b c d e f g e)
e f g (3)	13	(a b c d e f g h)
	14	(b c d e f g h)
	~~11~~	~~(a b c d e f g e)~~
e f h (1)	12	(a b c d e f h g)
	12	(a b c d e f h g)
f g h (3)	13	(a b c d e f g h)
	14	(b c d e f g h)

Centroid (size)	ID	Text (tokens)
l m n (1)	15	(l m n o p q r s)
m n o (1)	15	(l m n o p q r s)
n o p (1)	15	(l m n o p q r s)
o p q (1)	15	(l m n o p q r s)
p q r (1)	15	(l m n o p q r s)
q r s (1)	15	(l m n o p q r s)
u v w (2)	16	(u v w x y z a b)
	17	(u v w x y z a)
v w x (2)	16	(u v w x y z a b)
	17	(u v w x y z a)
	16	(u v w x y z a b)
w x y (3)	17	(u v w x y z a)
	18	(w x y z x y z)
	16	(u v w x y z a b)
x y z (3)	17	(u v w x y z a)
	18	(w x y z a x y z)
	~~18~~	~~(w x y z a x y z)~~
	16	(u v w x y z a b)
a y z (3)	17	(u v w x y z a)
	18	(w x a y z x y z)
a b z (1)	16	(u v w x y z a b)
a x z (1)	18	(w x y a x z y z)
a x y (1)	18	(w x y z a x y z)

In the next step we merge the overlapping clusters. Considering the clusters in Table 2 we identify some "similarity", e.g., the clusters with centroids *(b c d)*, *(c d e)*, and *(d e f)* are identical, whereas *(b c d)*, *(a b c)*, *(e f g)*, *(f g h)*, *(e f h)* are similar to a certain percentage. Similar cluster values are included in larger clusters, e.g., *(m n o)*, *(n o p)*, etc. are combined to *(l m n)*, cp. Table 3.

Table 3. Merging.

Centroid (size)	ID	Text (tokens)
	11	(a b c d e f g e)
b c d (4)	12	(a b c d e f h g)
	13	(a b c d e f g h)
	14	(b c d e f g h)
	16	(u v w x y z a b)
w x y (3)	17	(u v w x y z a)
	18	(w x y z a x y z)
l m n (1)	15	(l m n o p q r s)

Table 4. Discarding.

Centroid (size)	ID	Text (tokens)
	11	(a b c d e f g e)
b c d (4)	12	(a b c d e f h g)
	13	(a b c d e f g h)
	14	(b c d e f g h)
	16	(u v w x y z a b)
w x y (3)	17	(u v w x y z a)
	18	(w x y z a x y z)
~~l m n (1)~~	~~15~~	~~(l m n o p q r s)~~

Finally, all smaller clusters can be classified as unimportant and therefore are not used for summarization. E.g., if we use a minimum cluster size of $s = 3$, then *(l m n)* will be removed, cp. Table 4. At the end, the remaining $k = 2$ larger clusters are used for further processing.

6   Data Aggregation

Our approach for data aggregation in order to produce the final summarization is an extension of [10], cp. Sect. 3. In comparison to the original version, we trace several paths for the final message construction, and not only the path with the highest weight. In addition, the weights of the paths are calculated without stop words and weakly weighted nodes in order to produce more reliable results.

Algorithm: Data Aggregation

Input: One of the k largest clusters, cp. Sect. 5.

Step 1: *Build tweet graphs.* Each tweet is represented as a separate graph. Tokens are nodes and connected by directed edges according to the reading direction. Stop words are removed, tokens representing the cluster centre are combined to one node. If a cluster contains tweets that do not contain the centroid (or its permutation), they are not considered. Each node gets an initial weight of 1.

Step 2: *Merge the tweet graphs into a common cluster graph.* All tweet graphs are connected via the centroid as a common intersection. This is done by "superimposing". The combined centroid is assigned a new weight according to the number of combined tweets. Likewise, all identical sub-paths that begin or end at the centroid are superimposed and weighted.

If a tweet contains the centroid of its cluster n times, this tweet is also included n times in the combined cluster graph. If this results in an overlap with other nodes, their weight will be increased, if it was not already incremented before while one of the other $n - 1$ centroid's occurrence of the current tweet was processed. This ensures that all centroid occurrences in a tweet are treated equally, but the weight of the node in the tweet graph is not incremented repeatedly by a single tweet.

Step 3: *Reduce the cluster graph.* We reduce the cluster graph to its essence. *Strong weighted* nodes are considered *important* and *weakly weighted* nodes are considered *insignificant.* The centroid, which always has the maximum weight, represents the core content of the cluster while nodes that still have their initial weight of 1 are regarded as marginal information and can be removed.

Step 4: *Select m paths for the summarization.* In order to generate a summary having a maximum of information, several suitable paths are determined. For this, we start with the path having the *highest weight (main path).* Instead of using the paths with the next highest total weights afterwards, paths that *differ the most* from those used so far are selected. The path that has the least overlap or, in case of a tie, the higher weight, is selected as next sentence. The reason for this is that paths differing less have very similar content. In this way, the greatest possible diversity among the selected information can be achieved. If there are still unused paths afterwards, the procedure is repeated for each further sentence until a maximum of m paths is reached.

Step 5: *Build the final message* After selecting m paths, they are transformed into a human readable format. Each path is a concatenation of tokens, and hence replaced by one of the tweets whose paragraph they represent (e.g., by the last one that leads to an increasing node weight). The substitution is done using the lemmatized token sequences, which were saved during preprocessing and still contain stop words. This variant produces clearly better results concerning readability and comprehensibility of the message.

Output: Microblog summarization

Example 5. Assume a cluster *(d e f)* as one of the k largest clusters after the *data clustering* step as shown in Fig. 2 (not related to previous examples). Tweets are shown as sequences of their tokens, tokens are simplified as letters. Centroids are marked blue, tweets not containing a centroid are highlighted red):

centroid (size)	tweets	
	ID text (tokens)	ID text (tokens)
d e f (20)	21 (b c d e f g h i),	22 (c d e f gd e f),
	73 (a b c d e f),	23 (r u x d e f g h),
	54 (a b c d e f h g),	46 (c d e f h),
	92 (a b c d e f g h),	48 (v b c d e f g h),
	31 (l m n c d e f s t),	50 (m n c d e f s t u),
	51 (n c d e f s u t),	86 (m n c e d f h g),
	37 (c f d e g d),	76 (r u x d e f y z),
	95 (v b c d f e s t),	26 (d e f s t u v),
	34 (m n c d e f g h t),	91 (w x d e f s t u),
	97 (m n c d f e g h),	60 (a k l d h f g h)

Fig. 2. Input cluster.

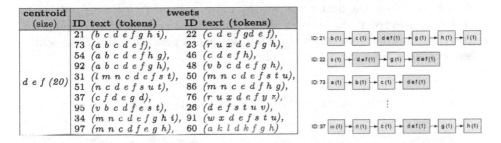

Fig. 3. Tweet graphs.

Based on the input data, we build *tweet graphs* (Step 1), cp. Fig. 3. ID 60 is not considered, because it does not contain the centroid. Each node gets an initial weight of 1. Afterwards we merge all tweet graphs into the *cluster graph* by superimposing (Step 2), cp. Fig. 4 (including the white nodes). The combined centroid gets a weight of 19. Also all sub-paths are superimposed and weighted. Removing all nodes with an initial weight of 1 leads to the *reduced graph* (Step 3, Fig. 4 without white nodes).

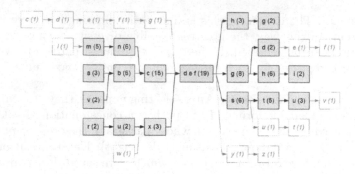

Fig. 4. Complete and reduced cluster graph (reduced nodes are white).

In Step 4 we select the paths for the $m = 4$ final messages, cp. Table 5. The most appropriate path in each phase is marked green. The *main path* has the highest total weight (top left table, *(m n c ...)*) and is added to the set of *selected paths*, cp. Table 6. The second path correspond the path with the *smallest overlap* (ovl.) in order to add the most valuable information. The third path correspond to the smallest overlap to all already selected paths, therefore we add *(a b c ...)* and *(v b c ...)* from the next table. Furthermore, we add *(v b c d e f g d)* as 4. path to the selected paths. Table 6 shows all selected paths after the complete aggregation process from which our final message is generated (inserting white token sequences from Fig. 4 (orange phrases)).

Table 5. Determine m paths for final message.

	Possible paths – 1. path		
	path	(weight)	ovl. to M
x	*(m n c d e f g h i)* - *(61)*		0
	(m n c d e f s t u) - *(59)*		0
	(a b c d e f g h i) - *(59)*		0
	...		...

	Possible paths – 3. path		
	path	(weight)	ovl. to M
	(a b c d e f h g) - *(48)*		$2/6 \approx 0.33$
	(v b c d e f h g) - *(47)*		$2/6 \approx 0.33$
x	*(a b c d e f g d)* - *(53)*		$3/6 = 0.5$
x	*(v b c d e f g d)* - *(52)*		$3/6 = 0.5$
	...		...

	Possible paths – 2. path		
	path	(weight)	ovl. to M
	(a b c d e f h g) - *(48)*		$2/6 \approx 0.33$
	(r u x d e f h g) - *(31)*		$1/6 \approx 0.17$
	(a b c d e f s t u) - *(57)*		$2/7 \approx 0.29$
x	*(r u x d e f s t u)* - *(40)*		$1/7 \approx 0.14$
	...		...

	Possible paths – 4. path		
	path	(weight)	ovl. to M
	(v b c d e f h g) - *(47)*		$5/6 \approx 0.83$
x	*(v b c d e f g d)* - *(52)*		$4/6 \approx 0.67$
	(v b c d e f g h i) - *(58)*		$6/7 \approx 0.86$
	...		...

Table 6. Creating summarization and final sentences.

nr.	Selected paths (M)		
	path	(weight)	
1	$(m\ n\ c\ d\ e\ f\ g\ h\ i)$ - (61)		→ $L\ m\ n\ c\ d\ e\ f\ g\ h\ i.$
2	$(r\ u\ x\ d\ e\ f\ s\ t\ u)$ - (40)		→ $R\ u\ x\ d\ e\ f\ s\ t\ u\ v.$
3	$(a\ b\ c\ d\ e\ f\ h\ g)$ - (48)		→ $A\ b\ c\ d\ e\ f\ h\ g.$
4	$(v\ b\ c\ d\ e\ f\ g\ d)$ - (52)		→ $V\ b\ c\ d\ e\ f\ g\ d\ e\ f.$

7 Experiments

Twitter provides a public API, which allows us to evaluate or summarization approach on real data. We implemented our technology in Java on an Intel Xeon "Skylake", 2.10 GHz, 192 GB DDR4, 2x 4 TB SATA3-HDD, Ubuntu Linux.

7.1 Data Analysis and Runtime

In this section we analyze the performance behavior of our approach. We measured the time from reading the tweet (stored in a file for repeatable experiments) til presenting the summarized messages. This process is repeated 12 times, whereby the best and the worst result is discarded and the average from the remaining ten values is calculated.

For our performance measurement we used "standard parameters": N-grams of size 3, clusters comprising less than 0.05% of the total number of all clustered tweets as well as those clusters that overlap by at least 60% are discarded. The 10 largest clusters are aggregated. In the reduction phase all nodes having $\leq 1.5\%$ of the centroid weights are removed. Finally, a summarization having a maximum of $m = 4$ sentences each is generated.

We run our experiments on 16 disjoint files, each containing between 27 000 and 4 300 000 English tweets. Table 7 shows our results on the *average runtime* for the summarization process. The table shows the number of tweets per file (*total*) as well as the *file size* in Mebibyte. *Clustering* correspond to the number of clustered tweets.

Noteworthy are the results for *thematically pre-filtered* tweets (grey lines). The corresponding messages were selected by a filter according to certain keywords, e.g., *covid-19* or *black lives matter*. Having about more than 0.2 ms difference per tweet, they are clearly higher than the values of their unfiltered counterparts. In addition, these files have also the highest percentage (over 95%) of tweets passing the data preprocessing step and therefore must be clustered afterwards. The average value for other files is less than 87%, cp. Table 8.

This is justified by longer text messages. Table 8 also shows the percentage of tweets participating in the clustering step, the percentage of retweets, and the

Table 7. Runtime performance with standard parameters.

File size		Tweets number		Average runtime		
File	MiB	Total	Clustering	s	min	ms/tweet
f1	158	27 268	27 041	5.89160	0.09819	0.21606
f2	410	74 033	63 113	11.52620	0.19210	0.15569
f3	926	165 822	143 175	25.42840	0.42381	0.15335
f4	1 061	166 382	160 776	28.62940	0.47716	0.17207
f5	919	172 507	170 575	36.98610	0.61644	0.21440
f6	981	173 358	147 577	26.47640	0.44127	0.15273
f7	986	179 608	177 294	37.28290	0.62138	0.20758
f8	1 127	182 426	174 611	32.24990	0.53750	0.17678
f9	1 554	277 741	241 272	41.54850	0.69248	0.14959
f10	2 348	408 521	352 172	61.15850	1.01931	0.14971
f11	4 348	799 004	682 682	109.06230	1.81771	0.13650
f12	5 422	962 521	821 616	135.03500	2.25058	0.14029
f13	6 634	1 160 599	1 000 558	169.80960	2.83016	0.14631
f14	18 567	3 281 852	2 788 772	461.83120	7.69719	0.14072
f15	21 338	3 721 695	3 174 048	538.39320	8.97322	0.14466
f16	24 691	4 253 183	3 628 391	609.02560	10.15043	0.14319

Table 8. Analysis of the underlying tweets.

File size		Number of	Duration	Tweet percentages			Text length
File	MiB	tweets	ms/tweet	Clustering	Retweets	Extended	Char/tweet
f1	158	27 268	0.21606	99.17%	68.56%	58.71%	188.50
f2	410	74 033	0.15569	85.25%	58.31%	32.91%	120.23
f3	926	165 822	0.15335	86.34%	60.59%	33.22%	121.93
f4	1 061	166 382	0.17207	96.63%	85.18%	58.40%	175.79
f5	919	172 507	0.21440	98.88%	68.93%	66.31%	187.45
f6	981	173 358	0.15273	85.13%	60.03%	32.54%	120.86
f7	986	179 608	0.20758	98.71%	68.51%	62.69%	182.37
f8	1 127	182 426	0.17678	95.72%	79.43%	47.76%	156.62
f9	1 554	277 741	0.14959	86.87%	59.09%	34.18%	123.39
f10	2 348	408 521	0.14971	86.21%	62.09%	32.58%	123.12
f11	4 348	799 004	0.13650	85.44%	57.09%	30.69%	116.55
f12	5 422	962 521	0.14029	85.36%	59.50%	30.63%	118.53
f13	6 634	1 160 599	0.14631	86.21%	60.10%	32.86%	122.25
f14	18 567	3 281 852	0.14072	84.98%	60.65%	28.71%	114.86
f15	21 338	3 721 695	0.14466	85.29%	60.00%	30.05%	116.96
f16	24 691	4 253 183	0.14319	85.31%	61.20%	29.98%	117.42
Average of the unfiltered files:				85.67%	59.88%	31.67%	119.65
Average of the filtered files:				97.82%	74.12%	58.77%	178.15

percentage of extended messages, i.e., posts having more than 140 characters. The last column (*text length*) shows the average tweet length per file. In conclusion, thematically pre-filtered phrases (grey lines) have above-average values in all criteria above and therefore lead to a higher runtime.

7.2   Aggregation and Summarization

In this section we describe the results of an assessment of tweets' aggregation. These results were obtained with a user study to identify the *quality of the summarization*. Since only a small number of people (10) took part in the survey, the results serve more as an orientation, rather than a representative study.

The study was split into two parts: In the *first part*, all users were asked to read all produced tweet clusters (five clusters between 45 and 80 tweets per topic) and write a short summary for each by hand. The clusters were selected to simulate the query result, but at the same time not to overwhelm the participants. The first cluster deals with the COVID-19 disease of the British Prime Minister *Boris Johnson* (45 tweets). The second cluster of 80 tweets deals with the death and the memory of the Swedish actor *Max von Sydow*, who died in March 2020. The 70 text messages of the third cluster, entitled *First day of summer*, is about the beginning of summer. The fourth cluster, *Warren drops out*, is about the departure of Senator Elizabeth Warren from the Democratic primaries for the US presidential election 2020 (75 tweets). The last cluster of the survey is entitled *Separating children* and contains 65 tweets dealing with the separation of children and their parents who are illegally in the US.

In the *second part*, our automatically generated summarization was presented to the users. With the help of five questions each, these were to be evaluated in terms of their comprehensibility and content.

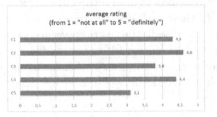

(a) "Do the individual aggregations contain the most important information of their clusters?"

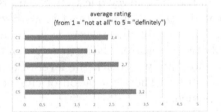

(b) "Is there any content missing in the individual aggregations that should necessarily be present?"

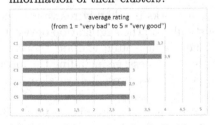

(c) "How do you rate the individual aggregations' comprehensibility?"

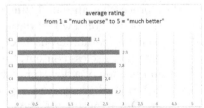

(d) "How do you rate the individual aggregations compared to your own?"

Fig. 5. Survey results on the quality of aggregation.

Figure 5 shows our results: All users agreed that our approach contains the *most important information* in the final aggregated message, cp. Fig. 5a. The lowest value in average was 3.1 for the 5th cluster (*Separating children*). However, the score received for this cluster also shows that the most important content was (at least partially) retrieved and the aggregation is acceptable.

We also asked for *missing content* (in comparison to the handwritten summary). Figure 5b shows that no mandatory information is missing (in particular cluster C2 and C4 with an average score of 1.7 and 1.8, resp.). The users were less positive about the automatic summaries of cluster $C1$ and $C3$. This is interesting for the aggregation of the first cluster (*Corona Boris Johnson*), as in the previous question the participants answered that this cluster contains the most important information. The opinion on the fifth cluster is again in line with the evaluation regarding the question about the most important contents. For this cluster the participants were most likely to identify shortcomings beforehand, so the tendency at this point is that more information has to be included. Overall, the question of missing essential content was answered negative in four out of five cases.

Apart from the content aspects, automatic summaries are required to be easy to read and understand by people. Figure 5c shows the result on *comprehensibility*: Four aggregations were rated with an average value of 3.0 or higher, which can be interpreted as rather good. Only one aggregation is below 3 and therefore has a moderate assessment w.r.t. comprehensibility. This can be explained by the fact that many words are reduced to their basic form.

In the final survey question, the users were asked to assess the automatically created aggregations in *direct comparison to* their *self-written counterparts*, cp. Fig. 5d. Most of the answers were rated round about the average value of 2.5. Only two are worse. The aggregation of the second cluster (*Max von Sydow*) was the most likely to reach the level of a hand-written summary with an average score of 2.9. The aggregation of cluster $C1$ received the worst average general assessment.

8   Summary and Conclusion

Stream data processing and analyzing social networks is a highly relevant topic nowadays. We focused on Twitter data, in particular on the aggregation of tweets in order to summarize numerous text messages, which often contain retweets, duplicates and other useless content, to a single short message including the most important information of a Twitter channel. For this, we presented an algorithm based on clustering N-grams and aggregating them using an extension of the PR algorithm. Our experiments show that our method is a promising approach to reach the claimed goal in reasonable time, e.g., for real time data analytics. However, an open issue is the readability of the final message, which should be improved in future work.

References

1. Ayers, J.W., et al.: Why do people use electronic nicotine delivery systems (electronic cigarettes)? A content analysis of Twitter, 2012–2015. PLoS ONE **12**(3), 1–8 (2017)
2. Cavazos-Rehg, P., et al.: A content analysis of depression-related tweets. Comput. Hum. Behav. **54**, 351–357 (2016)
3. Manning, C.D., Raghavan, P., Schütze, H.: Introduction to Information Retrieval. Cambridge University Press, Cambridge, April 2009. Online edition
4. O'Connor, B., Krieger, M., Ahn, D.: TweetMotif: exploratory search and topic summarization for Twitter. In: Proceedings of the International AAAI Conference on Weblogs and Social Media, Washington, DC, USA (2010)
5. Okazaki, M., Matsuo, Y.: Semantic Twitter: analyzing tweets for real-time event notification. In: Breslin, J.G., Burg, T.N., Kim, H.-G., Raftery, T., Schmidt, J.-H. (eds.) BlogTalk 2008-2009. LNCS, vol. 6045, pp. 63–74. Springer, Heidelberg (2010). https://doi.org/10.1007/978-3-642-16581-8_7
6. Parikh, R., Karlapalem, K.: ET: events from tweets. In: WWW (Companion Volume), pp. 613–620. ACM (2013)
7. Railean, C., Moraru, A.: Discovering popular events from tweets. In: Conference on Data Mining and Data Warehouses (SiKDD), October 2013
8. Rudenko, L., Haas, C., Endres, M.: Analyzing Twitter data with preferences. In: Darmont, J., Novikov, B., Wrembel, R. (eds.) ADBIS 2020. CCIS, vol. 1259, pp. 177–188. Springer, Cham (2020). https://doi.org/10.1007/978-3-030-54623-6_16
9. Sankaranarayanan, J., Samet, H., Teitler, B.E., Lieberman, M.D., Sperling, J.: TwitterStand: news in tweets. In: ACM 2009, pp. 42–51 (2009)
10. Sharifi, B.P., Inouye, D.I., Kalita, J.K.: Summarization of Twitter microblogs. Comput. J. **57**(3), 378–402 (2014)
11. Sutton, J., et al.: Lung cancer messages on Twitter: content analysis and evaluation. J. Am. Coll. Radiol. **15**, 210–217 (2017)
12. Takamura, H., Okumura, M.: Text summarization model based on the budgeted median problem. In: Proceedings of the 18th ACM Conference on Information and Knowledge Management (CIKM 2009), Hong Kong, China, pp. 1589–1592 (2009)

Indexes, Queries and Constraints

Inserting Keys into the Robust Content-and-Structure (RCAS) Index

Kevin Wellenzohn, Luka Popovic, Michael Böhlen, and Sven Helmer[(⊠)]

Department of Informatics, University of Zurich, Binzmühlestrasse 14,
8050 Zurich, Switzerland
{wellenzohn,boehlen,helmer}@ifi.uzh.ch, luka.popovic@uzh.ch

Abstract. Semi-structured data is prevalent and typically stored in formats like XML and JSON. The most common type of queries on such data are Content-and-Structure (CAS) queries, and a number of CAS indexes have been developed to speed up these queries. The state-of-the-art is the RCAS index, which properly interleaves content and structure, but does not support insertions of single keys. We propose several insertion techniques that explore the trade-off between insertion and query performance. Our exhaustive experimental evaluation shows that the techniques are efficient and preserve RCAS's good query performance.

Keywords: Indexing · Index updates · Semi-structured data

1 Introduction

A large part of real-world data does not follow the rigid structure of tables found in relational database management systems (RDBMSs). Instead, a substantial amount of data is semi-structured, e.g., annotated and marked-up data stored in formats such as XML and JSON. Since mark-up elements can be nested, this leads to a hierarchical structure. A typical example of semi-structured data are bills of materials (BOMs), which contain the specification of every component required to manufacture end products. Figure 1 shows an example of a hierarchical representation of three products, with their components organized under a node bom. Nodes in a BOM can have attributes, e.g., in Fig. 1 attribute @weight denotes the weight of a component in grams.

Semi-structured hierarchical data is usually queried via content-and-structure (CAS) queries [9] that combine a value predicate on the content of some attribute and a path predicate on the location of this attribute in the hierarchical structure. An example query for the BOM depicted in Fig. 1 that selects all car parts with a weight between 1000 and 3000 g has the form: Q (/bom/item/car//, [1000, 3000]), with "//" matching a node and all its descendants. To speed up this type of query, the Robust Content-and-Structure (RCAS) index has been proposed [17]. RCAS is based on a new interleaving scheme, called dynamic interleaving, that adapts to the distribution of the data and interleaves path and value dimension at their discriminative bytes.

© Springer Nature Switzerland AG 2021
L. Bellatreche et al. (Eds.): ADBIS 2021, LNCS 12843, pp. 121–135, 2021.
https://doi.org/10.1007/978-3-030-82472-3_10

Fig. 1. Example of a bill of materials (BOM).

So far, the RCAS index supports bulk-loading but it cannot be updated incrementally. We present efficient methods to insert new keys into RCAS without having to bulk-load the index again. We make the following contributions:

- We develop two different strategies for inserting keys into an RCAS index: strict and lazy restructuring.
- With the help of an auxiliary index, we mitigate the effects of having to restructure large parts of the index during an insertion. We propose techniques to merge the auxiliary index back into the main index if it grows too big.
- Extensive experiments demonstrate that combining lazy restructuring with the auxiliary index provides the most efficient solution.

2   Background

RCAS is an in-memory index that stores composite keys k consisting of two components: a path dimension P and a value dimension V that are accessed by $k.P$ and $k.V$, respectively. An example of a key (representing an entity from Fig. 1) is (/bom/item/car/bumper\$, *00 00 0A 8C*), where the blue part is the key's path and the red part is the key's value (in hexadecimal). Table 1 shows the keys of all entities from Fig. 1; the example key is k_7.

The RCAS index interleaves the two-dimensional keys at their discriminative path and value bytes. The discriminative byte $\mathsf{dsc}(K, D)$ of a set of keys K in a given dimension D is the position of the first byte for which the keys differ. That is, the discriminative byte is the first byte after the keys' longest common prefix in dimension D. For example, the discriminative path byte $\mathsf{dsc}(K^{1..7}, P)$ of the set of keys $K^{1..7}$ from Table 1 is the 13th byte. All paths up to the 13th byte share the prefix /bom/item/ca and for the 13th byte, key k_1 has value n, while keys $k_2, \ldots, k_7$ have value r. The dynamic interleaving is obtained by interleaving the keys alternatingly at their discriminative path and value bytes.

The dynamic interleaving adapts to the data: when interleaving at a discriminative byte, we divide keys into different partitions. If we instead use a byte that is part of the common prefix, all keys will end up in the same partition, which means that during a search we cannot filter keys efficiently. Our scheme guarantees that in each interleaving step we narrow down the set of keys to a smaller set of keys that have the same value for the discriminative byte. Eventually, the

Table 1. Set $K^{1..7} = \{k_1, \ldots, k_7\}$ of composite keys.

	Path Dimension P	Value Dimension V
k_1	/bom/item/canoe\$	69200 (00 01 0E 50)
k_2	/bom/item/carabiner\$	241 (00 00 00 F1)
k_3	/bom/item/car/battery\$	250714 (00 03 D3 5A)
k_4	/bom/item/car/battery\$	250800 (00 03 D3 B0)
k_5	/bom/item/car/belt\$	2890 (00 00 0B 4A)
k_6	/bom/item/car/brake\$	3266 (00 00 0C C2)
k_7	/bom/item/car/bumper\$	2700 (00 00 0A 8C)

set is narrowed down to a single key and its dynamic interleaving is complete. Switching between discriminative path and value bytes gives us a robust query performance since it allows us to evaluate the path and value predicates of CAS queries step by step in round-robin fashion.

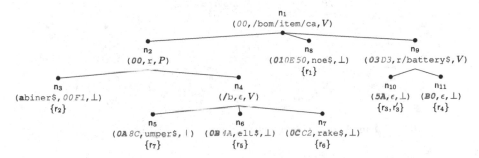

Fig. 2. The RCAS index for the keys in $K^{1..7}$.

We embed the dynamically interleaved keys $K^{1..7}$ from Table 1 into a trie data structure as shown in Fig. 2, building the final RCAS index. Each node n stores a path substring s_P (blue), a value substring s_V (red), and a dimension D. s_P and s_V contain the longest common prefixes in the respective dimensions of all the nodes in the subtree rooted at n. Dimension D determines the dimension that is used for partitioning the keys contained in the subtree rooted in n; D is either P or V for an inner node and $\perp$ for a leaf node. Leaf nodes store a set of references that point to nodes in the hierarchical document. In Fig. 2 node n_9 stores the longest common prefixes $s_P = $ r/battery\$ and $s_V = $ 03 D3. $n_9.D = V$, which means the children of n_9 are distinguished according to their value at the discriminative value byte (e.g., 5A for n_{10} and B0 for n_{11}). For more details on dynamic interleaving, building an RCAS index, and querying it efficiently, see [17]. Here we focus on inserting new keys into RCAS indexes.

3 Insertion of New Keys

We distinguish three insertion cases for which the effort varies greatly:

Case 1. The inserted key is a duplicate, i.e., there is already an entry in the index for the same key. Thus, we add a reference to the set of references in the appropriate leaf node. For instance, if we insert a new key k_3' that is identical to k_3, we only add the reference r_3' to the set of references of node n_{10} (see Fig. 2).

Case 2. The key to be inserted deviates from the keys in the index, but it does so at the very end of the trie structure. In this case, we add one new leaf node and a branch just above the leaf level. In Fig. 3 we illustrate RCAS after inserting key (/bom/item/car/bench\$, $00\ 00\ 19\ 64$) with reference r_9. We create a new leaf node n_{12} and add a new branch to its parent node n_4.

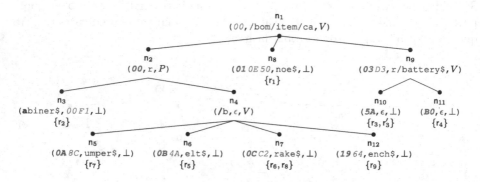

Fig. 3. Inserting a new key just above leaf level.

Case 3. This is the most complex case. If the path and/or the value of the new key results in a mismatch with the path and/or value of a node in the index, the index must be restructured. This is because position of a discriminative byte shifts, making it necessary to recompute the dynamic interleaving of a potentially substantial number of keys in the index. For example, if we want to insert key (/bom/item/cassette\$, $00\ 00\ AB\ 12$) with reference r_{10}, due to its value 00 at the discriminative value byte (the second byte), it has to be inserted into the subtree rooted at node n_2 (see Fig. 3). Note that the discriminative path byte has decreased by one position since the first s in cassette differs from r in the path substring $n_2.s_P$. This invalidates the current dynamic interleaving of the keys in the subtree rooted at n_2. Consequently, the whole subtree has to be restructured. As this is the most complicated case and there is no straightforward answer on how to handle it, we look at it in Sect. 4.

Insertion Algorithm. Algorithm 1 inserts a key into RCAS. The input parameters are the root node n of the trie, the key k to insert, and a reference r to the indexed element in the hierarchical document. The algorithm descends to the insertion point of k in the trie. Starting from the root node n, we compare the

---

Algorithm 1: Insert(n, k, r)

```
 1  while true do
 2  │   Compare n.s_P to relevant part of k.P
 3  │   Compare n.s_V to relevant part of k.V
 4  │   if k.P and k.V have completely matched n.s_P and n.s_V then        // Case 1
 5  │   │   Add reference r to node n
 6  │   └   return
 7  │   else if mismatch between k.P and n.s_P or k.V and n.s_V then       // Case 3
 8  │   │   // detailed description later
 9  │   │   Insert k into restructured subtree rooted at n
10  │   └   return
11  │   Let n_p = n
12  │   Let n be the child of n with the matching discriminative byte
13  │   if n = NIL then                                                     // Case 2
14  │   │   Let n = new leaf node
15  │   │   Initialize n.s_P and n.s_V with remainder of k.P and k.V
16  │   │   Set n.D to ⊥
17  │   │   Insert r into n
18  │   │   Insert n into list of children of n_p
19  └   └   return
```

---

current node's path and value substring with the relevant part in k's path and value (lines 2–3). As long as these strings coincide we proceed. Depending on the current node's dimension, we follow the edge that contains k's next path or value byte. The descent stops once we reach one of the three cases from above. In Case 1, we reached a leaf node and add r to the current node's set of references (lines 4–6). In Case 2, we could not find the next node to traverse, thus we create it (lines 13–19). The new leaf's substrings s_P and s_V are set to the still unmatched bytes in $k.P$ and $k.V$, respectively, and its dimension is set to ⊥. In Case 3 we discovered a mismatch between k and the current node's substrings (lines 7–10).

4 Index Restructuring During Insertion

4.1 Strict Restructuring

The shifting of discriminative bytes in Case 3 invalidates the current dynamic interleaving and if we want to preserve it we need to recompute it. An approach that achieves this collects all keys rooted in the node where the mismatch occurred (in the example shown above, the mismatch occurred in node n_2), adds the new key to it, and then applies the bulk-loading algorithm to this set of keys. This creates a new dynamic interleaving that is embedded in a trie and replaces the old subtree. We call this method *strict restructuring*. It guarantees a strictly alternating interleaving in the index, but the insertion operation is expensive if a large subtree is replaced. Figure 4 shows the RCAS index after inserting the key (/bom/item/cassette\$, *00 00 AB 12*).

Strict restructuring (Algorithm 2) takes four input parameters: the root node n of the subtree where the mismatch occurred, its parent node n_p (which is equal to NIL if n is the root), the new key k, and a reference r to the indexed element in the hierarchical document. See Sect. 6 for a complexity analysis.

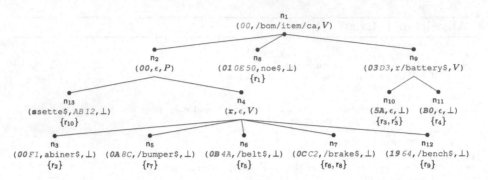

Fig. 4. Inserting a key with the strict restructuring method.

Algorithm 2: StrictRestructuring(n, n_p, k, r)

1 Let c = the set of all keys and their references rooted in n
2 Let $c = c \cup \{(k, r)\}$
3 Let $D = n.D$ // dimension used for starting interleaving
4 Let $n' = \text{bulkload}(c, D)$
5 **if** $n_p = \text{NIL}$ **then** replace original trie with n' // n is root node
6 **else** replace n with n' in n_p

4.2 Lazy Restructuring

Giving up the guarantee of a strictly alternating interleaving allows us to insert new keys more quickly. The basic idea is to add an intermediate node n'_p that is able to successfully distinguish its children: node n, where the mismatch happened and a new sibling n_k that represents the new key k. The new intermediate node n'_p will contain all path and value bytes that are common to node n and key k. Consequently, path and value substrings of n and n_k contain all bytes that are not moved to n'_p. Node n is no longer a child of its original parent n_p, this place is taken by n'_p. We call this method *lazy restructuring*. While it does not guarantee a strictly alternating interleaving, it is much faster than strict restructuring, as we can resolve a mismatch by inserting just two nodes: n'_p and n_k. Figure 5 shows RCAS after inserting the key (/bom/item/cassette\$, *00 00 AB 12*) lazily. Node n_{13} and its child n_2 partition the data both in the path dimension ($n.D = P$) and therefore violate the strictly alternating pattern.

Inserting a key with lazy interleaving introduces small irregularities that are limited to the dynamic interleaving of the keys in node n's subtree. These irregularities slowly *separate* (rather than *interleave*) paths and values if insertions repeatedly force the algorithm to split the same subtree in the same dimension. On the other hand, lazy restructuring can also repair itself when an insertion forces the algorithm to split in the opposite dimension. We show experimentally in Sect. 7 that lazy restructuring is fast and offers good query performance.

Algorithm 3 shows the pseudocode for lazy restructuring, it takes the same parameters as Algorithm 2. First, we create a new inner node n'_p and then determine which dimension to use for partitioning. If only a path mismatch

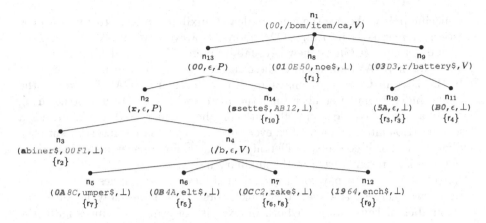

Fig. 5. Inserting a new key with lazy restructuring.

occurred between n and k, we have to use P. In case of a value mismatch, we have to use V. If we have mismatches in both dimensions, then we take the opposite dimension of parent node n_p to keep up an alternating interleaving as long as possible. The remainder of the algorithm initializes s_P and s_V with the longest common prefixes of n and k and creates two partitions: one containing the original content of node n and the other containing the new key k. The partition containing k is stored in a new leaf node n_k. We also have to adjust the prefixes in the nodes n and n_k. Finally, n and n_k are inserted as children of n_p', and n_p' replaces n in n_p. See Sect. 6 for a complexity analysis.

Algorithm 3: LazyRestructuring(n, n_p, k, r)

---
1 Let n_p' = new inner node
2 Let $n_p'.D$ = determineDimension()
3 Let $n_p'.s_P$ = longest common path prefix of n and k
4 Let $n_p'.s_V$ = longest common value prefix of n and k
5 Let n_k = new leaf node
6 Insert n and n_k as children of n_p'
7 Adjust s_P and s_V in n and n_k
8 Insert r into n_k
9 **if** n_p = NIL **then** replace original trie with n_p' // n is root node
10 **else** replace n with n_p' in n_p

---

5   Utilizing an Auxiliary Index

Using differential files to keep track of changes in a data collection is a well-established method (e.g., LSM-trees [12]). Instead of updating an index in-place, the updates are done out-of-place in auxiliary indexes and later merged according to a specific policy. We use the general idea of auxiliary indexes to speed up the insertion of new keys into an RCAS index. However, we apply this method slightly differently: we insert new keys falling under Case 1 and Case 2 directly into the main RCAS index, since these insertions can be executed efficiently. Only the keys in Case 3 are inserted into an auxiliary RCAS index. As the auxiliary index is much smaller than the main index, the strict restructuring method can be processed more efficiently on the auxiliary index. Sometimes a Case 3 insertion into the main index even turns into a Case 1/2 insertion into the auxiliary index, as it contains a different set of keys. For an even faster insertions we can use lazy restructuring in the auxiliary index.

There is a price to pay for using an auxiliary index: queries now have to traverse two indexes. However, this looks worse than it actually is, since the total number of keys stored in both indexes is the same. We investigate the trade-offs of using an auxiliary index and different insertion strategies in Sect. 7.

Using an auxiliary index only makes sense if the expensive insertion operations (Case 3) can be executed much more quickly on the auxiliary index. To achieve this, we have to merge the auxiliary index into the main index from time to time. This is more efficient than individually inserting new keys into the main index, though, as the restructuring of a subtree in the main index during the merge operation usually covers multiple new keys in one go rather than restructuring a subtree for every individual insertion. We consider two different merge strategies. The simplest, but also most time-consuming, method is to collect all keys from the main and auxiliary index and to bulk-load them into a new index.

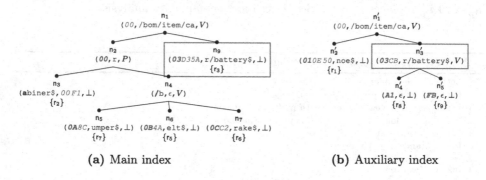

(a) Main index   (b) Auxiliary index

Fig. 6. A more sophisticated method merges only subtrees that differ.

A more sophisticated method traverses the main and auxiliary index in parallel and only if the path and/or value substrings of two corresponding nodes do not match, we restructure this subtree, bulk-load the keys into it, and insert it into the main index. Figure 6 illustrates this method. Since root nodes n_1 and n_1' match, the algorithm proceeds to its children. For child n_2' we cannot find a corresponding child in the main index, hence we relocate n_2' to the main index. For child n_3' we find child n_9 in the main index and since they differ in the value

---

Algorithm 4: Merge(n_m, n_a)

---

1 if $n_a \neq$ NIL then
2   if nodes n_m and n_a match then
3   foreach child c_a of n_a do
4   Find corresponding child c_m of n_m
5   if c_m does not exist then relocate c_a to n_m
6   else merge(c_m, c_a)
7   else
8   Let K = all keys in subtrees n_m and n_a
9   Let n'_m = bulkload(K)
10   Replace n_m with n'_m in main index

---

substring, the subtrees rooted in these two trees are merged. Notice that child n_2 in the main index is not affected by the merging. Algorithm 4 depicts the pseudocode. It is called with the root of the main index n_m and the root of the auxiliary index n_a. If n_m's and n_a's values of substrings s_P, s_V and dimension D match, we recursively merge the corresponding children of n_m and n_a. Otherwise, we collect all keys rooted in n_m and n_a and bulk-load a new subtree.

6   Analysis

We first look at the complexity of Case 1 and 2 insertions, which require no restructuring (see Sect. 3). Inserting keys that require no restructuring takes $O(h)$ time, where h is the height of RCAS, since Algorithm 1 descends the tree in $O(h)$ time and in Case 1 the algorithm adds a reference in $O(1)$ time, while in Case 2 the algorithm adds one leaf in $O(1)$ time. The complexity of Case 3, which requires restructuring, depends on whether we use lazy or strict restructuring.

Lemma 1. *Inserting a key into RCAS with lazy restructuring takes $O(h)$ time.*

Proof. The insertion algorithm descends the tree to the position where a path or value mismatch occurs in $O(h)$ time. To insert the key, lazy restructuring adds two new nodes in $O(1)$ time.

Lemma 2. *Inserting a key into RCAS with strict restructuring takes $O(l \cdot N)$ time, where l is the length of the longest key and N is the number of keys.*

Proof. Descending the tree to the insertion position takes $O(h)$ time. In the worst case, the insertion position is the root node, which means strict restructuring collects all keys in RCAS in $O(N)$ time, and bulk-loads a new index in $O(l \cdot N)$ time using the bulk-loading algorithm from [17].

The complexity of Case 3 insertions into the auxiliary index (if it is enabled) depends on the insertion technique and is $O(h)$ with lazy restructuring (Lemma 1) and $O(l \cdot N)$ with strict restructuring (Lemma 2). In practice, insertions into the auxiliary index are faster because it is smaller. This requires that the auxiliary index is merged back into the main index when it grows too big.

Lemma 3. *Merging an RCAS index with its auxiliary RCAS index using Algorithm 4 takes $O(l \cdot N)$ time.*

Proof. In the worst case, the root nodes of the RCAS index and its auxiliary RCAS index mismatch, which means all keys in both indexes are collected and a new RCAS index is bulk-loaded in $O(l \cdot N)$ time [17].

7 Experimental Evaluation

Setup. We use a virtual Ubuntu server with 8 GB of main memory and an AMD EPCY 7702 CPU with 1MB L2 cache. All algorithms are implemented in C++ and compiled with g++ (version 10.2.0). The reported runtime measurements represent the average time of 1000 experiment runs.

Dataset. We use the ServerFarm dataset from [17] that contains information about the files on a fleet of 100 Linux servers. The path and value of a composite key denote the full path of a file and its size in bytes, respectively. We eliminate duplicate keys because they trigger insertion Case 1, which does not change the structure of the index (see Sect. 3). Without duplicates, the ServerFarm dataset contains 9.3 million keys.

Reproducibility. The code, dataset, and instructions how to reproduce our experiments is available at: https://github.com/k13n/rcas_update.

7.1 Runtime of Strict and Lazy Restructuring

We begin by comparing the runtime of lazy restructuring (LR) and strict restructuring (SR) either applied on the main index directly, or applied on the combination of main and auxiliary index (Main+Aux). When the auxiliary index is used, insertion Cases 1 and 2 are performed on the main index, while Case 3 is performed on the auxiliary index with LR or SR. In this experiment we bulk-load 60% of the dataset (5 60 7400 keys) and insert the remaining 40% (3 738 268 keys) one-by-one. Bulk-loading RCAS with 5.6M keys takes 12 s, which means 2.15 µs per key. Figure 7a shows the average runtime ($\bar{x}$) and the standard deviation (σ) for the different insertion techniques. We first look at LR and SR

Approach	$\bar{x}$	σ
⊞ Bulk-load	2.15	N/A
▨ Main (LR)	3.18	4.11
▨ Main (SR)	4.75	41.71
▨ Main+Aux (LR)	4.65	3.47
▨ Main+Aux (SR)	5.98	34.98

(a) Average runtime $\bar{x}$ [µs]
Standard deviation σ [µs]

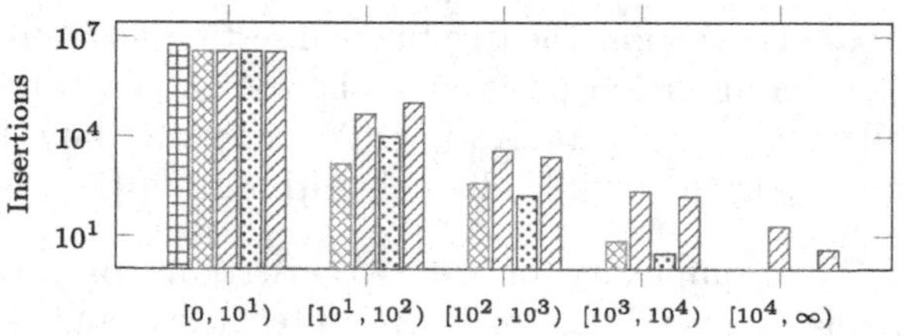

(b) Runtime distribution [µs]

Fig. 7. Runtime of insertions.

when they are applied to the main index only. LR is very fast with an average runtime of merely 3 μs per key. This is expected since LR only needs to insert two new nodes into the index. SR on the other hand, takes on average about 5 μs and is thus not significantly slower than LR, on average. The runtime of SR depends greatly on the level in the index where the mismatch occurs. The closer to the root the mismatch occurs, the bigger is the subtree this technique needs to rebuild. Therefore, we expect that even if the average runtime is low, the variance is higher. Indeed, the standard deviation of SR is 41 μs compared to 4 μs for LR. This is confirmed by the histogram in Fig. 7b, where we report the number of insertions that fall into a given runtime range (as a reference point, we report for bulk-loading that all 5.6M keys have a runtime of 2.15 μs per key). While most insertions are quick for all methods, SR has a longer tail and a significantly higher number of slow insertions (note the logarithmic axes). Applying LR and SR to the auxiliary index slightly increases the average runtime since two indexes must be traversed to find the insertion position, but the standard deviation decreases since there are fewer expensive updates to the auxiliary index, see Fig. 7b.

7.2 Query Runtime

We look at the query performance after updating RCAS with our proposed insertion techniques. We simulate that RCAS is created for a large semi-structured dataset that grows over time. For example, the Software Heritage archive [1,4], which preserves publicly-available source code, grows ca. 35% to 40% a year [15]. Therefore, we bulk-load RCAS with the at least 60% of our dataset and insert the remaining keys one by one to simulate a year worth of insertions. We expect SR to lead to better query performance than LR since it preserves the dynamic interleaving, while LR can introduce small irregularities. Further, we expect that enabling the auxiliary index does not significantly change the query runtime since the main and auxiliary indexes, when put together, are of similar size as the (main) RCAS index when no auxiliary index is used.

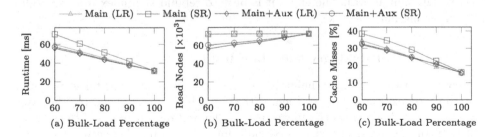

Fig. 8. Query performance.

In Fig. 8a we report the average runtime for the six CAS queries from [17]. For example, the first query looks for all files nested arbitrarily deeply in the /usr/include directory that are at least 5 KB large, expressed as (/usr/include//, [5000, ∞]). The results are surprising. First, SR in the main index leads to the worst query runtime and the remaining three approaches lead to faster query runtimes. To see why, let us first look at Fig. 8b that shows the number of nodes traversed during query processing (if the auxiliary index is enabled, we sum the number of nodes traversed in both indexes). The queries perform better when the auxiliary index is enabled because fewer nodes are traversed during query processing, which means subtrees were pruned earlier.

Figure 8b does not explain why LR leads to a better query performance than SR since with both approaches the queries need to traverse almost the same number of nodes. To find the reason for the better query runtime we turn to Fig. 8c, which shows that query runtime and the CPU cache misses[1] are highly correlated. SR leads to the highest number of cache misses due to memory fragmentation. When the index is bulk-loaded its nodes are allocated in contiguous regions of the main memory. The bulk-loading algorithm builds the tree depth-first in pre-order and the queries follow the same depth-first approach (see [17]). As a result, nodes that are traversed frequently together have a high locality of reference and thus range queries typically access memory sequentially, which is faster than accessing memory randomly [14]. Inserting additional keys fragments the memory. Strict restructuring (SR) deletes and rebuilds entire subtrees, which can leave big empty gaps between contiguous regions of memory and as a result experiences more cache misses in the CPU during query processing. LR causes fewer cache misses in the CPU than SR because it fragments the memory less. This is because LR always inserts two new nodes whereas SR inserts and deletes large subtrees, which can leave big gaps in memory.

The query runtime improves for all approaches as we bulk-load a larger fraction of the dataset because the number of cache misses decreases. Consider the strict restructuring method in the main index (green curve). By definition, SR structures the index exactly as if the index was entirely bulk-loaded. This can also be seen in Fig. 8b where the number of nodes traversed to answer the queries is constant. Yet, the query runtime improves as we bulk-load more of the index because the number of cache misses is reduced due to less memory fragmentation (see explanation above). Therefore, it is best to rebuild the index from scratch after inserting many new keys.

7.3 Merging of Auxiliary and Main Index

We compare two merging techniques: (a) the slow approach that takes all keys from both indexes and replaces them with a bulk-loaded index, and (b) the fast approach that descends both indexes in parallel and only merges subtrees that differ. In the following experiment we bulk-load the main index with a fraction of the dataset, insert the remaining keys into the auxiliary index, and merge

---

[1] We measure the cache misses with the perf command on Linux, which relies on the Performance Monitoring Unit (PMU) in modern processors to record hardware events like cache accesses and misses in the CPU.

the two indexes with one of the two methods. Figure 9a shows that fast merging outperforms the slow technique by a factor of three. This is because the slow merging needs to fully rebuild a new index from scratch, while the fast merging only merges subtrees that have actually changed. In addition, if fast merging finds a subtree in the auxiliary index that does not exist it the main index, it can efficiently relocate that subtree to the main index.

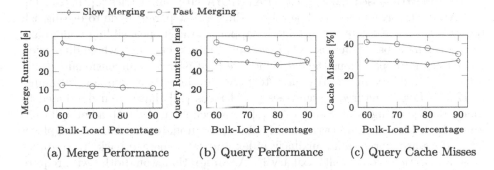

(a) Merge Performance   (b) Query Performance   (c) Query Cache Misses

Fig. 9. Merging and querying performance.

After merging the auxiliary index into the main index, we look at the query runtime of the main index in Fig. 9b. Slow merging leads to a better query performance than fast merging because slow merging produces a compact representation of the index in memory (see discussion above), while fast merging fragments the memory and leads to cache misses in the CPU (Fig. 9c).

7.4 Summary

Our experiments show that RCAS can be updated efficiently, but to guarantee optimal query performance it is recommended to rebuild the index occasionally. The best way to insert keys into the RCAS index is to use an auxiliary index with lazy restructuring (LR). LR is faster and leads to better query performance than strict restructuring since it causes fewer cache misses in the CPU during query processing. When the auxiliary index becomes too large, it is best to merge it back into the main RCAS index with the slow merging technique, i.e., the main index is bulk-loaded from scratch including all the keys from the auxiliary index.

8 Related Work

Updating RCAS is difficult due to its dynamic interleaving scheme that adapts to the data distribution [17]. Inserting or deleting keys can invalidate the position of the discriminative bytes and change the dynamic interleaving of other keys.

Interleaving bits and bytes is a common technique to build multi-dimensional indexes, e.g., the z-order curve [13] interleaves the dimensions bit-wise. These schemes are *static* since they interleave at pre-defined positions (e.g., one byte from one dimension is interleaved with one byte from another dimension). Because the interleaving is static, individual keys can be inserted and deleted without affecting the interleaving of other keys. QUILTS [11] devises static interleavings that optimize for a given query workload. However, Nishimura et al. [11] do not discuss what happens if the query workload changes and with it the static interleaving scheme, which affects the interleavings of *all* keys.

Existing trie-based indexes, e.g., PATRICIA [10], burst tries [5], B-tries [3], and ART [7], solve insertion Case 3 by adding a new parent node to distinguish between the node where the mismatch happened and its new sibling node. Lazy restructuring is based on this technique, but we must decide in which dimension the parent node partitions the data since we deal with two-dimensional keys.

Using auxiliary index structures to buffer updates is a common technique [6,12,16]. Log-structured merge trees (LSM-trees [12]) have been developed to ingest data arriving at high speed, see [8] for a recent survey. Instead of updating an index in-place, i.e., overwriting old entries, the updates are done out-of-place, i.e., values are stored in an auxiliary index and later merged back. We redirect Case 3 insertions to a small auxiliary RCAS index that would otherwise require an expensive restructuring of the main RCAS index.

The buffer tree [2] amortizes the cost of updates by buffering *all* updates at inner nodes and propagating them one level down when the buffers overflow. Instead, we apply the inexpensive Case 1 and 2 insertions immediately on the main RCAS index and redirect Case 3 insertions to the auxiliary RCAS index.

9   Conclusion and Outlook

We looked at the problem of supporting insertions in the RCAS index [17], an in-memory, trie-based index for semi-structured data. We showed that not every insertion requires restructuring the index, but for the cases where the index must be restructured we proposed two insertion techniques. The first method, called strict restructuring, preserves RCAS's alternating interleaving of the data's content and structure, while the second method, lazy restructuring, optimizes for insertion speed. In addition, we explore the idea of using an auxiliary index (similar to LSM-trees [8]) for those insertion cases that would require restructuring the original index. Redirecting the tough insertion cases to the auxiliary index leaves the structure of the main index intact. We proposed techniques to merge the auxiliary index back into the main index when the auxiliary index grows too big. Our experiments show that these techniques can efficiently insert new keys into RCAS and preserve its good query performance.

For future work we plan to support deletion. Three deletion cases can occur that mirror the three insertion cases. Like for insertion, the first two cases are simple and can be solved by deleting a reference from a leaf or the leaf itself if it contains no more references. The third case occurs when the dynamic interleaving is invalidated because the positions of the discriminative bytes shift. Deletion algorithms exist that mirror our proposed insertion techniques for the third case.

References

1. Abramatic, J., Cosmo, R.D., Zacchiroli, S.: Building the universal archive of source code. Commun. ACM **61**(10), 29–31 (2018). https://doi.org/10.1145/3183558
2. Arge, L.: The buffer tree: a technique for designing batched external data structures. Algorithmica **37**(1), 1–24 (2003). https://doi.org/10.1007/s00453-003-1021-x
3. Askitis, N., Zobel, J.: B-tries for disk-based string management. VLDB J. **18**(1), 157–179 (2009). https://doi.org/10.1007/s00778-008-0094-1
4. Di Cosmo, R., Zacchiroli, S.: Software heritage: why and how to preserve software source code. In: iPRES (2017)
5. Heinz, S., Zobel, J., Williams, H.E.: Burst tries: a fast, efficient data structure for string keys. ACM Trans. Inf. Syst. **20**(2), 192–223 (2002). https://doi.org/10.1145/506309.506312
6. Jagadish, H.V., Narayan, P.P.S., Seshadri, S., Sudarshan, S., Kanneganti, R.: Incremental organization for data recording and warehousing. In: VLDB, pp. 16–25 (1997)
7. Leis, V., Kemper, A., Neumann, T.: The adaptive radix tree: artful indexing for main-memory databases. In: ICDE, pp. 38–49 (2013). https://doi.org/10.1109/ICDE.2013.6544812
8. Luo, C., Carey, M.J.: LSM-based storage techniques: a survey. VLDB J. **29**(1), 393–418 (2019). https://doi.org/10.1007/s00778-019-00555-y
9. Mathis, C., Härder, T., Schmidt, K., Bächle, S.: XML indexing and storage: fulfilling the wish list. Comput. Sci. Res. Dev. **30**(1), 51–68 (2012). https://doi.org/10.1007/s00450-012-0204-6
10. Morrison, D.R.: PATRICIA - practical algorithm to retrieve information coded in alphanumeric. J. ACM **15**(4), 514–534 (1968). https://doi.org/10.1145/321479.321481
11. Nishimura, S., Yokota, H.: QUILTS: multidimensional data partitioning framework based on query-aware and skew-tolerant space-filling curves. In: SIGMOD, pp. 1525–1537 (2017). https://doi.org/10.1145/3035918.3035934
12. O'Neil, P.E., Cheng, E., Gawlick, D., O'Neil, E.J.: The log-structured merge-tree (LSM-tree). Acta Informatica **33**(4), 351–385 (1996). https://doi.org/10.1007/s002360050048
13. Orenstein, J.A., Merrett, T.H.: A class of data structures for associative searching. In: PODS 1984, New York, NY, USA, pp. 181–190 (1984). https://doi.org/10.1145/588011.588037
14. Piatov, D., Helmer, S., Dignös, A.: An interval join optimized for modern hardware. In: ICDE, pp. 1098–1109 (2016). https://doi.org/10.1109/ICDE.2016.7498316
15. Rousseau, G., Di Cosmo, R., Zacchiroli, S.: Software provenance tracking at the scale of public source code. Empirical Softw. Eng. **25**(4), 2930–2959 (2020). https://doi.org/10.1007/s10664-020-09828-5
16. Severance, D.G., Lohman, G.M.: Differential files: their application to the maintenance of large databases. ACM Trans. Database Syst. **1**(3), 256–267 (1976). https://doi.org/10.1145/320473.320484
17. Wellenzohn, K., Böhlen, M.H., Helmer, S.: Dynamic interleaving of content and structure for robust indexing of semi-structured hierarchical data. In: PVLDB, vol. 13, no. 10, pp. 1641–1653 (2020). https://doi.org/10.14778/3401960.3401963

Optimizing Execution Plans
in a Multistore

Chiara Forresi⊙, Matteo Francia⊙, Enrico Gallinucci(✉)⊙,
and Matteo Golfarelli⊙

University of Bologna, Cesena, Italy
{chiara.forresi,m.francia,enrico.gallinucci,matteo.golfarelli}@unibo.it

Abstract. Multistores are data management systems that enable query
processing across different database management systems (DBMSs);
besides the distribution of data, complexity factors like schema heterogeneity and data replication must be resolved through integration and data
fusion activities. In a recent work [2], we have proposed a multistore solution that relies on a dataspace to provide the user with an integrated view
of the available data and enables the formulation and execution of GPSJ
(generalized projection, selection and join) queries. In this paper, we propose a technique to optimize the execution of GPSJ queries by finding the
most efficient execution plan on the multistore. In particular, we devise
three different strategies to carry out joins and data fusion, and we build a
cost model to enable the evaluation of different execution plans. Through
the experimental evaluation, we are able to profile the suitability of each
strategy to different multistore configurations, thus validating our multi-
strategy approach and motivating further research on this topic.

Keywords: Multistore · NoSQL · Join optimization · Cost model

1 Introduction

The decline of the *one-size-fits-all* paradigm has pushed researchers and prac-
titioners towards the idea of *polyglot persistence* [19], where a multitude of
database management systems (DBMSs) are employed to support data storage
and querying. The motivations are manifold, including the exploitation of the
strongest features of each system, the off-loading of historical data to cheaper
database systems, and the adoption of different storage solutions by different
branches of the same company. This trend has also influenced the discipline of
data science, as analysts are being steered away from traditional data warehousing and towards a more flexible and lightweight approach to data analysis.
Multistore contexts are characterized by 1) the replication of data across different storage systems (i.e., there is no clean horizontal partitioning) with possibly
conflicting records (e.g., the same customer with a different country of residence
in different databases), and 2) a high level of schema heterogeneity: records of
the same real-world entity may be represented with different schema structures,
using different naming conventions for the same information and storing different

L. Bellatreche et al. (Eds.): ADBIS 2021, LNCS 12843, pp. 136–151, 2021.
https://doi.org/10.1007/978-3-030-82472-3_11

information in different databases. The large volume and the frequent evolution of these data hinder the adoption of a traditional integration approach.

In a recent work [2] we have proposed a multistore solution that relies on a dataspace to provide the user with an integrated view of the data. A *dataspace* is a lightweight integration approach providing basic query expressiveness on a variety of data sources, bypassing the complexity of traditional integration approaches and possibly returning best-effort or approximate answers [9]. The dataspace is built in accordance with a *pay-as-you-go* philosophy, i.e., by applying simple matching rules to recognize relationships between data structures and by letting the users progressively refine the dataspace as new relationships are discovered [13]. Users exploit the dataspace to formulate GPSJ (generalized projection, selection and join [12]) queries, i.e., the most common class of queries in OLAP applications. Queries are translated into execution plans that consist of many local computations (to be demanded to the single DBMSs) and a global computation (carried out by the middleware layer).

In this paper, we propose a technique to optimize the execution of GPSJ queries by finding the most efficient execution plan on the multistore. The main challenge lies in devising a cross-DBMS execution plan that couples data fusion operations (to reconcile replicated data) with the resolution of schema heterogeneity and efficiently provides a correct result. In particular, the paper provides the following contributions: (1) the extension of the multistore scenario presented in [2] to consider replicated data across different databases; (2) the introduction of three join strategies that define alternative query execution plans by relying on different schema representations; (3) the presentation of a multi-DBMS cost model to compare the complexity of execution plans in terms of disk I/O and choose the most efficient one; (4) the evaluation of the proposed join strategies on a representative example of two real-world entities (i.e., customers and orders) modeled with different schemas in different databases and linked by a many-to-one relationship.[1]

The paper is structured as follows. In Sect. 2 we introduce the background knowledge on our multistore; in Sect. 3 we introduce the join strategies and in Sect. 4 we present the cost model; the evaluation of the join strategies based on the cost model is given in Sect. 5. Section 6 discusses related work, and Sect. 7 draws the conclusions.

2   Multistore Preliminaries

In this section we provide the preliminary concepts to understand the multistore scenario; we refer the reader to [2] for further details. Figure 1 shows a functional overview of our prototypical implementation. The user interacts with the multistore by submitting GPSJ queries to the Query planner through a custom API service; the planner translates these queries into execution plans, which are

---

[1] Remarkably, many-to-one relationships are at the base of the multidimensional model and GPSJ queries [12], as well as our dataspace-based approach [2].

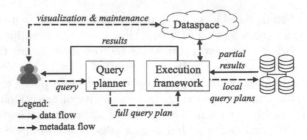

Fig. 1. Overview of our multistore.

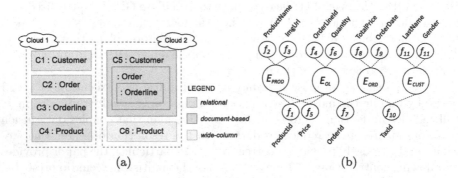

(a)   (b)

Fig. 2. Overview of our case study and the related dataspace.

formulated onto the Execution framework (i.e., Apache Spark in our implementation). Execution plans are composed of one or more local plans (to be submitted to the underlying DBMSs) and a global plan, that is run in the execution framework; the results are finally returned to the user. The case study is shown in Fig. 2a: it is a Unibench-based [22] multi-cloud scenario, where two branches of the same company store overlapping records of the same entities (i.e., customers, orders, orderlines, and products) on different DBMSs. The first branch relies on an RDBMS, the other on a document store and a wide-column store.

2.1 Basic Concepts

NoSQL DBMSs embrace a *soft-schema* approach that allows collections to contain records with different schemas. In [2] we describe how the multistore is able to manage schema heterogeneity; given that intra-collection schema heterogeneity does not affect execution plan optimization, we assume schema homogeneity among the records of the same collection. Here, we introduce a schema definition that provides a view of the records in first normal form by hiding the denormalization due to the nesting of records and exposing the relationships between schemas at different nesting levels.

Definition 1 (Schema). *A schema $S = \{a_1, \ldots, a_{|S|}\}$ is a set of attributes that applies to one or more records in a collection C. The attribute that uniquely*

Fig. 3. A sample JSON document corresponding to two records.

identifies the records with schema S is the key, *defined as* $key(S)$. *We use S^μ to denote the list of array attributes in C that must be unnested to unveil the records of S (if any).*

For the sake of simplicity, we assume all keys to be simple. Given a record r, its schema (denoted with S_r) is the set of attributes directly available in r (i.e., those in the top level). If r is contained within the array attribute a of record r', then (i) S_r also includes $key(S_{r'})$ (this is necessary to maintain the relationship between the schema of a nested record and the one of the parent record), and (ii) S_r^μ is built by extending $S_{r'}^\mu$ with a as the last attribute to be unnested.

Example 1. The JSON document in Fig. 3 is composed of two records, *cust* (in blue) and *ord* (in green; this is nested in *cust*), with the following schemas (keys are underlined): $S_{cust} = \{\underline{\text{cid}}, \text{firstName}, \text{address.street}, \text{orders} \}$, with $S_{cust}^\mu = []$; $S_{ord} = \{\text{cid}, \underline{\text{orders.oid}}, \text{orders.date}, \text{orders.price} \}$, with $S_{ord}^\mu = [\text{orders}]$.

2.2 Dataspace Modeling

The dataspace is defined by a set of abstract concepts named *features* and *entities*: the former provides a unique representation of semantically equivalent attributes, while the latter provides a representation of real-world entities. The composition of features and entities fundamentally relies on the recognition of relationships between attributes and schemas, which is done through mappings.

Definition 2 (Mapping). *A mapping m is a pair $m = (a_i, a_j)$ that expresses a semantic equivalence between two primitive attributes a_i and a_j. The existence of a mapping between a_i and a_j is indicated with $a_i \equiv a_j$.*

Mappings are specified between attributes of different schemas and they reveal the relationship between such schemas. Consider two schemas S_i and S_j. If $key(S_i) \equiv key(S_j)$, then we can infer a *one-to-one* relationship, represented as $S_i \leftrightarrow S_j$. If $a_k \equiv key(S_j) : a_k \in \{S_i \backslash key(S_i)\}$, then we can infer a *many-to-one* relationship from S_i to S_j, represented as $S_i \xrightarrow{a_k} S_j$. If $a_k \equiv a_l : a_k \in \{S_i \backslash key(S_i)\}, a_l \in \{S_j \backslash key(S_j)\}$, no direct relationship exists between the two schemas; *many-to-many* relationships are not considered.

Example 2. Consider the following two schemas, $S_1 = \{\underline{\text{cid}}, \text{firstName}\}$ modeling records of customers, and $S_2 = \{\underline{\text{oid}}, \text{orderDate}, \text{custId}, \text{custName}\}$ modeling records of orders. Two mappings can be defined on such schemas, i.e.,

$m_1 = (\underline{\text{cid}}, \text{custId})$, and $m_2 = (\text{firstName}, \text{custName})$. Since $key(S_1)$ is mapped to a non-key attribute of S_2, we can infer a many-to-one relationship between the two schemas. Mapping m_2 does not reveal any direct relationship, but it shows that S_2 is denormalized as it models customer information at the order level.

Mappings recognize that there is a semantic equivalence between two attributes in different schemas, thus we need to address all of them through a unique reference. This is the purpose of features.

Definition 3 (Feature). *A feature represents either a single attribute or a group of attributes mapped to each other. We define a feature as $f = (a, M, \mathbb{M})$, where a is the* representative *attribute of the feature; M is the set of mappings that link all the feature's attributes to the representative a; $\mathbb{M} : (v_i, v_j) \to v_k$ is an associative and commutative function that resolves the possible conflicts between the values of any two attributes (a_i, a_j) belonging to f and returns a single value v_k.*

Let $attr(f)$ be the set of attributes represented by f (i.e., the representative attribute plus those derived from the mappings). Given a record r, the conflict resolution function $\mathbb{M}$ can be applied to $r[a_i]$ and $r[a_j]$ if $\{a_i, a_j\} \subseteq attr(f)$; we refer the reader to [4] for an indication about different methods to define conflict resolution functions. Also, we remark that an attribute is always represented by one and only one feature; thus, for any two features f_i and f_j, it is $attr(f_i) \cap attr(f_j) = \varnothing$. We use $rep(f)$ to refer to the representative attribute of f, and $rep(a)$ as short for $rep(feat(a))$. As features are used to represent semantically equivalent attributes, we introduce the concept of *entity* to represent real-world entities (e.g. customers, orders).

Definition 4 (Entity). *An entity E is a representation of a real-world entity. It is identified by a feature that acts as a key in at least one schema; we refer to such feature as $key(E)$. Also, we use $feat(E)$ to refer to the set features whose attributes describe a property of E.*

For simplicity, we assume that all instances of the same entity are represented by same key feature. In particular, entities are obtained by detecting the features that act as a key in at least one schema. We can infer a many-to-one relationship from E_i to E_j based on a feature f if $key(E_j) = f$ and $f \in feat(E_i), f \neq key(E_i)$; we represent this as $E_i \xrightarrow{f} E_j$. Ultimately, the dataspace simply consists of the obtained entities and features. The dataspace corresponding to our case study is shown in Fig. 2b.

The dataspace is built semi-automatically in accordance with a pay-as-you-go philosophy: schemas are automatically extracted, while mappings are inferred by applying simple matching rules. Mappings are then used to recognize relationships between the schemas and to infer features and entities. At any time, the users may refine the dataspace as new relationships are discovered. Ultimately, the dataspace is exploited to formulate GPSJ queries, i.e., the most common class of queries in OLAP applications; a typical OLAP query consists of a group-by set (i.e., the features used to carry out an aggregation), one or more numerical features to be aggregated by some function (e.g., sum, average), and (possibly) some selection predicates. We refer the reader to [2] for details on the process to obtain the dataspace and to translate a query formulated on the dataspace into an execution plan.

2.3 Data Fusion Operations

Given the expressiveness of GPSJ queries, the execution plan of a query is formulated in the Nested Relational Algebra (NRA). Here, we slightly extend NRA to handle some operations required by our multistore scenario.

The most important addition to NRA is the extension of the join operator's semantics to handle data fusion. We do this by introducing an operator called *merge* ($\sqcup$) , i.e., an adaptation to our scenario of the *full outer join-merge* operator introduced in [18] to address the extensional and intensional overlap between schemas. In particular, the records belonging to the same entity (e.g., customers) can be partially overlapped, both in terms of instances (e.g., the same customer can be repeated across different schemas) and in terms of schemas (e.g., the name of the customer can be an attribute of two different schemas). We aim to keep as much information as possible when joining the records of two schemas, both from the extensional and the intensional points of view. The merge operator ($\sqcup$) answers this need by (i) avoiding any loss of records, (ii) resolving mappings by providing output in terms of features instead of attributes, and (iii) resolving conflicts whenever necessary. We define the merge operator as follows.

Definition 5 (Merge operation). *Let R_i and R_j be the recordsets of two schemas S_i and S_j, and consider $(a_k, a_l) \in (S_i, S_j)$ such that $a_k = a_l$, i.e., $\exists f : \{a_k, a_l\} \subseteq attr(f)$. The merge of the two recordsets $R_i \sqcup_f R_j$ produces a recordset R_{ij} with schema $S_{ij} = S_i^* \cup S_j^* \cup S_{ij}^\cap$ such that:*

- $S_i^* = \{a \in S_i : \nexists\, a' \in S_j \; s.t. \; a \equiv a'\}$
- $S_j^* = \{a' \in S_j : \nexists\, a \in S_i \; s.t. \; a \equiv a'\}$
- $S_{ij}^\cap = \{rep(a) : a \in S_i, \exists a' \in S_j \; s.t. \; a \equiv a'\}$

R_{ij} results in a full-outer join between R_i and R_j where the values of attributes linked by a mapping are merged through function $\mathcal{M}$. In particular, given a record $r \in R_{ij}$ obtained by joining $s \in R_i$ and $t \in R_j$ (i.e., $s[a_i] = t[a_j]$), it is $r[rep(a)] = \mathcal{M}(s[a], t[a']) \; \forall \; (a, a') \; s.t. \; a \in S_i, a' \in S_j, a \equiv a'$.

Example 3. Let $R_1 \sqcup_{f_{id}} R_2$, $s \in R_1$ and $t \in R_2$ two records with schema S_1 and S_2 respectively, $S_1 = \{a_1, a_3\}$, $S_2 = \{a_2, a_4\}$, $f_{id} = \{a_1, a_2\}$, $f_{name} = \{a_3, a_4\}$. Let $s[a_1] = t[a_2]$, $s[a_3] =$ "Smith" and $t[a_4] =$ "Smiht". The merge of s and t produces a record r where $r[a_3] = \mathcal{M}(s[a_3], t[a_4])$ and $\mathcal{M}$ is the a conflict resolution function that decides between "Smith" and "Smiht".

The merge operation is defined between recordsets, thus it is also applicable between the records of two arrays within the same collection. Consider a collection of customers with schema $S = \{\underline{cid}, o1, o2\}$, where o1 and o1 are arrays of

C^{Ne} (nested schema)

cid	firstName	address.street	orders		
C001	Alice	1, First St.	oid	date	Price
			O001	01/01/2020	10.00
			O002	01/02/2020	20.00
C002	Bob	2, Second Av.	oid	date	Price
			O003	02/01/2020	25.00

C^{NY} (normalized customer schema)

cid	firstName	address.street
C001	Alice	1, First St.
C002	Bob	2, Second Av.

C^{Fl} (flat schema)

cid	firstName	address.street	oid	date	price
C001	Alice	1, First St.	O001	01/01/2020	10.00
C001	Alyce	1, First St.	O002	01/02/2020	20.00
C002	Bob	2, Second Av.	O003	02/01/2020	25.00

C^{NX} (normalized order schema)

cid	oid	date	price
C001	O001	01/01/2020	10.00
C001	O002	01/02/2020	20.00
C002	O003	02/01/2020	25.00

Fig. 4. Three different schema representations of entities customer and orders.

orders. The merge operation is applicable between o1 and o2 to merge the records of orders. In the context of our multistore, this operation is always carried out in combination with the unnest of the merged array. Therefore, we introduce the *simultaneous unnest* operator $\overline{\mu}$ to carry out both operations, i.e., merging two (or more) array attributes and unnesting the result.

Definition 6 (Simultaneous unnest operation). *Let R_1 be a recordset with schema $S_1 = \{a_k, a_l, a_m\}$ where a_k is a primitive attribute, a_l and a_m are array attributes; also, let R_2 be the recordset in a_l with schema S_2, R_3 the recordset in a_m with schema S_3, $key(S_2) = key(S_3) = f$. The simultaneous unnest of a_l and a_m, declared as $\overline{\mu}_{[a_l,a_m]}(R_1)$, is translated to $\mu_{a_n}(R_1)$ where a_n is the result of $R_2 \sqcup_f R_3$.*

3   Query Plans and Optimization

In the multistore, the same real-world domain can be modeled in different ways in different DBMSs. The relational model favors normalized schemas (**NoS**), whereas non-relational models encourage different forms of denormalization, mainly nested schemas (**NeS**) and flat schemas (**FlS**). Figure 4 shows an example of these schema representations considering the relationship between customers and orders from our case study.

To define an efficient query plan we must consider that (1) a common schema representation must be chosen to join data, and (2) the query can either optimize data fusion activities or the push-down of operations to the local DBMSs, but not both of them. Indeed, data fusion is favored by normalizing all data (i.e., by choosing NoS as the common representation), whereas pushing operations down to the local DBMSs entails the transformation of data into NeS or FlS (as data in NeS/FlS represent the result of a nest/join operation between data in NoS). Therefore, the choice between the two optimizations is related to the choice of the common representation, each of which produces a different execution plan. The efficiency of the latter ultimately depends on the operations required by the query and on the original schema representation of the data. For this reason, the

Table 1. Schema alignment operations.

From schema	To schema	Operations
NoS (C^{NX}, C^{NY})	FlS (C^{Fl})	$(C^{NX}) \bowtie (C^{NY})$
	NeS (C^{Ne})	$v((C^{NX}) \bowtie (C^{NY}))$
NeS (C^{Ne})	FlS (C^{Fl})	$\mu(C^{Ne})$
	NoS (C^{NX})	$\pi(C^{Ne})$
	NoS (C^{NY})	$\mu(\pi(C^{Ne}))$
FlS (C^{Fl})	NoS (C^{NX})	$\gamma(\pi(C^{Fl}))$
	NoS (C^{NY})	$\pi(C^{Fl})$
	NeS (C^{Ne})	$v(C^{Fl})$

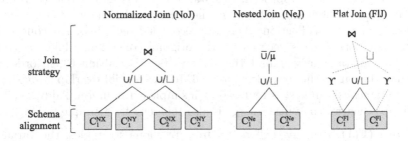

Fig. 5. Execution plan skeleton for each join strategy

query planner produces all three execution plans (one for each common schema representation that may be chosen) and later evaluates the most efficient one through the proposed cost model. Execution plans are composed of two steps.

1. A schema alignment step, where the data in each DBMS is transformed on-the-fly into the chosen reference schema representation.
2. A joining step to carry out the integration and merging of the data, including the data fusion and conflict resolution operations where necessary.

Table 1 shows the NRA operations required to compute a transformation from one schema representation to another (limited to two entities). These operations can be pushed down to the DBMSs if the latter support the former. Then, the strategy to join the aligned data depends on the common schema representation that is chosen. Figure 5 describes the skeleton of the execution plans for each strategy, considering two entities being stored on two DBMSs. Each plan may present some variations depending on the actual need for data fusion between the two entities. In particular, we outline three overlap scenarios: *full* (records of both E_Y and E_X may be replicated in different databases), *partial* (only records of E_Y may be replicated in different databases), or *absent*.

Variations in the execution plans are represented by (i) alternative operations: $\cup$ / $\sqcup$ is used to indicate that simple union $\cup$ is adopted when data fusion is not needed, merge $\sqcup$ otherwise (the same applies to $\overline{\cup}/\overline{\mu}$); (ii) additional operations: the dotted edges represent paths to optional operations that are carried out only when data fusion is needed. For each join strategy, we first discuss the execution plan in the full overlap scenario and then discuss the variations for the other scenarios.

Normalized Join (NoJ) Strategy. NoJ starts by separately merging the records belonging to the same entity (i.e., C_1^{NX} with C_2^{NX}, and C_1^{NY} with C_2^{NY}) and then joins the obtained results. This strategy follows the footsteps of a traditional integration approach, except that data fusion is carried out at query time. In partial (and no) overlap scenarios, the execution plan is modified by replacing the first merge operation on E_Y (and E_X) with a simple union.

Nested Join (NeJ) Strategy. The two nested collections can be joined directly by following a top-down approach. NeJ starts by merging the collections on the key of E_Y (thus applying data fusion to the upper level of the nested collection); this results in a new collection where the reconciled records of E_Y contain two arrays, each storing E_X's records for the original collections. The subsequent step is to simultaneously unnest these arrays (see Definition 6), in order and apply data fusion to the lower level as well. In the partial overlap scenario, the final simultaneously unnest is replaced by a simple array union. Additionally, in no overlap scenario, the initial merge is also replaced by a simple union.

Flat Join (FlJ) Strategy. Differently from previous strategies, the variations in presence or absence of data fusion need are more significant. In full overlap scenario, the execution plan requires to (i) separately aggregate both collections to extract a normalized view over E_Y; (ii) merge the obtained view to apply data fusion, (iii) join the reconciled records of E_Y with the reconciled records of E_X. The partial overlap scenario differs in the fact that records of E_X must not be reconciled, thus the first merge operation (i.e., the one between C_1^{Fl} and C_2^{Fl}) is replaced by a union. In no overlap scenario, all the optional operations in the execution plan (i.e., those necessary to reconcile E_Y's records) are not necessary, and it suffices to union C_1^{Fl} with C_2^{Fl}.

Remarkably, the efficiency of each strategy depends on the multistore configuration and the selected query. If the query involves data in a single schema representation, the respective join strategy is most likely to be the cheapest, as schema alignment is not necessary. Also, pushing operations (e.g., nest and join) down to the underlying DBMSs favors the usage of statistics and optimization the may not be available at the middleware level; however, by postponing the data fusion operations, the complexity of the execution plan increases (especially for FlJ, as seen above).

4   Cost Model

The identification of the most convenient join strategy to execute a query is demanded to a novel cost model that estimates the cost of our cross-DBMS GPSJ queries. In particular, it estimates the cost of every NRA operation (including the newly defined ones) by measuring the amount of data read and written to

Table 2. Cost model parameters and basic functions

Parameter/function	Description
$NR(C)$	Number of records in C
$NNR(C)$	If C is nested, number of nested records
$Len(C)$	Average byte length of a record in C
DPS	Size of a disk page
$PT(C)$	Number of partitions into which records in C are organized
NB	Number of memory buffers
$NP(C)$	Number of disk pages occupied by C: $\lceil \frac{NR(C) \cdot Len(C)}{DPS} \rceil$
$Part(C, nPart)$	Number of disk pages occupied by one of $nPart$ partitions of C

Table 3. Cost model for NRA operations and additional supporting operations

Operation	Description	Estimated cost	Sup.
$CA(C)$	Collection access	$NP(C)$	RMCS
$\pi(C)$	Projection	$NP(C)$	RMCS
$\gamma(C)$	Aggregation	$Sort(C) + NP(C)$	RM*S
$v(C)$	Nest	$Sort(C) + NP(C)$	RM-S
$\mu(C)$	Unnest	$NP(C)$	RM-S
$\overline{\mu}(C)$	Simult. unnest	$NR(C) \cdot SM(Part(C, \lceil \frac{NNR(C)}{NR(C)} \rceil))$	---S
$\overline{U}(C)$	Array union	$NP(C)$	RM-S
$(C_1) \bowtie (C_2)$	Join	$min(NLJ(C,C'), SMJ(C,C'), HJ(C,C'))$	RM-S
$(C_1) \sqcup (C_2)$	Merge	$min(NLJ(C,C'), SMJ(C,C'), HJ(C,C'))$	RM-S
$(C_1) \cup (C_2)$	Union	$NP(C) + NP(C')$	RM-S
$Shf(C)$	Data shuffle	$3 \cdot NP(C)$	-M-S
$SM(C)$	Sort-merge	$2 \cdot NP \cdot (\lceil log_{NB-1} NP \rceil + 1)$	RM-S
$Sort(C)$	Data sort (central.)	$SM(C)$	RM--
	Data sort (distrib.)	$Shf(R) + PT(C) \cdot SM(Part(C, PT(C)))$	---S
$HJ(C,C')$	Hybrid hash join	$3 \cdot (NP(C) + NP(C'))$	R---
$NLJ(C,C')$	Nested loops join	$NP(C) + NR(C) \cdot NP(C')$	R---
		$NP(C) + NR(C) \cdot NP(C') + Unnest(C'')$	-M--
$SMJ(C,C')$	Sort-merge join	$Sort(C) + Sort(C') + NP(C) + NP(C')$	R--S

disk (which is the slowest resource and is usually the bottleneck in typical GPSJ queries, even in a distributed framework like Apache Spark [20]). Building a custom cost model is necessary due to the variety of technologies in the multistore: although each execution engine adopts cost-based statistics to estimate query execution times, they are not directly comparable (e.g., MongoDB estimates execution times in milliseconds, while PostgreSQL uses arbitrary time units).

The cost model is focused on the technologies that we adopt in our implementation (see Sect. 2), i.e., RDBMSs in general, MongoDB, Apache Cassandra, and Apache Spark (which is used at the middleware level). To obtain the formulas we relied on existing literature on this subject (e.g., [7,17]) and on the tools' documentation. Table 2 shows the parameters required by the cost model, while Table 3 shows the core part, including the estimated cost for each NRA operation; the lower part of the latter introduces other supporting operations that are directly or indirectly used in the cost estimate for NRA operations. Table 3 also shows the support of each operation on the adopted technologies, i.e., RDBMSs (R), MongoDB (M), Apache Cassandra (C), and Apache Spark (S); symbol – indicates that the operation is not supported, while symbol * indicates that the operation is partially supported. Table 3 voluntarily omits for space reasons the formulas to estimate the number of records NR of the collection returned by each operation.

Given a query q submitted by the user, the query planner determines an execution plan for each join strategy defined in Sect. 3. Let P be the query plan for q, which can be decomposed into P_R, P_M, P_C (i.e., the portions of P to be executed on local DBMSs), and P_S (i.e., the portion to be executed on the middleware). The rationale of the decomposition is to push down to the local DBMSs as much computation as possible. Given the complexity of a multistore configuration comprising several technologies and concurrent computations in a distributed environment, we make a number of assumptions to simplify the calculation of $Cost(P)$. In particular, we assume that (i) global computations on the middleware begin after each local computation have been carried out, (ii) each DBMS runs in a non-distributed way on a separate machine, (iii) Apache Spark runs on a certain number of machines n_S,[2] and (iv) data is uniformly distributed across Spark's machines. Then, we calculate $Cost(P) = Cost(P_S)/n_S + \max_{i \in R,M,C} Cost(P_i)$.

5   Evaluation

The three join strategies are evaluated on a wide range of multistore configurations modeling the representative domain $E_X \to E_Y$ (where E_Y and E_X represent customers and orders, respectively) by running GPSJ queries that are devised in accordance with a reference model comprising two group-by features, one measure, and no selection predicates (e.g., the average price by product name and customer gender). The configurations vary on the following parameters.

- The number of records for each entity: either 10^2 or 10^5 for E_Y, either $NR_Y \cdot 10$ or $NR_Y \cdot 100$ for E_X.
- The ordering of records in each database: either ordered on $key(Y)$ (i.e., the customer key, which facilitates join and aggregation operations) or not.
- The overlap scenario (see Sect. 3): either absent, partial, or full; to estimate the cardinality we consider an overlap rate of 5% (i.e., 5% of customers on one collection overlap with the customers on the other).

The combination of these parameters determines 3072 physical configurations, which are hard to deploy and evaluate empirically. Thus, the join strategies are evaluated over all configurations by means of our cost model, while the accuracy of the latter is measured by deploying 6 representative configurations

---

[2] Although the level of parallelism in Spark is given in terms of CPU cores, we consider the number of machines because the cost model is focused on disk IO rather than on CPU computation.

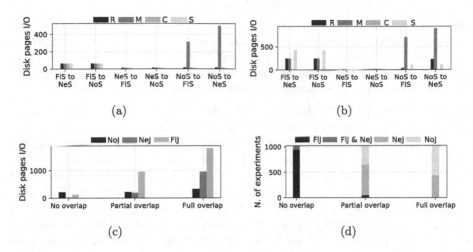

Fig. 6. Estimated cost of schema alignment on different execution engines with collections ordered (a) or not ordered (b) on the join attribute; estimated cost of join strategies (c); number of experiments won by each join strategy (d).

(i.e., all overlap scenarios, either with a low or high gap between the number of records of the two entities) consistently with the cost model assumptions (i.e., centralized DBMSs on separate machines, and Spark running on 4 machines). The results show that, in 83% of the experiments, the cost model identifies the strategy corresponding to the plan with the lowest execution time. With respect to having an oracle that always finds the best execution plan, the choices of our cost model cause an average overhead of 10%; conversely, always adopting a single join strategy returns an average overhead between 77% and 127%.

Single Step Evaluation. The first question we aim to answer is "Given a certain execution engine and a certain schema representation for the collections of E_Y and E_X, what is the cost of aligning both collections to a certain schema representation?". From the results (shown in Figs. 6a and 6b) we learn that NeS is generally the cheapest schema representation to move away from (as projections and unnest operation are the most simple ones) and the most expensive to align to (as nest requires an expensive aggregation operation); conversely, FlS is the most expensive to move away from, as it requires to carry out aggregations. We remark that MongoDB suffers in those transformations that require collections to be joined, due to its limited join capabilities; also, some costs are not estimated for Cassandra due to the lack of support to several operations.

The join strategies define operations that must be carried out in the middleware to consolidate the data obtained from the local DBMSs; therefore we evaluate the costs only with reference to Apache Spark. The results are shown in Fig. 6c. We observe that the cost for NoJ is quite stable over the different overlap scenarios, whereas the cost of NeJ and FlJ is more affected by the latter. As expected, FlJ is the one suffering the most the need to carry out data fusion. An interesting duality emerges by comparing these results with the above ones on schema alignment: NeS appears as the most expensive one to transform into and often the cheapest one to carry out the join, whereas FlS is exactly the opposite. These considerations confirm that the identification of the best execution plan will be significantly influenced by the characteristics of the dataset (in terms of the adopted schema representations, cardinality, and overlap scenarios).

Full Execution Plan Evaluation. Figure 6d shows, for each overlap scenario, the strategy that returns the minimum cost. The results indicate a clear distinction between the scenario with no overlap and the others. In the first case, FlJ emerges as a clear winner (except for a few cases where the estimated cost is the same for NeJ), indicating that DBMS locality can be fully exploited when there is no need to carry data fusion activities. In the other cases, NeJ and NoJ share an almost equal amount of wins, with NeJ slightly favoring the case of partial overlap (consistently with previous single-step results) and NoJ favoring the case where data fusion is needed for both entities (confirming the discussion made in Sect. 3). The main variable that pushes towards one of the two strategies in these configurations is the number of records in NeS and NoS: the higher the imbalance of data towards a certain schema representation, the lower the cost of the respective join strategy. Ultimately, these results validate the proposal of multiple join strategies (as neither of them is optimal under every circumstance) and motivate further research in this direction.

6   Related Work

The variety in terms of data models responds to different requirements of modern data-intensive applications, but providing transparent querying mechanisms to query large-scale collections on heterogeneous data stores is an active research area [21]. While many proposals answer the need for supporting multiple data models, there is a lack of solutions to address both schema heterogeneity and data fusion in polyglot systems. Remarkably, neglecting these issues may lead to incomplete and/or incorrect results.

A naive approach to solve the problem of querying several data models is to transform all datasets into a reference data model—usually the relational one [8]. This kind of solution leads to the loss of the schemaless flexibility and requires continuous maintenance to support schema evolution. A different approach is proposed by *multimodel* systems, which directly support several data models within the same platform (e.g., OrientDB, ArangoDB). Inter-data model querying is enabled by a custom query language to support nested structures and graph queries. An example is [3], which discusses a data warehousing approach relying on a multimodel system. Differently from our approach, these systems do not directly support the resolution of schema heterogeneity and data fusion— thus requiring manual activities (or additional tools) to clean either the original data or the query results.

In recent years, *multistores* and *polystores* have emerged to provide integrated access and querying to several heterogeneous stores through a mediator layer (middleware) [21]. The difference between multistores and polystores lies in whether they offer a single or multiple querying interfaces, respectively. Among the most notable are BIGDAWG [10], TATOOINE [6], and CloudMDsQL [14]. These systems vary in the functionalities they support (e.g., the available data models and storage systems, the support to the ingestion process, the expressiveness of the querying language, the possibility to move data from one DBMS to another). However, none of them supports data fusion.

Effectively supporting querying on a heterogeneous system with overlapping records requires the adoption of data fusion techniques [5]. The literature on this subject is very wide, thus we refer the reader to a recent survey [16]. Remarkably, related work in this area does not apply directly to a polyglot system. To the best of our knowledge, the only proposal that considers a scenario requiring data fusion in a polyglot system is QUEPA [15], where the authors present a polystore-based approach to support query augmentation. The approach is meant to complement other polystores that actually support cross-DBMS querying, and record linkage techniques are only used to find related instances in different DBMSs, but not to solve conflicts. Another work that proposes on-the-fly integration and schema heterogeneity resolution in an analytical context is [11]; however, the proposed approach is limited to document-oriented databases and does not consider data fusion.

7   Conclusions

In this work, we have extended our multistore approach [2] with a cost-based optimization of execution plans by devising and evaluating three join strategies in presence of data replication. The results demonstrate that, depending on the configuration of the multistore and the distribution of the data, different join strategies may emerge as the most convenient to follow to structure the query execution plan. This validates the multi-strategy approach and motivates further research in this direction. In future work, the first step will be to apply the join strategies on a wider domain including multiple entities. This step alone opens to several challenges, as the variety of schema representations will considerably increase and may impact significantly on the choice of the best strategy. The cost model can be also improved from many perspectives, by (i) considering the impact of distributed database implementations (other than the middleware execution engine), (ii) adopting finer modeling of concurrent computations, and (iii) integrating the cost model with the existing one for GPSJ queries on Apache Spark [1]. We plan to further evaluate the join strategies over a broader selection of queries, including selection predicates with varying selectivity, which will require additional statistics to be collected from the different DBMSs. Ultimately, we will consider the addition of partial aggregation push-down to the local databases to increase the efficiency of our multistore system.

References

1. Baldacci, L., Golfarelli, M.: A cost model for SPARK SQL. IEEE Trans. Knowl. Data Eng. **31**(5), 819–832 (2019)
2. Ben Hamadou, H., Gallinucci, E., Golfarelli, M.: Answering GPSJ queries in a polystore: a dataspace-based approach. In: Laender, A.H.F., Pernici, B., Lim, E.-P., de Oliveira, J.P.M. (eds.) ER 2019. LNCS, vol. 11788, pp. 189–203. Springer, Cham (2019). https://doi.org/10.1007/978-3-030-33223-5_16
3. Bimonte, S., Gallinucci, E., Marcel, P., Rizzi, S.: Data variety, come as you are in multi-model data warehouses. Inf. Syst. 101734 (2021)
4. Bleiholder, J., Naumann, F.: Declarative data fusion – syntax, semantics, and implementation. In: Eder, J., Haav, H.-M., Kalja, A., Penjam, J. (eds.) ADBIS 2005. LNCS, vol. 3631, pp. 58–73. Springer, Heidelberg (2005). https://doi.org/10.1007/11547686_5
5. Bleiholder, J., Naumann, F.: Data fusion. ACM Comput. Surv. (CSUR) **41**(1), 1–41 (2009)
6. Bonaque, R., et al.: Mixed-instance querying: a lightweight integration architecture for data journalism. Proc. VLDB Endow. **9**(13), 1513–1516 (2016)
7. DeWitt, D.J., et al.: Implementation techniques for main memory database systems. In: Proceedings of the 1984 SIGMOD Annual Meeting, pp. 1–8 (1984)
8. DiScala, M., Abadi, D.J.: Automatic generation of normalized relational schemas from nested key-value data. In: 2016 ACM SIGMOD International Conference on Management of Data, pp. 295–310. ACM (2016)
9. Franklin, M.J., Halevy, A.Y., Maier, D.: From databases to dataspaces: a new abstraction for information management. SIGMOD Rec. **34**(4), 27–33 (2005)
10. Gadepally, V., et al.: The BIGDAWG polystore system and architecture. In: 2016 IEEE High Performance Extreme Computing Conference, pp. 1–6. IEEE (2016)
11. Gallinucci, E., Golfarelli, M., Rizzi, S.: Approximate OLAP of document-oriented databases: a variety-aware approach. Inf. Syst. **85**, 114–130 (2019)
12. Golfarelli, M., Maio, D., Rizzi, S.: The dimensional fact model: a conceptual model for data warehouses. Int. J. Coop. Inf. Syst. **7**(2–3), 215–247 (1998)
13. Jeffery, S.R., Franklin, M.J., Halevy, A.Y.: Pay-as-you-go user feedback for dataspace systems. In: 2008 ACM SIGMOD International Conference on Management of Data, pp. 847–860. ACM (2008)
14. Kolev, B., et al.: CloudMDSQL: querying heterogeneous cloud data stores with a common language. Distrib. Parallel Databases **34**(4), 463–503 (2016)
15. Maccioni, A., Torlone, R.: Augmented access for querying and exploring a polystore. In: 34th IEEE International Conference on Data Engineering, ICDE 2018, pp. 77–88. IEEE Computer Society (2018)
16. Mandreoli, F., Montangero, M.: Dealing with data heterogeneity in a data fusion perspective: models, methodologies, and algorithms. In: Data Handling in Science and Technology, vol. 31, pp. 235–270. Elsevier (2019)
17. Mishra, P., Eich, M.H.: Join processing in relational databases. ACM Comput. Surv. **24**(1), 63–113 (1992)
18. Naumann, F., Freytag, J.C., Leser, U.: Completeness of integrated information sources. Inf. Syst. **29**(7), 583–615 (2004)
19. Sadalage, P.J., Fowler, M.: NoSQL Distilled: A Brief Guide to the Emerging World of Polyglot Persistence. Pearson Education, London (2013)
20. Shi, J., et al.: Clash of the titans: mapreduce vs. spark for large scale data analytics. Proc. VLDB Endow. **8**(13), 2110–2121 (2015)

21. Tan, R., Chirkova, R., Gadepally, V., Mattson, T.G.: Enabling query processing across heterogeneous data models: a survey. In: 2017 IEEE International Conference on Big Data, pp. 3211–3220. IEEE Computer Society (2017)
22. Zhang, C., Lu, J., Xu, P., Chen, Y.: UniBench: a benchmark for multi-model database management systems. In: Nambiar, R., Poess, M. (eds.) TPCTC 2018. LNCS, vol. 11135, pp. 7–23. Springer, Cham (2019). https://doi.org/10.1007/978-3-030-11404-6_2

Integrity Constraints for Microcontroller Programming in Datalog

Stefan Brass[✉] and Mario Wenzel

Martin-Luther-Universität Halle-Wittenberg, Institut für Informatik,
Von-Seckendorff-Platz 1, 06099 Halle (Saale), Germany
{brass,mario.wenzel}@informatik.uni-halle.de

Abstract. We consider microcontroller-programming with a declarative language based on the logic-programming language Datalog. Our prototype implementation translates a Datalog dialect to C-code for the Arduino IDE. In order to prove the correctness, one must ensure that the very limited memory of the microcontroller is sufficient for the derived facts. In this paper, we propose a class of constraints called "generalized exclusion constraints" that can be used for this task. Moreover, they are needed to exclude conflicting commands to the hardware, e.g. different output values on a pin in the same state. This class of constraints also generalizes keys and functional dependencies, therefore our results also help to prove such constraints for derived predicates.

1 Introduction

A microcontroller is a small computer on a single chip. For instance, the Amtel ATMega328P contains an 8-bit CPU, 32 KByte Flash Memory for the program, 2 KByte static RAM, 1 KByte EEPROM for persistent data, 23 general purpose I/O pins, timers, analog/digital-converters, pulse-width modulators, and support for serial interfaces. It costs less than 2 dollars and consumes little energy. Microcontrollers are used in many electronic devices.

For hobbyists, schools, and the simple development of prototypes, the Arduino platform is quite often used. It basically consists of a few variants of boards with the microcontroller, fitting hardware extension boards ("shields"), and an IDE with a programming language based on C.

The software for microcontrollers is often developed in Assembler or C. Declarative programming is an interesting option even for such small devices for the following reasons:

- Declarative programs are usually shorter than an equivalent program in a procedural language. This enhances the productivity of the programmers.
- There can be no problems with uninitialized variables or dangling pointers.
- The language is relatively simple, therefore it can be used also by non-experts (e.g., Arduino boards are a nice device to be used in school).
- The language has a mathematically precise semantics based on logic, which makes programs easier to verify.

© Springer Nature Switzerland AG 2021
L. Bellatreche et al. (Eds.): ADBIS 2021, LNCS 12843, pp. 152–166, 2021.
https://doi.org/10.1007/978-3-030-82472-3_12

- The simple semantics also permits powerful optimization, e.g. in [14], we translate a subclass of programs to a finite automaton extended with a fixed set of variables (i.e. we use "parameterized states").
- Many programs become easier to understand and more flexible by a data-driven architecture. E.g., the configuration data for a home-automation system used as an example in [14] is basically a small database.

In [13,14], we proposed a language "Microlog" for programming Microcontrollers like on the Arduino. The language is based on Datalog (simple logical rules). More specifically, we were inspired by the language Dedalus [1]. One reason for the current revival of Datalog is that it is used also for applications that are not typical database applications, such as static analysis of program code [9], cloud computing [10], and semantic web applications [3,5].

While classic Datalog is not turing-complete, we use it on an infinite sequence of states (similar to the language Dedalus [1]). If one ignores technical restrictions such as the restricted memory and the limited range of the clock, it would be possible to simulate a turing machine. Therefore, using Datalog to specify the input-output-behaviour of a microcontroller is not restricted to toy applications.

We have a prototype implementation that compiles our Datalog-based language "Microlog" into C code for the Arduino IDE. In order to be sure that the program will never stop working, one has to prove that the memory is sufficient for storing all derived facts for the current and the next state. While restricted memory is in principle a problem for many programs, the danger of insufficient memory is quite real on this small hardware. The solution in our paper [14] is fully automatic, but works only for a restricted set of programs. In this paper, we follow a different path based on integrity constraints. They have to be specified manually, but if the set is sufficiently complete, the method presented here can prove that the constraints hold in all states.

We call the class of constraints studied in this paper "generalized exclusion constraints" (GECs). Each instance expresses that two facts cannot occur together in a model. This includes key constraints: There, different facts with the same key value cannot both be true in the same state. Whereas keys are local to one relation, GECs can be specified also for facts from different relations. Exclusion constraints appear already in [4,8,11]. They require that projections of two relations are disjoint: $\pi_{A_{i_1},...,A_{i_n}}(R) \cap \pi_{B_{j_1},...,B_{j_m}}(S) = \emptyset$. Of course, such constraints are a special case of the constraints studied here. Exclusion constraints in PostgreSQL are keys with a user-defined comparison operator. Furthermore, GECs are similar to "negative constraints" in [3,5], but GECs include keys/FDs.

Constraints can be used in every different ways. For instance, [8] modifies specifications of operations in state oriented systems such that they cannot violate constraints (invariants). This is a kind of active integrity enforcement. In [5] constraints are used to ignore inconsistent data (violating the constraints) during query answering. There is a large body of work to compute implied updates in order to specialize integrity constraint checking for a given update, see, e.g., [2]. In our case, we try to prove that no state reachable by executing the Datalog program can violate the constraints. This is a program verification task.

In Sect. 2, we define a rule-based language for programming microcontrollers and its translation into pure Datalog. In Sect. 3, we define the type of constraints that is investigated in this paper, and show how they can be used for the task at hand. In Sect. 4, we give the tools to prove that the constraints are indeed satisfied for a given program. While we focus in this paper on microcontroller programming, the technique is applicable to any Datalog program. Therefore, it is an interesting alternative to our previous work on computing functional dependencies for derived predicates [6].

2   A Datalog-Variant for Microcontroller Systems

2.1   Standard Datalog

Let us first quickly repeat the definition of standard Datalog. The Datalog dialect for Arduino microcontroller systems will be translated to a standard Datalog program in order to define its semantics. Also the generalized exclusion constraints will be defined for standard Datalog, which makes them applicable for all applications of Datalog, not only in microcontroller programming.

A Datalog program is a finite set of rules of the form $A \leftarrow B_1 \wedge \cdots \wedge B_n$, where the head literal A and the body literals B_i are atomic formulas $p(t_1, \ldots, t_m)$ with a predicate p and terms $t_1, \ldots, t_m$. Terms are constants or variables. Rules must be range-restricted, i.e. all variables appearing in the head A must also appear in at least one body literal B_i. This ensures that all variables are bound to a value when the rule is applied. The requirement will be slightly modified for rules with built-in predicates, see below. A fact is a rule with an empty body, i.e. it has the form $p(c_1, \ldots, c_m)$ with constants c_i.

In order to work with time, we need some built-in predicates for integers. Whereas normal predicates are defined by rules (or facts) as above, built-in predicates have a fixed semantics that is built into the system. They can only appear in rule bodies and have additional requirements for the range-restriction so that the rule body is evaluable at least in the sequence from left to right.

- $\mathsf{succ}(\mathsf{T}, \mathsf{S})$: This returns the next point in time (state) S for a given state T. Therefore, the variable T must appear in a literal to the left of this literal in the rule body so that it is bound when this literal is executed. We use $\mathbb{N}_0$ as logical time, and $\mathsf{succ}(\mathsf{T}, \mathsf{S})$ is true iff $\mathsf{S} = \mathsf{T} + 1 \wedge \mathsf{T} \geq 0$.
- $t_1 < t_2$, and the same with the other comparison operators $=, \neq, \leq, >, \geq$. If the terms t_1 or t_2 are variables, the variable must appear already in a body literal to the left (and therefore be bound to a value).
- $t_1 + t_2 < t_3$ which ensures that t_3 is more than t_2 time units (milliseconds) after t_1. Again variables must be bound to the left. The delay t_2 must be ≥ 0.
- $t_1 + t_2 \geq t_3$ (t_3 is not more than t_2 milliseconds after t_1, possibly before t_1).

2.2   Datalog with States

The program on a microcontroller must act in time. It basically runs forever (until the power is switched off), but the time-dependent inputs lead to some state change, and outputs depend on the state and also change over time. We do not assume knowledge about the outside world, but it is of course possible that the outputs influence future inputs. So it is quite clear that a programming language for microcontrollers must be able to define a sequence of states.

We borrow from Dedalus$_0$ [1] the idea to add a time (or state) argument to every predicate. Note that this is logical time, the numbers have no specific meaning except being a linear order.

Every predicate that looks like having n arguments really has $n + 1$ arguments with an additional "zeroth" time argument in front. For a literal A of the form $p(t_1, \ldots, t_n)$ let $\hat{A}$ be $p(\mathsf{T}, t_1, \ldots, t_n)$ with a fixed special variable T that cannot be used directly in the program. For a normal rule $A \leftarrow B_1 \wedge \cdots \wedge B_m$, all time arguments are this same variable T, i.e. the rule describes a deduction within a state. Thus, the rule is an abbreviation for the standard Datalog rule $\hat{A} \leftarrow \hat{B}_1 \wedge \cdots \wedge \hat{B}_m$.

In order to define the next state, we also permit rules with the special mark "@next" in the head literal:

$$p(t_1, \ldots, t_n)@\mathsf{next} \leftarrow B_1 \wedge \cdots \wedge B_m.$$

This rule is internally replaced by:

$$p(\mathsf{S}, t_1, \ldots, t_n) \leftarrow \hat{B}_1 \wedge \cdots \wedge \hat{B}_m \wedge \mathsf{succ}(\mathsf{T}, \mathsf{S}).$$

Note that @next can only be applied in the head, i.e. we can transfer information only forward in time. All conditions can only refer to the current point in time.

Facts can be marked with @start, in which case the constant 1 is inserted for the time argument, i.e. $p(c_1, \ldots, c_n)@\mathsf{start}$ is replaced by $p(1, c_1, \ldots, c_n)$. Since sometimes setup settings must be done before the main program can start, we also permit @init which uses the time constant 0. This pre-state is also necessary because the results of calls are only available in the next state. For instance, we will need the real-time as returned by `millis()` in every state. However, to be available in the start state 1, the function must be called in state 0.

Facts without this mark hold in all states (they are time-independent). However, since all predicates have a time argument, and we want rules to be range-restricted, we define a predicate always as

always@init.	% always(0).
always@next ← always.	% always(S) ← always(T) $\wedge$ succ(T, S).

A fact $p(c_1, \ldots, c_m)$ is replaced by $p(\mathsf{T}, c_1, \ldots, c_n) \leftarrow$ always(T). (A possible optimization would be to compute time-independent predicates and remove the time argument from them.)

The minimal model of such a program is usually infinite (at least with always or similar predicates), therefore the iteration of the T_P-operator to compute derived facts does not stop. However, this is no real problem, since we actually compute derived facts state by state. We forbid direct access to the succ-relation and to the special variables T and S. Therefore, within a state, only finitely many facts are derivable. After we reached a fixpoint, we apply the rules with @next in the head to compute facts for the next state. When that is done, we can forget the facts in the old state, and switch to the new state. Within that state, we can again apply the normal rules to compute all facts true in that state.

2.3   Interface Predicates

A Datalog program for a Microcontroller must interface with the libraries for querying input devices and performing actions on output devices. A few examples of interface functions (from the `Arduino.h` header file) are:

```
#define HIGH   0x1      void pinMode(uint8_t pin, uint8_t mode);
#define LOW    0x0      void digitalWrite(uint8_t pin, uint8_t val);
#define INPUT  0x00     int  digitalRead(uint8_t pin);
#define OUTPUT 0x01     unsigned long millis(void);
```

For each function f that can be called, there is a special predicate call_f with a reserved prefix "call_". The predicate has the same arguments as the function to be called and in addition the standard time argument. E.g. derived facts about the predicate call_digitalWrite(T, Port, Val) lead to the corresponding calls of the interface faction `digitalWrite` in state T. The implementation ensures that duplicate calls are eliminated, i.e. even if there are different ways to deduce the fact, only one call is done.

The sequence of calls is undefined. If a specific sequence is required, one must use multiple states. Conflicts between functions (where a different order of calls has different effects) can be specified by means of our exclusion constraints.

If an interface function f returns a value, there is a second predicate ret_f that contains all parameters of the call and a parameter for the return value. For instance, for the function `digitalRead`, there are two predicates:

- call_digitalRead(T, Port), and
- ret_digitalRead(S, Port, Val).

If the call is done in one state, the result value is available in the next state. This ensures, e.g., that the occurrence of a call cannot depend on its own result.

Since calls of interface functions usually have side effects and cannot be taken back, it is important to clearly define which calls are actually done. In contrast, the evaluation sequence of literals in a rule body can be chosen by the optimizer. Therefore the special call_f predicate can be used only in rule heads. We use the syntax $f(t_1, \ldots, t_n)$@call, which is translated to call_$f(t_{i_1}, \ldots, t_{i_k})$, where $i_1 < i_2 < \cdots < i_k$ are all arguments that are not the special marker?. For instance, a rule that calls `digitalRead` is written as

$$\text{digitalRead}(\text{Port}, ?)@\text{call} \leftarrow \ldots$$

It seems more consistent if the call and the result look like the same predicate with the same number of arguments. Correspondingly, $f(t_1, \ldots, t_n)$@ret is replaced by ret_$f(t_1, \ldots, t_n)$. It can only appear in rule bodies.

For calls that should occur in the initialization state, the suffixes @call@init could be used together, but this does not look nice. We use @setup in this case.

Finally, we need also constants from the interface definition. If our Datalog program contains e.g. #HIGH, this corresponds to the constant HIGH in the generated C-code. We assume that different symbolic constants denote different values (unification will fail for them). Thus, the programmer may not use synonyms.

2.4   Real Time

So far, we have just a sequence of states. How much time it really takes from one state to the next depends on the necessary deductions in the state and the time needed for the interface function calls. Many control programs need real time. This can be achieved with the interface function millis() that returns the number of milliseconds since the program was started.

For common patterns of using real time information, we should define abbreviations. For instance, delaying a call to a predicate for a certain number of milliseconds can be written as follows:

$$p(t_1, \ldots, t_n)@\text{after}(\text{Delay}) \leftarrow A_1, \ldots, A_m.$$

This is internally translated to the following rules:

$$\text{delayed\_}p(t_1, \ldots, t_n, \text{From}, \text{Delay})@\text{next} \leftarrow$$
$$A_1 \wedge \cdots \wedge A_m \wedge \text{millis@ret}(\text{From}).$$
$$\text{delayed\_}p(X_1, \ldots, X_n, \text{From}, \text{Delay})@\text{next} \leftarrow$$
$$\text{delayed\_}p(X_1, \ldots, X_n, \text{From}, \text{Delay}) \wedge$$
$$\text{millis@ret}(\text{Now}) \wedge \text{From} + \text{Delay} < \text{Now}.$$
$$p(X_1, \ldots, X_n)@\text{next} \leftarrow$$
$$\text{delayed\_}p(X_1, \ldots, X_n, \text{From}, \text{Delay}) \wedge$$
$$\text{millis@ret}(\text{Now}) \wedge \text{From} + \text{Delay} \geq \text{Now}.$$
$$\text{millis}(?)@\text{call}.$$

The function millis() is called in every state so that there is always the current time available. Since we do not exactly know how long the processing for one state takes, we cannot be sure that we really get every milliseconds value. Therefore, the comparisons are done with $\leq$ and $>$ instead of $=$ and $\neq$.

Example 1. Most Arduino boards have an LED already connected to Port 13. With the following program we can let this LED blink with 1000 ms on, then 1000 ms off, and so on. The similar program BinkWithoutDelay from the Arduino tutorial has 16 lines of code.

```
pinMode(13, #OUTPUT)@setup.
turn_on@start.

turn_off@after(1000)          ← turn_on.
turn_on@after(1000)           ← turn_off.

digitalWrite(13, #HIGH)@call ← turn_on.
digitalWrite(13, #LOW)@call  ← turn_off.
```

The internal Datalog version (with all abbreviations expanded) of the program is shown in Fig. 1.   □

(1) call_pinMode(0, 13, #OUTPUT).

(2) turn_on(1).

(3) delayed_turn_off(S, From, 1000) ←
         turn_on(T) ∧ ret_millis(T, From) ∧ succ(T, S).

(4) delayed_turn_off(S, From, Delay) ←
         delayed_turn_off(T, From, Delay) ∧
         ret_millis(T, Now) ∧ From + Delay ≥ Now ∧ succ(T, S).

(5) turn_off(S) ←
         delayed_turn_off(T, From, Delay) ∧
         ret_millis(T, Now) ∧ From + Delay < Now ∧ succ(T, S).

(6) delayed_turn_on(S, From, 1000) ←
         turn_off(T) ∧ ret_millis(T, From) ∧ succ(T, S).

(7) delayed_turn_on(S, From, Delay) ←
         delayed_turn_on(T, From, Delay) ∧
         ret_millis(T, Now) ∧ From + Delay ≥ Now ∧ succ(T, S).

(8) turn_on(S) ←
         delayed_turn_on(T, From, Delay) ∧
         ret_millis(T, Now) ∧ From + Delay < Now ∧ succ(T, S).

(9) call_digitalWrite(T, 13, #HIGH) ←
         turn_on(T).

(10) call_digitalWrite(T, 13, #LOW) ←
         turn_off(T).

(11) always(0).

(12) always(S) ← always(T) ∧ succ(T, S).

(13) call_millis(T) ← always(T).

Fig. 1. Blink Program from Example 1 with all appreviations expanded

3   Generalized Exclusion Constraints

Obviously, it should be excluded that `digitalWrite` is called in the same state and for the same port with two different values. Since no specific sequence is defined for the calls, it is not clear whether the output will remain high or low (the last call overwrites the value set by the previous call). What is needed here is a key constraint. In this section, we consider only standard Datalog. Therefore, we must look at the translated/internal version of the example. There, the predicate is call_digitalWrite(T, Port, Val), and we need that the first two arguments are a key for all derivable facts. In logic programming and deductive databases, constraints are often written as rule with an empty head (meaning "false"). Thus, a constraint rule like the following should never be applicable:

$$\leftarrow \text{call\_digitalWrite}(T, \text{Port}, \text{Val}_1) \wedge \text{call\_digitalWrite}(T, \text{Port}, \text{Val}_2) \wedge \text{Val}_1 \neq \text{Val}_2.$$

If we look at the program, we see that a violation of this key could only happen if turn_on and turn_off would both be true in the same state. Thus, we need also this constraint:

$$\leftarrow \text{turn\_on}(T) \wedge \text{turn\_off}(T).$$

The common pattern is that there are conflicts between two literals, such that the existence of a fact that matches one literal excludes all instances of the other literal. This leads to the following definition:

Definition 1 (Generalized Exclusion Constraint). *A "Generalized Exclusion Constraint" (GEC) is a formula of the form*

$$\leftarrow p(t_1, \ldots, t_n) \wedge q(u_1, \ldots, u_m) \wedge \varphi$$

and φ is either true *or a disjunction of inequalities $t_{i_\nu} \neq u_{j_\nu}$ for $\nu = 1, \ldots, k$.*

The implicit head of the rule is false, so the constraint is satisfied in a Herbrand interpretation $\mathcal{I}$ iff there is no ground substitution θ for the two body literals such that $p(t_1, \ldots, t_n)\theta \in \mathcal{I}$ and $q(u_1, \ldots, u_m)\theta \in \mathcal{I}$ and φ is true or there is $\nu \in \{1, \ldots, k\}$ with $t_{i_\nu}\theta \neq u_{j_\nu}\theta$.

Instead of a disjunction of inequalities in the body, one could equivalently use a conjunction of equalities in the head. However, in contrast to a normal deductive rule, a constraint cannot be used to derive new facts: Since the interpretation of equality is given, such an integrity rule can only yield an inconsistency.

Example 2. The "generalized exclusion constraints" are really a generalization of the exclusion constraints of [4,8,11]: For instance, consider relations $r(A, B)$ and $s(A, B, C)$ and the exclusion constraint $\pi_A(r) \cap \pi_A(s) = \emptyset$. In our formalism, this would be expressed as $\leftarrow r(A, \_) \wedge s(A, \_, \_) \wedge$ true.

As in Prolog, every occurrence of "_" denotes a new variable (a placeholder for unused arguments). It is a violation of the constraint if the same value A appears as first argument of r and as first argument of S.   □

In the following, when we say simply "exclusion constraint" or even "constraint", we mean "generalized exclusion constraint". We also allow to drop "∧ true" in the constraint formula.

Example 3. We already illustrated with digitalWrite above that our constraints can express keys. We can also express any functional dependency. For instance, consider $r(A, B, C)$ and the FD $B \longrightarrow C$. This is the same as the generalized exclusion constraint $\leftarrow r(\_, B, C_1) \wedge r(\_, B, C_2) \wedge C_1 \neq C_2$.   □

Example 4. For the original task, to check that memory is sufficient to represent all facts in a single state, we need in particular the following constraint:

$$\leftarrow \text{delayed\_turn\_on}(T, \text{From}_1, \text{Delay}_1) \wedge \text{delayed\_turn\_on}(T, \text{From}_2, \text{Delay}_2) \wedge$$
$$(\text{From}_1 \neq \text{From}_2 \vee \text{Delay}_1 \neq \text{Delay}_2).$$

This is actually a key constraint and means each state contains at most one delayed_turn_on-fact. Of course, we need the same for delayed_turn_off. With that, the potentially unbounded set of facts in a state already becomes quite small. The implicit state argument is no problem, because we compute only facts for the current state and for the next state. Also arguments filled with constants in the program cannot lead to multiple facts in the state. Furthermore, function calls have unique results, i.e. the functional property holds. E.g. constraints like the following for the millis() function can be automatically generated:

$$\leftarrow \mathsf{ret\_millis}(T, \mathsf{Now}_1) \wedge \mathsf{ret\_millis}(T, \mathsf{Now}_2) \wedge \mathsf{Now}_1 \neq \mathsf{Now}_2.$$

With these constraints, we already know that a state for the Blink program can contain at most one fact of each predicate. This certainly fits in memory.

The full set of constraints for the Blink program from Example 1 is shown in Fig. 2. Five of the constraints are keys, but (C) to (H) state that no two of the predicates turn_on, turn_off, delayed_turn_on, delayed_turn_off occur in the same state. There should be an abbreviation for such a constraint set: "For every T, at most one instance of turn_on(T), turn_off(T), delayed_turn_on(T, From, Delay), delayed_turn_off(T, From, Delay) is true." This includes also the keys (I) and (J). The keys (A) and (B) could come from a library, and keys of type (K) should be automatic for all ret_f predicates.   □

(A)   ← call_digitalWrite(T, Port, Val$_1$) ∧ call_digitalWrite(T, Port, Val$_2$) ∧
        Val$_1$ ≠ Val$_2$.

(B)   ← call_pinMode(T, Port, Mode$_1$) ∧ call_pinMode(T, Port, Mode$_2$) ∧
        Mode$_1$ ≠ Mode$_2$.

(C)   ← turn_on(T) ∧ turn_off(T).

(D)   ← turn_on(T) ∧ delayed_turn_off(T, From, Delay).

(E)   ← turn_off(T) ∧ delayed_turn_on(T, From, Delay).

(F)   ← delayed_turn_on(T, From$_1$, Delay$_1$) ∧ delayed_turn_off(T, From$_2$, Delay$_2$).

(G)   ← turn_on(T) ∧ delayed_turn_on(T, From, Delay).

(H)   ← turn_off(T) ∧ delayed_turn_off(T, From, Delay).

(I)   ← delayed_turn_off(T, From$_1$, Delay$_1$) ∧ delayed_turn_off(T, From$_2$, Delay$_2$) ∧
        (From$_1$ ≠ From$_2$ ∨ Delay$_1$ ≠ Delay$_2$).

(J)   ← delayed_turn_on(T, From$_1$, Delay$_1$) ∧ delayed_turn_on(T, From$_2$, Delay$_2$) ∧
        (From$_1$ ≠ From$_2$ ∨ Delay$_1$ ≠ Delay$_2$).

(K)   ← ret_millis(T, Now$_1$) ∧ ret_millis(T, Now$_2$) ∧ Now$_1$ ≠ Now$_2$.

Fig. 2. Constraints for the Blink Program

4 Refuting Violation Conditions

4.1 Violation Conditions

A "violation condition" describes the situation where two rule applications lead to facts that violate a constraint. Our task will be to show that all violation conditions themselves violate a constraint or are otherwise inconsistent or impossible to occur. Basically, we get from a constraint rule to a violation condition if we do an SLD resolution step (corresponding to unfolding) on each literal:

Definition 2 (Violation Condition). *Let a Datalog program P and a generalized exclusion constraint $\leftarrow A_1 \wedge A_2 \wedge \varphi$ be given. Let*

- *$A_1' \leftarrow B_1 \wedge \cdots \wedge B_m$ ($m \geq 0$) be a variant with fresh variables of a rule in P,*
- *$A_2' \leftarrow C_1 \wedge \cdots \wedge C_n$ ($n \geq 0$) be a variant with fresh variables of a rule in P (it might be the same or a different rule), such that*
- *(A_1, A_2) is unifiable with (A_1', A_2'). Let θ be a most general unifier.*

Then the violation condition is:

$$(B_1 \wedge \cdots \wedge B_m \wedge C_1 \wedge \cdots \wedge C_n \wedge \varphi)\theta.$$

The "fresh variables" requirement means that the variables are renamed so that the constraint and the two rules have pairwise disjoint variables.

The disjunction $\varphi\theta$ can be simplified by removing inequalities $t_i \neq u_i$ that are certainly false, because t_i and u_i are the same variable or the same constant. If the disjunction becomes empty in this way, it is false, and we do not have to consider the violation condition further. If t_i and u_i are distinct constants for some i, the inequality and thus the whole disjunction can be simplified to true.

Example 5. Consider constraint (A), the key constraint for call_digitalWrite:

$$\leftarrow \text{call\_digitalWrite}(\mathsf{T}, \text{Port}, \text{Val}_1) \wedge \text{call\_digitalWrite}(\mathsf{T}, \text{Port}, \text{Val}_2) \wedge \text{Val}_1 \neq \text{Val}_2.$$

The two rules with matching head literals are rules (9) and (10):

$$\text{call\_digitalWrite}(\mathsf{T}, 13, \#\texttt{HIGH}) \leftarrow \text{turn\_on}(\mathsf{T}).$$
$$\text{call\_digitalWrite}(\mathsf{T}, 13, \#\texttt{LOW}) \leftarrow \text{turn\_off}(\mathsf{T}).$$

We rename the variables of the rules so that the constraint and the two rules have pairwise disjoint variables (we start with index 3, since 1 and 2 appear in the constraint):

$$\text{call\_digitalWrite}(\mathsf{T}_3, 13, \#\texttt{HIGH}) \leftarrow \text{turn\_on}(\mathsf{T}_3).$$
$$\text{call\_digitalWrite}(\mathsf{T}_4, 13, \#\texttt{LOW}) \leftarrow \text{turn\_off}(\mathsf{T}_4).$$

Now we do the unification of the head literals with the literals from the constraint. A possible most general unifier (MGU) is

$$\{\mathsf{T}_3/\mathsf{T}, \mathsf{T}_4/\mathsf{T}, \text{Port}/13, \text{Val}_1/\#\texttt{HIGH}, \text{Val}_2/\#\texttt{LOW}\}.$$

MGUs are unique modulo a variable renaming. Now the violation condition is

$$\text{turn\_on}(\mathsf{T}) \land \text{turn\_off}(\mathsf{T}) \land \#\text{HIGH} \neq \#\text{LOW}.$$

Since $\#\text{HIGH} \neq \#\text{LOW}$ is true, the violation condition can be simplified to

$$\text{turn\_on}(\mathsf{T}) \land \text{turn\_off}(\mathsf{T}).$$

This is what we would expect: It should never happen that turn_on and turn_off are true in the same state.

It would also be possible to match the two literals of the constraint with different variants (with renamed variables) of the same rule, but in this example, that would give conditions like $\#\text{HIGH} \neq \#\text{HIGH}$, which are false. Such obviously inconsistent violation conditions do not have to be considered.   □

Violation conditions express the conditions under which the result of a derivation step violates an exclusion constraint:

Theorem 1. $\mathsf{T}_P(\mathcal{I})$ *violates an exclusion constraint* $\leftarrow A_1 \land A_2 \land \varphi$ *if and only if there is a violation condition for P and* $\leftarrow A_1 \land A_2 \land \varphi$ *which is true in $\mathcal{I}$.*

The T_P operator, well known in logic programming, yields all facts that can be derived by a single application of the rules in P, given the facts that are true in the input interpretation. One starts with the empty set of facts $\mathcal{I}_0$ which certainly satisfies all exclusion constraints. Then one iteratively applies the T_P operator, i.e. $\mathcal{I}_{i+1} := \mathsf{T}_P(\mathcal{I}_i)$, to get the minimal model $\mathcal{I}_\omega := \bigcup_{i \in \mathbb{N}} \mathcal{I}_i$, which is the intended interpretation of P.

Theorem 2. *Let P be a Datalog program, $\mathcal{C}$ be a set of generalized exclusion constraints, and $\mathcal{H}$ be some set of Herbrand interpretations that includes at least all interpretations that occur in the iterative computation of the minimal model. If all violation conditions for P and constraints from $\mathcal{C}$ are false in all $\mathcal{I} \in \mathcal{H}$ that satisfy $\mathcal{C}$, then the minimal Herbrand model $\mathcal{I}_\omega$ of P satisfies $\mathcal{C}$.*

Thus, we have to show that the violation conditions are unsatisfiable assuming the constraints. However, it turns out that this does not work well in the initialization state 0 and the start state 1. Therefore, the theorem permits to throw in additional knowledge formalized as some set of Herbrand interpretations $\mathcal{H}$ that is a superset of the relevant interpretations. In the example, we need that ret_f-predicates cannot occur in state 0: This is obvious, because there is no previous state that might contain a call. One could also precompute all predicates that might occur in state 0 and 1 and use this knowledge to restrict $\mathcal{H}$.

4.2   Proving Violation Conditions Inconsistent

The consistency check for the violation conditions is done by transforming the task to a formula that can be checked by a constraint solver for linear arithmetic constraints [7,12]. Since we assume that all constraints were satisfied before the derivation step that is described by the violation condition, we can exclude any match of two literals A_1 and A_2 from the violation condition with a constraint:

Definition 3 (Match Condition). *Let two literals A_1 and A_2 and an exclusion constraint $\leftarrow C_1 \wedge C_2 \wedge \gamma$ be given. Let $\leftarrow C_1' \wedge C_2' \wedge \gamma'$ be a variant of the constraint with fresh variables (not occurring in A_1 and A_2). If (A_1, A_2) are unifiable with (C_1', C_2') there is a match condition for (A_1, A_2) and this constraint, computed as follows:*

- *Let θ be a most general unifier without variable-to-variable bindings from variables of (A_1, A_2) to variables of (C_1', C_2') (since the direction of variable-to-variable bindings is arbitrary, this is always possible).*
- *Let A_1 be $p(t_1, \ldots, t_n)$ and A_2 be $q(u_1, \ldots, u_m)$.*
- *Then the match condition is*

$$t_1 = t_1\theta \wedge \cdots \wedge t_n = t_n\theta \wedge u_1 = u_1\theta \wedge \cdots \wedge u_m = u_m\theta \wedge \gamma'\theta.$$

The requirement on the direction of variable-to-variable bindings ensures that the match condition contains only variables that also occur in A_1 or A_2.

Again, some parts of the condition can be immediately evaluated. The formula basically corresponds to the unification (plus the formula from the constraint). Most conditions will have the form $X = X$ and can be eliminated. However, if the literals from the constraint contain constants or equal variables, the condition becomes interesting. Note that we cannot simply apply the unification as in Definition 2, because we finally need to negate the condition: We are interested in values for the variables that are possible without violating the exclusion constraint.

Definition 4 (Violation Formula). *Let a violation condition*

$$A_1 \wedge \cdots \wedge A_m \wedge B_1 \wedge \cdots \wedge B_n \wedge \varphi$$

be given, where $A_1, \ldots, A_m$ have user-defined predicates and $B_1, \ldots, B_m$ have built-in predicates. The violation formula for this violation condition is a conjunction ($\wedge$) of the following parts:

- *φ*
- *For each B_i its logical definition. If B_i has the form $\mathsf{succ}(t_1, t_2)$, the logical definition is $t_2 = t_1 + 1 \wedge t_1 \geq 0$. For $t_1 + t_2 \geq t_3$ and $t_1 + t_2 < t_3$, we take that and add $t_2 \geq 0$. For other built-in predicates, it is B_i itself.*
- *For all possible match conditions μ of a constraint $\leftarrow C_1 \wedge C_2 \wedge \gamma$ with two literals A_i and A_j, the negation $\neg\mu$.*

Example 6. This example continues Example 5 with the violation condition:

$$\mathsf{turn\_on}(T) \wedge \mathsf{turn\_off}(T).$$

We use constraint (C): $\leftarrow \mathsf{turn\_on}(T) \wedge \mathsf{turn\_off}(T)$. Formally, we have to rename the variable in the constraint, e.g. to T_1, and then compute the unifier T_1/T of the constraint literals with the literals in the violation condition. The match condition is $T = T \wedge T = T$, which can be simplified to true. Since there is no other matching constraint, the violation formula, which requires that the violation condition does not violate the constraint, is ¬true, i.e. false. Therefore, the violation condition cannot be satisfied. We can stop as soon as we know that the violation formula is unsatisfiable. Thus, even if there were other matching constraints, we would not have to consider them.   □

Example 7. For a more complex case, let us consider Constraint (J) which ensures that there can be only one fact about delayed_turn_on in each state:

$$\leftarrow \text{delayed\_turn\_on}(T, \text{From}_1, \text{Delay}_1) \wedge \text{delayed\_turn\_on}(T, \text{From}_2, \text{Delay}_2) \wedge$$
$$(\text{From}_1 \neq \text{From}_2 \vee \text{Delay}_1 \neq \text{Delay}_2).$$

In order to generate violation conditions, all possibilities for matching rule heads with the two literals of the constraint must be considered. In this case, facts that might violate the constraint can be derived by applying Rule (6) and Rule (7) (see Fig. 1). For space reasons, we consider only the violation condition that corresponds to the case that both constraint literals are derived with different instances of Rule (6): We rename the variables once to S_3, From_3, T_3 (i.e. the head of Rule (6) becomes delayed_turn_on($S_3, \text{From}_3, 1000$)) and once to S_4, From_4, T_4. An MGU is

$$\{S_3/T, \text{From}_3/\text{From}_1, \text{Delay}_1/1000, S_4/T, \text{From}_4/\text{From}_2, \text{Delay}_2/1000\}.$$

Thus, the resulting violation condition is:

$$\text{turn\_off}(T_3) \wedge \text{ret\_millis}(T_3, \text{From}_1) \wedge \text{succ}(T_3, T) \wedge$$
$$\text{turn\_off}(T_4) \wedge \text{ret\_millis}(T_4, \text{From}_2) \wedge \text{succ}(T_4, T) \wedge$$
$$(\text{From}_1 \neq \text{From}_2 \vee 1000 \neq 1000)$$

Of course, $1000 \neq 1000$ is false and can be removed. Now we want to compute the violation formula. The easy parts are:

- The formula part of the violation condition: $\text{From}_1 \neq \text{From}_2$.
- The definition of the built-in succ-literals:

$$T = T_3 + 1 \wedge T_3 \geq 0 \wedge T = T_4 + 1 \wedge T_4 \geq 0.$$

Note that $T_3 = T_4$ can be derived from this.

Furthermore, we have to add the negation of all possible match conditions for constraints matching two literals in the violation condition (we might stop early as soon as we have detected the inconsistency). In this case, there is only one possible constraint, namely (K). A variant with fresh variables is:

$$\leftarrow \text{ret\_millis}(T_5, \text{Now}_5) \wedge \text{ret\_millis}(T_5, \text{Now}_6) \wedge (\text{Now}_5 \neq \text{Now}_6)$$

An MGU with variable-to-variable bindings directed towards the violation condition is $\{T_5/T_3, \text{Now}_5/\text{From}_1, T_4/T_3, \text{Now}_6/\text{From}_2\}$. This gives the following match condition:

$$T_3 = T_3 \wedge \text{From}_1 = \text{From}_1 \wedge T_4 = T_3 \wedge \text{From}_2 = \text{From}_2 \wedge \text{From}_1 \neq \text{From}_2.$$

With the trivial equalities removed, this is $\mathsf{T}_4 = \mathsf{T}_3 \wedge \mathsf{From}_1 \neq \mathsf{From}_2$. The negation is added to the violation formula. Thus the total violation formula is:

$$\mathsf{From}_1 \neq \mathsf{From}_2 \wedge$$
$$\mathsf{T} = \mathsf{T}_3 + 1 \wedge \mathsf{T}_3 \geq 0 \wedge \mathsf{T} = \mathsf{T}_4 + 1 \wedge \mathsf{T}_4 \geq 0 \wedge$$
$$\neg(\mathsf{T}_4 = \mathsf{T}_3 \wedge \mathsf{From}_1 \neq \mathsf{From}_2).$$

This is easily discovered to be inconsistent. Thus, Constraint (J) cannot be violated if both literals are derived with Rule (6). The other cases can be handled in a similar way. □

Theorem 3. *Let $A_1 \wedge \cdots \wedge A_m \wedge B_1 \wedge \cdots \wedge B_m \wedge \varphi$ be a violation condition and ψ be its violation formula with respect to constraints C. There is a variable assignment $\mathcal{A}$ that makes ψ true in the standard interpretation of arithmetics if and only if there is a Herbrand interpretation $\mathcal{I}$ satisfying C with the standard interpretation of the built-in predicates such that the violation condition is true in $\mathcal{I}$ for some extension of $\mathcal{A}$ (not all variables of the violation condition might be in ψ).*

5 Conclusions

We are investigating the programming of microcontrollers in Datalog. We have discussed an interesting class of constraints which we called "generalized exclusion constraints". They contain keys, but can specify uniqueness of facts also between different relations. In particular, the constraints can be used to ensure that each state does not contain "too many" facts, e.g. more than what fits in the restricted memory of a microcontroller. But they also can express conflicts between different interface functions that cannot be called in the same state.

This class of constraints is also interesting, because for the most part, they are able to reproduce themselves during deduction. We have introduced the notion of a "violation condition" as a tool for checking this. Violation conditions can be reduced to a "violation formula" that can be checked for consistency by a constraint solver for linear arithmetics. If the violation formula should be consistent, the violation condition can be shown to the user who might then add a constraint to prove that the violation can never occur. A prototype implementation is available at: https://users.informatik.uni-halle.de/~brass/micrologS/.

References

1. Alvaro, P., Marczak, W.R., Conway, N., Hellerstein, J.M., Maier, D., Sears, R.: Dedalus: Datalog in time and space. In: de Moor, O., Gottlob, G., Furche, T., Sellers, A.J. (eds.) Datalog Reloaded – First International Workshop, Datalog 2010. LNCS, vol. 6702, pp. 262–281. Springer, Heidelberg (2011). https://doi.org/10.1007/978-3-642-24206-9_16, http://www.neilconway.org/docs/dedalus_dl2.pdf
2. Bry, F., Manthey, R., Martens, B.: Integrity verification in knowledge bases. In: Voronkov, A. (ed.) RCLP -1990. LNCS, vol. 592, pp. 114–139. Springer, Heidelberg (1992). https://doi.org/10.1007/3-540-55460-2_9

3. Calì, A., Gottlob, G., Lukasiewicz, T.: A general Datalog-based framework for tractable query answering over ontologies. In: Proceedings of the 28th ACM SIGMOD-SIGACT-SIGART Symposium on Principles of Database Systems (PODS 2009), pp. 77–86. ACM (2009)
4. Casanova, M.A., Vidal, V.M.P.: Towards a sound view integration methodology. In: Proceedings of the 2nd ACM SIGACT-SIGMOD Symposium on Principles of Database Systems (PODS 1983), pp. 36–47 (1983)
5. Chabin, J., Halfeld-Ferrari, M., Markhoff, B., Nguyen, T.B.: Validating data from semantic web providers. In: Tjoa, A.M., Bellatreche, L., Biffl, S., van Leeuwen, J., Wiedermann, J. (eds.) SOFSEM 2018. LNCS, vol. 10706, pp. 682–695. Springer, Cham (2018). https://doi.org/10.1007/978-3-319-73117-9_48
6. Engels, C., Behrend, A., Brass, S.: A rule-based approach to analyzing database schema objects with Datalog. In: Fioravanti, F., Gallagher, J.P. (eds.) LOPSTR 2017. LNCS, vol. 10855, pp. 20–36. Springer, Cham (2018). https://doi.org/10.1007/978-3-319-94460-9_2
7. Imbert, J.-L., Cohen, J., Weeger, M.D.: An algorithm for linear constraint solving: its incorporation in a Prolog meta-interpreter for CLP. J. Log. Program. **16**, 235–253 (1993). https://core.ac.uk/download/pdf/82420821.pdf
8. Schewe, K.D., Thalheim, B.: Towards a theory of consistency enforcement. Acta Informatica **36**, 97–141 (1999). https://doi.org/10.1007/s002360050155
9. Scholz, B., Jordan, H., Subotić, P., Westmann, T.: On fast large-scale program analysis in Datalog. In: Proceedings of the 25th International Conference on Compiler Construction (CC 2016), pp. 196–206. ACM (2016)
10. Shkapsky, A., Yang, M., Interlandi, M., Chiu, H., Condie, T., Zaniolo, C.: Big data analytics with Datalog queries on Spark. In: Proceedings of the 2016 International Conference on Management of Data (SIGMOD 2016), pp. 1135–1149. ACM (2016). http://yellowstone.cs.ucla.edu/~yang/paper/sigmod2016-p958.pdf
11. Thalheim, B.: Dependencies in Relational Databases. Teubner, Germany (1991)
12. Van Hentenryck, P., Graf, T.: Standard forms for rational linear arithmetic in constraint logic programming. Ann. Math. Artif. Intell. **5**(2), 303–319 (1992). https://doi.org/10.1007/BF01543480
13. Wenzel, M., Brass, S.: Declarative programming for microcontrollers - Datalog on Arduino. In: Hofstedt, P., Abreu, S., John, U., Kuchen, H., Seipel, D. (eds.) INAP/WLP/WFLP -2019. LNCS (LNAI), vol. 12057, pp. 119–138. Springer, Cham (2020). https://doi.org/10.1007/978-3-030-46714-2_9. https://arxiv.org/abs/1909.00043
14. Wenzel, M., Brass, S.: Translation of interactive Datalog programs for microcontrollers to finite state machines. LOPSTR 2020. LNCS, vol. 12561, pp. 210–227. Springer, Cham (2021). https://doi.org/10.1007/978-3-030-68446-4_11

Chance Constraint as a Basis for Probabilistic Query Model

Maksim Goman$^{(\boxtimes)}$

Johannes Kepler University, 4040 Linz, Austria
Maksim.Goman@jku.at
http://www.ie.jku.at

Abstract. We consider basic principles of probabilistic queries. Decomposition of a generic probabilistic query with conditioning in SQL-like syntax shows that data comparison operators are the only difference to the deterministic case. Any relational algebra operators presume comparison of attribute values. Probabilistic relational algebra operators are not comparable to deterministic ones due to uncertainty factor – they process distribution functions instead of unit values. We argue that chance constraint is a useful principle to build the basic set of binary probabilistic comparison operators (BPCO), the respective probabilistic relational algebra operators and their query syntax for query language implementations.

We argue that these BPCO should be based on principles of probability theory. We suggest generic expressions for the BPCO as counterparts for deterministic ones. Comparison of two random variables and a random variable to a scalar are considered. We give examples of BPCO application to uniformly distributed random variables and show how to build more complex probabilistic aggregation operators.

One of the main concerns is compatibility of uncertain query processing with query processing in modern deterministic relational databases. The advantage is knowledge continuity for developers and users of uncertain relational databases. With our approach, only addition of a probabilistic threshold to parameters of relational query operations is required for implementation. We demonstrate that the BPCO based on chance constraints maintain consistency of probabilistic query operators with the syntax of deterministic query operators that are common in today's database industrial query languages like SQL.

Keywords: Uncertain databases · Probabilistic databases · Uncertain comparison · Uncertain query · Binary order relation

1 Introduction

Research on uncertain data models for uncertain or probabilistic databases began in 1980s. One example is Barbará et al. [1], where a data model and extended relational algebra were made with probability theory. The work operates with

© Springer Nature Switzerland AG 2021
L. Bellatreche et al. (Eds.): ADBIS 2021, LNCS 12843, pp. 167–179, 2021.
https://doi.org/10.1007/978-3-030-82472-3_13

discrete distributions, introduces comparison of probability distributions for conditioning, defines comparison operations for that and uses the total variation distance to compare a given distribution to a "standard" distribution.

Most of the existing studies on probabilistic databases focus on the discrete probabilistic attributes, employing possible worlds semantics (PWS) [1–6], and due to the problem complexity, heuristics and simplifications are used, such as computation of a couple of the principal moments of resulting distributions [5]. Grouping probabilistic tuples is a challenging task, because tuples may belong to many groups with different probabilities. In other words, using PWS for a probabilistic query produces exponentially many deterministic data realizations, each occurring with some probability, derived from marginal individual probabilities of attributes or tuples. Uncertain attributes with continuous distributions are considered a difficult problem because PWS is not applicable there. Unfortunately, attributes with continuous distributions did not receive enough attention.

Uncertain attributes behave themselves differently in tuple existence probability (TEP) model where every value becomes inherently conditional on TEP. Uncertain attributes and TEP form a joint event where the tuple exists with probability p. Thus, even deterministic attributes become a Bernoulli variable given TEP. This creates problems for processing queries, including the simplest COUNT operation in relational algebra.

Uncertainty usually presents in data from imprecise measurements, ambiguous observations, forecasts and estimations, inconsistent models and the like, where noise, errors and incompleteness are considered essential properties. Among applications of imprecise data can be found object geolocation problems [14], event monitoring and sensor data processing systems (including stream data processing) [7], uncertain scientific data arrays [6], industrial sensor networks [3], text recognition, data indexing, expression of confidence in data correctness or similarity [15] (an example of TEP), and others.

For example, consider missing values in data. This is a known issue in data processing, management, and queries. It is possible to include such missing values in data processing, if it were possible to represent them as uncertain values based on certain knowledge of the nature of the data or its statistical properties, information about possible errors, etc. Then, one could add more tuples with such uncertain values into queries, where it may be useful. Another origin of uncertain data is information (e.g. measurement) that may be imprecise or faulty. Finally, data presuming errors with known distributions like estimations based on a priori information of possible outcomes or interpolation (or extrapolation) with a given (or assumed) bias. Thus, uncertain data might be included in queries.

Transformation to deterministic data is one possible way to design queries on uncertain data [5,7]. This is done through substitution of averages instead of distribution function (DF) or in similar manner. Another way to perform probabilistic querying is to compute the resulting distributions explicitly, mainly by means of simulations due to absence of analytical solutions for many DFs and discrete distributions where PWS usually becomes a computational problem [2,5,6]. Although it can be slow, the latter approach produces an accurate result.

However, algorithms and implementations must be fast enough to effectively meet time constraints on software response time.

A threshold query is a fundamental query type which retrieves the objects qualifying a set of predicates with certain threshold guarantees [8]. The threshold query can be regarded as an essential tool for data analysis because predicates can be specifically defined for various applications. We consider that the meaning and value of the threshold in queries have been underestimated in uncertain databases. We will consider the following statement in the paper: A probabilistic threshold query (PTQ) should have an additional reliability threshold parameter and should retrieve all the results satisfying the threshold requirements with minimum given reliability. The reliability threshold has the meaning of a minimum probability of assuring a satisfactory query result. Therefore, processing of probabilistic queries must conform to norms of probability calculus. Moreover, this alone allows to extend the usual semantics of various deterministic relational queries (e.g., simple and conditional selection, joins, top-k, aggregations (SUM, MAX), etc.) to probabilistic (uncertain) relational queries.

We consider queries involving conditioning (SELECT and GROUP BY) and aggregation operations (e.g. SUM) on uncertain data in this paper. Reasonable trade-off between sufficient precision, accuracy or uniqueness of the answer to the query and tolerance to ambiguity and uncertainty of the answer is expressed by the reliability threshold in PTQ. We assume that values of uncertain attributes are independent random variables with known probability distributions. Generalization to dependent attributes should follow in later research. We aim at maintaining SQL-like query semantics because it is familiar in the industry. As a result, we will develop a simple and transparent relational query model on the basis of chance constraint method [9, 11, 12]. We give a brief description of chance constraints in Sect. 3.

Uncertain conditioning is the main topic of the paper. On the example of SQL-like query, we will show that conditioning can be represented as a sequence of chance constraints. While the approach is general and works with any DF of uncertain attribute instances, we will assume continuous DF types. A discrete DF is also possible and only DF type is different – probability mass function (PMF). The only operations that are needed for that are binary probabilistic comparison operators (BPCO) for uncertain data types. Usually, relational algebra operators have parameters, e.g. constants, thresholds, etc. These parameters are used in BPCO. Addition of only one extra query parameter – a reliability threshold – is enough to produce any type of probabilistic relational queries. We derive these operators in general form. This enables us to have simple semantic for uncertain queries well supported by probability theory. Later, a formulation of uncertain queries as optimization problems can be useful for higher level query processing models. Several examples will demonstrate our approach to BPCO application in uncertain relational queries with conditioning as well as construction of more complex query operators.

The paper is organized as follows: after formulation of PTQ in Sect. 2 we give the chance constraint model for the probabilistic query in Sect. 3. After that, we define generic BPCO in Sect. 3. Then we discuss their operational aspects in Sect. 4. Section 5 contains examples of application of the BPCO in a query. Conclusion gives summary of the work.

Material in Sects. 2 through 5 is new and completely original. To the best of our knowledge, this is the first research in relational probabilistic or uncertain databases that use chance constraint method for conditioning on uncertain attributes with continuous distributions. This work shows that the problem of probabilistic conditioning is tractable with probability calculus. Moreover, this approach is generalizable to attributes with discrete distributions and TEP.

2   Problem Formulation

An uncertain relation R in probabilistic data model (PDM) [1] contains tuples $(t_1, t_2, ..., t_n)$ that conform to the schema $A^d \cup A^p$. Attributes in the set A^d are deterministic attributes and in A^p are uncertain attributes modeled as random variables with given probability density function (PDF). We consider continuous PDFs in this paper, but it is generalizable to discrete ones. Thus, each tuple has k continuous uncertain attributes in the set A^p. The uncertainty is represented by the PDFs $f_{X_i}(x)$ of random attribute variables $X_i, i = 1, \ldots, k$ in this tuple.

According to mathematical traditions, we use capital letters to denote random variables, constants, parameters and *attribute names* with uncertain data type (e.g. C). All deterministic variables, parameters and constants will be written in lower case as well as *names of attributes* that have deterministic data types (e.g. a). We use lower case characters for reserved words in *SQL-like syntax*, e.g. "select", "sum", "from", "where", etc., but the key keywords are upper case letters *in the text*, e.g. "SELECT", "SUM", "FROM", "WHERE", etc. Query parameters are put in angular brackets $\langle \rangle$, i.e. values that are supplied into the query as parameters. The same uppercase name (e.g. Y) can be used in formulas and text with the meaning of attribute value instance *from a tuple* as well as in the sense of attribute names of uncertain data type like in SQL-like templates. Because we consider uncertain data in the terms of probability theory, all terms with the words like "probabilistic" and "uncertain" have the same meaning of uncertainty model, e.g. probabilistic attribute and uncertain attribute are synonyms in the paper.

TEP is an independent random variable from other attributes A^p in this model. It expresses tuple-level uncertainty. Bernoulli or discrete TEP also transforms deterministic attributes A^d of the tuple to discrete random variables. We are not going to consider the discrete case of TEP in details, but our approach is the same for the discrete case. TEP random variable Y_i with PMF $\phi_{Y_i}(y)$ generates a new random variable $Z_i = X_i Y_i$, i.e. a product of the attribute random variable and TEP. The joint mixed PDF of Z of two independent random variables X and Y is $f_Z(x, y) = f_X(x)\phi_Y(y)$. Without loss of generality, we will drop possible TEP for tuples in the rest of the paper.

A PTQ query is represented as an SQL query template of the following type:

(Q) : select id, Y, sum(X) from $\langle R \rangle$ where $(X \leq \langle a \rangle)$ and $(X > \langle C \rangle)$ group by
id, Y having $(Y \leq \langle b \rangle)$ or $(Y > \langle B \rangle)$ order by sum(X),

    where
    id   is a deterministic key attribute;
    a and b are deterministic constant parameters;
    R   is a relation parameter (table name);
    X, Y, B, C represent independent random variables, including
    X, Y are attributes with uncertain data type, and
    B, C are given probabilistic constant parameter.

We will refer to the PTQ query prototype above as (Q). The SELECT-WHERE, GROUP-BY and HAVING operators above represent conditioning. Hence, one needs comparison operators to compare random variables (and their distributions). So, we need to define these comparison operators and then to apply them to parameters of query operators. The works [1, 10] represented some probabilistic conditional operators for a discrete case. We generalize the approach to continuous random variables and formulate conventional conditional operators for common query languages. Now, after introduction of problem model, we will show that because of probability properties, measuring closeness of probability distributions does not need any other metric, but probability, and we suggest additional reliability threshold in order to measure *how much* the random variables (distributions) are different.

A conditioning in a deterministic query presumes that every tuple belongs to only one group with probability 1. This is because conventional order relations for deterministic data types (e.g. real numbers) assure the only binary outcome of operations "more than" $(>)$, "less than" $(<)$ and "equal to" $(=)$. We consider that the equality operator $=$ is equivalent to approximate equality $\approx$ for uncertain values, so we will continue with this sign in the paper. However, there is no such one-to-one order relation for random variables. Because uncertainty of attribute variables, every tuple in probabilistic query can belong to many groups at the same time. Similarly, each attribute value can participate in many aggregations, e.g. sum$(X > 2)$ and sum$(X < 2)$.

The binary maximization operator for two real numbers is naturally based on conventional order relation of real numbers, and the result of this operation is selection of one of them, namely the larger number. On the contrary, the binary operation of maximizing two random variables can only assure that one of the variables is larger than the other with certain probability distribution, because comparison of random variables is only possible for their distributions. We can not simply select one of the two random variables based on that: they can be both larger than another one to some extent at the same time (due to possible DF overlap) unless we consider samples from their marginal distributions. Operationally, we compare them by creating a new (third) random variable as a difference of the old ones and with the help of this third random variable we can conclude something about order relation of the old two. Fortunately, if we add a probabilistic threshold to the uncertain comparison operator, we can employ chance constraint approach and return one of the variables as the larger with the required reliability level.

We consider two uniformly distributed independent uncertain attribute values $U(a, b)$ with given bounds in the examples because they are naturally very useful for many real-life problems as they model cases of the largest uncertainty. Two or more dimensional random variables should be processed according to principles of probability calculus, because the only difference is their DF.

3   Chance Constraint Model and Probabilistic Comparison Operators

A chance constraint for (Q) is the following inequality [9,11,12]:

$$Pr\{X \leq \beta\} \geq \alpha, \tag{1}$$

where
X is a random variable;
β is a parameter, i.e. a deterministic scalar or a random variable;
$\alpha \in [0, 1]$ is a threshold (reliability level).

Chance constraint is interpreted like this: probability, that X is less or equal to the given value β must be greater than the reliability level (threshold) α.

We will use the following notation in uncertain queries in order to express the threshold α for a chance constraint in relational operators in our SQL-like notation: operator_α. Unlike traditional notation from relational algebra, where operators are expressed with Latin letters, English names will be used in capitals here. This is because we have a lot of mathematical notations from probability theory that use Latin letters. For instance, sign σ denotes standard deviation in probability theory and the same letter means SELECT in relational algebra. Nevertheless, probabilistic relational algebra operators can be built in the same manner with our BPCO. The work is to be done in future.

Then, the uncertain query (Q) is represented as follows:

(Q') : select$_{\langle\alpha1\rangle}$ id, Y, sum$_{\langle\alpha2\rangle}(X)$ from $\langle R \rangle$ where $(X \leq \langle a \rangle)$ and $(X > \langle C \rangle)$ group by$_{\langle\alpha3\rangle}$ id, Y having$_{\langle\alpha4\rangle}(Y \leq \langle b \rangle)$ or $(Y > \langle B \rangle)$ order by$_{\langle\alpha5\rangle}$ sum(X).

Coefficients α_i, $i = 1, \ldots, 5$ can be all different or the same. In case of only one α for all operators, it can be given with the main SELECT keyword. In order to build such uncertain queries we need to begin with BPCO $<_\alpha, \approx_{\epsilon,\alpha}, >_\alpha$ to compare random attribute values of tuples.

Comparison of a Random Variable to a Scalar. For a random variable X with PDF $f_X(x)$, cumulative distribution function (CDF) $F_X(x)$, reliability threshold $\alpha \in [0, 1]$ and a scalar $c \in \mathbb{R}$ we denote:

– Operator "$<_\alpha$": $Pr(X < c) > \alpha \Leftrightarrow F_X(c) > \alpha \Rightarrow X < c$;
– Operator "$>_\alpha$": $Pr(X > c) > \alpha \Leftrightarrow 1 - F_X(c) > \alpha \Rightarrow X > c$;
– Operator "$\approx_{\varepsilon,\alpha}$": We allow some small distinction between X and c, i.e.
   $\forall \varepsilon > 0, |X - c| < \varepsilon$. This is equivalent to
   $Pr((X > c - \varepsilon) \cap (X < c + \varepsilon)) > \alpha \Leftrightarrow F_X(c + \varepsilon) - F_X(c - \varepsilon) > \alpha \Rightarrow X \approx c$.

Comparison of Two Random Variables. For random variables X with PDF $f_X(x)$ and CDF $F_X(x)$, Y with PDF $f_Y(y)$ and CDF $F_Y(y)$, and reliability threshold $\alpha \in [0,1]$, there is a new random variable $Z = X - Y$ with CDF $F_Z(X,Y)$. Usually, we should derive CDF of the new variable as a convolution of the old ones: $F_Z = X * (-Y)$. Then we denote:

– Operator "$<_\alpha$": $Pr(X < Y) > \alpha \Leftrightarrow F_Z(0) > \alpha \Rightarrow X < Y$;
– Operator "$>_\alpha$": $Pr(X > Y) > \alpha \Leftrightarrow 1 - F_Z(0) > \alpha \Rightarrow X > Y$;
– Operator "$\approx_{c,\alpha}$": We allow some small distinction between X and Y, i.e.
   $\forall \varepsilon > 0, |Z| < \varepsilon$. Thus,
   $Pr((Z > -\varepsilon) \cap (Z < \varepsilon)) > \alpha \Leftrightarrow F_Z(\varepsilon) - F_Z(-\varepsilon) > \alpha \Rightarrow X \approx Y$.

Derivation of DF of the Difference of Random Variables. In case of comparison of two random variables, the CDF of their difference $Z = X - Y$ should be known or derived. The difference of two independent normally distributed variables is another random variable Z with normal distribution. However, other DFs and their combinations should be considered for every practical application accordingly. We consider the case of two independent uniformly distributed random variables in examples in Sect. 5. The same is true for discrete distributions and this is a way to reconsider current PWS view on discrete random attributes. It is worth to note that addition of TEP is nothing else as generation of a new random attribute where the new random variable is a product of the respective TEP and the attribute's random variable.

4   Conditioning as Application of Chance Constraints

Relational operators return new relations, i.e. sets or bags of tuples. According to our model, uncertain relational algebra or SQL operators should return sets of tuples that satisfy chance constraints on certain attributes with given reliability. In the most general case, once filtering, grouping or aggregation operators have identified tuples whose attributes satisfy the probabilistic condition (expressed as a chance constraint), we can return the tuples unchanged for further processing. We call the approach probabilistic conditioning.

There are other approaches, e.g. given in [2,5], where conditional operators truncate original distributions. Although we find it arguable, it can be application-dependent. They return only parts of the distribution of random variables (truncated distributions) after conditioning and we call the approach truncating conditioning. However, even if truncated distributions are meant as the result of conditioning operators, we still can employ our BPCO for that.

Obviously, the chance constraint satisfies the criterion for a hash function: it must depend on the grouping attributes only. In conformance with the threshold, tuples that likely belong to the same group will get in the same bucket.

We consider, that the number of groups can be larger in probabilistic case because it depends on interpretation of uncertainty in the problem to which the data belong. We believe that there are at least two possibilities how to treat group identifiers. The first one is when an identifier of every group is a union of uncertain values of probabilistically equal attribute values forming the group and the number of groups can grow enormously in this case obtained with the operation $\approx_{\epsilon,\alpha}$.

The second one is when the number of groups is the same as in deterministic case. Each value of the uncertain attribute vector (excluding duplicates) is assumed to be the group identifier. In both the cases, depending on the setup of probabilistic equality operator, the number of values in any group can be larger than in deterministic case. When grouping attribute is probabilistic and no grouping parameters are given, the number of groups can be determined after exhaustive cross pair-wise comparison of all tuples in the query in the worst case.

All in all, group membership is determined using probabilistic equality operator as a probabilistic similarity operator applied to distributions of attribute values and using conditioning parameters. As a result, every uncertain value can belong to many groups (to all in the worst case) and following aggregations can be very different from deterministic ones. Evidently, the probabilistic model is very relaxed and requirements for memory and processing power are larger for probabilistic databases in general.

Grouping probabilistic tuples is considered hard in the literature because tuples may belong to many groups with different probabilities. However, applying our chance constraint approach, grouping and aggregation in a query is conceptually done in the same way as for deterministic queries (e.g. see one-pass algorithm for unary, full-relation operations in [8]). GROUP BY operator can be seen as repeated selections with a different condition per group (group identifier) with given reliability threshold α. The only difference from conventional deterministic case is that we need the threshold α (the same for all groups or different). Let id be a deterministic attribute with the meaning of batch identifier, DEFECT_FREE – an uncertain attribute with the meaning of estimated number of high-quality items in the batch and PRODUCTION is an uncertain attribute meaning estimation of a total number of items in the batch. All the attributes are numerical. In this way, probabilistic counterpart to deterministic grouping algorithm is as follows:

Step 1. Select all rows that satisfy the condition specified in the WHERE clause. This presumes application of the chance constraint to the values of the uncertain attribute of tuples and use of BPCO to compare attribute random values to the given conditioning parameter, e.g. for query template (Q'):

$$\text{select}_{\langle \alpha 1 \rangle} \text{ id, DEFECT\_FREE, sum}_{\langle \alpha 2 \rangle}(\text{PRODUCTION}) \text{ from } \langle R \rangle \text{ where}$$
$$(\text{PRODUCTION} \leq 100) \text{ and } (\text{PRODUCTION} > C \sim U(50, 55))$$

is equivalent to applying the following chance constraint to the uncertain attribute PRODUCTION:

$$(Pr(\text{PRODUCTION} \leq 100) > \alpha 1) \cap (Pr(\text{PRODUCTION} > C) > \alpha 1).$$

Step 2. Form groups from the rows obtained in step 1 according to the GROUP BY clause for the uncertain attribute: group by$_{\langle\alpha 3\rangle}$ DEFECT_FREE. Again, this means application of chance constraint and grouping criterion (identifier) to the value of the respective attribute DEFECT_FREE of each tuple t:

$$t.\text{DEFECT\_FREE} \approx_{\varepsilon,\alpha 3} \text{group\_DEFECT\_FREE\_id.}$$

The required chance constraint can be constructed and resolved using our *probabilistic equality* comparison operator.

Step 3. Discard all groups that do not satisfy the condition in the HAVING clause. This implies application of chance constraint to the set of uncertain tuples produced on the previous step 2, i.e.:

$$\text{having}_{\langle\alpha 4\rangle} \text{ DEFECT\_FREE } \leq 5 \Leftrightarrow Pr(\text{DEFECT\_FREE} \leq 5) > \alpha 4$$

Step 4. Apply aggregation functions to each group. An uncertain aggregation function produces a single uncertain value, some information about resulting distribution or full distribution as the output. Aggregation functions MIN, MAX need the reliability threshold as a parameter; SUM and AVG do not need it because of their nature: these functions account for full distributions of operands including TEP were TEP is given (AVG needs COUNT indirectly). Based on the meaning of the uncertain operator COUNT in a specific application problem, the reliability threshold may be needed as a parameter. However, issues of uncertain aggregations are outside of the scope of the current paper.

Step 5. Application of probabilistic ordering to the output relation is possible to accomplish with BPCO $<_\alpha$, $\approx_{\varepsilon,\alpha}$ and $>_\alpha$. In fact,

$$\text{order by}_{\langle\alpha 5\rangle} \text{ sum(PRODUCTION)}$$

is nothing else as building precedence order (group_i) $\prec$ (group_j) for output groups of tuples based on comparison of aggregation SUM(PRODUCTION) for each group:

$$\text{sum(PRODUCTION} \in \text{group\_i)} <_{\alpha 5} \text{sum(PRODUCTION} \in \text{group\_j)},$$

$\forall$ group_i, group_j $\in G$, $i \neq j$, where G is the set of all groups.

Step 6. Retrieve values or relations for the columns and aggregations listed in the SELECT clause.

5   Examples

We illustrate the simplicity of any conditioning operators based on application of BPCO derived in Sect. 3 to attribute values in query model (Q').

Let R be a relation, and A_1 and A_2 be two values from different tuples of an uncertain attribute A from the set of all uncertain attributes A^p of R. The two uncertain instances of the attribute will have uniform distributions in the example, but with different parameters: $A_1 \sim U(a_1, b_1)$, $A_2 \sim U(a_2, b_2)$. We need to derive the PDF and CDF for the difference $Z = A_1 - A_2$. After that, we can use the BPCO with the expression for $F_Z(z)$ for the case of A_1 and A_2: $Z = A_1 + A'_2$.

A sum of two uniformly distributed random variables has a triangular distribution and for a uniformly distributed X and $\forall k, l \in \mathbb{R}$, a new random variable $Y = kX + l$ is possible. For the current study, we have only the coefficient $k = -1 < 0$. Thus, PDF and CDF are reversed, e.g. $f_Y(x) = 1 - f_X(x)$. It means the change of end points a_2 and b_2 of the uniform distribution $A_2(a_2, b_2)$: $a'_2 = -a_2, b'_2 = -b_2$. Because initially $b_2 \geq a_2$, it follows that $a'_2 \geq b'_2$ and we obtain the convolution of the original A_1 and $A'_2 \sim U(b'_2, a'_2)$.

Using the approach from [13], we obtain the expression for $f_Z(z)$ for the case of difference of uniform distributions with lower bound strictly equal to zero, i.e. $Y_1 \sim U(0, c_1)$ and $Y_2 \sim U(0, c_2)$:

$$f_Z(z) = \frac{1}{c_1 c_2 (n-1)!} (z - (z - c_1)_+ - (z - c_1)_+ + (z - c_1 - c_2)_+), \qquad (2)$$

where $0 \leq z \leq c_1 + c_2$, $z \in \mathbf{R}$ and $x_+ = max(0, x) \, \forall x \in \mathbf{R}$.

After introduction of a new variable $c_i = b_i - a_i$, $i = 1, 2$, we obtain a new respective random variable $Y_i \sim U(0, c_i) = A_i - a_i$, $i = 1, 2$. This is a shift of the first and the second distribution by a constant a_1 or b'_2 respectively. Original values are obtained by the reverse transformation: $A_i = Y_i + a_i$ $i = 1, 2$. It is possible to process the random parts of Y_i with known PDFs and then apply correction to the result by adding $a_1 + b'_2$. CDF $F_Z(Z) = \int_l^u f_Z(z)dz$, where l is the known lower bound and u is the known upper bound.

Now, as we know the CDF $F_Z(z)$, depending on a_1, b_1, a_2, b_2:

- Operator "$<_\alpha$": $Pr(A_1 < A_2) > \alpha \Leftrightarrow F_Z(0) > \alpha \Rightarrow A_1 < A_2$.
- Operator "$>_\alpha$": $Pr(A_1 > A_2) > \alpha \Leftrightarrow 1 - F_Z(0) > \alpha \Rightarrow A_1 > A_2$;
- Operator "$\approx_{\varepsilon,\alpha}$": $Pr(A_1 = A_2) > \alpha \Leftrightarrow F_Z(\varepsilon) - F_Z(-\varepsilon) > \alpha \Rightarrow A_1 \approx A_2$.

Example 1. For a uniformly distributed value $A_1 \sim U(2, 6)$ and $c = 3 \in \mathbb{R}$ the following operators return FALSE and the tuple with the value A_1 is not added to the result set of conditioning in both cases below ($\alpha = 0.8$, $\varepsilon = 2$):

$$A_1 <_{0.8} 3 \Leftrightarrow Pr(X < 3) > 0.8 \Leftrightarrow F_{A_1}(A_1 < 3) = 0.25 < 0.8 \Rightarrow FALSE$$

$$A_1 \approx_{2,0.8} 3 \Leftrightarrow Pr(X - 3 < 2) \cap Pr(A_1 - 3 > -2) > 0.8 \Leftrightarrow$$
$$\Leftrightarrow F_{A_1}(5) - F_{A_1}(1) = 0.75 - 0 = 0.75 < 0.8 \Rightarrow FALSE$$

Example 2. For two independent uniformly distributed values $A_1 \sim U(2, 5), A_2 \sim U(3, 8)$ the comparison operators return FALSE and the tuple with the value A_1 is not added to the result set of conditioning in both cases below ($\alpha = 0.9, \varepsilon = 1$).

$$A_1 <_{0.9} A_2 \Leftrightarrow Pr(A_1 < A_2) > \alpha \Leftrightarrow F_Z(0) = 0.87 < 0.9 \Rightarrow FALSE$$
$$A_1 \approx_{1,0.9} A_2 \Leftrightarrow Pr(A_1 - A_2 < 1) \cap Pr(A_1 - A_2 > -1) > 0.9 \Leftrightarrow$$
$$\Leftrightarrow F_Z(1) - F_Z(-1) = 0.27 < 0.9 \Rightarrow FALSE$$

Example 3. Other relational algebra operations are easy to implement with our approach. For instance, the conditioning operator IN that needs a boolean conditioning result of the following type in SQL-like notation is of the form:

$$\text{select}_{\langle \alpha \rangle} * \text{ from } \langle Measures \rangle \ t \text{ where VAL in}_{\langle \varepsilon \rangle} (1, 2, 3)$$

is equivalent to:

$$(t.VAL \approx_{\varepsilon,\alpha} 1) \ || \ (t.VAL \approx_{\varepsilon,\alpha} 2) \ || \ (t.VAL \approx_{\varepsilon,\alpha} 3),$$

where t denotes a table and VAL is its uncertain attribute. The comparison operators in this model use the threshold α from the related parent statement, e.g. operator IN uses the threshold α from operator SELECT. Parameter ε can have a default predefined value for a data type (and therefore, optional in the IN operator) or directly supplied with the IM operator for each query. The chance constraint is applied to each tuple in t and tuples with attribute VAL satisfying it are selected for output.

6 Conclusion

In this paper, we focused on probabilistic query model, and suggested BPCO for it. We have presented basic principles for building probabilistic relational algebra and query language implementation. To the best of our knowledge, this is the first approach enabling comprehensible, generalizable and effective grouping on uncertain attributes. We believe that the major advantages of our model are generality, simplicity and strong mathematical support. Probability naturally expresses uncertainty in most of practical situations and provides well established mathematical tools to process uncertain data.

We introduced chance constraint model for probabilistic query operators, defined BPCO, gave SQL-like query templates and discussed operational aspects for their implementation. It turns out that chance constraint approach makes the query model transparent and opens possibilities to adjust the quality of relational query to the special aspects of the practical problem with reliability coefficients α. This makes probabilistic conditioning easier to model and implement. In this way, any known relational (especially conditional) operators are possible to formulate for probabilistic data.

We suggested principles and expressions of the BPCO based on probabilistic order relations as counterparts for deterministic ones. Any relational algebra operators presume comparison of attribute values. We argue that probability calculus and chance constraints are enough to compare distributions of probabilistic data values, and the reliability threshold α is the only extra parameter required. Thus, probabilistic queries are always threshold queries. Cases of comparison of two random variables and a random variable to a scalar were considered.

Examples were given that show the usage of our BPCO in the query context for uniformly distributed uncertain data. Construction of more complex probabilistic relational operators (e.g. aggregations) was shown as well.

The described approach opens ways to creation of detailed probabilistic relational algebra. Much work is required in the context of probabilistic data models in order to assure effective implementations. Other issues like null values, concept of missing probability, multivariate distributions and TEP are easier to model with chance constraints, yet are waiting for further research.

Finally, our probabilistic approach maintains consistency in semantics with existing deterministic relational algebra operators that are common in today's database query languages like SQL. Polymorphism makes it possible to have the same query operations for probabilistic data types. Our approach enables preservation of the modern conventional SQL syntax that is important for iterative knowledge development.

The future work includes implementation and verification of the proposed approach in a prototype, and comparison performance with different DF types. Specific attention will be given to discrete distributions and comparison to PWS model. We already have early experience with implementation of certain parts of the approach in a data stream processing framework PipeFabric [16].

Initially, the implementation of the proposed concept as a data query tool, its performance evaluation, and validation of the probabilistic query model can be done on the basis of a general purpose framework. At the same time, we know already from our experience, that required data structures are to be critically analyzed during the implementation in the chosen framework, and specific perspective ones should be selected for the experimental system to assure good performance of the conditioning operations.

Another direction of the future work is development of the basics of probabilistic relational algebra and full range of prototypes of SQL-like operators for it using the concepts of the current work.

References

1. Barbará, D., Garcia-Molina, H., Porter, D.: The management of probabilistic data. IEEE Trans. Knowl. Data Eng. **4**(5), 487–502 (1992). https://doi.org/10.1109/69.166990
2. Tran, T.L.T., McGregor, A., Diao, Y., Peng, L., Liu, A.: Conditioning and aggregating uncertain data streams: going beyond expectations. PVLDB **3**(1), 1302–1313 (2010). https://doi.org/10.14778/1920841.1921001
3. Wang, Y., Li, X., Li, X., Wang, Y.: A survey of queries over uncertain data. Knowl. Inf. Syst. **37**(3), 485–530 (2013). https://doi.org/10.1007/s10115-013-0638-6

4. Van den Broeck, G., Suciu, D.: Query processing on probabilistic data: a survey. Found. Trends Databases **7**(3–4), 197–341 (2017). https://doi.org/10.1561/1900000052

5. Tran, T.L.T., Peng, L., Diao, Y., McGregor, A., Liu, A.: CLARO: modeling and processing uncertain data streams. VLDB J. **21**(5), 651–676 (2012). https://doi.org/10.1007/s00778-011-0261-7

6. Ge, T., Zdonik, S.: Handling uncertain data in array database systems. In: Alonso, G., Blakeley, J. A., Chen, A.L.P. (eds.) ICDE 2008, pp. 1140–1149. IEEE Computer Society (2008). https://doi.org/10.1109/ICDE.2008.4497523

7. Dezfuli, M.G., Haghjoo, M.S.: Xtream: a system for continuous querying over uncertain data streams. In: Hüllermeier, E., Link, S., Fober, T., Seeger, B. (eds.) SUM 2012. LNCS (LNAI), vol. 7520, pp. 1–15. Springer, Heidelberg (2012). https://doi.org/10.1007/978-3-642-33362-0_1

8. Garcia-Molina, H., Ullman, J.D., Widom, J.: Database Systems - The Complete Book. 2nd edn. Pearson Education (2009)

9. Henrion, R.: Chance constrained problems. https://www.stoprog.org/sites/default/files/tutorials/SP10/Henrion.pdf. Accessed 21 May 2021

10. Fuhr, N.: A probabilistic framework for vague queries and imprecise information in databases. In: McLeod, D., Sacks-Davis, R., Schek, H.J. (eds.) VLDB 1990, pp. 696–707. Morgan Kaufmann (1990). http://www.vldb.org/conf/1990/P696.PDF

11. Geletu, A., Klöppel, M., Zhang, H., Li, P.: Advances and applications of chance-constrained approaches to systems optimisation under uncertainty. Int. J. Syst. Sci. **44**(7), 1209–1232 (2013). https://doi.org/10.1080/00207721.2012.670310

12. Prékopa, A.: Stochastic Programming. Springer, Dordrecht (2011). https://doi.org/10.1007/978-94-017-3087-7

13. Sadooghi-Alvandi, S.M., Nematollahi, A.R., Habib, R.: On the distribution of the sum of independent uniform random variables. Stat. Papers **50**(1), 171–175 (2007). https://doi.org/10.1007/s00362-007-0049-4

14. Cheng, R., Kalashnikov, D.V., Prabhakar, S.: Querying imprecise data in moving object environments. IEEE Trans. Knowl. Data Eng. **16**(9), 1112–1127 (2004). https://doi.org/10.1109/TKDE.2004.46

15. Fuhr, N., Thomas Rölleke, T.: A probabilistic relational algebra for the integration of information retrieval and database systems. ACM Trans. Inf. Syst. **15**(1), 32–66 (1997). https://doi.org/10.1145/239041.239045

16. Goman, M.: Efficient aggregation methods for probabilistic data streams. In: Shishkov, B. (ed.) BMSD 2018. LNBIP, vol. 319, pp. 116–132. Springer, Cham (2018). https://doi.org/10.1007/978-3-319-94214-8_8

High-Dimensional Data and Data Streams

Unsupervised Feature Selection for Efficient Exploration of High Dimensional Data

Arnab Chakrabarti[1(✉)], Abhijeet Das[1], Michael Cochez[2],
and Christoph Quix[3,4]

[1] RWTH Aachen University, Aachen, Germany
chakrabarti@dbis.rwth-aachen.de, abhijeet.das@rwth-aachen.de
[2] Vrije Universiteit Amsterdam, Amsterdam, Netherlands
m.cochez@vu.nl
[3] Hochschule Niederrhein, University of Applied Sciences, Krefeld, Germany
christoph.quix@hs-niederrhein.de
[4] Fraunhofer Institute for Applied Information Technology FIT,
Sankt Augustin, Germany

Abstract. The exponential growth in the ability to generate, capture, and store high dimensional data has driven sophisticated machine learning applications. However, high dimensionality often poses a challenge for analysts to effectively identify and extract relevant features from datasets. Though many feature selection methods have shown good results in supervised learning, the major challenge lies in the area of unsupervised feature selection. For example, in the domain of data visualization, high-dimensional data is difficult to visualize and interpret due to the limitations of the screen, resulting in visual clutter. Visualizations are more interpretable when visualized in a low dimensional feature space. To mitigate these challenges, we present an approach to perform unsupervised feature clustering and selection using our novel graph clustering algorithm based on Clique-Cover Theory. We implemented our approach in an interactive data exploration tool which facilitates the exploration of relationships between features and generates interpretable visualizations.

1 Introduction

The ability to collect and generate a wide variety of complex, high-dimensional datasets continues to grow in the era of Big Data. Increasing dimensionality and the growing volume of data pose a challenge to the current data exploration systems to unfold hidden information in high dimensional data. For example, in the field of data visualization human cognition limits the number of data dimensions that can be visually interpreted. The potential amount of overlapping data points projected on to a two-dimensional display hinders the interpretation of meaningful patterns in the data. Though dimensionality reduction has proved to be a promising solution to this problem, there exists the risk of discarding interesting

© Springer Nature Switzerland AG 2021
L. Bellatreche et al. (Eds.): ADBIS 2021, LNCS 12843, pp. 183–197, 2021.
https://doi.org/10.1007/978-3-030-82472-3_14

properties of the data. There are two prominent approaches for dimensionality reduction: *Feature Extraction* and *Feature Selection*. Feature extraction strategies such as Principle Component Analysis (PCA), Linear Discriminant Analysis (LDA), or Multidimensional Scaling (MDS), try to mitigate the effect by projecting a high-dimensional feature space into a lower dimensional space which in turn results in information loss due to the transformation of the locally relevant dimensions. Hence, these methods are often not suitable for data exploration tasks, especially when the user is interested to explore the local structure of the data. On the other hand, feature selection focuses on finding meaningful dimensions, thereby removing irrelevant and redundant features [13], while maintaining the underlying structure. Feature selection methods can be classified as supervised and unsupervised; the latter has gained popularity in recent years.

In this paper, we propose a novel graph clustering approach for unsupervised feature selection using the concept of *"Clique-Cover"* as an underlying foundation. A clique, for an undirected graph, is a subgraph where any two vertices of the subgraph are adjacent to each other. To enumerate such a graph in order to find the largest clique (a clique with most vertices) is termed as the *maximal-clique problem* in graph theory. The maximal-clique model has been studied extensively to detect clusters in large graphs and has found its application in varied domains such as information retrieval [4] or pattern recognition [15].

The contributions of this paper are (i) the integration of Clique-Cover theory in an advanced feature selection pipeline, and (ii) a detailed evaluation of the approach with various experiments using real-world datasets. In our approach, we transform the problem space into a complete graph where the features are nodes and the edge weights denote the degree of correlation between the features. Then, we apply our proposed *maximal-clique* based algorithm for non-overlapping cluster detection. Finally, we select highly relevant features from the detected clusters using *graph-centrality measures*. The algorithm is embedded in a novel *Feature Selection Pipeline* to select features from datasets lacking class labels. This main contribution of the paper is presented in Sect. 3, after we introduced the basics of Clique-Cover theory and discussed related work in Sect. 2.

To verify the efficiency of our approach, we performed experiments to compare our results with that of the existing approaches using real-world datasets. Our experiments presented in Sect. 4 demonstrate that the proposed method performs better than baseline approaches in terms of clustering and classification accuracy. Furthermore, by evaluating our model in terms of computational efficiency and robustness we report the scalability of our model towards increasing dimensionality.

2   Background and Related Work

Clique-Cover is a graph clustering approach based on the underlying notion of maximal cliques [8]. A *Clique* for an undirected graph $G = (V, E)$ is defined as the set of vertices C such that each of the distinct pair of vertices in C is adjacent (i.e., there exists an edge connecting the pairs). A Clique, which is not a subset of a larger clique, is known as a maximal clique. Thus, given a graph G, a subgraph H of a graph G is a maximal clique if H is isomorphic to a complete graph, and there is no vertex $v \in V(G)$ such that v is adjacent to each vertex of H. In other words, a subgraph H of a graph G is a maximal clique if H is a clique, and there is no vertex in G that sends an edge to every vertex of H. In this work, we have extended the concept of maximal cliques to the edge-weighted cliques. A maximal clique having the maximum sum of edge-weights highlights the notion of a cluster. The recursive process of determining such cliques leads to the generation of clusters of different sizes. In terms of graph theory, a cluster can be termed as a cover on the respective nodes of the graph such that the subset of nodes is strongly connected within the cover. Thus a *Clique-Cover* is formally defined as follows: *Let* G *be a graph. A clique of a graph* G *is a nonempty subset* S *of* $V(G)$ *where* S *is a complete graph. A set* ϑ *of cliques in* G *is a clique cover of* G *if for every* $u \in V(G)$ *there exists* $S \in \vartheta$ *such that* $u \in S$.

Feature Clustering algorithms localize the search for relevant features and attempt to find clusters that exist in multiple overlapping subspaces. There are two major branches of feature clustering: (i) The bottom-up algorithms find dense regions in low dimensional spaces and combine them to form clusters. (ii) The top-down algorithms start with the full set of dimensions as the initial cluster and evaluate the subspaces of each cluster, iteratively improving the results. *Clustering in Quest(CLIQUE)* [2] is a bottom-up approach that uses a static grid size to determine the clusters within the subspace of the dataset. It combines density and grid-based clustering and uses an a-priori-style technique to identify clusters in subspaces. Tuning the parameters for grid size and the density threshold is difficult in CLIQUE. *PROjected CLUstering(PROCLUS)* [1] is a top-down algorithm, which samples the data, selects a set of k medoids and iteratively improves the clustering. Although we can achieve an enhanced cluster quality, it depends on parameters like the number of clusters and the size of the subspaces, which are difficult to determine in advance.

Unsupervised Feature Selection can be broadly classified into three main approaches: *Filter*, *Wrapper*, and *Hybrid*. *Filter methods* select the most relevant features from the data itself without using any clustering algorithm. However, they are unable to model feature dependencies and yield better results mostly with supervised data. Relief [16], Laplacian Score [10], Spectral feature selection [23] are some of the filter methods. *Wrapper methods*, on the other hand, use the results of a specific clustering algorithm to evaluate feature subsets. Although they can model feature dependencies, the main disadvantage of wrapper approaches is that they have a high computational cost and are prone to overfitting. *Hybrid methods* combine filter and wrapper models and aim at achieving a compromise between efficiency and effectiveness (significance of the feature subsets) by using feature ranking metrics and learning algorithms. As highlighted in [18], the limitation of these models is that they require the specification of the hyper-parameters in advance. Moreover, most of the traditional methods are designed to handle only numerical data, whereas the data gener-

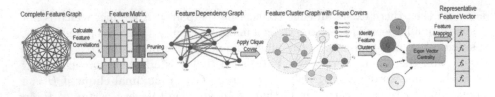

Fig. 1. Feature selection pipeline

ated in real-world applications is a combination of numerical and non-numerical features. In the next section we present our proposed graph clustering algorithm based on the Clique-Cover theory. A weighted feature graph is constructed where the nodes represent the feature set and the edges represent the feature correlation measures.

3   Unsupervised Feature Selection with Clique Covers

Our approach is unsupervised as it does not require class label information. The main idea is to model the dependency between features by clustering them. Interpretability of features is retained as features are not transformed but only selected. To prove the effectiveness of our approach in the domain of data visualization, we provide an interface to visualize the *Representative Features*. The interface allows the user to explore the intermediate results, visualize feature graphs, and visually inspect the data of the resulting feature sets.

We depict the complete workflow of our feature selection pipeline in Fig. 1. As a first step, we create a **Complete Feature Graph** from the dataset. Next, we assign weights to the feature graph using feature correlation measures. These weights are stored in the **Feature Matrix** which acts as the internal data structure for our **Feature Correlation Graph**. In the next step, we apply our graph pruning algorithm to detect and remove weakly connected edges from the complete Feature Correlation Graph and generate the **Feature Dependency Graph**. As a next step, we iteratively apply our *Clique-Cover algorithm* to the Feature Dependency Graph to identify the *clique-covers*. From these clusters, we now apply our algorithm for *Representative Feature Selection*, using *eigen-vector centrality measures*, to construct the **Representative Feature Vector**, which gives us the dimensionality-reduced feature space. In the following subsections, we describe each of the steps in detail.

Data Model and Preprocessing. We assume the data to be in tabular format, where the columns represent the *features* and the rows represent the *data points*. After the data is cleaned and pre-processed, we split the features in categorical and numerical features. For data pre-processing, we perform the following steps: 1. Data Cleaning for the removal of empty and duplicate columns, 2. Data Normalization for standardizing both numerical and the categorical data, 3. Data

Imputation for dealing with missing values by using the principle of predictive mean matching [21], and 4. Data Segregation for identifying numerical and categorical features. The reason to segregate is that we apply the most suitable correlation measures in the respective groups in order to capture the maximum trends of association. As discussed in the following section, a single correlation measure cannot work well with both groups. A selection of appropriate measures is required for the proper construction of the feature graph.

Construction of the Feature Correlation Graph. First, we need to determine the pairwise feature correlations. In the feature graph, the nodes are the features, and the edge-weights are the correlation or association coefficients between the features. As described above, we construct two feature correlation graphs, one for numerical and one for categorical features. To calculate the weights of the edges for these graphs we use the following correlation measures: (i) The Chi-square test of association followed by Cramer's V for categorical feature groups. (ii) Maximal Information Coefficient (MIC) for numerical feature groups. *The Chi-square test* is used to determine the correlation between categorical variables. While it is advantageous because it is symmetric in nature and invariant with respect to the order of the categories, it suffers from certain weaknesses. For example, it fails to specify the strength of the association between the variables and it is sensitive to the sample size. To address this challenge we use a further test known as the *Cramer's V*. This is an essential test that we conduct in order to determine feature correlation as it is immune to the sample size and provides a normalized value, where 0 implies no association and 1 implies a strong association between the attributes. We use *MIC* to capture non-linear trends between variables of numerical feature groups by using the concept of Information Entropy. However, in high-dimensional space this method becomes computationally expensive [19]. To overcome this, we calculate MIC using the normalized Mutual Information. A square matrix is created using the MIC pairs that represents the correlations between the numerical feature groups.

At the end of this step, we get two weighted square Feature Matrices for each feature correlation graphs. Both feature groups were handled independently and they undergo identical processes in the feature selection pipeline. In the rest of the paper, for the purpose of explainability, we describe a common feature selection process (as in Fig. 1). This represents the overall workflow for feature selection using our proposed approach.

Feature Pruning. The complete feature graph obtained from the previous step may contain weakly connected edges between the nodes. We identify a *weak-edge* as those edges whose weights are below the *Threshold Coefficient*. The Threshold Coefficients are determined using the concepts of K-Nearest Neighbors [3]. The KNN method is a common approach in graph algorithms to determine the proximity of nodes [14]. The reason for using the KNN algorithm is that it does not require any assumptions or training steps to build the model. Moreover, it is easy to implement and robust to noisy data as well. The value of K is set as $K = \sqrt{N}$, where N is the number of features in each of the feature sets.

Algorithm 1: Identifying Threshold Coefficient

Procedure : $makeAffinity$
Input: $corrMat$ (MIC and/or Cramer) and K;
Output: affinitymatrix($affMat$);
$totalNodes \leftarrow length(corrMat)$;
if $K > $ totalNodes **then**
  | $affMat \leftarrow corrMat$;
end
else
  | /* Determine strong connections for every feature node   */
  | **foreach** i-th feature in totalNodes **do**
  | $strongConnections \leftarrow sort(corrMat[i,], decreasing = TRUE)[1:K]$;
  | /* Make the affinity matrix symmetric in nature   */
  | **foreach** s-th feature in strongConnections **do**
  | | $j \leftarrow position(corrMat[i,] == s)$; $affMat[i,j] \leftarrow corrMat[i,j]$;
  | | $affMat[j,i] \leftarrow corrMat[i,j]$;
  | **end**
  | **end**
end
return $affMat$;

After determining the threshold coefficients, the K strongest connections for each feature are retained and the others are pruned, resulting in the *Feature Dependency Graph*. We store the Feature Dependency Graph in the form of an *affinity matrix* which is symmetric in nature. The steps of this process are shown in Algorithm 1, which takes the correlation matrix ($corrMat$) and K (described above) as inputs and gives the *affinity matrix* ($affMat$) as the output. The correlation matrices (*MIC and Cramer*) are square weighted adjacency matrices obtained by applying correlation measures on the Feature Correlation Graphs.

Feature Clustering. To identify relevant clusters in our Feature Dependency Graph, we have used the "Clique Cover Theory" [8]. For our approach of identifying the maximal cliques with respect to the maximum sum of the edge-weights from the undirected edge-weighted Feature Dependency Graphs, we evaluate the sub-graphs satisfying the following properties: (i) Internal homogeneity: Elements belonging to a group have high associations with each other. (ii) Maximality: A maximal clique cannot be further extended by introducing external elements. These properties emphasize the notion of a cluster. Such a cluster is termed as *Clique-Cover* in graph theory which partitions an undirected graph into cliques of various sizes. To explain the use of this approach for constructing our proposed algorithm of finding feature clusters, let us consider the example of a Feature Dependency Graph as shown in Fig. 2.

The example has seven nodes, representing the features of the dataset, and the edge-weight corresponds to the correlation coefficient between the feature pairs. The algorithm initially determines the cliques from the graph and further determines the maximal cliques. It then proceeds to incorporate the edge-weights

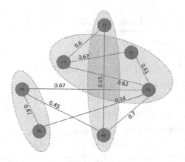

Fig. 2. Identification of cliques covers on a feature dependency graph

of the maximal cliques. The maximal clique with respect to the maximum sum of edge-weight is identified as a cluster. In the graph from Fig. 2 we can see that there exists many cliques such as {3, 6}, {1, 7},{5, 6},{3, 5, 6}. However only five maximal cliques can be identified namely, {3, 4, 6}, {1, 4}, {2, 3, 7}, {3, 5, 6} and {1, 7}. We assign the weight of the maximal clique to be equal to the sum of the weights of the edges in that clique. So the corresponding weight of the 5 maximal cliques is 1.82, 0.65, 1.90, 1.42, and 0.60, respectively. In this case, {2, 3, 7} is the maximal clique with respect to the maximum weight of 1.90. This clique satisfies the properties of "internal homogeneity" and "maximality", because it has strong interconnections and is maximal. This can be termed as the first cluster or the *Clique Cover*. We now remove the clustered nodes and edges from the existing graph by dynamically truncating the affinity matrix and updating the dimensions. Then, the new feature dependency graph contains the remaining four nodes with features F1, F4, F5, F6 respectively. The cluster identification is applied recursively on the remaining subgraph, and it outputs two more clusters {1, 4} and {5, 6}. Therefore, the Clique Cover graph clustering algorithm generates three clusters {2, 3, 7}, {1, 4} and {5, 6} of sizes 3, 2 and 2 respectively. It can be seen that, the *Clique Cover* always creates non-overlapping/exclusive clusters, which is evident from the fact that none of the features can be present in more than one cluster. Moreover, the approach does not require a prior estimation of the number of clusters. The number of clusters and the size of each cluster is determined dynamically from the intrinsic properties of the graph.

Algorithm 2 presents our feature clustering approach. As an input to the algorithm we give the weighted adjacency matrix obtained from the Feature Correlation step. It initializes two output lists; one for storing the cluster node IDs and the other for storing the cluster node labels. Initially, the remaining dimensions are set to the total dimensions of the feature graph. The algorithm proceeds by identifying the threshold coefficient for each node and generates a feature dependency graph. Next, the algorithm determines the cliques, maximal cliques, and the total number of maximal cliques in the Feature Dependency Graph. It then iterates through all of the maximal cliques and identifies the maximal clique having the maximal weight by summing up the edge-weights in

---

Algorithm 2: Unsupervised Feature Clustering w. Clique Cover Theory

---

Procedure : *FeatureClustering*;
Input : Weighted Adjacency Matrix obtained from Feature Correlation
Output : ClusterNodeIds and ClusterNodeLabels
Initialize: ClusterNodeIds ← (); ClusterNodeLabels ← (); remainDim ← totalDim;
Step 1: Identify threshold coefficient
Step 2: Generate a feature dependency graph
Step 3: Determine Cliques Q, Maximal Cliques Q_i and # of Maximal Cliques
Step 4: Determine the weight of all the Maximal Cliques
Step 5: Determine the Maximal Clique with maximum weight and set it as the first cluster or the Clique Cover
Step 6: Update the output with the cluster node Ids and labels
Step 7: Remove the clustered nodes and edges from the feature graph
Step 8: Update the feature graph with remaining dimensions
Step 9: Recursive call to *FeatureClustering* procedure
Step 10: If there is one feature node present, then update the output with the last node

---

the maximal clique. This maximal clique is the first cluster or Clique Cover. It updates the output list with the corresponding node Ids and labels of the first cluster. The algorithm then removes the clustered nodes and edges and updates the feature graph with the remaining dimensions. It recursively calls the *FeatureClustering* procedure to generate more clusters. This way, the algorithm recursively reduces the size of the remaining dimensions and assigns the feature nodes as part of some clusters. The terminating condition for the recursive process is reached when there is a single node. It terminates by updating the output list with node Ids and labels of the last node.

Feature Mapping. In the last step, we map the features from the high dimensional feature space to the *representative features* in the low dimensional space. These features are selected from each of the generated feature clusters. The selection is made using the concepts of graph centrality. Centrality in social networks is an important measure of the influence of a node in the network [7]. In our approach, we have used Eigenvector Centrality to determine the importance of a node in a cluster. It is a globally based centrality measure based on the principle that a node is important if it is linked by other important nodes. Bonacich, in his work [5] has shown that Eigenvector Centrality gives better results when clusters are formed by the determination of maximal cliques. In our approach, the process of determining the Eigenvector Centrality score is carried out for all nodes within each cluster. The maximum score corresponds to the node, which is the most central node in the cluster. The central node is termed as the representative feature.

4   Evaluation

We have evaluated our approach over ten datasets and compared with five of the most prominent unsupervised feature selection methods. We demonstrate that our approach discovers more meaningful feature clusters from complex datasets and gives good results in terms of clustering and classification accuracy. From visualization perspective, we show that by using our approach the visualizations render much less clutter and in turn making high dimensional data much easier and intuitive to explore.

Experimental Setting. We have conducted our experiments in a server running Ubuntu 14.04, with two Intel Xeon X5647@2.93 GHz CPUs (8 logical cores/CPU) and 16G RAM.

Datasets.[1] For the evaluation, we have considered high-dimensional datasets from various categories. The datasets also have different aspects like binary class, multi-class, missing values, and skewed classes. This enables us to perform a stress test in order to compare with existing approaches. For the quantitative evaluation, supervised datasets are selected because the class labels are needed to evaluate the classification and clustering accuracy, and also for the cost-sensitive analysis. Since our approach is unsupervised, we conducted the following steps: 1. we have removed the class labels from the selected datasets, 2. we run our algorithms for feature selection on the unsupervised datasets, 3. the class labels are then appended to the results obtained from each of the feature selection approaches, and 4. the supervised reduced feature sets obtained are then used for quantitative evaluation. Table 1 shows the list of the selected datasets used for evaluation along with the time taken to construct the reduced feature set using our proposed feature selection pipeline.

4.1   Baseline Algorithms

We compare the performance of our proposed Clique-Cover based Unsupervised Feature Selection against the following five baseline algorithms. (1) Laplacian Score for Feature Selection [10], (2) Spectral Feature Selection for Supervised and Unsupervised Learning [23], (3) l2, 1-Norm Regularized Discriminative Feature Selection for Unsupervised Learning (UDFS) [22], (4) Unsupervised Feature Selection Using Nonnegative Spectral Analysis (NDFS) [11]., (5) Unsupervised feature selection for multi-cluster data (MCFS) [6].

Evaluation Metrics. The reduced feature sets obtained from each approach are quantitatively evaluated using these metrics:

- **Evaluation using Classification Accuracy** - The accuracy of the reduced feature sets are evaluated using classifiers: Naive Bayes, Support Vector Machine (SVM), Random Forests and Logistic Regression. K-fold cross validation is used to evaluate the classifiers.

---

[1] Data Repository: https://figshare.com/s/1807247ef2165735465c.

Table 1. Experimental results for selected datasets. Dimensions are the total number of features in the dataset and #Features are the final set of selected features after the application of our feature selection algorithm.

Dataset	Dimensions	Time (in seconds)	#Features
Automobile	25	0.10	9
QSAR Biodegradation	41	0.16	12
Emotions	78	0.97	17
Robot failure	91	1.08	27
Yeast	116	2.42	20
Musk	168	11.61	32
Arrhythmia	280	22.52	44
AirlineTicketPrice	417	43.59	37
GAMETES Genome	1000	111.50	70
Colon	2000	576.27	115

- **Evaluation using Clustering Accuracy** - The accuracy of the reduced feature sets are evaluated using two clustering algorithms: K-means and Expectation Maximization clustering approaches. The Clustering Accuracy metric is used for assessing the clustering quality. The number of clusters is set to the number of classes present in the respective datasets.
- **Evaluation in terms of the redundancy of the Selected Features** - We have used "Representation Entropy" [13] as a metric to evaluate the redundancy of the selected features. Let the eigenvalues of the $d \times d$ covariance matrix of a feature set of size d be λ_j, where $j = 1...d$ and $\tilde{\lambda}_j = \frac{\lambda_j}{\sum_{j=1}^{d} \lambda_j}$ where $0 \leq \tilde{\lambda}_j \leq 1$, then we define *Representation Entropy* as: $H_R = \sum_{j=1}^{d} \tilde{\lambda}_j log \tilde{\lambda}_j$ The Representation Entropy (H_R) measures of the amount of information compression achieved by dimensionality reduction. This is equivalent to the amount of redundancy present in the reduced feature set. The goal of our approach is to have a low value of H_R for the individual clusters but a high H_R for the final reduced feature set, which in turn would indicate that the representative feature set has low information redundancy.
- **Evaluation using ROC Curves for cost-sensitive analysis:** ROC curve is used to check the performance of a classification model. We have used this metric for cost-sensitive analysis. The higher AUC signifies the better performance of the classifier corresponding to relevant features in the dataset. We have considered all the classifiers mentioned above and plotted the ROC curve for each of the reduced feature sets obtained from different approaches.

Because of limited space, we describe the evaluation result only from one experiment. However, the extensive evaluation report using the remaining nine datasets can be found here (https://figshare.com/s/01d10e873bd0896fa30a). Below, we show the performance of our model and the comparisons with the baseline

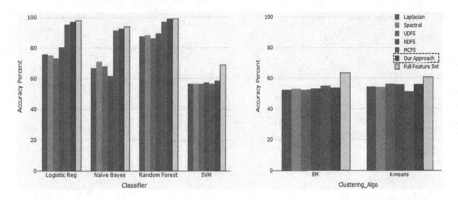

Fig. 3. Classification and clustering accuracy with the Colon Tumor dataset

approaches using the 'Colon Tumor' dataset[2] as it has the highest number of features (2000 features).

The classification and the clustering accuracy are depicted in Fig. 3. From the results, we can conclude that the classification accuracy of the reduced feature space from our proposed approach has shown relatively better results in all the four selected classifiers in comparison with the baseline methods. Regarding clustering accuracy, although the overall clustering accuracy is low as compared to the classification accuracy, the relative performance of our approach is good. The low accuracy is because the number of clusters in the data are different from what we have assigned. As seen in Fig. 3, we have determined the clustering and the classification accuracy using the *Full Feature Set* in order to estimate the relative accuracy of our proposed method.

In Fig. 4, we plot the ROC curves of the reduced feature sets measured using different classifiers which shows that our approach outperforms the selected methods. Whereas, Fig. 5 gives the *Representation Entropy* (H_R) obtained from the reduced feature sets of our approach along with the corresponding values obtained from the baseline methods. The resulting Representation Entropy of our proposed approach is higher, which indicates that the features selected by our method have a relatively low information redundancy rate.

4.2   Performance Measure

The computational complexity is regarded starting after the ingestion and the feature correlation phase. We have determined the computational complexity from the construction of the Complete Feature Graph until we obtain the Representative Feature Vector. The recursive process of determining the feature clusters mainly depends on three steps: identifying the threshold coefficient using K-NN method, maximal clique determination, and finding the weight of each

---

[2] Colon Tumor Data: http://csse.szu.edu.cn/staff/zhuzx/Datasets.html.

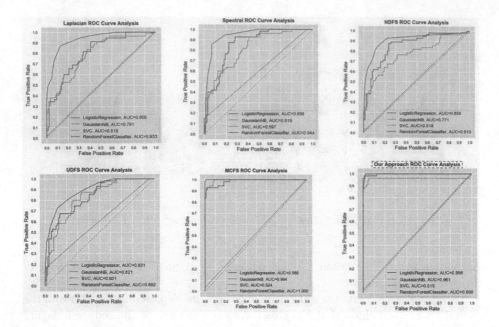

Fig. 4. ROC plots using the Colon Tumor dataset

	Laplacian	Spectral	UDFS	NDFS	MCFS	Our Approach
Rep Entropy	0.91315	0.90626	0.84794	0.7526	0.94620	1.0111

Fig. 5. Representation entropy (Colon Tumor dataset)

maximal clique. In our case, the complexity of identifying the threshold coefficient depends on the number of nodes in the complete feature graph(n) and the value of k (k is the number of nearest neighbors). The complexity is given as $O(kn)$. It has already been proved that the complexity of maximal clique determination is equal to $O(2^{n/3})$, where n is the number of nodes [20]. The complexity of finding the weights of each of the maximal clique depends on the number of edges(e), and is equivalent to $O(e)$. After the feature clusters are determined, the algorithm identifies representative features from each cluster based on the Eigenvector Centrality measure. The complexity of determining Eigenvector Centrality is $O(qE)$, where q is the number of iterations needed before convergence, and E is the number of edges in each cluster. The combined computational complexity for feature clustering and selection can be written as: $[O(kn) + O(2^{n/3}) + (p \times O(e))] + O(qE)$ where n is the total number of features in the feature graph, k is the number of nearest neighbors, p is the number of intermediate maximal cliques obtained, e is the number of edges in each maximal clique, q is the number of iterations required to determine Eigenvector Centrality and E is the number of edges in the cluster. The core complexity of this step is represented by the exponential function to determine maximal cliques in the graph. This indicates that the time complexity to determine maximal cliques increases exponentially with the number of features. To investigate the practical consequences, we have calculated the time taken to process the feature graph to determine the Representative Features. As seen in the Table 1, the time taken increases exponentially with respect to the number of features in the dataset. On analyzing the time taken for processing the features, the run time of the algorithm is found to be $t = 1.38^n$.

We would like to mention that the enumeration of maximal cliques has been proven as an NP-hard combinatorial optimization problem. Over the past decade, several algorithms have been designed to address this issue. However, most of these heuristic algorithms fail for massive graphs. Lately, pruning based exact and parameterized algorithms have been proposed which are able to achieve linear runtime scaling for massive graphs [9,12,17]. For the purpose of determining the maximal cliques in our proposed feature selection pipeline, we have used the *Parallel Maximum Clique Solver*[3] which have implemented the algorithms presented in the work of Rossi et al. [17].

5   Conclusion

In this work, we have presented a novel graph-based clustering algorithm based on the *Clique Cover Theory*. The number of clusters along with their size is determined dynamically using the intrinsic properties of the data without any prior estimation from the user. The approach was also evaluated on several datasets having a varying number of features and properties. The results indicate that our proposed approach can be used in an effective way for selecting important features in an unsupervised manner, thus proving to be an efficient strategy for dimensionality reduction.

To identify meaningful features from high dimensional data sets and to visualize them efficiently we have tested the implementation of our approach with an interactive data exploration tool[4]. Our visualization tool provides two main functionalities: 1. Explore Data Features and 2. Visualize data in the reduced feature space. With the help of this tool, the features are visualized using feature graphs like cluster feature graphs and representative feature graphs. The correlation between features is explored using correlation heatmaps. The data points in the reduced feature space are visualized using standard methods. The reduced dimensional space allows many visualization techniques to demonstrate various characteristics of the data.

With this tool, we have presented an interface for the efficient exploration of large multidimensional data. One limitation of our approach is that we have segregated the datasets into numerical and categorical feature groups and the feature clusters are determined separately for these individual groups. In the future, we plan to extend our approach so that the resulting clusters are a mix of

---

[3] https://github.com/ryanrossi/pmc.

[4] VizExploreTool: http://dbis.rwth-aachen.de/cms/staff/chakrabarti/unsupervised-feature-selection/eval/view.

both the feature groups. We are currently investigating techniques to determine clusters by incorporating correlation measures that determine the relationship between numerical and categorical features. Another interesting direction would be to extend the feature selection to deal with skewed clusters. For example, suppose a dataset has 24 features, and in the clustering phase, 20 features become a part of the first cluster, and the remaining four features are part of the second cluster. Since there are only two clusters, there will be two representative features from each cluster. Thus, the resulting feature set can have very low accuracy. Instead, more than one representative feature for the skewed clusters could be considered.

Acknowledgment. This work was funded by the Deutsche Forschungsgemeinschaft (DFG, German Research Foundation) under Germany's Excellence Strategy – EXC-2023 Internet of Production – 390621612.

References

1. Aggarwal, C.C., Wolf, J.L., Yu, P.S., Procopiuc, C., Park, J.S.: Fast algorithms for projected clustering. ACM SIGMOD Rec. **28**(2), 61–72 (1999)
2. Agrawal, R., Gehrke, J., Gunopulos, D., Raghavan, P.: Automatic subspace clustering of high dimensional data for data mining applications. In: Proceedings ACM SIGMOD Conference, pp. 94–105 (1998)
3. Altman, N.S.: An introduction to kernel and nearest-neighbor nonparametric regression. Am. Stat. **46**(3), 175–185 (1992)
4. Augustson, J.G., Minker, J.: An analysis of some graph theoretical cluster techniques. J. ACM (JACM) **17**(4), 571–588 (1970)
5. Bonacich, P.: Some unique properties of eigenvector centrality. Soc. Netw., 555–564 (2007)
6. Cai, D., Zhang, C., He, X.: Unsupervised feature selection for multi-cluster data. In: Proceedings ACM SIGKDD, pp. 333–342 (2010)
7. Elgazzar, H., Elmaghraby, A.: Evolutionary centrality and maximal cliques in mobile social networks. Int. J. Comput. Sci. Inf. Tech. **10** (2018)
8. Erdös, P., Goodman, A.W., Pósa, L.: The representation of a graph by set intersections. Can. J. Math. **18**, 106–112 (1966)
9. Gramm, J., Guo, J., Hüffner, F., Niedermeier, R.: Data reduction and exact algorithms for clique cover. J. Exp. Algorithmics (JEA) **13**, 2 (2009)
10. He, X., Cai, D., Niyogi, P.: Laplacian score for feature selection. In: Advances in Neural Information Processing Systems, pp. 507–514 (2006)
11. Li, Z., Yang, Y., Liu, J., Zhou, X., Lu, H.: Unsupervised feature selection using nonnegative spectral analysis. In: Proceedings 26th AAAI Conference (2012)
12. Lu, C., Yu, J.X., Wei, H., Zhang, Y.: Finding the maximum clique in massive graphs. PVLDB **10**(11), 1538–1549 (2017)
13. Mitra, P., Murthy, C., Pal, S.K.: Unsupervised feature selection using feature similarity. IEEE Trans. Pattern Anal. Mach. Intell. **24**(3), 301–312 (2002)
14. Paredes, R., Chávez, E.: Using the k-nearest neighbor graph for proximity searching in metric spaces. In: Consens, M., Navarro, G. (eds.) SPIRE 2005. LNCS, vol. 3772, pp. 127–138. Springer, Heidelberg (2005). https://doi.org/10.1007/11575832_14

15. Pavan, M., Pelillo, M.: A new graph-theoretic approach to clustering and segmentation. In: Proceedings IEEE Conference Computer Vision & Pattern Recognition (2003)
16. Robnik-Šikonja, M., Kononenko, I.: Theoretical and empirical analysis of ReliefF and RReliefF. Mach. Learn. **53**(1–2), 23–69 (2003)
17. Rossi, R.A., Gleich, D.F., Gebremedhin, A.H., Patwary, M.M.A.: Fast maximum clique algorithms for large graphs. In: Proceedings WWW, pp. 365–366 (2014)
18. Solorio-Fernández, S., Carrasco-Ochoa, J.A., Martínez-Trinidad, J.F.: A review of unsupervised feature selection methods. Artif. Intell. Rev. **53**(2), 907–948 (2019). https://doi.org/10.1007/s10462-019-09682-y
19. Speed, T.: A correlation for the 21st century. Science **334**(6062), 1502–1503 (2011)
20. Tarjan, R.E., Trojanowski, A.E.: Finding a maximum independent set. SIAM J. Comput. **6**(3), 537–546 (1977)
21. Wright, M.N., Ziegler, A.: ranger: A fast implementation of random forests for high dimensional data in C++ and R. arXiv preprint arXiv:1508.04409 (2015)
22. Yang, Y., Shen, H.T., Ma, Z., Huang, Z., Zhou, X.: L2, 1-norm regularized discriminative feature selection for unsupervised. In: Proceedings IJCAI (2011)
23. Zhao, Z., Liu, H.: Spectral feature selection for supervised and unsupervised learning. In: Proceedings International Conference on Machine Learning, pp. 1151–1157. ACM (2007)

MuLOT: Multi-level Optimization of the Canonical Polyadic Tensor Decomposition at Large-Scale

Annabelle Gillet[(✉)], Éric Leclercq, and Nadine Cullot

LIB EA 7534 Univ. Bourgogne Franche Comté, Dijon, France
annabelle.gillet@depinfo.u-bourgogne.fr,
{eric.leclercq,nadine.cullot}@u-bourgogne.fr

Abstract. Tensors are used in a wide range of analytics tools and as intermediary data structures in machine learning pipelines. Implementations of tensor decompositions at large-scale often select only a specific type of optimization, and neglect the possibility of combining different types of optimizations. Therefore, they do not include all the improvements available, and are less effective than what they could be. We propose an algorithm that uses both dense and sparse data structures and that leverages coarse and fine grained optimizations in addition to incremental computations in order to achieve large scale CP (CANDE-COMP/PARAFAC) tensor decomposition. We also provide an implementation in Scala using Spark, MuLOT, that outperforms the baseline of large-scale CP decomposition libraries by several orders of magnitude, and run experiments to show its large-scale capability. We also study a typical use case of CP decomposition on social network data.

Keywords: Tensor decomposition · Data mining · Multi-dimensional analytics

1 Introduction

Tensors are powerful mathematical objects, which bring capabilities to model multi-dimensional data [8]. They are used in multiple analytics frameworks, such as Tensorflow [1], PyTorch [23], Theano [3], TensorLy [18], where their ability to represent various models is a great advantage. Furthermore, associated with powerful decompositions, they can be used to discover the hidden value of Big Data. Tensor decompositions are used for various purposes such as dimensionality reduction, noise elimination, identification of latent factors, pattern discovery, ranking, recommendation and data completion. They are applied in a wide range of applications, including genomics [14], analysis of health records [29], graph mining [28] and complex networks analysis [4,19]. Papalexakis et al. in [21] review major usages of tensor decompositions in data mining applications.

Most of tensor libraries that include decompositions work with tensors of limited size, and do not consider the large-scale challenge. However, as tensors

© Springer Nature Switzerland AG 2021
L. Bellatreche et al. (Eds.): ADBIS 2021, LNCS 12843, pp. 198–212, 2021.
https://doi.org/10.1007/978-3-030-82472-3_15

model multi-dimensional data, their global size varies exponentially depending on the number and size of their dimensions, making them sensitive to large-scale issues. Some intermediate structures needed in the algorithms result in data explosion, such as the Khatri-Rao product in the canonical polyadic decomposition [15]. Thus, analyzing Big Data with tensors requires optimization techniques and suitable implementations, able to scale up. These optimizations are directed toward different computational aspects, such as the memory consumption, the execution time or the scaling capabilities, and can follow different principles, such as coarse grained optimizations, fine grained optimizations or incremental computations.

In this article we focus on the canonical polyadic decomposition (also known as CANDECOMP/PARAFAC or CP decomposition) that allows to factorize a tensor into smaller and more usable sets of vectors [17], and which is largely adopted in exploratory analyzes. Our contribution is twofold: 1) we propose an optimized algorithm to achieve large scale CP decomposition, that uses dense or sparse data structures depending on what suits best each step, and that leverages incremental computation, coarse and fine grained optimizations to improve every computation in the algorithm; and 2) we provide an implementation in Scala using Spark that outperforms the state of the art of large-scale tensor CP decomposition libraries. The implementation is open source and available on Github[1], along with experimental evaluations to validate its efficiency especially at large scale.

The rest of the article is organized as follows: Sect. 2 presents an overview of tensors including the CP decomposition, Sect. 3 introduces a state of the art of tensor manipulation libraries, Sect. 4 describes our scalable and optimized algorithm, Sect. 5 details the experiments we ran to compare our algorithm to other large-scale CP decomposition libraries, Sect. 6 presents a study on real data performed with our algorithm and finally Sect. 7 concludes.

2   Overview of Tensors and CP Decomposition

Tensors are general abstract mathematical objects which can be considered according to various points of view such as a multi-linear application, or as the generalization of matrices to multiple dimensions. We will use the definition of a tensor as an element of the set of the functions from the product of N sets $I_j, j = 1, \ldots, N$ to $\mathbb{R} : \mathcal{X} \in \mathbb{R}^{I_1 \times I_2 \times \cdots \times I_N}$, where N is the number of dimensions of the tensor or its order or its mode. Table 1 summarizes the notations used in this article.

Tensor operations, by analogy with operations on matrices and vectors, are multiplications, transpositions, unfolding or matricizations and factorizations (also named decompositions) [8,17]. The reader can consult these references for an overview of the major operators. We only highlight the most significant operators on tensors which are used in our algorithm. The mode-n matricization of a tensor $\mathcal{X} \in \mathbb{R}^{I_1 \times I_2 \times \cdots \times I_N}$ noted $\mathcal{X}_{(n)}$ produces a matrix $\mathbf{M} \in \mathbb{R}^{I_n \times \Pi_{j \neq n} I_j}$.

---

[1] https://github.com/AnnabelleGillet/MuLOT.

The Hadamard product of two matrices having the same size (i.e., $I \times J$) noted $\mathbf{A} \circledast \mathbf{B}$ is the elementwise matrix product. The Kronecker product between a matrix $\mathbf{A} \in \mathbb{R}^{I \times J}$ and a matrix $\mathbf{B} \in \mathbb{R}^{K \times L}$ noted $\mathbf{A} \otimes \mathbf{B}$ gives a matrix $\mathbf{C} \in \mathbb{R}^{(IK) \times (JL)}$, where each element of $\mathbf{A}$ is multiplied by $\mathbf{B}$. The Khatri-Rao product of two matrices having the same number of columns noted $\mathbf{A} \odot \mathbf{B}$ is a columnwise Kronecker product.

Table 1. Symbols and operators used

Symbol	Definition	Symbol	Definition
$\mathcal{X}$	A tensor	$\circ$	Outer product
$\mathcal{X}_{(n)}$	Matricization of a tensor $\mathcal{X}$ on mode-n	$\otimes$	Kronecker product
		$\circledast$	Hadamard product
a	A scalar	$\oslash$	Hadamard division
$\mathbf{v}$	A column vector	$\odot$	Khatri-Rao product
$\mathbf{M}$	A matrix	$\dagger$	Pseudo inverse

The canonical polyadic decomposition allows to factorize a tensor into smaller and more exploitable sets of vectors [13,25]. Given a N-order tensor $\mathcal{X} \in \mathbb{R}^{I_1 \times I_2 \times \cdots \times I_N}$ and a rank $R \in \mathbb{N}$, the CP decomposition factorizes the tensor $\mathcal{X}$ into N column-normalized factor matrices $\mathbf{A}^{(i)} \in \mathbb{R}^{I_i \times R}$ for $i = 1, \ldots, N$ with their scaling factors $\lambda \in \mathbb{R}^R$ as follows:

$$\mathcal{X} \simeq [\![\lambda, \mathbf{A}^{(1)}, \mathbf{A}^{(2)}, \ldots, \mathbf{A}^{(N)}]\!] = \sum_{r=1}^{R} \lambda_r a_r^{(1)} \circ a_r^{(2)} \circ \cdots \circ a_r^{(N)}$$

where $a_r^{(i)}$ are columns of $\mathbf{A}^{(i)}$.

Algorithm 1. CP-ALS

Require: Tensor $\mathcal{X} \in \mathbb{R}^{I_1 \times I_2 \times \cdots \times I_N}$ and target rank R
1: Initialize $\mathbf{A}^{(1)}, \ldots, \mathbf{A}^{(N)}$, with $\mathbf{A}^{(n)} \in \mathbb{R}^{I_n \times R}$
2: **repeat**
3:    **for** $n = 1, \ldots, N$ **do**
4:        $\mathbf{V} \leftarrow \mathbf{A}^{(1)T} \mathbf{A}^{(1)} \circledast \cdots \circledast \mathbf{A}^{(n-1)T} \mathbf{A}^{(n-1)} \circledast \mathbf{A}^{(n+1)T} \mathbf{A}^{(n+1)} \circledast \cdots \circledast \mathbf{A}^{(N)T} \mathbf{A}^{(N)}$
5:        $\mathbf{A}^{(n)} \leftarrow \mathcal{X}_{(n)} (\mathbf{A}^{(N)} \odot \cdots \odot \mathbf{A}^{(n+1)} \odot \mathbf{A}^{(n-1)} \odot \cdots \odot \mathbf{A}^{(1)}) \mathbf{V}^\dagger$
6:        normalize columns of $\mathbf{A}^{(n)}$
7:        $\lambda \leftarrow$ norms of $\mathbf{A}^{(n)}$
8:    **end for**
9: **until** < convergence >

Several algorithms have been proposed to compute the CP decomposition [26], we focus on the alternating least squares (ALS) one, described above in Algorithm 1. The Matricized Tensor Times Khatri-Rao Product (MTTKRP, line 5 of the Algorithm 1) is often the target of optimizations, because it involves the tensor matricized of size $\mathbb{R}^{I_n \times J}$, with $J = \Pi_{j \neq n} I_j$, as well as the result of the Khatri-Rao product of size $\mathbb{R}^{J \times R}$. It is thus computationally demanding and uses a lot of memory to store the dense temporary matrix resulting of the Khatri-Rao product [24].

3   State of the Art

Several tensor libraries have been proposed. They can be classified according to their capability of handling large tensors or not.

rTensor (http://jamesyili.github.io/rTensor/) provides users with standard operators to manipulate tensors in R language including tensor decompositions, but does not support sparse tensors. Tensor Algebra Compiler (TACO) provides optimized tensor operators in C++ [16]. High-Performance Tensor Transpose [27] is a C++ library only for tensor transpositions, thus it lacks lots of useful operators. Tensor libraries for MATLAB, such as TensorToolbox (https://www.tensortoolbox.org/) or MATLAB Tensor Tools (MTT, https://github.com/andrewssobral/mtt), usually focus on operators including tensor decompositions with optimization on CPU or GPU. TensorLy [18], written in Python, allows to switch between tensor libraries back-ends such as TensorFlow or PyTorch. All of these libraries do not take into account large tensors, which cannot fit in memory.

On the other hand, some implementations focus on performing decompositions on large-scale tensors in a distributed setting. HaTen2 [15] is a Hadoop implementation of the CP and Tucker decompositions using the map-reduce paradigm. It was later improved with BigTensor [22]. SamBaTen [12] proposes an incremental CP decomposition for evolving tensors. The authors developed a Matlab and a Spark implementations. Gudibanda et al. in [11] developed a CP decomposition for coupled tensors using Spark (i.e., different tensors having a dimension in common). ParCube [20] is a parallel Matlab implementation of the CP decomposition. CSTF [5] is based on Spark and proposes a distributed CP decomposition.

As a conclusion, the study of the state of the art shows some limitations of the proposed solutions. A majority of frameworks are limited to 3 or 4 dimensions which is a drawback for analyzing large-scale, real and complex data. They focus on a specific type of optimization, and use only sparse structures to satisfy the sparsity of large tensors. This is a bottleneck to performance, as they do not consider all the characteristics of the algorithm (i.e., the factor matrices are dense). Furthermore, they are not really data centric, as they need an input only with integer indexes, for dimensions and for values of dimensions. Thus it reduces greatly the user-friendliness as the mapping between real values (e.g., user name or timestamp) and indexes has to be supported by the user. The Hadoop implementations need a particular input format, thus necessitate data transformations to execute the decomposition and to interpret the results, leading to laborious prerequisites and increasing the risk of mistakes when working with the results. Moreover, not all of the implementations are open-source, some only give the binary code.

4   Distributed, Scalable and Optimized ALS for Apache Spark

Optimizing the CP ALS tensor decomposition induces several technical challenges, that gain importance proportionally to the size of the data. Thus, to compute the decomposition at large scale, several issues have to be resolved.

First, the **data explosion of the MTTKRP** is a serious computational bottleneck (line 5 of Algorithm 1), that can overflow memory, and prevent to work with large tensors, even if they are extremely sparse. Indeed, the matrix produced by the Khatri-Rao has $J \times R$ non-zero elements, with $J = \Pi_{j \neq n} I_j$, for an input tensor of size $\mathbb{R}^{I_1 \times I_2 \times \cdots \times I_N}$. We propose to reorder carefully this operation, in order to avoid the data explosion and to improve significantly the execution time (see Algorithm 3).

The main operations in the ALS algorithm, i.e., the update of the factor matrices, **are not themselves parallelizable** (lines 4 and 5 of Algorithm 1). In such a situation, it is profitable to think of other methods to take advantage of parallelism, that could be applied on fine grained operations. For example, leveraging parallelism for matrices multiplication is an optimization that can be applied in many situations. This also eases the reuse of such optimizations, without expecting specific characteristics from the algorithm (see Sect. 4.2).

The **nature of data structures used in the CP decomposition are mixed**: tensors are often sparse, while factor matrices are dense. Their needs to be efficiently implemented diverge, so rather than sticking globally to sparse data structures to match the sparsity of tensors, each structure should take advantage of their particularities to improve the whole execution (see Sect. 4.1). To the best of our knowledge, this strategy has not been explored by others.

The **stopping criterion** can also be a bottleneck. In distributed implementations of the CP ALS, the main solutions used to stop the algorithm are to wait for a fixed number of iterations, or to compute the Frobenius norm on the difference between the input tensor and the tensor reconstructed from the factor matrices. The first solution severely lacks in precision, and the second is computationally demanding as it involves outer products between all the factor matrices. However, an other option is available to check the convergence, and consists in measuring the similarity of the factor matrices between two iterations, evoked in [8,17]. It is a very efficient solution at large-scale, as it merges precision and light computations (see Sect. 4.3).

Finally, the implementation should facilitate the **data loading**, and avoid data transformations only needed to fit the expected input of the algorithm. It should also produce easily interpretable results, and minimize the risk of errors induced by laborious data manipulations (see Sect. 4.4). The study of the state of the art of tensor libraries shows that tensors are often used as multi dimensional arrays, that are manipulated through their indexes, even if they represent real world data. The mapping between indexes and values is delegated to the user, although being an error-prone step. As it is a common task, it should be handled by the library.

To tackle these challenges, we leverage three optimization principles to develop an efficient decomposition: coarse grained optimization, fine grained optimization, and incremental computation. The coarse grained one relies on specific data structures and capabilities of Spark to efficiently distribute operations. The incremental computation is used to avoid to compute the whole Hadamard product at each iteration. The fine grained optimization is applied on the MTTKRP to reduce the storage of large amount of data and costly computations. For this, we have extended Spark's matrices with the operations needed for the CP decomposition. In addition, we choose to use an adapted converging criteria, efficient at large-scale. For the implementation of the algorithm, we take a data centric point of view to facilitate the loading of data and the interpretation of the results. Our CP decomposition implementation is thus able to process tensors with billions of elements (i.e., non zero entries) on a mid-range workstation, and small and medium size tensors can be processed in a short time on a low-end personal computer.

4.1 Distributed and Scalable Matrix Data Structures

A simple but **efficient sparse matrix storage structure** is COO (COOrdinate storage) [2,10]. The `CoordinateMatrix`, available in the mllib package of Spark [6], is one of those structures, that stores only the coordinates and the value of each existing element in a RDD (Resilient Distributed Datasets). **It is well suited to process sparse matrices.**

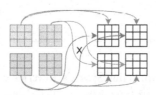

Fig. 1. Blocks mapping for a multiplication between two `BlockMatrix`

Another useful structure is the `BlockMatrix`. It is composed of multiple blocks containing each a fragment of the global matrix. Operations can be parallelized by executing it on each sub-matrix. For binary operations such as multiplication, only blocks from each `BlockMatrix` that will be associated are sent to each other, and the result is then aggregated if needed (see Fig. 1). **It is thus an efficient structure for dense matrices**, and allows distributed computations to process all blocks.

Unfortunately, only some basic operations are available for `BlockMatrix`, such as multiplication or addition. The more complex ones, such as the

Hadamard and Khatri-Rao products, are missing. We have extended Spark `BlockMatrix` with more advanced operations, that keep the coarse grained optimization logic of the multiplication. We also added new operations, that involve `BlockMatrix` and `CoordinateMatrix` to take advantage of the both structures for our optimized MTTKRP (see below).

4.2 Mixing Three Principles of Optimization

Tensors have generally a high level of sparsity. In the CP decomposition, they only appear under their matricized form, thus they are naturally manipulated as `CoordinateMatrix` in our implementation. On the other hand, the factor matrices $\mathbf{A}$ of the CP decomposition are dense, because they hold information for each value of each dimension. They greatly benefit from the capabilities of the extended `BlockMatrix` we developed. By using the most suitable structure for each part of the algorithm, we leverage specific optimizations that can speed up the whole algorithm.

Algorithm 2. CP-ALS adapted to Spark

Require: Tensor $\mathcal{X} \in \mathbb{R}^{I_1 \times I_2 \times \cdots \times I_N}$ and target rank R
1: Initialize $\mathbf{A}^{(1)}, \ldots, \mathbf{A}^{(N)}$, with $\mathbf{A}^{(n)} \in \mathbb{R}^{I_n \times R}$
2: $\mathbf{V} \leftarrow \mathbf{A}^{(1)T} \mathbf{A}^{(1)} \circledast \cdots \circledast \mathbf{A}^{(N)T} \mathbf{A}^{(N)}$
3: **repeat**
4:   **for** $n = 1, \ldots, N$ **do**
5:     $\mathbf{V} \leftarrow \mathbf{V} \oslash \mathbf{A}^{(n)T} \mathbf{A}^{(n)}$
6:     $\mathbf{A}^{(n)} \leftarrow MTTKRP(\mathcal{X}_{(n)}, (\mathbf{A}^{(N)}, \ldots, \mathbf{A}^{(n+1)}, \mathbf{A}^{(n-1)}, \ldots, \mathbf{A}^{(1)}))\mathbf{V}^{\dagger}$
7:     $\mathbf{V} \leftarrow \mathbf{V} \circledast \mathbf{A}^{(n)T} \mathbf{A}^{(n)}$
8:     normalize columns of $\mathbf{A}^{(n)}$
9:     $\lambda \leftarrow$ norms of $\mathbf{A}^{(n)}$
10:   **end for**
11: **until** $<$ convergence $>$

Besides to using and improving Spark's matrices according to the specificities of data, we also have introduced fine grained optimization and incremental computing into the algorithm to avoid costly operations in terms of memory and execution time. Those improvements are synthesized in Algorithm 2 and explained below.

First, to avoid computing $\mathbf{V}$ completely at each iteration for each dimension, we propose to do it incrementally. Before iterating, we calculate the Hadamard product for all $\mathbf{A}$ (line 2 of the Algorithm 2). At the beginning of the iteration, $\mathbf{A}^{(n)T} \mathbf{A}^{(n)}$ is element-wise divided from $\mathbf{V}$, giving the expected result at this step (line 5 of the Algorithm 2). At the end of the iteration, the Hadamard product between the new $\mathbf{A}^{(n)T} \mathbf{A}^{(n)}$ and $\mathbf{V}$ prepares $\mathbf{V}$ for the next iteration (line 7 of the Algorithm 2).

The MTTKRP part (line 6 of the Algorithm 2) is sensitive to improvement, as stated in Sect. 2. Indeed, by focusing on the result rather than on the operation, it can be easily reordered. For example, if we multiply a 3-order tensor matricized on dimension 1 with the result of $\mathbf{A}^{(3)} \odot \mathbf{A}^{(2)}$, we can notice that in the result, the indexes of the dimensions in the tensor $\mathcal{X}$ correspond directly to those in the matrices $\mathbf{A}^{(3)}$ and $\mathbf{A}^{(2)}$. This behaviour is represented below—with notation shortcut $B_i = \mathbf{A}^{(2)}(i, 1)$ and $C_i = \mathbf{A}^{(3)}(i, 1)$—in an example simplified with only one rank:

$$
\begin{bmatrix} a_1b_1c_1 & a_1b_2c_1 & a_1b_1c_2 & a_1b_2c_2 \\ a_2b_1c_1 & a_2b_2c_1 & a_2b_1c_2 & a_2b_2c_2 \end{bmatrix} \times \begin{bmatrix} B_1C_1 \\ B_2C_1 \\ B_1C_2 \\ B_2C_2 \end{bmatrix}
$$

$$
= \begin{bmatrix} a_1b_1c_1.B_1C_1 + a_1b_2c_1.B_2C_1 + a_1b_1c_2.B_1C_2 + a_1b_2c_2.B_2C_2 \\ a_2b_1c_1.B_1C_1 + a_2b_2c_1.B_2C_1 + a_2b_1c_2.B_1C_2 + a_2b_2c_2.B_2C_2 \end{bmatrix}
$$

Thus, rather than computing the full Khatri-Rao product and performing the multiplication with the matricized tensor, we apply a fine grained optimization that takes advantage of the mapping of indexes, and that anticipates the construction of the final matrix. For each entry of the `CoordinateMatrix` of the matricized tensor (i.e., all non-zero values), we find in each factor matrix $\mathbf{A}$ which element will be used, and compute elements of the final matrix (Algorithm 3).

Algorithm 3. Detail of the MTTKRP

Require: The index of the factor matrix n, the matricized tensor $\mathcal{X}_{(n)} \in \mathbb{R}^{I_n \times J}$ with
$\quad J = \mathit{\Pi}_{j \neq n} I_j$ and $\mathbf{A}^{(1)}, \ldots, \mathbf{A}^{(n-1)}, \mathbf{A}^{(n+1)}, \ldots, \mathbf{A}^{(N)}$, with $\mathbf{A}^{(i)} \in \mathbb{R}^{I_i \times R}$
1: Initialize $\mathbf{A}^{(n)}$ at 0, with $\mathbf{A}^{(n)} \subset \mathbb{R}^{I_n \times R}$
2: **for each** (x, y, v) in $\mathcal{X}_{(n)}$ with x, y the coordinates and v the value **do**
3:     **for** $r = 1, \ldots, R$ **do**
4:        $value \leftarrow v$
5:        **for each** $\mathbf{A}^{(i)}$ with $i \neq n$ **do**
6:           $c \leftarrow$ extract $\mathbf{A}^{(i)}$ coordinate from y
7:           $value \leftarrow value \times \mathbf{A}^{(i)}(c, r)$
8:        **end for**
9:        $\mathbf{A}^{(n)}(x, r) \leftarrow \mathbf{A}^{(n)}(x, r) + value$
10:    **end for**
11: **end for**

4.3 Stopping Criterion

To evaluate the convergence of the algorithm and when it can be stopped, a majority of CP decomposition implementations uses the Frobenius norm on the difference between the original tensor and the reconstructed tensor from the factor matrices. However, at large-scale the reconstruction of the tensor from the factor matrices is an expensive computation, even more than the naive MTTKRP. Waiting for a predetermined number of iterations is not very effective to avoid unnecessary iterations. Thus, other stopping criteria such as the evaluation of the difference between the factor matrices with those of the previous iteration [8,17] are much more interesting, as they work on smaller chunks of data. To this end, we use the Factor Match Score (FMS) [7] to measure the difference between factor matrices of the current iteration ($[\![\lambda, \mathbf{A}^{(1)}, \mathbf{A}^{(2)}, \ldots, \mathbf{A}^{(N)}]\!]$) and those of the previous iteration ($[\![\hat{\lambda}, \hat{\mathbf{A}}^{(1)}, \hat{\mathbf{A}}^{(2)}, \ldots, \hat{\mathbf{A}}^{(N)}]\!]$). The FMS is defined as follows:

$$FMS = \frac{1}{R} \sum_{r=1}^{R} \left(1 - \frac{\xi - \hat{\xi}}{max(\xi, \hat{\xi})} \right) \prod_{n=1}^{N} \frac{a_r^{(n)T} \hat{a}_r^{(n)}}{\|a_r^{(n)}\| . \|\hat{a}_r^{(n)}\|}$$

where $\xi = \lambda_r \prod_{n=1}^{N} \|a_r^{(n)}\|$ and $\hat{\xi} = \hat{\lambda}_r \prod_{n=1}^{N} \|\hat{a}_r^{(n)}\|$.

4.4   Data Centric Implementation

Our implementation of the CP decomposition, in addition to being able to run with any number of dimensions, is data centric: it takes a Spark `DataFrame` as input to execute the CP directly on real data. Thus, it benefits from Spark capabilities to retrieve data directly from various datasources.

A specific column of the `DataFrame` contains the values of the tensor and all the other columns contain the values for each dimension. The CP operators returns a map associating the original names of the dimensions to a new `DataFrame` with three columns for each dimension: the dimension's values, the rank, and the value computed by the CP decomposition. By using `DataFrame` as input, we allow the use of any type as dimensions' values. For example, users could create a `DataFrame` with four columns: username, hashtag, time and value, with username and hashtag being of type `String` in order to easily interpret the decomposition result. This avoids having to handle an intermediate data structure containing the mapping between indexes and real values, and thus reduces the risk of mistakes when transforming data.

5   Experiments

To validate our algorithm, we have run experiments on tensors produced by varying the size of dimensions and the sparsity, on a Dell PowerEdge R740 server (Intel(R) Xeon(R) Silver 4210 CPU @ 2.20 GHz, 20 cores, 256 GB RAM). We compare our execution time to those of the baseline of distributed CP tensor decomposition libraries available: HaTen2 [15], BigTensor [22], SamBaTen [12] and CSTF [5]. Hadoop 2.6.0 was used to execute HaTen and BigTensor. We also study the scalability of MuLOT by varying the number of cores used by Spark.

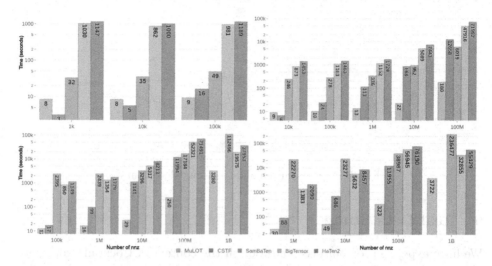

Fig. 2. Execution time for tensors with 3 dimensions of size 100 (top-left), 1 000 (top-right), 10 000 (bottom-left) and 100 000 (bottom-right). CSTF produces an Out Of Memory exception for tensors with 1B elements

Tensors were created randomly with 3 dimensions of the same size, from 100 to 100k. The sparsity ranges from 10^{-1} to 10^{-9}, and tensors were created only if the number of non-zero elements is superior to $3 \times size$ and inferior or equal to 1B (with dimensions of size 100 and 1 000, tensors can only have respectively 10^6 and 10^9 non-zero elements at most, with a sparsity up to 10^{-1} they cannot reach 1B elements, but respectively 10^5 and 10^8 non-zero elements). We have run the CP decomposition for 5 iterations, and have measured the execution time. Results are shown in Fig. 2. The source code of the experiments and the tool used to create tensors are available at https://github.com/AnnabelleGillet/MuLOT/tree/main/experiments.

Our implementation clearly outperforms the state of the art, with speed-up reaching several order of magnitude. CSTF keeps up concerning the execution time of small tensors, but is no match for large tensors, and cannot compute the decomposition for tensors with 1B elements. Execution times of MuLOT are nearly linear following the number of non-zero elements. The optimization techniques applied show efficient results even for very large tensors of billion elements, with a maximum execution time for a 3-order tensor with dimensions of size 100k of 62 min, while the closest, BigTensor, takes 547 min. It also does not induce a high overhead for small tensors, as the decomposition on those with dimensions of size 100 takes less than 10 s.

We also studied the scalability of our algorithm (Fig. 3). We measured the speed-up depending on the number of cores used by Spark. Our algorithm shows a sub-linear scalability, but without a big gap. The scalability is an important property for large-scale computations.

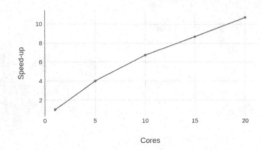

Fig. 3. Near-linear scalability of our algorithm

6   Real Data Study

We have experimented our decomposition in the context of Cocktail[2], an inter-disciplinary research project aiming to study trends and weak signals in discourses about food and health on Twitter. In order to test our decomposition on real data, we focus on french tweets revolving around COVID-19 vaccines, harvested with Hydre, a high performance plateforme to collect, store and analyze tweets [9]. The corpus contains 9 millions of tweets from the period of November 18th 2020 to January 26th 2021.

We would like to study the communication patterns in our corpus. To this end, we have built a 3-order tensor, with a dimension representing the users, another the hashtags and the last one the time (with a week granularity). For each user, we kept only the hashtags that he had used at least five times on the whole period. The size of the tensor is $10340 \times 5469 \times 80$, with 135k non-zero elements. We have run the CP decomposition with 20 ranks.

This decomposition allowed us to discover meaningful insights on our data, some of the most interesting ranks have been represented in Fig. 4 (the accounts have been anonymised). We have a background discourse talking about lockdown and curfew, with some hashtags related to media and the French Prime Minister. It corresponds to the major actuality subjects being discussed around the vaccines.

It also reveals more subject-oriented patterns, with one being anti-Blanquer (the French Minister of Education), where accounts that seem to belong to high-school teachers use strong hashtags against the Minister (the translation of some of the hashtags are: Blanquer lies, Blanquer quits, ghost protocol, the protocol refers to the health protocol in french schools). We can identify in this pattern a strong movement of disagreement, with teachers and parents worrying about the efficiency and the applicability of the measures took to allow schools to stay open during the pandemic.

Another pattern appears to be anti-government, with some signs of conspiracy. They use hashtags such as health dictatorship, great reset, deep state corruption, wake up, we are the people, disobey, etc. Indeed, the pandemic inspired

---

[2] https://projet-cocktail.fr/.

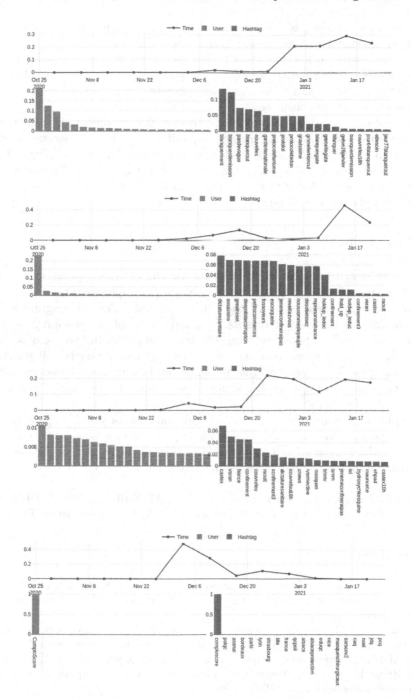

Fig. 4. Communication patterns in the vaccine corpus (from top to bottom): the anti-Blanquer, the conspirators/anti-government, the background speech, and a bot to measure conspiracy score of tweets

a rise in doubt and opposition to some decisions of the government to handle the situation, that sometimes lead to conspiracy theories.

It is interesting to see that the CP decomposition is able to highlight some isolated patterns. With this capability, we identify a bot in our corpus, that quotes tweets that it judges as conspiracy-oriented, and gives them a score to measure the degree of conspiracy.

The CP decomposition is well-suited to real case studies. It is a great tool for our project, as it shows promising capabilities to detect patterns in data along tensor dimensions, with a good execution time. The results given by the decomposition can be easily interpreted and visualized: they can be shared with researchers in social science to specify the meaning of each rank, and thus giving valuable insights on the corpus.

7   Conclusion

We have proposed an optimized algorithm for the CP decomposition at large-scale. We have validated this algorithm with a Spark implementation, and shows that it outperforms the state of the art by several orders of magnitude. We also put data at the core of tensors, by taking care of the mapping between indexes and values without involving the user, thus allowing to focus on data and analyses. Through experiments, we proved that our library is well-suited for small to large-scale tensors, and that it can be used to run the CP decomposition on low-end computers for small and medium tensors, hence making possible a wide range of use cases.

We plan to continue our work on tensor decompositions by 1) exploring their use in social networks analyzes; 2) developing other tensor decompositions such as Tucker, HOSVD or DEDICOM; and 3) studying the impact of the choice of the norm for the scaling of the factor matrices.

Acknowledgments. This work is supported by ISITE-BFC (ANR-15-IDEX-0003) coordinated by G. Brachotte, CIMEOS Laboratory (EA 4177), University of Burgundy.

References

1. Abadi, M., et al.: TensorFlow: a system for large-scale machine learning. In: 12th USENIX Symposium on Operating Systems Design and Implementation, pp. 265–283 (2016)
2. Ahmed, N., Mateev, N., Pingali, K., Stodghill, P.: A framework for sparse matrix code synthesis from high-level specifications. In: Proceedings of the 2000 ACM/IEEE Conference on Supercomputing, SC 2000, pp. 58–58. IEEE (2000)
3. Al-Rfou, R., et al.: Theano: a Python framework for fast computation of mathematical expressions. arXiv:1605.02688 (2016)
4. Araujo, M., et al.: Com2: fast automatic discovery of temporal ('Comet') communities. In: Tseng, V.S., Ho, T.B., Zhou, Z.-H., Chen, A.L.P., Kao, H.-Y. (eds.) PAKDD 2014. LNCS (LNAI), vol. 8444, pp. 271–283. Springer, Cham (2014). https://doi.org/10.1007/978-3-319-06605-9_23

5. Blanco, Z., Liu, B., Dehnavi, M.M.: CSTF: large-scale sparse tensor factorizations on distributed platforms. In: Proceedings of the 47th International Conference on Parallel Processing, pp. 1–10 (2018)
6. Bosagh Zadeh, R., et al.: Matrix computations and optimization in apache spark. In: Proceedings of the 22nd ACM SIGKDD International Conference on Knowledge Discovery and Data Mining, pp. 31–38 (2016)
7. Chi, E.C., Kolda, T.G.: On tensors, sparsity, and nonnegative factorizations. SIAM J. Matrix Anal. Appl. **33**(4), 1272–1299 (2012)
8. Cichocki, A., Zdunek, R., Phan, A.H., Amari, S.: Nonnegative Matrix and Tensor Factorizations: Applications to Exploratory Multi-way Data Analysis and Blind Source Separation. Wiley (2009)
9. Gillet, A., Leclercq, É., Cullot, N.: Lambda+, the renewal of the lambda architecture: category theory to the rescue (to be published). In: Conference on Advanced Information Systems Engineering (CAiSE), pp. 1–15 (2021)
10. Goharian, N., Jain, A., Sun, Q.: Comparative analysis of sparse matrix algorithms for information retrieval. Computer **2**, 0–4 (2003)
11. Gudibanda, A., Henretty, T., Baskaran, M., Ezick, J., Lethin, R.: All-at-once decomposition of coupled billion-scale tensors in apache spark. In: High Performance Extreme Computing Conference, pp. 1–8. IEEE (2018)
12. Gujral, E., Pasricha, R., Papalexakis, E.E.: SamBaTen: sampling-based batch incremental tensor decomposition. In: International Conference on Data Mining, pp. 387–395. SIAM (2018)
13. Harshman, R.A., et al.: Foundations of the PARAFAC procedure: models and conditions for an "explanatory" multimodal factor analysis (1970)
14. Hore, V., et al.: Tensor decomposition for multiple-tissue gene expression experiments. Nat. Genet. **48**(9), 1094–1100 (2016)
15. Jeon, I., Papalexakis, E.E., Kang, U., Faloutsos, C.: Haten2: billion-scale tensor decompositions. In: International Conference on Data Engineering, pp. 1047–1058. IEEE (2015)
16. Kjolstad, F., Kamil, S., Chou, S., Lugato, D., Amarasinghe, S.: The tensor algebra compiler. In: OOPSLA, pp. 1–29 (2017)
17. Kolda, T.G., Bader, B.W.: Tensor decompositions and applications. SIAM Rev. **51**(3), 455–500 (2009)
18. Kossaifi, J., Panagakis, Y., Anandkumar, A., Pantic, M.: TensorLy: tensor learning in Python. J. Mach. Learn. Res. **20**(1), 925–930 (2019)
19. Papalexakis, E.E., Akoglu, L., Ience, D.: Do more views of a graph help? Community detection and clustering in multi-graphs. In: International Conference on Information Fusion, pp. 899–905. IEEE (2013)
20. Papalexakis, E.E., Faloutsos, C., Sidiropoulos, N.D.: ParCube: sparse parallelizable CANDECOMP-PARAFAC tensor decomposition. ACM Trans. Knowl. Discov. From Data (TKDD) **10**(1), 1–25 (2015)
21. Papalexakis, E.E., Faloutsos, C., Sidiropoulos, N.D.: Tensors for data mining and data fusion: Models, applications, and scalable algorithms. Trans. Intell. Syst. Technol. (TIST) **8**(2), 16 (2016)
22. Park, N., Jeon, B., Lee, J., Kang, U.: BIGtensor: mining billion-scale tensor made easy. In: ACM International on Conference on Information and Knowledge Management, pp. 2457–2460 (2016)
23. Paszke, A., et al.: PyTorch: an imperative style, high-performance deep learning library. In: Advances in Neural Information Processing Systems, pp. 8024–8035 (2019)

24. Phan, A.H., Tichavský, P., Cichocki, A.: Fast alternating LS algorithms for high order CANDECOMP/PARAFAC tensor factorizations. Trans. Sig. Process. **61**(19), 4834–4846 (2013)
25. Rabanser, S., Shchur, O., Günnemann, S.: Introduction to tensor decompositions and their applications in machine learning. arXiv preprint arXiv:1711.10781 (2017)
26. Sidiropoulos, N.D., De Lathauwer, L., Fu, X., Huang, K., Papalexakis, E.E., Faloutsos, C.: Tensor decomposition for signal processing and machine learning. Trans. Sig. Process. **65**(13), 3551–3582 (2017)
27. Springer, P., Su, T., Bientinesi, P.: HPTT: a high-performance tensor transposition C++ library. In: ACM SIGPLAN International Workshop on Libraries, Languages, and Compilers for Array Programming, pp. 56–62 (2017)
28. Sun, J., Tao, D., Faloutsos, C.: Beyond streams and graphs: dynamic tensor analysis. In: ACM SIGKDD International Conference on Knowledge Discovery and Data Mining, pp. 374–383. ACM (2006)
29. Yang, K., et al.: TaGiTeD: predictive task guided tensor decomposition for representation learning from electronic health records. In: Proceedings of the Thirty-First AAAI Conference on Artificial Intelligence (2017)

From Large Time Series to Patterns Movies: Application to Airbus Helicopters Flight Data

Benjamin Chazelle[1], Pierre-Loic Maisonneuve[2], Ammar Mechouche[2], Jean-Marc Petit[1], and Vasile-Marian Scuturici[1(✉)]

[1] Univ Lyon, INSA Lyon, LIRIS (UMR 5205 CNRS), Villeurbanne, France
{jean-marc.petit,marian.scuturici}@liris.cnrs.fr
[2] Airbus Helicopters, Marignane, France
{pierre-loic.maisonneuve,ammar.mechouche}@airbus.com

Abstract. Huge amount of multivariate time series (TS) data are recorded by helicopters in operation, such as oil temperature, oil pressure, altitude, rotor speed to mention a few. Despite the effort deployed by Airbus Helicopters towards an effective use of those TS data, getting meaningful and intuitive representations of them is a never ending process, especially for domain experts who have a limited time budget to get the main insights delivered by data scientists.

In this paper, we introduce a simple yet powerful and scalable technique for visualizing large amount of TS data through *patterns movies*. We borrow the co-occurrence matrix concept from image processing, to create 2D pictures, seen as *patterns*, from any multivariate TS according to two dimensions over a given period of time. The cascade of such patterns over time produces so-called *patterns movies*, offering in a few seconds a visualisation of helicopter' parameters in operation over a long period of time, typically one year.

We have implemented and conducted experiments on Airbus Helicopters flight data. First outcomes of domain experts on patterns movies are presented.

Keywords: Data visualization · Data streams · Database applications

1 Introduction

For safety and maintenance reasons, many physical sensors have been installed on operating helicopters. From a data perspective, the Flight Data Continuous Recorder (FDCR) collects Time Series (TS) from physical sensors of the machine, usually at a frequency of 2 hertz (Hz). Over the last decade, Airbus Helicopters have gathered data on hundreds of thousands flight hours, over hundreds of helicopters operated by different customers worldwide, on many different types of missions. To face with such huge amount of TS data, a Big Data platform has been deployed to enable the storing and processing capabilities, offering

© Springer Nature Switzerland AG 2021
L. Bellatreche et al. (Eds.): ADBIS 2021, LNCS 12843, pp. 213–226, 2021.
https://doi.org/10.1007/978-3-030-82472-3_16

new opportunities to domain experts, especially for troubleshooting and predictive maintenance [7]. Time series analysis is still an active research domain, see for example [1,2] or [3,10] for a survey. Despite the effort deployed by Airbus Helicopters towards an effective use of those TS data, getting meaningful and intuitive representations of them remains a never ending process.

In the past, data were mainly used for troubleshooting purposes, for instance to understand the conditions triggering an unexpected incident. The process was limited to the exploitation of data from the flight where the incident occurred or the flight before, analyzed using classical TS visualization softwares such as Grafana[1], Kibana[2] or in-house dedicated tools.

For years, data collected from helicopters are also used to better understand the real usage spectrum of the different helicopters sub-systems (such as lubrication system, starter generator, hydraulic pump, landing gear...). Understanding the behaviour of these sub-systems in different contexts allows us to optimize their future (re)-design.

Now, more and more efforts are made to develop predictive maintenance capabilities for helicopters systems, based on the whole in-service data made available. However, this is a more challenging topic which requires a strong involvement of System Design Responsible (SDR) experts who have a deep knowledge of their respective systems.

Moreover, SDR do not have time – neither necessarily the required data science skills – to mine, quickly and autonomously, massive collected TS data. Thus, it is quite important to provide them with relevant and adequate artefacts that allow them to get a simplified access and analysis of their TS data.

Predictive maintenance algorithms consist in general of monitoring "quantities" that should respect some conditions which can be considered as the *normal operating behaviour* of the monitored system. Then when this quantity no longer respects the conditions, an alert is raised. Also, often, such conditions come from hypothesis formulated by SDR, and consist in general of correlations that should be preserved over time between certain flight parameters under certain flight conditions, such as time between pilot actions and systems reactions, correlations between systems temperatures and pressures etc. Quick testing/verification/validation of SDR hypothesis is then very important for their efficient involvement in the predictive maintenance development. Nevertheless, turning large TS into useful knowledge for domain experts is clearly not an easy task at all.

In this paper, we introduce a simple yet powerful and scalable technique for visualizing large TS data through *patterns movies*. An overview of our approach is given in Fig. 1. The basic idea relies on the visualization of correlations between two (flight) parameters over a large period of time. This large period is split into non-overlapping time windows. For each time window we build one image (or pattern), corresponding to the co-occurrence matrix of the two parameters, aggregating the TS information from this time window. By assembling successive images, one for each time window, we obtain a so-called "patterns movie".

---

[1] https://grafana.com/.
[2] https://www.elastic.co/fr/kibana.

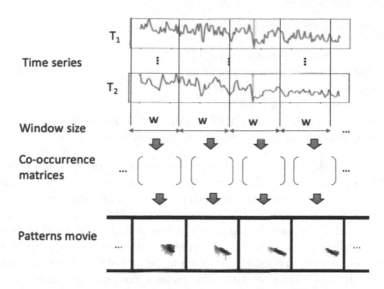

Fig. 1. Sketch of patterns movie construction

The resulting movie points out how patterns slowly evolve over time. Domain experts have the opportunity to visualize in a short period of time – typically less than a minute – millions of records and observe trends related to helicopter usage.

We have implemented and conducted experiments on Airbus Helicopters flight data. First outcomes of domain experts on patterns movies are presented.

To the best of our knowledge, the use of co-occurrence matrix for aggregating large TS data and their visualization with patterns movies is a new contribution which has many advantages:

- Pattern movies are very convenient for domain experts to better understand their TS data
- The proposed process turns out to be scalable, almost linear in the size of the TS data.

2   From TS Data to Patterns Videos

Let (T_1, T_2) be two numerical TS variables over the same period of time $\mathcal{T}$ and $w_1, w_2, \ldots, w_n$ a succession of non-overlapping time windows of the same size, with $w_i << \mathcal{T}$ for each $i \in \{1, \ldots, n\}$.

We denote by $\hat{T}_1$ and $\hat{T}_2$ a discretization of these TS. Many techniques could be applied such as equal-width discretization or equal-frequency discretization. Furthermore, external knowledge provided by experts should be taken into account. Details are omitted.

For a time window w, we denote by T_1^w, T_2^w the part of (T_1, T_2) that fall into w.

The proposed process applied on every time window w is as follows:

1. Discretize T_1^w and T_2^w into $\hat{T}_1^w$ and $\hat{T}_2^w$
2. Count the number of occurrences of any pairs of values from $(\hat{T}_1^w, \hat{T}_2^w)$.
3. Build the co-occurrence matrix $\hat{M}_w$
4. Generate a picture associated to $\hat{M}_w$
5. Integrate the picture into an MPEG file, i.e. the movie file is composed by successive frames, one frame for each time window $w_1, \ldots, w_n$

We reuse classical notions of co-occurrence matrix from image processing, useful in texture analysis of 2D images [4]. In our case, we consider that each co-occurrence matrix is a simple image which captures useful information (*patterns*) about the process of interest. The co-occurrence matrix can be seen also as a multidimensional frequency histogram. The cascade of such patterns over time produces so-called *patterns movies*, offering in a few seconds a visualisation of helicopter' parameters in operation over a long period of time, typically one year.

It is worth noting that the time dimension is lost on each time window w, making it possible to aggregate the studied parameters and to erase the local specificities. Each generated picture turns out to deliver a *time-agnostic* pattern, while the time dimension is still present in the "patterns movies". In other words, a patterns movie can be seen as a sequence of time-agnostic patterns, allowing to visualize how patterns slowly evolve over time.

A Running Example

In the sequel, we consider a running example to explain how a picture is built from two TS variables over one time window only, i.e. $w = T$. The five steps described previously are exemplified on data depicted in Table 1(a).

Step 1 (Discretization): We consider here a simple discretization, the rounding function $D(x) = \lfloor x \rceil$. For sake of readability, each pair of values in $\hat{T}_1$ and $\hat{T}_2$ has got a particular colour, as shown in Table 1(b)

Step 2 (Counting): A new dimension is added to count how many times a given pair of values appears in $(\hat{T}_1^w, \hat{T}_2^w)$, depicted in Table 1(c).

Step 3 (Co-occurrence matrix): A co-occurrence matrix is built. Rows refers to $\hat{T}_1$ values, i.e. $\langle 5, 6, 7, 8, 9 \rangle$, and columns to $\hat{T}_2$ values, i.e. $\langle 1, 2, 3, 4 \rangle$. A pair of values (u, v) refers to the counting associated to that pair in the time window w (cf step 3). The co-occurrence matrix obtained is depicted in Table 1(d). This representation plays the role of a two-dimensional histogram, where the time dimension is lost.

Step 4 (Picture generation): From the previous co-occurrence matrix of size $n \times m$, we sketch how pictures of size $n \times m$ can be generated. The main idea is that the larger the value of a matrix at (i, j), the darker the (i, j) pixel in the 2D-picture. In order to protect the observer from possible bias of reading and consequently of interpretation, we have adopted a normalization by distribution intervals to better reflect the real data density, i.e. the number of data per unit area [11].

Table 1. Running example

(a)

T_1^w	5,3	4,7	5,5	5,8	6,1	7	8,2	8	8,3	8,6
T_2^w	1,9	1,5	3	3,4	4	3,1	3,6	3,9	4,2	0,5

⇓ (b)

$\widehat{T}_1^w$	5	5	6	6	6	7	8	8	8	9
$\widehat{T}_2^w$	2	2	3	3	4	3	4	4	4	1

⇓ (c)

$T_1^{\hat{w}}$	5	6	6	7	8	9
$T_2^{\hat{w}}$	2	3	4	3	4	1

Count	2	2	1	1	3	1

⇓ (d)

$$
\hat{M}_w \qquad
\begin{array}{c|cccc}
 & \multicolumn{4}{c}{T_2^{\hat{w}} \text{ values}} \\
 & 1 & 2 & 3 & 4 \\
\hline
5 & 0 & 2 & 0 & 0 \\
6 & 0 & 0 & 2 & 1 \\
T_1^{\hat{w}} \text{ values} \quad 7 & 0 & 0 & 1 & 0 \\
8 & 0 & 0 & 0 & 3 \\
9 & 1 & 0 & 0 & 0 \\
\end{array}
$$

A typical 2D-picture is given in Fig. 2, which corresponds to a pattern on two variables: the oil pressure and the oil temperature observed in the main gear box. The discretization is produced by partitioning the values of each attribute in $K = 100$ equal length intervals.

Step 5 (Pattern movie generation): This step is simple as it consists to generate such pictures over different time windows in order to produce a movie. The time dimension is taken into account here at a coarser granularity, allowing to study the global trends of different parameters. An example is shown in Fig. 3.

In Fig. 3, we display some frames from a patterns movie built from data corresponding to only one aircraft. The studied TS variables are "Oil temperature" (x-axis) and "Oil pressure" (y-axis). The middle frame from the last row corresponds to a time window where an operating incident was reported.

Computational Considerations

Generating patterns movies scales well over very large TS since each transformation has a complexity linear or quasi linear in the size of the input. Moreover parallelisation can be applied. Details are omitted.

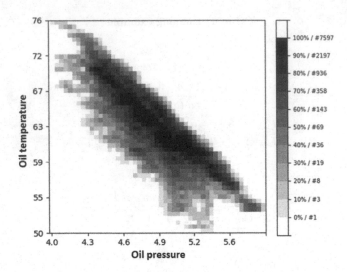

Fig. 2. Co-occurrence matrix 100 × 100, all in-flight data from aircraft A, "Oil temperature" *vs* "Oil pressure"

3   Implementation and Experimentations

The implementation has been done with `Python 3.6.7` with libraries `Pandas 0.24.1` for tabular data, `NumPy 1.16.2` for math operations, and `Matplotlib 3.0.3` for dataviz. Animated renderings use the FFmpeg encoder[3] for the generation of MPEG-4 video files[4].

Experiments were executed on an Intel(R) Core(TM) i7-8750H CPU @ 2.20 GHz with 16 Go RAM.

We studied several datasets, two of them are described below. The first one comes from a unique helicopter with over 45 days in operation, resulting in 76 flight hours and 550,000 records obtained at a frequency 2 Hz. 24 parameters were recorded into attributes such as oil pressure, oil temperature or altitude. The second one was bigger with more than 118 million records, corresponding to 16,000 flight hours of 33 helicopters, recorded over a period of 20 months. On average we had 500 flight hours per aircraft.

The first dataset allowed an initial exploration by generating co-occurrence matrices between all possible pairs of attributes in a few minutes. For example, Fig. 2 shows a relationship between the oil temperature and its pressure, with an equal-width dicretization of 100 bins in each dimension.

Similarly, Fig. 4 shows a correlation between attributes playing a role in the mechanics of the helicopter. These first results were expected by business experts, and judged as promising to visualize TS data.

---

[3] Bellard, F, FFmpeg, ffmpeg.org, 2019.

[4] The Moving Picture Experts Group, M. MPEG-4 mpeg.chiariglione.org/standards/ mpeg-4/mpeg-4.htm, 1998.

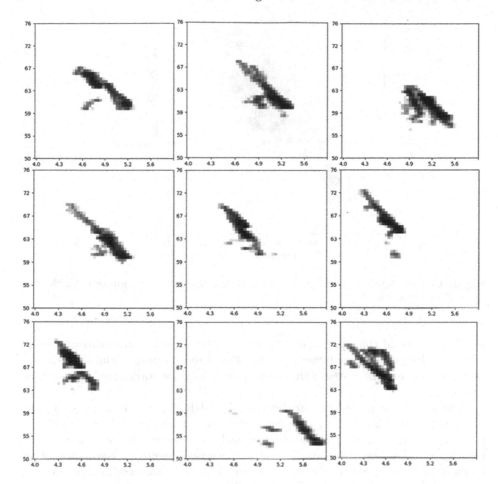

Fig. 3. Snapshot of a patterns movie at different points in time

New visualizations of static and animated co-occurrence matrices were then regenerated on the new dataset. Two main observations can be drawn. First, on each device a global normality appears on the *kernels* of the representations, i.e. the region with the most frequent co-occurrences. We observe a great similarity of the most frequent data in Fig. 5 (a) and (b) (the darkest part).

Second, data at the periphery of the kernel, ie the less frequent data, ranging from white to gray, do not follow the same distribution from one device to another, and represent a large region of the co-occurrence matrix. On the other side, the kernel part of this representation seems to be invariant.

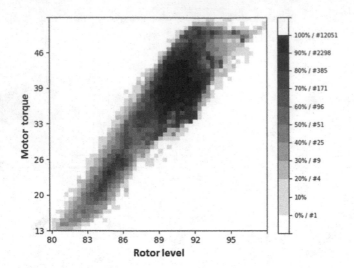

Fig. 4. Co-occurrence matrix 100 × 100, all in-flight data from aircraft A, "Motor torque" *vs* "Rotor level"

Experts found this approach easy to use, giving them convenient and intuitive visualization of very large TS data. These results were useful in verifying hypotheses about the system behaviour, quite complementary of existing propositions [5, 6, 8].

The prototype is intended to be used by SDR experts as a decision support system: It allows them to quickly comfort or invalidate their "implicit" hypothesis. Then, in case of comforted hypothesis, a more complex analysis and investigation are required in order to either precisely identify a root cause of an incident or tune a predictive maintenance indicator for the studied system.

4 Evolution in Time of the Centroid of Co-occurrence Matrices

Splitting temporal data using time windows generates a multitude of successive ordered co-occurrence matrices. One of our goals is to better understand the evolution of these matrices with respect to the time dimension. The most intuitive way to do this is to compare the different matrices with each other. To do so, we look for a numerical measure between these matrices.

After exploring some classical distances adapted to matrices, like Jaccard or Manhattan, an euclidean distance based on matrix centroids has been chosen by domain experts for its simplicity of interpretation and visualization potential.

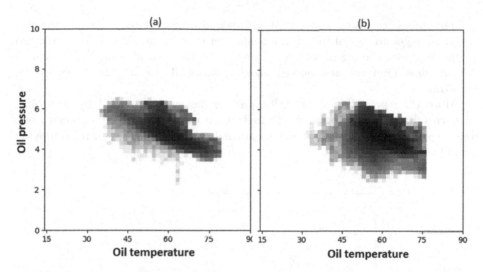

Fig. 5. Co-occurrence matrix 50 × 50, "Oil temperature" *vs* "Oil pressure", all in-flight data from aircraft B (a) and from aircraft C (b).

Let $C \in \mathbb{R}^{w \times h}$ be a matrix. The point $(\overline{x}, \overline{y})$ is the centroid of C if:

$$\overline{x} = \frac{\sum_{i=1}^{w} i \times \sum_{j=1}^{h} C(i,j)}{\sum_{i=1}^{w} \sum_{j=1}^{h} C(i,j)} \qquad \overline{y} = \frac{\sum_{j=1}^{h} j \times \sum_{i=1}^{w} C(i,j)}{\sum_{j=1}^{h} \sum_{i=1}^{w} C(i,j)}$$

For example, for the matrix:

$$\begin{bmatrix} 10 & 0 & 0 \\ 0 & 5 & 0 \\ 0 & 15 & 30 \end{bmatrix}$$

the corresponding centroid is:

$$\overline{x} = \frac{1 \times 10 + 2 \times 5 + 3 \times (15 + 30)}{10 + 5 + 15 + 30} = \frac{155}{60}$$

$$\overline{y} = \frac{1 \times 10 + 2 \times (5 + 15) + 3 \times 30}{10 + 5 + 15 + 30} = \frac{140}{60}$$

Let $A, B \in \mathbb{R}^{w \times h}$ and $(\overline{x}_A, \overline{y}_A)$ and $(\overline{x}_B, \overline{y}_B)$ their corresponding centroids. We define the distance between A and B as the normalized euclidean distance between the corresponding centroids:

$$dist(A, B) = \frac{1}{\sqrt{w^2 + h^2}} \times \sqrt{(\overline{x}_A - \overline{x}_B)^2 + (\overline{y}_A - \overline{y}_B)^2}$$

The idea is to visualize the path followed by the centroids of co-occurrence matrices to get an idea of their movements over time. Centroids can be visualized statically by displaying all of them in order to have an idea of their os-called *transit zone*. They can also be visualized dynamically to show how they evolve over time.

More than providing information on the distances travelled by centroids, such visualizations also provide information on their direction and transit area. Transit zones can be used to represent normality and highlight centroids moving away from it.

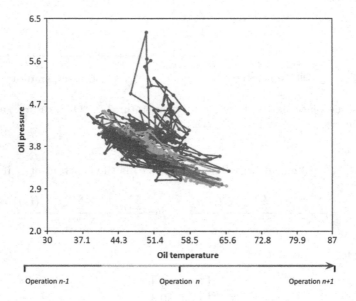

Fig. 6. Centroids for co-occurrence matrix 50 × 50, all in-flight data from aircraft A, "Oil temperature" *vs* "Oil pressure", window size of 30 min

The path followed by centroids before and after maintenance operations has been analyzed in order to detect trends and patterns with respect to the studied maintenance intervention (see Figs. 6, 7, 8, 9).

Figure 6 shows the path of the centroids around a given n-th maintenance operation. The path of the centroids before the maintenance operation n (intervention on the dial) is drawn in red. The previous operation $n - 1$ concerned an intervention on the gearbox. The operation $n + 1$ concerns also an intervention on the dial, and the centroid path between n and $n + 1$ is displayed in blue. Centroids are calculated on 50 × 50 oil temperature and pressure matrices, within a window size of 30 min. We observe a variation of the transit zone taken by the centroids over time.

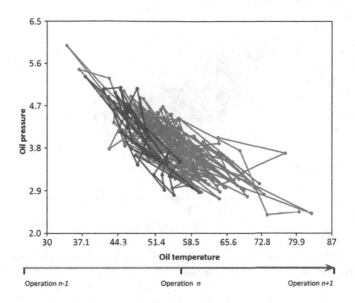

Fig. 7. Centroids for co-occurrence matrix 50 × 50, all in-flight data from aircraft B, "Oil temperature" *vs* "Oil pressure", window size of 30 min

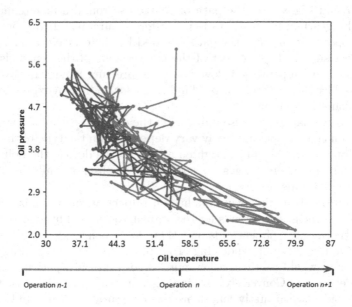

Fig. 8. Centroids for co-occurrence matrix 50 × 50, all in-flight data from aircraft C, "Oil temperature" *vs* "Oil pressure", window size of 30 min

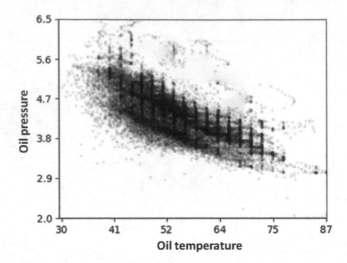

Fig. 9. Centroids for co-occurrence matrix 50×50, all in-flight data from aircraft D, "Oil temperature" *vs* "Oil pressure", window size of 3 min

The downside of the visualisation based on centroids is that it requires a lot of data to be relevant. If maintenance operations are too close in time, the small number of centroids tracing the path may not be sufficient to obtain a sufficiently precise idea of the transit zones they use.

Figure 7 and Fig. 8 show the path of centroids around a maintenance operation on the gearbox lubrication of two different aircrafts. In red is the path before the operation, in blue, the path followed by the centroid after operation. We observe a similar displacement of the transit zone of the centroids towards a zone where the temperature is lower and the pressure higher. In this case the path followed by the centroid is a good indicator for an human expert to validate the maintenance operation.

Some external factors are also influencing the centroid path. For example, the effect of an oil change operation may vary depending on the type of the used oil. Even if an operation was only to tighten a bolt on the device, the bolt could be tightened in many different ways. Nevertheless, we observe similar maintenance operations in our experiments.

The duration of the time windows has an impact on the visualization generated. Although the general trends for the transit zones used by centroids remain the same, the number of centroids and their local behaviors are affected by a change in the frequency of windowing. Too high a frequency would aggregate a lot of data and would result in a low number of centroids, perhaps too low to capture an evolution. Conversely, too fine a granularity would increase the number of centroids, which firstly lengthens the computation time, and can cause the appearance of artefacts. Figure 9 illustrates this phenomenon. It represents all the centroids of the 50 × 50 co-occurrence matrices, relating to the temperature of the oil and its pressure, obtained from a windowing with a frequency of 3 min. We observe the appearance of vertical line explained by the fact that the variability of the data on the oil pressure attribute becomes locally in time so small, that the horizontal position of the centroid is forced to fix on an integer value (the sensor precision is at 1 unit).

5   Conclusion

We introduced a technique for visualizing large TS data as patterns movies. On the basis of a division of the TS into time windows, co-occurrence matrices are built, allowing to display a representation of the underlying data distribution. The time dimension is lost locally at each matrix, but is kept globally throughout the windowing, in the produced pattern movie. Many experiments were conducted with TS data from Airbus Helicopters, from which we presented and discussed the main outcomes. In addition, we were able to aggregate further the visualization by focusing on centroids of co-occurrence matrix only. Such an abstraction turned out to be very useful to study the normal behavior of the studied phenomenon with transit zone of centroids.

To sum up, this approach proposes to capture the evolution of trends observed over time windows in TS. Therefore, the main perspective is to be able to detect deviations with respect to the normal behavior of operating helicopters. Whenever these changes are detected, an alert could be raised to anticipate and better organize maintenance actions. The overall objective is to improve safety in order to avoid potential incidents, and allow customers to increase the availability of their helicopters. Experts found this approach very promising, intuitive, easy to use, allowing rapid testing of hypotheses on large collections of TS.

Many perspectives remain to be addressed: first, human perception of those pattern movies could be evaluated more thoroughly to define new visual quality metrics [9]. Second, patterns movies could be used to anomaly detection, not by experts' eyes, but with automatic techniques on the co-occurrence matrices. Third, more research also deserves to be done to help domain experts to find appropriate tradeoffs to get meaningful pattern movies, for example to select the two parameters for the 2D visualization, to define an appropriate time window and also to discretize the data. Finally, co-occurence matrix can be extended to a set of dimensions for the x-axis and to another set of dimensions for the y-axis, instead of a single dimension for both axis as we do.

Acknowledgements. Part of this work has been funded by the Datavalor initiative of the LIRIS laboratory.

References

1. Boniol, P., Palpanas, T.: Series2Graph: graph-based subsequence anomaly detection for time series. Proc. VLDB Endow. **13**(11), 1821–1834 (2020)
2. Dang, X., Shah, S.Y., Zerfos, P.: Seq2Graph: discovering dynamic non-linear dependencies from multivariate time series. In: 2019 IEEE International Conference on Big Data (Big Data), Los Angeles, CA, USA, 9–12 December 2019, pp. 1774–1783. IEEE (2019)
3. Esling, P., Agón, C.: Time-series data mining. ACM Comput. Surv. **45**(1), 12:1–12:34 (2012)
4. Haralick, R.M., Shanmugam, K.S., Dinstein, I.: Textural features for image classification. IEEE Trans. Syst. Man Cybern. **3**(6), 610–621 (1973)
5. Keim, D.A., Mansmann, F., Schneidewind, J., Thomas, J., Ziegler, H.: Visual analytics: scope and challenges. In: Simoff, S.J., Böhlen, M.H., Mazeika, A. (eds.) Visual Data Mining. LNCS, vol. 4404, pp. 76–90. Springer, Heidelberg (2008). https://doi.org/10.1007/978-3-540-71080-6_6
6. Kumar, N., Lolla, V.N., Keogh, E.J., Lonardi, S., Ratanamahatana, C.A.: Time-series bitmaps: a practical visualization tool for working with large time series databases. In: Kargupta, H., Srivastava, J., Kamath, C., Goodman, A. (eds.) Proceedings of the 2005 SIAM International Conference on Data Mining, SDM 2005, Newport Beach, CA, USA, 21–23 April 2005, pp. 531–535. SIAM (2005)
7. Mechouche, A., Daouayry, N., Cameini, V.: Helicopter big data processing and preditive analytics: feedback and perspectives. In: European Rotorcraft Forum, Warsaw, Poland, September 2019, p. 6 (2019)
8. Peng, R.: A method for visualizing multivariate time series data. J. Stat. Softw. Code Snippets **25**(1), 1–17 (2008)
9. Tatu, A., Bak, P., Bertini, E., Keim, D.A., Schneidewind, J.: Visual quality metrics and human perception: an initial study on 2D projections of large multidimensional data. In: Santucci, G. (ed.) Proceedings of the International Conference on Advanced Visual Interfaces, AVI 2010, Roma, Italy, 26–28 May 2010, pp. 49–56. ACM Press (2010)
10. Torkamani, S., Lohweg, V.: Survey on time series motif discovery. Wiley Interdiscip. Rev. Data Min. Knowl. Discov. **7**(2), e1199 (2017)
11. Tufte, E.R.: The Visual Display of Quantitative Information. Graphics Press (1992)

Data Integration

Experimental Evaluation Among Reblocking Techniques Applied to the Entity Resolution

Laís Soares Caldeira[1]([✉])[iD], Guilherme Dal Bianco[2][iD], and Anderson A. Ferreira[1][iD]

[1] Universidade Federal de Ouro Preto, Ouro Preto, Minas Gerais, Brazil
`lais.caldeira@aluna.ufop.edu.br`, `anderson.ferreira@ufop.edu.br`
[2] Universidade Federal da Fronteira Sul, Chapecó, Santa Catarina, Brazil
`guilherme.dalbianco@uffs.edu.br`

Abstract. Entity Resolution (ER) is an essential task in the data integration process, by identifying records that refer to the same object in the real world. In a naive approach, ER needs to compare all pairs of records in a dataset. This process has a high cost, especially for large-scale datasets. Several techniques have been proposed in the literature to restrict the comparison among records grouped in the same blocks to mitigate such a cost. In order to further reduce the number of comparisons, some approaches, named reblocking, focus on blocking reprocessing. The reblocking techniques include two major groups: meta-blocking and filtering. Meta-blocking reduces the number of comparisons based on blocks shared by the records. On the other hand, filtering focuses on providing pairs of records for comparison based on the degree of similarity between them. Although both approaches have the same goal, as far as we know, no work in the literature experimentally compares the reblocking techniques. Filling this gap, in this research, we present a qualitative and comparative analysis of techniques in the state-of-the-art of reblocking approaches. With this analysis, we provide different characteristics to assess issues of effectiveness and efficiency of the techniques. Finally, we specify appropriate scenarios for each evaluated technique.

Keywords: Entity resolution · Blocking · Blocking reprocessing · Filtering techniques · Meta-blocking techniques

1 Introduction

The continuous growth in the volume of data generated and shared by information systems (e.g., social media, management systems, and Web systems),

The authors thank CAPES, CNPq, FAPEMIG and the Federal University of Ouro Preto (UFOP) for supporting this work. This study was partially funded by CAPES - Brazil - Finance Code 001.

© Springer Nature Switzerland AG 2021
L. Bellatreche et al. (Eds.): ADBIS 2021, LNCS 12843, pp. 229–243, 2021.
https://doi.org/10.1007/978-3-030-82472-3_17

the diversity of representation structures, and the different descriptions of information are challenges faced in the data integration process [7]. This process is essential for achieving a unified view of heterogeneous data from different sources [8]. However, many datasets contain erroneous, missing, or duplicate values, making them difficult to use. With the popularization of data-dependent activities, it is necessary to increase the importance of the quality and integrity of the information available.

Entity Resolution (ER) is a central task in the data integration process, and has important practical implications in a wide variety of commercial, scientific, governmental, medical, criminal, and security domains [4]. ER identifies records that refer to the same object in the real world [6]. In a naive approach, ER compares all records from one or more datasets to identify matching pairs, that is, pairs of records belonging to the same entity. Thus, it results in a quadratic number of comparisons in relation to the number of records. This exhaustive approach is very costly, especially when applied to large volume of data. One of the main challenges in ER is to identify all (or almost all) matching pairs, avoiding the quadratic computational cost [15].

Several techniques have been proposed to restrict the comparison between records by grouping similar records in blocks, called *Blocking*. Only records within the same block are compared, reducing the computational cost substantially. Traditionally, the blocks are constructed with some indexing strategies with low computational cost (e.g., the inverted index strategy and tree-based indexing). Those blocks may be, optionally, reprocessed for decreasing even more the number of comparisons. This stage, called *Reblocking*, aims at removing the unnecessary comparisons improving the computational effectiveness. Reblocking has stood out in recent years with competitive techniques, most of them focused on two approaches: *Meta-blocking* and *Filtering*. In relevant papers on meta-blocking and filtering techniques, better results were identified compared with traditional block construction techniques, successfully alleviating the problem of quadratic growth of comparisons when the data increase in size [11,16].

Meta-blocking techniques [2,14,19] are based on the principle of sharing blocks between pairs of records as evidence of correspondence. The meta-blocking approach aims to reduce redundant comparisons (same records compared several times) and superfluous comparisons (between records belonging to different entities) [12]. On the other hand, the filtering techniques [23,25] select matching candidate pairs based on the degree of similarity. For example, by sharing rare tokens[1], record size, the position of tokens in prefixes or suffixes of records, among others. Thus, such techniques address the problem in different ways but have the same goal, which is to reduce the number of comparisons between records.

The comparative analysis of techniques can be done in a qualitative way (analyzing strengths, weaknesses, differences and similarity of the techniques), in a quantitative way (carrying out experiments and comparing the results) or both. In [5,16], the authors compare qualitatively and quantitatively block-

---

[1] Token corresponds to a substring/term from a record attribute value.

ing and meta-blocking techniques. In [10], Köpcke et al. compare blocking and filtering techniques. And, in [9,11], the authors compare qualitatively and quantitatively filtering techniques. It is worth mentioning that several other works propose new methods and compare them with existing techniques. However, the works mentioned above that comprise reblocking, do not describe new proposals and only compare techniques that already exist in the literature. Attempt to address the gap that encompasses comparisons between meta-blocking and filtering techniques, in [15], the authors compare qualitatively such approaches, without delving into experimental comparisons. As far as we know, meta-blocking and filtering techniques, besides having the same goal, have not yet been compared experimentally, demonstrating which approach is more promising.

Our work aims to fill this gap by presenting a quantitative and qualitative comparison between relevant unsupervised techniques of meta-blocking and filtering applied to reblocking. We analyze experimentally seven recent state-of-the-art approaches, named PPJoin [25], PPJoin+ [25], AdaptJoin [23], Reciprocal WNP [14], Reciprocal CNP [14], PBBRT [2] and BLAST [19]. By comparing meta-blocking and filtering, we aim at providing new insights into the strengths and weaknesses of reblocking techniques that can guide professionals in selecting appropriate techniques for various scenarios.

The rest of this paper is structured as follows: Sect. 2 describes some important concepts. Section 3 reviews related work. Section 4 describes the reblocking techniques evaluated in this work. Section 5 discusses our experimental evaluation, presents the results and analyzes them in a quantitative and qualitative way. Finally, Sect. 6 concludes the paper and present possible future works.

2 Preliminaries

2.1 Entity Resolution

The entity resolution task aims to identify all matching pairs of records in one or more datasets [6]. More formally, let $R = \{r_1, r_2, \cdots, r_n\}$ be a dataset with n records. Two records, r_i and r_j with $i \neq j$, are considered corresponding (matching) if both represent to the same real entity ($r_i \equiv r_j$).

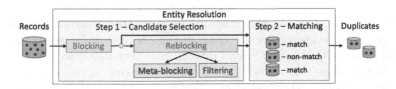

Fig. 1. Workflow for entity resolution

Figure 1 illustrates the entity resolution processes. ER receives a set of records as input and returns as output a set of pairs of records that ideally correspond to the same entity, called duplicates. ER can be split into two steps [15]: (1) the candidate selection step, and (2) the candidate matching step, i.e., matching. The latter step compares records for determining which ones represent the same entities, dominating the overall cost of ER [6,7]. ER usually becomes efficient and scalable through the first step, which selects the pairs of records most likely to refer to the same entity [15]. This step eliminates less promising candidate pairs, preventing them from being compared. Several works address the strategy of selecting candidate pairs using different techniques that belong to two main stages, usually called blocking and reblocking (see Fig. 1). Initially, a blocking technique groups candidate records to belong to the same entity, and later a reblocking technique may optionally decrease the pairs of candidate records generated in such groups.

2.2 Blocking

As previously mentioned, blocking techniques group records into blocks that have some evidences of representing similar information [4]. Several blocking techniques have been proposed in the literature to support heterogeneous data, with noise and without structure [5]. Applying blocking techniques, comparisons between records carried out at the ER matching step only occur inside the blocks. It reduces the number of comparisons substantially compared with the exhaustive approach. However, blocking may still result in a high amount of unnecessary comparisons when applied to large datasets [14]. A second stage, known as reblocking, aims to discard unnecessary comparisons.

2.3 ReBlocking

The blocks produced by the blocking stage may be refined by reblocking techniques. It is designed to decrease the number of unnecessary comparisons between candidate pairs, becoming indispensable for a good balance between the effectiveness and efficiency of the ER task [15,16]. In Fig. 1, we expand reblocking in meta-blocking and filtering to show in which stage of the ER task both techniques fit into, not limiting the reblocking to them. Meta-blocking and filtering are the main focus of this work.

Meta-Blocking. Meta-blocking attempts to eliminate redundant and superfluous comparisons between pairs of records in the ER task. It focuses on maintain candidate pairs with a higher probability of matching based on the amount of blocks shared by pair of records [12,20]. Meta-blocking appears as one of the most promising approaches concerning to efficiency [14].

Several Meta-blocking techniques have been proposed by more recent works [2,14,19]. Most of them run in main memory and are based on graph representation to redefine the blocks. A vertex represents a record. An edge connects vertices if their corresponding records share blocks in common. A weighting function captures the likelihood of matching records for labeling the edges. A pruning strategy removes light edges from the graph. Meta-blocking weighting and pruning strategies considerably eliminate unnecessary comparisons between records. The remaining edges indicates the set of candidate pairs, whose corresponding records need to be compared with.

Filtering. Filtering has been described in the literature as similarity join techniques [11]. Its assumption is that records referring to the same real-world object are highly similar each other [15]. Techniques filtering [9,23,25] may use several types of filters to reduce the candidate pairs by following a pipeline model. For example, a technique may filter out a pair of records if its prefixes do not have tokens in common. In general, filters use similarity functions along with a threshold to quantify the similarity between two records. In this work, we focus on filtering techniques that use token-based similarity functions (e.g. Jaccard and Cosine [11]).

It is worth to notice that the filtering approaches are usually applied to pairs of records that have already been generated by an indexing/blocking technique [11]. As Fig. 1 shows, the blocking output feeds the filtering approach. Besides that, the filtering approach performs both steps: candidate generation and matching step (Step 1 and 2 of Fig. 1). However, in this work, we only focus on generating a set of candidate pairs of filtering techniques to produce a fair comparison with other approaches.

3 Related Work

Some works [5,9,11,16] compare techniques that focus on reducing the number of candidate pairs belonging to the same entity. Such works provide theoretical and experimental surveys on several techniques, highlighting their characteristics, strengths, weaknesses, complexity, performance and scalability. However, those works describe experimental evaluations between blocking and meta-blocking techniques [5,16], between blocking and filtering techniques [10], or only between filtering techniques [9,11]. None of them experimentally evaluate meta-blocking and filtering techniques.

Few works present new blocking techniques and compare them experimentally with filtering techniques [21,22]. However, such works do not take account meta-blocking techniques in their experimental evaluation. There also exist some works that qualitatively relate the filtering techniques in the same context as the blocking/meta-blocking techniques, but without delving into experimental comparisons [6,15]. Thus, our work differs from the above mentioned by evaluating experimentally both, quantitatively and qualitatively, meta-blocking and filtering techniques as reblocking.

4 Inside the Techniques

In this section, we describe in detail the unsupervised reblocking techniques necessary to properly understand our experimental analyses. Such techniques have been cited as state-of-the-art approaches in recent works and are generally used as a basis for experimental evaluations [9,11,18–20,24].

4.1 Filtering Techniques

The PPJoin (PPJ) [25], PPJoin+ (PPJ+) [25], and AdaptJoin (ADP) [23] techniques eliminate candidate pairs with low probability to be a duplicate. Their filters are based on both similarity function (tuned by thresholds provided by the user) and tokens frequency. Two records are considered similar whether they have overlaps that exceed the threshold (e.g., Jaccard or Cosine). A pre-processing step is necessary to employ the filters. For instance, based on the global token frequency, in each record, its tokens are sorted. This strategy makes the less frequent tokens, considered rare tokens, stay in the prefixes of the records, being a prerequisite for processing some of the filters.

When blocking is performed, very frequent tokens generate blocks with many records, which results in a significant overload when processed. *Prefix Filtering* of PPJ algorithm addresses this problem by indexing only the less frequent tokens of each record, i.e., the less frequent tokens and the most informative [25]. The produced candidate pairs are sent to the next filters, *Length Filtering* and *Positional Filtering*. Length Filtering removes candidate pairs when the difference in the size of the token set between records is above a defined threshold. Positional Filtering assesses whether the distance from the common token between the candidate pair respects an inferred limit.

PPJ+ is an extension of PPJ with addition of the *Suffix Filtering* [25]. The suffix filter is a generalization of the Positional Filtering for the tokens of the suffixes of the records, in order to further filter the candidate pairs that survive the previous filters. All tokens that have not been classified as prefixes are considered a record suffix. The suffix of each record is recursively partitioned into two similar parts and PPJ+ calculates the number of tokens in common in each corresponding partitions between two records, until the pair candidate is filtered using an inferred threshold value. ADP [23] extends the Prefix Filtering by dynamically calculating the prefix size. The intuition behind it is that the adaptive prefix size can be more flexible to prune non-matching pairs.

4.2 Meta-Blocking Techniques

As stated in Subsect. 2.3, meta-blocking techniques are conceptually based on graphs, where vertices represent the records and edges connect vertices of two records that appear in the same block. Each edge has a weight that reflects the probability of matching the records represented by its connected vertices. Low-weight edges are removed from the graph. The edge weights are based on information obtained from the blocks. For instance, by capturing the intuition that the amount of blocks two records share can indicates matching probability. Pruning schemes eliminate edges with low values.

Reciprocal Weighted Node Pruning (RecWNP) [14] considers the neighborhood of a given vertex (i.e., pairs of candidate records), weights the edges that interconnect the vertices and prunes the edges below an inferred local threshold. Kept edges that connect vertices that represent pairs of non-redundant records are also discarded. Redundant candidate pairs are treated as a strong indication of being a pair of records with high chances of matching. Reciprocal Cardinality Node Pruning (RecCNP) [14] differs in the strategy of ordering all neighboring edges of a given vertex in decreasing weight and maintaining the $top - k$.

In [19] is proposed a strategy based on LSH (Locality-Sensitive Hashing), called BLAST, to collect statistical information directly from the data in a scalable way. First, the attributes are grouped according to their similarity, and then the blocking is performed by exploring the attributes partitioning. Thus, only records whose tokens belong to attributes on the same partition will be considered candidate pairs in blocking. BLAST measures an attribute's information content using entropy [17], which identifies the most informative attributes and improves the edges' weight when reblocking.

Before representing the records in a graph, RecWNP, RecCNP and BLAST, specifically, employ two steps before reblocking: Block Purging and Block Filtering. Block Purging discards large blocks, i.e., blocks that exceed a maximum number of records per block. Block Filtering aims to restructure the set of blocks by eliminating unnecessary records in the blocks, e.g., records that are contained in many blocks. Block Filtering uses a filtering rate (r), defined in the interval $[0; 1]$, as a parameter to eliminate such records. The survived set of restructured blocks are the meta-blocking input. The application of such pre-processing techniques, as well as those used in filtering techniques, can lead to better results, since they reduce the number of candidate pairs [14, 19].

Blocking Process Based on Relevance of Terms (PBBRT) [2] removes blocks based on token entropies [17]. Tokens with high entropies are more relevant to matching, that is, when a token becomes more frequent, its amount of information decreases. Using this intuition, PBBRT removes blocks whose token entropy is below the average of all token entropy values, reducing the number of blocks. For reblocking, blocks obtained using tokens with low frequency (i.e., the token can be highly informative) may provide pair of records as strong matching candidates. This way, the edge that connects the vertices representing this pair of records can receive a greater weight so that the pruning scheme maintains the edge. PBBRT is a meta-blocking technique that has not yet been compared with other reblocking techniques.

5   Experimental Evaluation

In this section, we discuss the experimental results and analyses. We begin with the description of the datasets and metrics used to evaluate the results. Next, we detail the experimental setup. Finally, we discuss the outcomes, and comparatively analyze the performance of the techniques evaluated.

5.1   Datasets

We use seven semi-structured datasets, four real datasets (R1, R2, R3 and R4) and three synthetic datasets (S1, S2 and S3), which vary in size, domain, and characteristics. The datasets are publicly available[2]. Table 1 shows the characteristics of these datasets.

Table 1. Characteristics about the datasets: number of records ($|R|$), total number of matching pairs ($|D(R)|$), total number of attribute-value pairs ($|AV(R)|$), average number of attribute-value pairs per records ($|AVR(R)|$) and number of comparisons performed by the brute force approach ($|BF(R)|$).

	Real Datasets				Synthetic Datasets		
	R1	R2	R3	R4	S1	S2	S3
$|R|$	4, 910	63, 869	50, 797	3, 354, 773	10, 000	100, 000	1, 000, 000
$|D(R)|$	2, 224	2, 308	22, 863	892, 579	8, 705	85, 497	857, 538
$|AV(R)|$	19, 626	208, 065	971, 445	19, 064, 747	106, 108	1, 061, 421	10, 617, 729
$|AVR(R)|$	4.0	3.3	19.1	15.5	10.6	10.6	10.6
$|BF(R)|$	$1.21 \cdot 10^7$	$2.04 \cdot 10^9$	$1.29 \cdot 10^9$	$5.63 \cdot 10^{12}$	$5.00 \cdot 10^7$	$5.00 \cdot 10^9$	$5.00 \cdot 10^{11}$

About the real datasets, R1 contains data from DBLP and the ACM digital library. R2 contains records from DBLP and Google Scholar. R3 contains records about films from IMDB and DBPedia. R4 contains records from two different snapshots from English Wikipedia. The synthetic datasets were generated creating original records, without duplicates, based on a real-world vocabularies that includes person names and address, for instance. Those original records are randomly modified (e.g., excluding words and inserting characters) to produce their corresponding record pairs (i.e., duplicates). The synthetic datasets contain 60% and 40% of original and duplicate records, respectively, with up to nine matches per original record. The ground truth is known for all datasets.

The R4 and S3 datasets have the largest number of data, which allows us to evaluate the techniques in terms of scalability. All datasets have been widely used to evaluate meta-blocking and filtering approaches [1,11,14,16,20,25].

5.2   Evaluation Metrics

We may evaluate the quality of blocking and reblocking by the Pair Completeness (PC), Pair Quality (PQ) and F metrics [1,5,14,19]. Blocking and reblocking techniques generate the set C of candidate pairs to be duplicates from the R input record set. Let $|C|$ be the total number of candidate pairs, $|D(C)|$ the number of duplicates in C, and $|D(R)|$ the total number of correct duplicates in R, Thus, we have:

- *Pairs Completeness (PC)* is similar to recall and measures the ratio of detectable duplicates in relation to existing ones, $PC = \frac{|D(C)|}{|D(R)|}$.

---

[2] https://sourceforge.net/projects/erframework/files/DirtyERDatasets/.

- *Pairs Quality (PQ)* is similar to precision and measures the ratio of candidate pairs that correspond to real duplicates, $PQ = \frac{|D(C)|}{|C|}$.
- *F_β-measure (F-measure)* is the harmonic mean of PQ and PC, $F_\beta = (1+\beta^2) \cdot \frac{PQ \cdot PC}{(\beta^2 \cdot PQ) + PC}$. We may weigh PQ and PC in *F-measure*, giving us flexibility to use in different contexts. Two commonly used values for β are 2, which weighs PC twice as much as PQ, and 0.5, which weighs PC with half as important as PQ. If PQ e PC have the same weight for the final measure, use $\beta = 1$ [3]. *F-measure* takes values in the range $[0, 1]$.

The total number of candidate matching pairs $|C|$ will be used as metric to measure the computational cost for duplicate detection, i.e., the amount of comparisons in the ER task. The objective is to maximize PC and PQ and, thus, minimizes $|C|$ and maximize the number of detected duplicates $|D(C)|$. However, high number of candidate pairs usually leads to detect more duplicates, increasing PC, but reducing PQ [5]. Therefore, blocking and reblocking techniques are successful whether they achieve a good balance between PC and PQ.

5.3   Experimental Setup

Our experimental evaluation aims to compare relevant techniques applied to reblocking. The autors of RecWNP [14], RecCNP [14], PBBRT [2], BLAST [19], PPJ [25] and PPJ+ [25] provided to us the source code, and for ADP [23], we obtained the source code by the authors of [11]. Meta-blocking techniques were implemented in Java 8 and filtering techniques in C++[3].

We performed Token Blocking [13] for all evaluated techniques in the blocking stage. We chose Token Blocking because the high degree of redundancy produced prevents some errors in the records (e.g., typographical errors, missing fields and attributes inversions) may impact the blocking quality [1]. We represent each record by a set of its tokens.

For experimental analysis, we follow other works and compare the techniques by their *Effectiveness* and *Efficiency* [14,15]. Effectiveness refers to how many duplicates are detected, estimated by the PC. Effective techniques must have their PC values at least equals to 0.95. Efficiency refers to the computational cost to detect duplicates - usually estimated by the number of candidate pairs $|C|$ and by PQ. More formally, the goal of an efficient technique is to maximize PQ having its PC value equals at least to 0.80 [14]. F_β-measure makes it possible to assess whether the techniques have a good balance between effectiveness (PC) and efficiency (PQ). To give greater weight to effectiveness, we define $\beta = 2$, and to assign greater weight to efficiency, we define $\beta = 0.5$ [3].

Thus, we split the reblocking techniques into techniques favorable to the effectiveness and efficiency of the ER:

---

[3] All experimental results were obtained using an Intel Xeon (R) computer E5-2660 v2 2.20 GHz × 40 with 378 GB of RAM, running CentOS Linux 7.

- RecCNP and PBBRT are considered by their authors as good techniques for applications where *efficiency* is required, as it minimizes the number of candidate pairs generated in most cases.
- RecWNP is a good choice for applications that aim for *effectiveness*, as it maximizes the number of duplicates found.
- BLAST can adapt to both *efficiency* and *effectiveness* contexts, according to its authors.
- PPJ, PPJ+, and ADP adapt to *efficiency* and *effectiveness* contexts by varing their similarity thresholds.

The techniques that fit in both effectiveness and efficiency are differentiated by the input parameter used.

Table 2. The hyperparameter analysis for each reblocking technique (r to meta-blocking and t to filtering) in all datasets.

			Datasets						
			R1	R2	R3	R4	S1	S2	S3
Meta-blocking	ETS	RecWNP	r = 0.8	r = 0.8	r = 0.8	r = 0.8	r = 0.95	r = 0.95	r = 0.95
		BLAST	r = 0.8	r = 0.8	r = 0.8	r = 0.8	r = 0.95	r = 0.95	r = 0.95
	ECY	BLAST	r = 0.8	r = 0.8	r = 0.8	r = 0.8	r = 0.8	r = 0.8	r = 0.8
		RecCNP	r = 0.8	r = 0.8	r = 0.8	r = 0.8	r = 0.8	r = 0.8	r = 0.8
		PBBRT	–	–	–	–	–	–	–
Filtering	ETS	PPJ	t = 0.7	t = 0.6	t = 0.2	t = 0.3	t = 0.4	t = 0.4	t = 0.5
		PPJ+	t = 0.6	t = 0.4	t = 0.1	t = 0.3	t = 0.3	t = 0.3	t = 0.3
		ADP	t = 0.4	t = 0.2	t = 0.1	t = 0.3	t = 0.3	t = 0.3	t = 0.3
	ECY	PPJ	t = 0.8	t = 0.7	t = 0.3	t = 0.7	t = 0.5	t = 0.6	t = 0.6
		PPJ+	t = 0.7	t = 0.6	t = 0.2	t = 0.6	t = 0.4	t = 0.4	t = 0.5
		ADP	t = 0.6	t = 0.4	t = 0.1	t = 0.5	t = 0.5	t = 0.5	t = 0.5

Table 2 shows optimum hyperparameters configuration used by reblocking techniques for the EffecTivenesS (ETS) and EffiCiencY (ECY) in all datasets. RecWNP, RecCNP and BLAST filter out records specifying the r value, that is a filtering rate to eliminate such records. We varied the r value and, for $r = 0.80$, we obtained the satisfactory results in the real datasets for both effectiveness and efficiency techniques. In synthetic datasets, we found $r = 0.95$ for effectiveness techniques and $r = 0.80$ for efficiency techniques. For filtering techniques, we report the results by using cosine similarity function. We also experiment Jaccard coefficient but the results were similar. About the similarity threshold t, we range from 0.1 to 0.9 and report the best results. PBBRT infers its threshold values directly from the data, without the need for input parameters.

5.4 Performance of Techniques

We first examine the techniques that favor effectiveness and then the techniques for the ER task's efficiency. In Tables 3 and 4, the up arrow (↑) indicates that

PC met the restriction and the down arrow ($\downarrow$) indicates that it did not meet restriction. For the techniques that the constraint has been met, we consider the best value of the F_β metric (in bold) to identify the best technique for each dataset. We use real datasets to perform a deeper analysis on each technique and the synthetic datasets with a focus on scalability analysis.

Effectiveness. Table 3 shows the experimental results of the effectiveness techniques (RecWNP, BLAST, PPJ, PPJ+, ADP) in the real datasets. Analyzing the results of the F_β for techniques that meet the effectiveness constraint, it is possible to observe that RecWNP achieves better results than the others in two datasets (R2 and R4). On the other hand, RecWNP does not meet the restriction of effectiveness in R3. It can be explained because R3 is composed of more dirty data (records highly similar that are non-matching and pairs of records with little similarity refers to matching), which leads to a reduction in the value of PC. PPJ achieves the best F_β in R3 with a drawback of large number of candidate pairs (i.e., 5$\times$ greater than RecWNP). In the end, BLAST has the best F_β performance in R1. However, it shows an unstable effectiveness in the other datasets (i.e., it does not meet the PC effectiveness restriction).

Table 3. The performance of effectiveness techniques applied to real datasets. The best results of the F_β metric are highlighted.

		Effectiveness				
		RecWNP	BLAST	PPJ	PPJ+	ADP
	|C|	$2.91 \cdot 10^4$	$9.33 \cdot 10^3$	$2.76 \cdot 10^4$	$1.57 \cdot 10^4$	$8.59 \cdot 10^4$
R1	PC	$0.98 \uparrow$	$0.98 \uparrow$	$0.95 \uparrow$	$0.95 \uparrow$	$0.97 \uparrow$
	PQ	$8.18 \cdot 10^{-2}$	$2.34 \cdot 10^{-1}$	$7.57 \cdot 10^{-2}$	$1.34 \cdot 10^{-1}$	$2.52 \cdot 10^{-2}$
	F_β	0.3065	**0.5994**	0.2871	0.4281	0.1140
	|C|	$2.30 \cdot 10^6$	$1.22 \cdot 10^6$	$2.99 \cdot 10^6$	$6.28 \cdot 10^6$	$1.17 \cdot 10^8$
R2	PC	$0.95 \uparrow$	$0.93 \downarrow$	$0.96 \uparrow$	$0.98 \uparrow$	$0.98 \uparrow$
	PQ	$1.32 \cdot 10^{-3}$	$1.76 \cdot 10^{-3}$	$7.39 \cdot 10^{-4}$	$3.59 \cdot 10^{-4}$	$1.93 \cdot 10^{-5}$
	F_β	**0.0066**	0.0087	0.0037	0.0018	0.0001
	|C|	$1.90 \cdot 10^7$	$4.79 \cdot 10^5$	$9.82 \cdot 10^7$	$1.58 \cdot 10^8$	$9.10 \cdot 10^7$
R3	PC	$0.92 \downarrow$	$0.81 \downarrow$	$0.95 \uparrow$	$0.97 \uparrow$	$0.85 \downarrow$
	PQ	$1.88 \cdot 10^{-3}$	$3.86 \cdot 10^{-2}$	$2.20 \cdot 10^{-4}$	$1.41 \cdot 10^{-4}$	$2.15 \cdot 10^{-4}$
	F_β	0.0093	0.1621	**0.0011**	0.0007	0.0011
	|C|	$7.55 \cdot 10^9$	$1.81 \cdot 10^9$	$1.37 \cdot 10^{11}$	$9.63 \cdot 10^{10}$	$8.79 \cdot 10^9$
R4	PC	$0.97 \uparrow$	$0.93 \downarrow$	$0.98 \uparrow$	$0.96 \uparrow$	$0.95 \uparrow$
	PQ	$5.71 \cdot 10^{-4}$	$4.56 \cdot 10^{-4}$	$6.39 \cdot 10^{-6}$	$8.94 \cdot 10^{-6}$	$9.66 \cdot 10^{-5}$
	F_β	**0.0028**	0.0023	0.00003	0.0004	0.0005

The PC of the techniques, in general, present values above 95%. On the other hand, ADP and BLAST did not achieve good results for PC in R3. It can be explained because R3 has more attribute-value pairs per record ($|AVR(R)|$) than other datasets. In BLAST, it impacts when similar attributes are grouped and in ADP when defining the prefix length value. In both cases, the number of candidate pairs is decreased, and consequently, duplicates pairs are missed, which leads to a decrease in the value of PC.

Qualitatively, we can analyze that, despite the good performance of the filtering techniques (i.e., PPJ and PPJ+) for some datasets, there are scenarios that limit the power of discarding candidate pairs. More homogeneous datasets (i.e., datasets whose records share many tokens and have many similar record pairs) result in a few pairs of records discarded. For example, Length Filtering loses its effectiveness when the records in a dataset have slight variation in size (e.g., the synthetic datasets), causing multiple pairs of records to be considered candidates, often not being matched. In other words, if the filters fail, many candidate pairs will be accepted at the end of the algorithm's execution. It can be considered a weak point, explaining the low efficiency in the sets with long records and a lot of data (e.g., R3).

To analyze the techniques' scalability, we performed experiments on three sets of synthetic data ranging the size. Figure 2(a) shows the results for the effectiveness techniques. We can see better scalability of the RecWNP meta-blocking technique regarding the filtering techniques (PPJ, PPJ+, and ADP). BLAST was not plotted on the chart because it does not meet the PC restriction for effectiveness in all synthetic datasets.

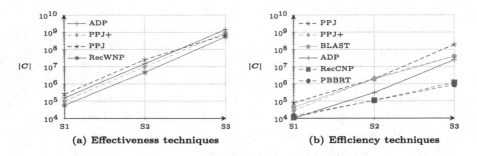

(a) Effectiveness techniques   (b) Efficiency techniques

Fig. 2. Scalability in synthetic data for (a) effectiveness and (b) efficiency techniques.

In short, meta-blocking techniques (e.g., RecWNP) achieves the best results in the datasets analyzed. RecWNP, in addition to being scalable for the large datasets, performs among the best in F_β metrics. On the other hand, filtering techniques (e.g., PPJ and PPJ+) are competitive with meta-blocking in datasets with small dataset sizes, achieving a good trade-off between the number of candidate and matching pairs.

Table 4. The performance of efficiency techniques applied to real datasets. The best results of the F_β metric are highlighted.

		Efficiency					
		RecCNP	BLAST	PBBRT	PPJ	PPJ+	ADP
R1	|C|	$1.19 \cdot 10^4$	$9.33 \cdot 10^3$	$1.12 \cdot 10^4$	$8.93 \cdot 10^3$	$4.93 \cdot 10^3$	$1.06 \cdot 10^4$
	PC	0.96 ↑	0.98 ↑	0.96 ↑	0.80 ↑	0.83 ↑	0.83 ↑
	PQ	$1.81 \cdot 10^{-1}$	$2.34 \cdot 10^{-1}$	$1.91 \cdot 10^{-1}$	$1.99 \cdot 10^{-1}$	$3.74 \cdot 10^{-1}$	$1.73 \cdot 10^{-1}$
	F_β	0.2163	0.2762	0.2280	0.2342	**0.4197**	0.2055
R2	|C|	$1.18 \cdot 10^5$	$1.22 \cdot 10^6$	$8.32 \cdot 10^4$	$8.46 \cdot 10^5$	$3.34 \cdot 10^5$	$3.35 \cdot 10^6$
	PC	0.84 ↑	0.93 ↑	0.85 ↑	0.88 ↑	0.81 ↑	0.80 ↑
	PQ	$1.69 \cdot 10^{-2}$	$1.76 \cdot 10^{-3}$	$2.35 \cdot 10^{-2}$	$2.39 \cdot 10^{-3}$	$5.60 \cdot 10^{-3}$	$5.48 \cdot 10^{-4}$
	F_β	0.0210	0.0022	**0.0291**	0.0030	0.0070	0.0007
R3	|C|	$2.89 \cdot 10^5$	$4.79 \cdot 10^5$	$2.24 \cdot 10^5$	$4.76 \cdot 10^7$	$6.92 \cdot 10^7$	$9.10 \cdot 10^7$
	PC	0.64 ↓	0.81 ↑	0.75 ↓	0.81 ↑	0.91 ↑	0.85 ↑
	PQ	$5.55 \cdot 10^{-2}$	$3.86 \cdot 10^{-2}$	$7.60 \cdot 10^{-2}$	$3.90 \cdot 10^{-4}$	$3.00 \cdot 10^{-4}$	$2.15 \cdot 10^{-4}$
	F_β	0.0680	**0.0477**	0.0926	0.0005	0.0004	0.0003
R4	|C|	$8.06 \cdot 10^6$	$1.81 \cdot 10^9$	$4.73 \cdot 10^6$	$1.44 \cdot 10^9$	$2.23 \cdot 10^9$	$2.78 \cdot 10^9$
	PC	0.89 ↑	0.93 ↑	0.94 ↑	0.82 ↑	0.83 ↑	0.84 ↑
	PQ	$9.99 \cdot 10^{-2}$	$4.56 \cdot 10^{-4}$	$1.78 \cdot 10^{-1}$	$5.07 \cdot 10^{-4}$	$3.34 \cdot 10^{-4}$	$2.70 \cdot 10^{-4}$
	F_β	0.1215	0.0006	**0.2120**	0.0006	0.0004	0.0003

Efficiency. Table 4 shows the experimental results of the efficiency techniques (RecCNP, BLAST, PBBRT, PPJ, PPJ+, ADP) in the real datasets. Considering the F_β metric, PBBRT is the technique that stands out with the best performance in two datasets (R2 and R4), followed by RecWNP. The PBBRT shows a F_β improvement compared to RecWNP in 38.6% and 74.5% in R2 and R4 datasets, respectively. PPJ+ has the best result in R1. It confirms the earlier conclusions about filtering techniques performing satisfactorily in datasets with a smaller amount of data and more homogeneous. The meta-blocking techniques RecWNP and PBBRT do not meet the restriction from PC to R3 ($PC \geq 0.8$). It can be explained because R3 is made up of dirtier data (as stated earlier). This can lead to the underweight of the corresponding record pairs, which causes the missing of matching pairs. BLAST achieves the best performance for R3. In this case, the BLAST attribute similarity analysis may have contributed to finding a more significant number of matching pairs. The Meta-blocking efficiency can be explained by the easy extraction of valuable information, directly from the data and the graph, about the relationship of the records to identify those with the most potential for correspondence. PBBRT obtains the best results among the analyzed techniques mainly because of the efficient strategy of choosing tokens to be used in the blocking and reblocking stage. Also, PBBRT does not require the user-defined parameter, which is a strong point concerning other techniques.

Figure 2(b) shows the scalability focus on efficiency techniques in synthetic datasets. PBBRT and RecCNP have the best scalability concerning the others when the datasets' size increases. It is explained by using the efficient strategies used to improve the pruning process of candidate pairs. ADP increase in the number of candidate pairs is because adaptive prefix produce more candidate pairs when the data increases.

In short, meta-blocking techniques excel in the analysis of efficiency, with PBBRT obtaining the best performance in F_β, in addition to being scalable for the large datasets tested. The PPJ and PPJ+ filtering techniques are positioned competitively with meta-blocking techniques in the smaller datasets evaluated.

6   Conclusions

This paper presents a comparative analysis of reblocking stage involving meta-blocking and filtering techniques. Reblocking stage aims at reducing the number of comparisons of the ER task. Meta-blocking focuses on reducing the number of comparisons based on the blocks shared by the records. On the other hand, filtering techniques reduce the number of comparisons based on the records' degree of similarity. These techniques were analyzed in the context of applications for the effectiveness and efficiency of ER in real and synthetic datasets. The results show that the filtering techniques are competitive with the meta-blocking techniques in smaller datasets, achieving good results. However, the filtering techniques did not adjust well to the large datasets evaluated. On the other hand, meta-blocking techniques maintained good performance in most of the evaluated datasets.

We believe that scalability remains an open challenge for the filtering approach techniques. Also, there is room for effectiveness and efficiency improvements in the meta-blocking techniques. For future work, we intend to explore reblocking in a real-time ER context, which aims to identify matching pairs in the shortest time.

References

1. Bianco, G.D., Goncalves, M.A., Duarte, D.: Bloss: effective meta-blocking with almost no effort. Inf. Syst. **75**, 75–89 (2018)
2. Caldeira, L.S., Ferreira, A.A.: Improvements in the blocking process for entity resolution based on the term relevance. In: SBBD, pp. 61–72 (2018). (in Portuguese)
3. Chinchor, N., Sundheim, B.M.: MUC-5 evaluation metrics. In: Proceedings of the Fifth Message Understanding Conference (MUC-5), pp. 22–29 (1993)
4. Christen, P.: Data Matching: Concepts and Techniques for Record Linkage, Entity Resolution, and Duplicate Detection. Springer, Heidelberg (2012). https://doi.org/10.1007/978-3-642-31164-2
5. Christen, P.: A survey of indexing techniques for scalable record linkage and deduplication. TKDE **24**(9), 1537–1555 (2012)
6. Christophides, V., Efthymiou, V., Stefanidis, K.: Entity Resolution in the Web of Data. Morgan & Claypool Publishers, San Rafael (2015)

7. Dong, X.L., Srivastava, D.: Big Data Integration. Morgan & Claypool Publishers, San Rafael (2015)
8. Golshan, B., Halevy, A., Mihaila, G., Tan, W.C.: Data integration: after the teenage years. In: PODS, pp. 101–106 (2017)
9. Jiang, Y., Li, G., Feng, J., Li, W.S.: String similarity joins: an experimental evaluation. PVLDB 7(8), 625–636 (2014)
10. Köpcke, H., Thor, A., Rahm, E.: Evaluation of entity resolution approaches on real-world match problems. PVLDB 3(1–2), 484–493 (2010)
11. Mann, W., Augsten, N., Bouros, P.: An empirical evaluation of set similarity join techniques. PVLDB 9(9), 636–647 (2016)
12. O'Hare, K., Jurek-Loughrey, A., Campos, C.: A review of unsupervised and semi-supervised blocking methods for record linkage. In: P, D., Jurek-Loughrey, A. (eds.) Linking and Mining Heterogeneous and Multi-view Data. USL, pp. 79–105. Springer, Cham (2019). https://doi.org/10.1007/978-3-030-01872-6_4
13. Papadakis, G., Ioannou, E., Niederée, C., Fankhauser, P.: Efficient entity resolution for large heterogeneous information spaces. In: WSDM, pp. 535–544 (2011)
14. Papadakis, G., Papastefanatos, G., Palpanas, T., Koubarakis, M.: Scaling entity resolution to large, heterogeneous data with enhanced meta-blocking. In: EDBT, pp. 221–232 (2016)
15. Papadakis, G., Skoutas, D., Thanos, E., Palpanas, T.: Blocking and filtering techniques for entity resolution: a survey. CSUR 53(2), 1–42 (2020)
16. Papadakis, G., Svirsky, J., Gal, A., Palpanas, T.: Comparative analysis of approximate blocking techniques for entity resolution. PVLDB 9(9), 684–695 (2016)
17. Shannon, C.E.: A mathematical theory of communication. ACM SIGMOBILE Mob. Comput. Commun. Rev. 5(1), 3–55 (2001)
18. Silva, L.F., Canalle, G.K., Salgado, A.C., Lóscio, B.F., Moro, M.M.: An experimental analysis of the impact of attribute selection on entity resolution processes. In: SBBD, pp. 37–48 (2019). (in Portuguese)
19. Simonini, G., Bergamaschi, S., Jagadish, H.: Blast: a loosely schema-aware meta-blocking approach for entity resolution. PVLDB 9(12), 1173–1184 (2016)
20. Simonini, G., Gagliardelli, L., Bergamaschi, S., Jagadish, H.: Scaling entity resolution: a loosely schema-aware approach. Inf. Syst. 83, 145–165 (2019)
21. Song, D., Heflin, J.: Automatically generating data linkages using a domain-independent candidate selection approach. In: Aroyo, L., et al. (eds.) ISWC 2011. LNCS, vol. 7031, pp. 649–664. Springer, Heidelberg (2011). https://doi.org/10.1007/978-3-642-25073-6_41
22. Song, D., Luo, Y., Heflin, J.: Linking heterogeneous data in the semantic web using scalable and domain-independent candidate selection. TKDE 29(1), 143–156 (2017)
23. Wang, J., Li, G., Feng, J.: Can we beat the prefix filtering? an adaptive framework for similarity join and search. In: SIGMOD, pp. 85–96 (2012)
24. Wang, X., Qin, L., Lin, X., Zhang, Y., Chang, L.: Leveraging set relations in exact and dynamic set similarity join. VLDB J. 28(2), 267–292 (2018). https://doi.org/10.1007/s00778-018-0529-2
25. Xiao, C., Wang, W., Lin, X., Yu, J.X., Wang, G.: Efficient similarity joins for near-duplicate detection. TODS 36(3), 1–41 (2011)

FiLiPo: A Sample Driven Approach for Finding Linkage Points Between RDF Data and APIs

Tobias Zeimetz[(✉)] and Ralf Schenkel

Trier University, 54286 Trier, Germany
{zeimetz,schenkel}@uni-trier.de

Abstract. Data integration is an important task in order to create comprehensive RDF knowledge bases. Many data sources are used to extend a given dataset or to correct errors. Since several data providers make their data publicly available only via Web APIs they also must be included in the integration process. However, APIs often come with limitations in terms of access frequencies and speed due to latencies and other constraints. On the other hand, APIs always provide access to the latest data. So far, integrating APIs has been mainly a manual task due to the heterogeneity of API responses. To tackle this problem we present in this paper the FiLiPo (**Fi**nding **Li**nkage **Po**ints) system which automatically finds connections (i.e., linkage points) between data provided by APIs and local knowledge bases. FiLiPo is an open source sample-driven schema matching system that models API services as parameterized queries. Furthermore, our approach is able to find valid input values for APIs automatically (e.g. IDs) and can determine valid alignments between KBs and APIs. Our results on ten pairs of KBs and APIs show that FiLiPo performs well in terms of precision and recall and outperforms the current state-of-the-art system.

Keywords: Data integration · Schema mapping · Relation alignment

1 Introduction

RDF knowledge bases (KBs) are used in many domains, e.g. bibliographic, medical, and biological data. Most knowledge bases face the problem that they are potentially incomplete, incorrect or outdated. Considering how much new data is generated daily it is highly desirable to integrate missing data provided by external sources. Thus, data integration approaches [3,7,8,11,13] are used to expand KBs and correct erroneous data. The usual process of data integration is to download data dumps and align the schemas of a local KB and these dumps. "Aligning" describes the process by which relations and classes from the local KB are mapped to relations and entities of external sources, thus creating a mapping between the local and the external data schemas. Afterwards, the integration process can be done and the data of the KB is expanded or updated.

© Springer Nature Switzerland AG 2021
L. Bellatreche et al. (Eds.): ADBIS 2021, LNCS 12843, pp. 244–259, 2021.
https://doi.org/10.1007/978-3-030-82472-3_18

However, data dumps are often updated only infrequently. Using live data through APIs instead of dumps [7, 8] allows access to more recent data. In addition, the number of potential data sources becomes much larger when using APIs since most data providers share their data not via dumps, but via APIs. According to Koutraki et al. [8], *APIs seem to be a sweet-spot between making data openly accessible and protecting it.* The problems of data integration, i.e. how two different schemas can be mapped, remain. In the worst case, the schema of an external source has a completely different structure than the local KB. Hence, data integration remained a manual task for most parts [8].

Motivation. Connecting KBs with data behind APIs can significantly improve existing intelligent applications. As a motivating example, we consider dblp[1], a bibliographic database of computer science publications. It accommodates different meta data about publications, e.g., titles, publisher names, and author names and can be represented as an RDF KB. Data from dblp is often used for reviewer, venue or paper recommendation, and extending dblp with information from APIs like CrossRef, or SciGraph, for example titles or abstracts, can improve these applications. Missing information about authors like ORCIDs (an ORCID is a code to uniquely identify scientific authors) can be supplemented by these APIs and help to disambiguate author profiles. Furthermore, such information is also useful for a user querying dblp for authors or publications, where missing information can be completed using external data sources. Therefore it is important that multiple APIs can be used and missing data can be integrated from many different sources. Additionally, the determined alignments can be used to identify erroneous data and correct it if necessary.

Contributions. We present FiLiPo (**Fi**nding **Li**nkage **Po**ints)[2], a system to automatically discover alignments between KBs and APIs, focusing on detecting property/path alignments. We omit aligning classes because classes and types (in terms of semantic classes, e.g. URLs) do not exist in typical API responses. FiLiPo is designed to work with single record response APIs, i.e. APIs that return only a single record as response and not a list of most similar search results, and works for datasets of arbitrary domains. In contrast to other systems [13], users of FiLiPo only require knowledge about a local KB (e.g. class names) but no prior knowledge about the APIs' data structure. To the best of our knowledge, FiLiPo is the first aligning system that automatically detects what information from a KB has to be used as input of an API to retrieve responses. Thus end users do not have to determine the best input, significantly reducing manual effort. In contrast to other state-of-the-art systems [8], FiLiPo uses fifteen different string similarity metrics to find an alignment between the schema of a KB and that of an API. A single string similarity method is not suited to compare different kinds of data, for example both ORCIDs (requiring exact matches), ISBNs (with some variation) and abbreviated names. A user only needs to specify the number of requests sent to the API in order to keep the approach simple.

---

[1] https://dblp.uni-trier.de/.
[2] Code available at https://github.com/dbis-trier-university/FiLiPo.

2   Problem Statement

This paper addresses five challenges when aligning local KBs with APIs. The first challenge is to determine which input values (e.g. DOI, etc.) have to be sent to the API to retrieve a valid response. A valid response is a response that contains information about the requested entity. In contrast, invalid responses contain information about similar entities (e.g. a list of most similar search results) or an error message. Note that the user has to specify the URL and the parameter of an API (e.g. `www.example.com/api?q=`). When a resource is requested that is unknown to the API, it can respond in several ways. The classic case is that it returns an HTTP status code (e.g. `404`). The more complicated case is a JSON response that contains an error message or returns information on a "similar" resource (e.g., with a similar DOI). This cannot be easily distinguished from a "real" response which contains data about the requested resource.

An alignment between the schemata of an API and a KB are determined by collecting several responses from an API and comparing these information with the one stored in a KB. Semantically equal data values between API responses and KB entities are denoted as (sample) matches (e.g. the match of a DOI value). In order to determine such matches, the second challenge is that the same value may be represented slightly differently in the KB than in the API (e.g., names with and without abbreviated first names), hence the comparison needs to apply string similarity methods. The various existing similarity methods have different strengths and weaknesses. For example, Levenshtein distance is good for comparing the titles of a paper or movie, but performs poorly when comparing names of authors or actors because names are often abbreviated and first and last names may be in different order. Hence, a suitable similarity method needs to be determined automatically for each type of data.

A special case of this challenge is comparing identifiers, e.g. ISBNs. Identifiers need to be equal in order to yield as match. However, the ISBN of a book can be written in different forms (e.g. without hyphens) but should be considered equal. For this reason a simple check for equality is not sufficient, otherwise possible alignments are lost. Note that such identifiers (e.g. IBANs, tax numbers and others) also exist in other domains.

Finding a match between the information of KBs and APIs can be particularly problematic if APIs respond with records similar to the requested one. For example, a request for a book with title "*Some example Title*" may lead to an API response of a book with title "*Some Title*". The information of the API and the KB may overlap, especially for values that appear in many entities (e.g. year). Thus, the fourth challenge is to check if APIs respond with the requested information. Koutraki et al. [8] state that if KBs and APIs share the same domain, it is likely that the data of their entities overlap. This means that if the information of the API and the KB overlaps sufficiently, the API has probably responded with the requested record.

The last challenge is that some data values are contained in an API response several times, e.g. year values. In this case, they may represent a different piece of information, e.g. some bibliographic APIs respond with data containing references and citations of a paper, which often include author names and publication years. During the matching process, care must be taken as to which information is matched. Just because the values match, they do not form a valid match (e.g. matching a papers author names with the author names of the papers references). Hence the semantics and structure of the paths should be considered but API responses do not always have a clear or a directly resulting semantics.

3   Related Work

Web Data Alignment. Next to FiLiPo (which was already presented in a demonstration [17]), DORIS [8,9] is the only system that has dealt with the alignment of KBs and APIs so far. DORIS builds upon the schema of an existing KB and during the alignment process, it sends several requests to an API. Users only have to specify the input class for the API and a request limit. The input class specifies which form of entities the API responds to (e.g. publications). Then the label information of instances is used as input for APIs, which is often not the appropriate input for an API (e.g. some APIs expect DOIs, etc.). In contrast, FiLiPo is able to detect automatically appropriate input values.

A key assumption of DORIS is that it is more likely to find information about popular entities (e.g. famous actors) via API calls. From this follows the assumption that KBs contain more facts of well-known entities and hence it ranks entities by descending number of facts. These entities will then be used for the alignment. This approach has major drawbacks, e.g. the number of facts for a publication stored by a bibliographic KB is often determined by the meta data of that publication, not by its popularity (unless citations etc. are stored). To compare data values during the alignment DORIS uses equality (ignoring punctuation and case). This limitation becomes clear when examining, for example, author names. They are often abbreviated and DORIS' matching approach will fail since it performs exact match on normalised names. In contrast, FiLiPo uses a set of similarity methods and picks randomly chosen entities of a KB.

Wrapper Inference. The problem of aligning KBs and APIs shares similarities with various other fields [3,8,14] like schema alignment, query discovery and wrapper inference approaches. Wrapper inference approaches [12,15] face similar problems as alignment systems from other fields. Senellart et al. [15] present an approach which uses domain knowledge (concept names and instance data) in order to identify the input of form fields. They assume that there are no specifically required fields in the form. However, this does not apply to the majority of APIs, since most have a mandatory parameter. Afterwards the structure of the data behind the form fields is aligned with concept names by exploiting the semantics of form fields and web tables (e.g. labels, table headers, etc.). Since paths in API responses do not always have a clear or any semantic at all, FiLiPo does not use path semantics. Derouiche et al. [12] also use domain knowledge to extract data from Web sources. Additionally, they use for every concept (e.g. date) a form of regular expression. Since users have to specify these expressions, this approach significantly raises the manual effort and the needed knowledge.

Schema/Ontology Alignment. Aligning data of KBs and APIs has similar problems as schema/ontology alignment. The major difference is that API responses often do not have explicit semantics or any semantics at all, and the data schema of the API is often not directly accessible to external parties. In addition, names of the paths are often ambiguous. Semantics in form of rules (as with RDF/OWL) does not exist in API responses. Also, responses usually do not provide information about classes/relations that can be used for the alignment process. When using APIs, only instance information is available and hence classical schema/ontology approaches are not suitable. Additionally, Madhavan et al. [10] state that KBs often contain multiple schemas to materialise similar concepts and hence build variations in entities and their relations. This makes schema-based matching inaccurate, which must therefore be supported by evidence in form of instances.

Instance-Based Alignment. Instance-based alignment systems use the information bound to instances in KBs in order to find shared relations and classes between two KBs. These approaches can be divided into instance-based class alignment approaches and instance-based relation alignment approaches. The main difference between class and relation alignment lies in the fact that relations have a domain and range. Even if relations share the same value, they can have different semantics (e.g. editor and author).

A lot of works [4,6,10,13] focus on instance-based relation alignment between KBs. Most of them focus on finding 1:1 matches, e.g. matching publicationYear to year. The iMAP system [4] semi-automatically determines 1:1 matches, but also considers 1:n matches. iMAP consists of a set of search modules, called searchers. Each of the searchers handles specific types of attribute combinations (e.g. a text searcher). FiLiPo follows a similar approach. Instead of searchers, FiLiPo only distinguishes between the type of information (numeric, string, or is it a key). Then, in case of strings, a number of different similarity methods are considered, and the best method is automatically determined and used.

Similar to iMAP, MWEAVER [13] also needs user assistance. MWEAVER realises a sample-driven schema mapping approach which automatically constructs schema mappings from sample target instances given by the user. The idea of this system is to allow the user to implicitly specify mappings by providing sample data. However, this approach needs significant manual effort. The user must be familiar with the target schema in order to provide samples. In contrast to this approach, FiLiPo draws the sample data randomly from the KB and thus tries to cover a wide range of information.

SOFYA [6] is an instance-based on-the-fly approach for relation alignment between two KBs. The approach works with data samples from both KBs in order to identify matching relations. The core aspect of SOFYA is that the standard relation "sameAs" is used to find identical entities in two different KBs. However, this mechanism cannot be used for the alignment of KBs and APIs, because APIs do not contain standardised "sameAs" links.

The Cupid system [11] is used to discover an alignment between KBs based on the names of the schema elements, data types, constraints and structure. It combines a broad set of techniques of various categories (e.g. instance-based, schema alignment, etc.). The system uses a linguistic and structural approach in order to find a valid alignment. Furthermore, Cupid leverages a corpus of schemas and mappings to improve the robustness of the schema matching algorithms. Unfortunately, this approach cannot be used when aligning KBs and APIs, since often there is no formally defined schema for an API.

4 Preliminaries

Knowledge Bases. An RDF KB can be represented as graph with labelled nodes and edges. A KB consists of triples of the form (s, p, o) which represent a fact in the KB. The subject (start node) s describes the entity the fact is about, e.g. a paper entity. An entity is represented by an URI, which is an identifier of a real-world entity such as a paper or an abstract concept (e.g. a conference). The predicate p describes the relation between the subject and the object, e.g. `title`. The object (target node) o describes an entity, e.g. an author, or is a literal, e.g. the title of a publication. A class in a KB is an entity that represents a group of entities. Entities assigned to a class are instances of that class. In Fig. 1b, the entity `PaperEntity` is an instance of the class `Publication`.

Relations. Since this paper focuses on aligning relations, we introduce a formal definition for relation (paths). Given a KB K, if $(s, r, o) \in K$, we say that s and o are in relation r, or formally $r(s, o)$; in other words, there is a path from s to o with label r. Also, we write $r_1.r_2.....r_n(s, o)$ to denote that there exists a path of relations $r_1, r_2, ..., r_n$ in K from subject s to object o visiting every node only once. For example, in Fig. 1b the relation `year(PaperEntity,"2020")` describes the path from the entity `PaperEntity` to the value `"2020"`. In the following we will refer to $r_1.r_2.....r_n(s, o)$ as relation-value path.

Identifier Relations. Some KBs contain globally standardised identifiers such as DOIs, IBANs (International Bank Account Numbers), tax numbers and others. Identifiers are only bound to a single entity and should be unique. Therefore, relations r that model identifier relations have the constraint that their inverse relations (r^{-1}) are "quasi-functions", i.e., their inverse relations have a high functionality. Many works [5,8,16] have used the following definition for determining the functionality of relations:

$$ fun(r) := \frac{|\{x : \exists y : r(x, y)\}|}{|\{(x, y) : r(x, y)\}|} $$

Since real world KBs are designed by humans identifier relations are often error-prone which is why some identifier values may appear more than once. Hence, we consider every relation r contained in K with $fun(r^{-1}) \geq \theta_{id}$, where $\theta_{id} \in [0, 1]$ is a threshold, as *identifier relation*. From now on we denote R_K^{id} as the set of all identifier relations (e.g., `doi`, `isbn`, etc.) contained in a KB K. Note that we ignore identifier relations that are composed of several relations.

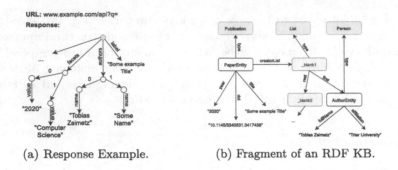

(a) Response Example.   (b) Fragment of an RDF KB.

Fig. 1. Record of a KB and the corresponding API response.

Web API. A Web service can provide one or multiple APIs to access data. APIs are called via parameterised URLs (see Fig. 1a). As shown in Fig. 1a the response of an API can be represented as an unordered and labelled tree. Inner nodes in the tree represent an object (similar to an entity in a KB) or an array, leaf nodes represent values. The path to a node represents a relation between an instance (similar to an entity in a KB) and another instance or value. To avoid confusion we will describe these relations in a response only as paths.

Path-Value-Pairs. In order to find valid alignments between KBs and APIs the information in the API responses has to be compared with the values of the corresponding entities in a KB. Since comparing objects and arrays from the API response with entities from the KB to determine alignments is not promising, only paths to leafs (literals) have to be considered. Given an API response res we will write $p_1.p_2.....p_n(o)$ to denote that there is a path $p_1, p_2, ..., p_n$ in res from the root of the response to the leaf o with these labels. For example, in Fig. 1a the path `label("Some example Title")` describes the path from the root of the API response to the leaf `"Some example Title"` via the path `label`.

Branching Points. A branching point in an API response indicates that there are several outgoing edges from one node, labelled by numeric index values 0 to n. These branching points represent arrays. In the example in Fig. 1a, the path `authors.0.name("Tobias Zeimetz")` contains a branching point. To indicate a branching point, we will use the symbol $*$ instead of the numeric index in paths; in the example, we will write `authors.*.name("Tobias Zeimetz")`. Using the same logic, a relation in a KB that points to a set of entities is considered to be a branching point (e.g. `creatorList` in Fig. 1b). Additionally, we write $P*$ to indicate a path $P * p$ that has P as prefix and p as suffix, with a branching point separating the two parts.

5   Schema Matching and Mapping

FiLiPo operates in two phases. First (*probing phase*), FiLiPo sends various information (e.g. DOIs, titles, etc.) to an API to determine which information the

API responds to. Afterwards (*aligning phase*), the information returned is used to guess the API's schema and to determine an alignment between the local and external data. The input of the aligning process is the URL of the API (see Fig. 1a) and the corresponding input classes in the KB. An input class is a class of entities that will be used to request the API. An extended version of this paper with a detailed description of the algorithm can be found at arXiv[3].

5.1 Probing Phase

The probing phase is used to find the set R_{in} of relations of the input class that point to values which can be used to request the API successfully (e.g., a DOI relation). Note that we only consider APIs with one input parameter (API tokens and similar do not count as input parameter since they are constants), otherwise the runtime will increase extremely, because of the combination possibilities. To illustrate the probing with an example, we assume that the input class of the API whose result is shown in Fig. 1a is `Publication`. The illustrated fragment in Fig. 1b has five relations to describe the metadata of a publication but the API only responds to DOIs. First, all relations that are not connected to literals (e.g. `type`) are ignored. This is done because almost all APIs expect a literal as input value (e.g. DOI, title, etc.) and not classes encoded as URL entities.

In addition, values that occur more than once in the KB (e.g. year numbers such as 2021, ambiguous titles such as "Editorial" and names) are not used as input values because more than one record can be returned and possibly a not matching one is returned. Afterwards n_p initial requests are sent to the API for each remaining relation of the input class (i.e. `title` and `doi`). The created URL to request the API is a concatenation of the API URL specified by the user (see Fig. 1a and values for the corresponding input relations, e.g. for `doi` an example call URL is www.example.com/api?q=10.1145/3340531.3417438.

The input values for each relation are picked uniformly at random from entities of the input class in the KB. This is done to prevent the entities from being very similar to each other and thus increase the probability of an response. For example, assuming that an API only responds to entities with a specific publisher, e.g. Springer. If entities are selected in any non-random way, e.g. according to the amount of facts, it is possible that no entities with publisher Springer are included, and the API cannot respond and no aligning can be done.

After requesting an API it can respond in several ways, i.e. with the HTTP status code 200 `OK` or with an HTTP error code. Relations $r \in R_{in}$ that lead to responses are considered as valid input relations. All other relations will no longer be considered as input relations and hence, unnecessary requests are prevented. Next, the alignment phase begins, considering only the set R_{in} of relations that led to valid answers. The aligning phase itself is divided into two parts: (1) determining candidate alignments and (2) determining the final alignments.

---

[3] Link to the extended paper version: https://arxiv.org/abs/2103.06253.

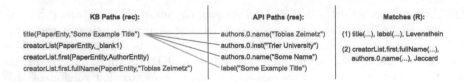

Fig. 2. Fragment of a KB Record and an API Response

5.2   Aligning Phase: Candidate Alignment

This phase takes as input the set of valid input relations R_{in}, a KB K and the corresponding identifier relations R_K^{id}. For each input relation $r_{in} \in R_{in}$, the algorithm sends n_r further requests to the API. For each request, it chooses a random entity e from the input class. It then calls the API with values v_{req} of the input relation r_{in} of e and stores the response in res (see Fig. 2, middle part; note that, for the sake of simplicity, not the full KB and API paths are shown in Fig. 2). Next, FiLiPo retrieves the set rec of all facts that K contains for e in form of relation-value paths $r(e, l)$ (see Fig. 2, left side). Note that r can be a path of multiple relations, e.g. $r_1.r_2...r_n(e, l)$. Like Koutraki et al. [8] we take only facts into account up to depth three, because all other facts usually do not make statements about the entity e. To exclude the case that entities are connected in only one direction, inverse relations are also considered.

The next step is to find all relation matches R between rec and res (see Fig. 2, right side). The set res encodes information from the response as path-value pairs of the form $p(v)$ where p is the path in the response from the root to the value v. Note that p can be a path of multiple components, e.g. $p_1.p_1...p_n(v)$. All values l of rec must be compared with all values v of res. Figure 2 presents an example for the title relation. The coloured lines represent comparisons between the values, red lines denote invalid matches and the green line represents a valid match. For each pair $(r(e, l), p(v))$, a suitable similarity method is determined. If l or v is an IRI, it is important that they are compared with **equals** as IRIs are identifiers and hence only the same if they are identical. The same holds for numerical values. In all other cases FiLiPo uses a set M_{sim} of fifteen different similarity methods[4] with several variants since one string similarity method is not sufficient to compare several data types. The method $m \in M_{sim}$ returning the largest similarity of l and v is considered (temporarily) to be a suitable method to compare both values and is stored for the later process.

We used the string similarity library developed by Baltes et al. [2] since it contains all major similarity methods, divided into three categories: equal, edit and set based. Since fuzzy methods are not appropriate for identifier relations and comparing them for equality would be too strict, identifier relations in R_K^{id} are therefore compared with a gradient boosting classifier working on Flair [1] embeddings. We use Flair embeddings since this framework is character-based

---

[4] All used similarity methods are listed in our manual at https://github.com/dbis-trier-university/FiLiPo/blob/master/README.md.

and therefore suits better for the comparison of identifier values. Once the best similarity method has been determined, and if it yields a similarity of at least θ_{str}, the triple (r, p, m) is created and added to the set of record matches R.

If enough matches are found, it is assumed that the input entity e and the API response overlap in their information (the overlapping information is highlighted in Fig. 2 in blue) and that the API has responded with information about the requested entity. We compute the overlap by dividing the number of matches $|R|$ by the number of entries of the smallest record rec or rcs. If the overlap is greater than a threshold θ_{rec}, the overlap is considered sufficient and the matches R will be added to $A_{r_{in}}$ (an example of overlapping values/paths is presented in blue in Fig. 2 and an example of $A_{r_{in}}$ is presented in Fig. 3). This set represents matches found for the input relation r_{in}. If not enough matches are found, it is assumed that the API has responded with information of a different entity; in this case, any matches found between the records must be ignored.

5.3 Aligning Phase: Final Alignment

Afterwards $A_{r_{in}}$ is used to determine the final alignment. For each relation in $A_{r_{in}}$ the best path match on the API side is searched (if existing). It is easy to match relations and paths without branching points, e.g. label or title in Fig. 2 (see (1)). However, for matches with a branching point path (see (2)), we need to decide if all entries of the corresponding array provide the same type of information or different types. In the first case, e.g. an array specifying the authors of a paper, we need to match *all paths* that are equal (index values omitted) of the API response with the same relation. This is the case in the example in Fig. 1a for the path authors.*.name. In the last case, where every entry of the array has a different type, each different index value at the branching point should be mapped to one specific relation, possibly different relations for the different index values. In the example, facets.0.value("2020") always denotes the year of the publication, whereas facets.1.value("Computer Science") denotes the genre of the publication. Therefore, matching either the year or the genre relation of K to facets.*.value is incorrect and should be prevented.

In order to solve these problems, FiLiPo distinguishes two cases: fixed path matches (FPM) and branching point matches (BPM). First, for every relation r for which at least one tuple (r, p, m) exists in $A_{r_{in}}$ we determine the path $P*$ (index values are replaced by the wild card symbol) that was matched most often in $A_{r_{in}}$, regardless of which similarity method m was used.

Next it is determined if $(r, P*) \in A_{r_{in}}$ is a BPM or FPM. Hence, it is checked if the path $P*$ that was matched to r in $A_{r_{in}}$ only had one index value at the branching point or multiple different ones (see $A_{r_{in}}$ in Fig. 3, blue highlighted lines). An example of a fixed path is facets.0.value in the set $A_{r_{in}}$ in Fig. 3. To indicate the year, always the same path is used in the API response. The first entry of the array facets always describes the year of a publication. If only one index value is found, it is considered as FPM. To ensure that it is a valid FPM, a confidence score for this match is determined. If a path was found only a few times, a match is not convincing. Hence, we calculate a confidence score

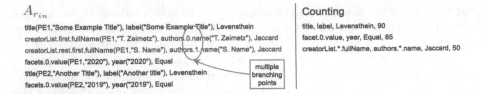

Fig. 3. Example Fragment of $A_{r_{in}}$ with abbreviated names for readability.

for the matching by dividing the number of valid matches for r by the number of responses. This confidence must be greater than the confidence threshold θ_{rec}. We reuse θ_{rec} based on the assumption that the overlapping of records is also reflected in the overlapping of relations. In the example in Fig. 3 (right side) it is shown that for `facet.0.value` and `year` 85 matches (using Equal) are found. Assuming that 100 requests are sent to the API and all are answered, this results in a confidence of $\frac{85}{100} = 0.85$. If the score is greater than or equal to θ_{rec}, it will yield as valid FPM and the relation-path match is added to the final alignment set. Note that another example for a FPM is the match of `title` and `label`.

Some relations and paths are dependent on the previous entity. For example, to match the name path for an author we have to include the whole author array of the API response because matching only one specific path (e.g. `authors.0.name`) excludes information of other authors. Hence, if more than one index value was found for $P*$ it is possible that $(r, P*)$ is a BPM. A match of r and a branching point path $P*$ is considered valid if the following two conditions are satisfied: (1) if the relation r has led to a match often enough, i.e. the previously computed confidence value is $\geq \theta_{rec}$, and (2) if the matched $(r, P*)$ occurs frequently enough in all matches $A_{r_{in}}$. If both conditions are met, the match $(r, P*)$ is considered a BPM and added to the final alignment set.

For the sake of simplicity, one aspect has yet not been considered in detail. Some relations can potentially be matched with multiple paths in the API response. For example, the relation for the publication year could be incorrectly matched with the path to the publication years of the article's references. As already indicated in the problem statement, just because the values match, it does not mean that it is a valid match. Hence the semantics of the paths should be considered but API responses do not always have a clear or a directly resulting semantics. To mitigate this, a reciprocal discount is used, i.e. the number n of matches found for a possibly incorrect path p and a relation r is discounted by the length difference of the paths to $n/|(len(r) - len(p))|$. Thus paths with the same length (and potentially same structure) as the KB are preferred. In this way, the structure of the data is taken into account, but there is no dependence on the paths having unambiguous and clear semantics. At the end the final alignment set contains all valid matches found for the input relation r_{in}.

6   Evaluation

Many systems [4,13] in Sect. 3 work semi-automatically with user assistance and are mostly designed for data of the same format. Some of the systems exploit schema information, use semantics or "sameAs" relations to find alignments. However, schema information exists rarely on the API side and using semantics or relations is difficult since API responses do not always have clear semantics. Furthermore, "sameAs" predicates are a concept of RDF and not present in classical API responses. Thus, we only use DORIS as a baseline system.

Datasets. We evaluated DORIS and FiLiPo on three KBs, seven bibliographic and two movie APIs. One KB is an RDF version of dblp[5]. The other KBs are Linked Movie DB[6] and a self-created RDF version of IMDB. The used APIs are SciGraph, CrossRef, Elsevier, ArXiv, two APIs provided by Semantic Scholar (one with DOIs and one with ArXiv keys as input parameters) and the COCI API of Open Citations. All of these APIs respond with metadata about scientific articles. To align the movie KBs we used the APIs of the Open Movie Database (OMDB) and The Movie Database (TMDB). They respond with metadata about movies, e.g. movie director and movie genres.

As a gold standard[7], we manually determined the correct path alignments for each suitable combination of KB and API. Alignments were ignored that could not be determined based on the data, but for which a human may have been able to draw a connection. For example sameAs relations, in most cases, cannot be determined automatically since the URLs may differ completely.

FiLiPo Evaluation. In order to find a suitable configuration (sample size and similarity thresholds) that works for most APIs, we performed several experiments. FiLiPo works with two different thresholds: the string similarity θ_{str} and the record overlap θ_{rec}. To identify a combination that provides good alignment results, we tested several combinations of values for both thresholds (steps of 0.1) and calculated precision, recall and F1 score. The found alignments had a very high precision for θ_{str} between 1.0 and 0.5; recall was significantly better at 0.5. This is mainly due to the fact that data which are slightly different (e.g. names) can still be matched. For large values of θ_{rec}, many alignments are lost, because the data of a KB and an API overlap only slightly in the worst case. Here, a value of 0.1 to 0.2 was already sufficient to prevent erroneous matching. Hence, we used $\theta_{str} = 0.5$ and $\theta_{rec} = 0.1$ in the experiments. Regarding the sample size we determined that 25 probing and 75 additional requests (sample size of 100) is suitable for most APIs. However, since some KBs and APIs have little data in common, the sample size may need to be adjusted.

We assume that users have no in-depth knowledge of used APIs, but are familiar with the structure of the KB, and that users have domain knowledge and hence understand common data structures from the genre of the KB (e.g.

---

[5] Provided by dblp: https://basilika.uni-trier.de/nextcloud/s/A92AbECHzmHiJRF.
[6] http://www.cs.toronto.edu/~oktie/linkedmdb/linkedmdb-18-05-2009-dump.nt.
[7] Code and gold standard can be found at https://zenodo.org/record/4778531.

Table 1. Probing Time (PT), Alignment Time (AT), (Average) Alignments (A), (Mean) Precision (P), (Mean) Recall (R), (Mean) F1 Score (F1)

Data Sets	FiLiPo							DORIS			
	Requests	PT	AT	A	P	R	F1	A	P	R	F1
dblp ↔ CrossRef	25/75	18.0	4.0	18	0.97	0.78	**0.91**	9	0.89	0.36	0.51
dblp ↔ SciGraph	25/75	14.5	2.5	18	0.96	0.78	**0.86**	11	1.00	0.38	0.55
dblp ↔ S2 (DOI)	25/75	24.5	8.0	15	0.89	0.87	**0.88**	12	0.83	0.47	0.60
dblp ↔ S2 (ArXiv)	25/75	24.5	9.0	7	1.00	0.88	**0.94**	6	0.83	0.33	0.47
dblp ↔ COCI	25/75	23.0	19.0	16	1.00	0.78	**0.88**	9	1.00	0.33	0.50
dblp ↔ Elsevier	25/375	17.5	5.5	13	0.92	0.92	**0.92**	–	–	–	–
LMDB ↔ TMDB	25/75	4.5	2.0	6	0.94	1.00	**0.97**	7	0.57	0.80	0.67
dblp ↔ ArXiv	25/75	11.5	3.5	8	0.83	0.86	**0.85**	5	1.00	0.43	0.60
LMDB ↔ OMDB	25/75	36.5	3.5	14	0.93	0.95	**0.94**	11	0.55	0.56	0.55
IMDB ↔ OMDB	25/75	4.0	14.5	9	0.73	0.66	0.69	9	1.00	0.90	**0.95**

bibliographic meta data). Additionally, users can make further settings (e.g., changing the sample size) to fine-tune FiLiPo. All APIs were executed with default settings, i.e. 25 probing with 75 additional requests (in total 100 requests) are made for every valid input relation. There are two exceptions: Since dblp contains relatively few publications by Elsevier, we set the number of additional requests to 375. For IMDB, we use a record overlap threshold of 0.3 since IMDB contains several relations with low functionality (e.g. movieLanguage) and hence incorrect matches would be tolerated. In contrast, DORIS excludes all relations with a low functionality from the alignment process. Hence, it prevents the result for erroneous matches but also loses some matches.

Since FiLiPo pulls random records from a KB and uses them to request an API, the alignments found may differ slightly between different runs. Hence, the evaluation was performed three times for each combination of KB and API. The average runtime was approx. 25 min. If input relations are known, as is the case with DORIS, then the system usually needs no longer than a few minutes because the probing phase can be skipped. The probing phase is expensive in runtime because an API is requested a significant number of times (see Table 1).

FiLiPo was able to identify all correct input relations for almost all APIs. The only exception is the combination of IMDB and OMDB: IMDB contains a relation (alternativeVersion) to specify an alternative version of a movie (e.g. a directors cut is an alternative version of a movie) which is a valid input for OMDB. Of four possible input relations, it was able to identify all (alternative) title relations (title, label and alternativeTitle) as input relation in all runs, but only determined in 60% of the runs the alternativeVersion as input. The reason for this is that especially the alternative version of lesser-known movies are unknown to OMDB. It can be summarised that *in all cases a valid input was found* but only in 9 of 10 cases *all* valid input relations were found.

For the evaluation we used the metrics precision, recall and F1 Score. FiLiPo was able to achieve a precision between 0.73 to 1.00 and a recall between 0.66

to 1.00. Values close to 1.0 are achieved mainly because there are only a few possible alignments. The F1 scores for FiLiPo are between 0.69 and 0.95.

Baseline Evaluation. We re-implemented DORIS for our evaluation. It uses label information of instances as its predefined input relation for APIs. Since this is not always the appropriate input parameter for an API (e.g. some APIs expect DOIs as input) we modified DORIS such that the input relation can be specified by the user. Compared to FiLiPo, DORIS has an advantage in the evaluation, since it does not have to determine valid input relations for the used APIs. In contrast to FiLiPo, these input relations must be specified by the user and hence the runtime is shorter and there is no risk of alignment with wrong input relations. DORIS uses two different confidence metrics to determine an alignment: the overlap and PCA confidence. We assessed that the PCA confidence delivers better results for the alignment and hence DORIS is able to match journal-related relations. Since most of the entities in dblp are conference papers, journal specific relations are lost when using the overlap confidence. The downside is that a path that was found only once in the responses only needs to match once to achieve a high confidence. In such cases it is risky to trust the match and hence a re-probing is performed which increases the runtime considerably, since entities that share the matched relation are subsequently searched and ranked. DORIS has been configured in order to send 100 requests to the APIs. The threshold for the PCA confidence has been set to 0.1 based on a calibration experiment similarly to FiLiPo testing several threshold values between 0.1 and 1.0 (in steps of 0.1). With threshold 0.1, no erroneous alignments were made; recall was significantly larger at 0.1 than with larger values.

FiLiPo outperforms DORIS in terms of precision in most cases and clearly in terms of recall and F1. This is mainly caused by the two disadvantages of DORIS discussed before: First, aligning with entities with most facts often misses rare features of entities (e.g. a specific publisher like Elsevier). As a result, it is not possible to determine an alignment for Elsevier's API (see Table 1). However, in order to be able to evaluate the alignment process, we restricted DORIS in the case of Elsevier to only use journals published by Elsevier which resulted in an F1 score of 0.85. Second, using only one similarity method results in a relatively high precision, but is also too rigid to recognise slightly different data (e.g. abbreviations of author names), thus leading to low recall. Only with IMDB, DORIS was able to achieve better results, mainly because DORIS excludes all relations with a very low functionality from the alignment process. This is also the reason why DORIS was significantly worse in terms of recall in the other alignment tests. However, since OMDB responds with only a small amount of information, in which no information with a high functionality was included, this limitation does not have a negative effect but rather a positive one.

7   Conclusion

We presented FiLiPo, a system to automatically discover alignments between KBs and APIs. A user only needs knowledge about a KB but no prior knowledge about an APIs data schema. In contrast to the DORIS system, our system is additionally able to determine valid input relations for APIs which significantly reduces manual effort by the user. In all cases a valid input relation was found by FiLiPo but only in 9 of 10 cases *all* input relations were found. Our evaluation showed that FiLiPo outperformed DORIS and delivered better alignment results in all but one case. In contrast to DORIS, it determined an alignment in all cases.

References

1. Akbik, A., Blythe, D., Vollgraf, R.: Contextual string embeddings for sequence labeling. In: COLING, pp. 1638–1649 (2018)
2. Baltes, S., Dumani, L., Treude, C., Diehl, S.: SOTorrent: reconstructing and analyzing the evolution of stack overflow posts. In: MSR, pp. 319–330. ACM (2018)
3. Bernstein, P.A., Madhavan, J., Rahm, E.: Generic schema matching, ten years later. Proc. VLDB Endow. 4(11), 695–701 (2011)
4. Dhamankar, R., Lee, Y., Doan, A., Halevy, A.Y., Domingos, P.M.: iMAP: discovering complex mappings between database schemas. In: SIGMOD, pp. 383–394. ACM (2004). https://doi.org/10.1145/1007568.1007612
5. Hogan, A., Polleres, A., Umbrich, J., Zimmermann, A.: Some entities are more equal than others: statistical methods to consolidate linked data. In: 4th Workshop on New Forms of Reasoning for the Semantic Web: Scalable & Dynamic (2010)
6. Koutraki, M., Preda, N., Vodislav, D.: SOFYA: semantic on-the-fly relation alignment. In: EDBT, pp. 690–691 (2016). https://doi.org/10.5441/002/edbt.2016.89
7. Koutraki, M., Preda, N., Vodislav, D.: Online relation alignment for linked datasets. In: Blomqvist, E., Maynard, D., Gangemi, A., Hoekstra, R., Hitzler, P., Hartig, O. (eds.) ESWC 2017. LNCS, vol. 10249, pp. 152–168. Springer, Cham (2017). https://doi.org/10.1007/978-3-319-58068-5_10
8. Koutraki, M., Vodislav, D., Preda, N.: Deriving intensional descriptions for web services. In: CIKM, pp. 971–980. ACM (2015). https://doi.org/10.1145/2806416.2806447
9. Koutraki, M., Vodislav, D., Preda, N.: DORIS: discovering ontological relations in services. In: ISWC. CEUR Workshop Proceedings, vol. 1486 (2015)
10. Madhavan, J., Bernstein, P.A., Doan, A., Halevy, A.Y.: Corpus-based schema matching. In: ICDE, pp. 57–68 (2005). https://doi.org/10.1109/ICDE.2005.39
11. Madhavan, J., Bernstein, P.A., Rahm, E.: Generic schema matching with cupid. In: VLDB, pp. 49–58. Morgan Kaufmann (2001)
12. Derouiche, N., Cautis, B., Abdessalem, T.: Automatic extraction of structured web data with domain knowledge. In: ICDE. IEEE Computer Society (2012). https://doi.org/10.1109/ICDE.2012.90
13. Qian, L., Cafarella, M.J., Jagadish, H.V.: Sample-driven schema mapping. In: SIGMOD, pp. 73–84. ACM (2012). https://doi.org/10.1145/2213836.2213846
14. Rahm, E., Bernstein, P.A.: A survey of approaches to automatic schema matching. VLDB J. 10(4), 334–350 (2001). https://doi.org/10.1007/s007780100057

15. Senellart, P., Mittal, A., Muschick, D., Gilleron, R., Tommasi, M.: Automatic wrapper induction from hidden-web sources with domain knowledge. In: WIDM. ACM (2008). https://doi.org/10.1145/1458502.1458505
16. Suchanek, F.M., Abiteboul, S., Senellart, P.: PARIS: probabilistic alignment of relations, instances, and schema. Proc. VLDB Endow. 5(3), 157–168 (2011). https://doi.org/10.14778/2078331.2078332
17. Zeimetz, T., Schenkel, R.: Sample driven data mapping for linked data and web apis. In: CIKM, pp. 3481–3484. ACM (2020). https://doi.org/10.1145/3340531. 3417438

SMAT: An Attention-Based Deep Learning Solution to the Automation of Schema Matching

Jing Zhang[1]([✉]), Bonggun Shin[2], Jinho D. Choi[1], and Joyce C. Ho[1]

[1] Emory University, Atlanta, GA 30329, USA
{jing.zhang2,jinho.choi,joyce.c.ho}@emory.edu
[2] Deargen Inc., Seoul, South Korea
bonggun.shin@deargen.me

Abstract. Schema matching aims to identify the correspondences among attributes of database schemas. It is frequently considered as the most challenging and decisive stage existing in many contemporary web semantics and database systems. Low-quality algorithmic matchers fail to provide improvement while manually annotation consumes extensive human efforts. Further complications arise from data privacy in certain domains such as healthcare, where only schema-level matching should be used to prevent data leakage. For this problem, we propose SMAT, a new deep learning model based on state-of-the-art natural language processing techniques to obtain semantic mappings between source and target schemas using only the attribute name and description. SMAT avoids directly encoding domain knowledge about the source and target systems, which allows it to be more easily deployed across different sites. We also introduce a new benchmark dataset, OMAP, based on real-world schema-level mappings from the healthcare domain. Our extensive evaluation of various benchmark datasets demonstrates the potential of SMAT to help automate schema-level matching tasks.

Keywords: Schema-level matching · Natural language processing · Attention over attention

1 Introduction

The tremendous growth and availability of data can benefit a broad range of applications such as healthcare, energy, transportation, and smart buildings. Unfortunately, across many domains, data is collected using a wide variety of database systems with customized schemas developed for each company or purpose. The customized databases can hinder data exchange, data integration, and large-scale analytics. Schema matching aims to establish the correspondence between the fields of a source and target database schema – a decisive initial step in the standardization of different databases. Automation of the schema matching task has received steady attention in the database and AI communities over the years. It has also been adopted as a practical and principled tool

© Springer Nature Switzerland AG 2021
L. Bellatreche et al. (Eds.): ADBIS 2021, LNCS 12843, pp. 260–274, 2021.
https://doi.org/10.1007/978-3-030-82472-3_19

to improve the modeling and implementation of data exchange and data integration [2, 21, 26]. Yet, this problem remains largely unsolved and still requires significant manual labor.

Given the importance of schema matching and the time-intensive nature of the task, it is crucial to develop new methods to help expedite the process. Several automated schema matching methods have been proposed, including constraint-based approaches [5, 13, 33] and linguistic-based approaches [18, 20, 23, 38]. While the existing methods have achieved high performance in different domains, they suffer from several limitations. The constraint-based approaches analyze the element contents, which is not always guaranteed to be the same across the two schemas. Moreover, it assumes the data on both sides can be queried, which can violate privacy constraints. For the linguistic approaches, the relations are hand-coded between the two schemas or may not properly capture the similarity between the field descriptions. Numerous matching tools (matchers) can generate correspondences between pairs of schemas [6, 13]. Yet they rely on heuristic techniques. Recently, a deep neural network (DNN)-based model, ADnEV, was proposed to utilize similarity from existing matchers and post-process the results to work across domains [35]. However, ADnEV is limited by the capability of existing matchers and may not generalize to all domains.

Given the rising importance of schema integration involving sensitive data, such as in healthcare, we focus on schema-level matching rather than instance-level or hybrid schema matching. This paper posits that the schema matching process (i.e., source schema elements to target schema elements and its attributes matching) can be viewed as inferring the relatedness (or similarity) between the source and target fields. We propose SMAT, a DNN-based model with attention that extends recent advances in natural language processing and sentiment analysis. SMAT captures the semantic correlation from the source schema attributes to the target schema attributes based on the name and descriptions. Moreover, our model can be used to automatically generate the matching between the source and target schemas without encoding domain knowledge. We also introduce a new publicly available dataset that annotates several source to target conversions in the healthcare domain. We perform extensive evaluations of SMAT on a variety of datasets.

2   Related Work

This section describes the existing works related to schema-level matching that only considers schema information and not instance data. For a detailed survey on schema matching, we refer the reader to [33]. Table 1 provides a brief comparison of some related works and our model along four categories (i.e., whether it is schema-level matching, what the match cardinality is, whether it captures rich text, and whether it utilizes deep-learning framework).

One line of schema matching work is the constraint-based approach. Most schemas contain constraints to define the attributes such as data types and value ranges, uniqueness, optionality, relationship types and cardinalities [33].

Table 1. Comparison between different approaches on various categories.

Approach	Schema-level	Cardinality	Rich text	Deep learning
Constraint-based [3]	No	1:n	No	No
Linguistic content-based [23]	Yes	n:1	No	No
ADnEV [35]	Yes	n:1	No	Yes
DITTO [26]	No	n:1	Yes	Yes
SMAT	Yes	n:1	Yes	Yes

Similarity can be measured by data types and domains, key characteristics (e.g., unique, primary, foreign), and relationship cardinality [1,14,28]. Recently, [3] proposes a hybrid of the constraint-based approach using key characteristics and the instance itself to create the meta-schema. Unfortunately, such approaches cannot readily handle the n:1 scenario that can be found in schema matching. For example, if the source schema contains "starttime" and "endtime" and the target schema contains "Duration", the meta-schema mapping can not generate and convert the two attributes into the single target.

An alternative method is the linguistic content-based approach, which utilizes names and text to explore semantically similar schema elements. There are two primary linguistic data mapping techniques: name matching and description matching. The idea behind these techniques is to calculate similarity based on either the name of the fields or the description of the fields, respectively. In name matching, the similarity of names can be defined and measured through equality of names, equality of synonyms, similarity of names based on common substrings and user-provided name matches. However, consulting a synonym lexicon has limitations since it is common to use abbreviations for attribute names (e.g., DOB for date of birth, SSN for Social Security number, etc.) and may not identify the relationships.

Description matching is based on the idea that schemas usually contain element and attribute names in natural language to express the intended semantics of schema elements. The process involves the identification of two semi-related data objects and the creation of mappings between them. In a recent work [23], the authors utilized the UMBC EBIQUITY-CORE technique [19] to obtain the similarity of the comments of schemas. Yet, it may not capture the similarity between the descriptions. For example, the similarity score between "the comment of the book" and "the review of the article" is 0.39 (1 is the same and 0 is dissimilar). Another work used word embeddings to link datasets [15]; however it only embeds the table name which may not yield sufficient information.

With the development of DL techniques, entity matching [4,26], ontology alignment [24], and instance-level schema-matching [25] can utilize rich textual information to provide better solutions. However, both entity matching and instance-level schema matching assume the data can be queried on both sides, which can violate data privacy constraints. For schema-level matching, [30] proposed a probabilistic graphical model and achieved a good score on precision and recall. Recently, ADnEV was proposed to utilize a DL technique to post-process the matching results from other matchers and outperformed existing models. However, the quality of the matchers limits the potential of the model.

3   SMAT: A DNN Model

3.1   Problem Statement

Given two table descriptions S_{TS} and S_{TT}, two attributes names N_{F1} and N_{F2}, and their descriptions S_{F1} and S_{F2} from the source and target schema respectively, we construct two sets of sentences. The source sentence set $S_S = \{N_{F1}, S_{TS} + S_{F1}\} = \{w_1, w_2, ..., w_n\}$ consists of n words, and the target sentence set $S_T = \{N_{F2}, S_{TT} + S_{F2}\} = \{w_1, w_2, ..., w_{n'}\}$ consists of n' words. For the training data, there is an annotated label $L(S_S, S_T)$ where 0 denotes two fields are not related (i.e., not mapped to each other), and 1 denotes two sentences are related (i.e., corresponding attribute-to-attribute matching). Table 2 provides an example of the sentence pair. Thus the task objective is to classify the semantic relation of each sentence pair to reveal the attribute-to-attribute matching.

3.2   Overview

The task of determining the relatedness between two attributes descriptions can be viewed as inferring the similarity of two sentence pairs in NLP tasks. Since DNNs can be trained end-to-end without any prior knowledge (i.e., no need to implement feature engineering), they have been utilized for text similarity tasks. For sentiment classification, InferSent introduced an end-to-end DNN and achieved a higher performance than existing sentiment analysis models [8]. Yet there are two major limitations to adopting such models for the schema matching task. First, the element and attribute description may not contain sufficient information to distinguish it from others. Second, the descriptions may have abbreviations or words that have unknown word representations.

To address the above limitations, SMAT consists of 4 major modules (shown in Fig. 1). First, the input embedding of the sentences utilizes a hybrid encoding to deal with large vocabularies for any input text. Second, bidirectional Long short term memory (BiLSTM) networks are used to capture the hidden semantics of the words in the description and the column name separately. Third, the attention over attention (AOA) mechanism [9] is adopted to model the correlation between the column name and its description to obtain a better sentence representation.

The final prediction layer uses the sentence representations to make an accurate classification. We also introduce data augmentation and controlled batch sample ratios (CBSR) to deal with the class imbalance problem that is present in schema matching tasks.

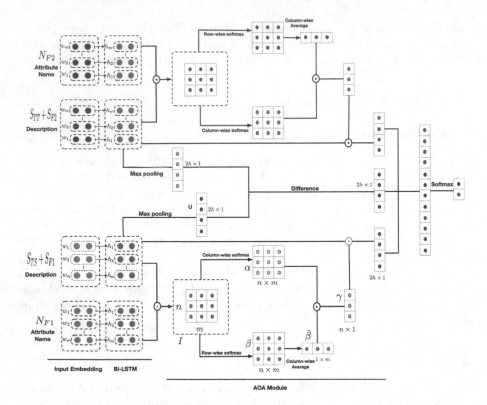

Fig. 1. Illustration of SMAT's structure

3.3   Input Embedding and BiLSTM

Existing word embedding models such as GloVe [32] are limited by vocabulary size or the frequency of word occurrences. As a result, rare words like *ICD-9* result in unknown tokens. Byte-Pair Encoding (BPE) is a hybrid between character- and word-level representations which can deal with the large vocabularies common in natural language corpora [34]. Instead of full words, BPE learns sub-words units to tokenize any input text without introducing any "unknown" tokens.

Thus, SMAT uses BPE to tokenize the input text. Each word/sub-word w_i in the sentence $S_1 = \{w_1, w_2, ..., w_n\}$ is then mapped to a high-dimensional vector e_i, using GloVe embeddings. While we use GloVe due to its popularity, any word embedding representation can be used.

To capture the contextual nature of the text, a BiLSTM network is utilized to capture the hidden semantics. Compared with the standard LSTM, BiLSTM can utilize both the past and the future information to yield better sentence representations. Thus, after the word embedding is obtained for each set of words (i.e., attribute name or attribute description), the embeddings are fed to a BiLSTM network.

3.4   Attention-over-Attention (AOA)

The output of the BiLSTM is dealt with using two approaches. All the information in the sequence is captured using the max-pooling operator to compress the sequence into a single unified vector. However, one limitation of this representation is the inability to capture interactions between the attribute name and its description. The second approach uses an attention over attention (AOA) module to model this interaction. AOA was first proposed for the question answering task [9]. Since calculating the dot product and difference of two sentence representations fail to capture fine-grained relations on the word level, the AOA module introduces mutual attention to simultaneously capture the relationships between attribute name to description and description to attribute name.

Our AOA module captures the correlations between the attribute names and the text using two mechanisms. Let $h_c \in R^{m \times 2h}$ denote the attribute name representation, where m is the attribute name length (i.e., number of words in the attribute name) and h is the hidden dimension. Let $h_s \in R^{n \times 2h}$ denote the element-attribute description representation, where n is the description length and h is the hidden dimension. The module first calculates the pair-wise interaction matrix $I = h_s \cdot h_c^T$, where the value of each entry represents the correlation of each word pair between the description and attribute name. A column-wise softmax and row-wise softmax is applied to the interaction matrix I, to obtain the attribute name to description attention, α, and description to attribute name attention, β, respectively. Thus for the tth attribute word and k^{th} text description, the associated attentions are:

$$\alpha(t) = softmax(I(1,t), I(2,t), \cdots, I(m,t)) \tag{1}$$

$$\beta(k) = softmax(I(k,1), I(k,2), \cdots, I(k,n)) \tag{2}$$

Then, the attribute name-level attention $\bar{\beta}$ is calculated using a column-wise averaging of β. This attention indicates the important words in the attribute name. Finally, the sentence-level attention $\gamma \in R^n$ can be obtained by a weighted sum of each individual attribute name to description attention α. By considering the contribution of each word explicitly, the AOA module learns the important weights for each word in the sentence.

$$\alpha_{ij} = \frac{\exp(I_{ij})}{\sum_i \exp(I_{ij})}$$

$$\beta_{ij} = \frac{\exp(I_{ij})}{\sum_j \exp(I_{ij})}$$

$$\bar{\beta} = \frac{1}{n} \sum_i \beta_{ij}$$

$$\gamma = \alpha \cdot \bar{\beta}^T$$

The two sets of final description level attentions for the source and target, γ_s and γ_t, are concatenated along with the difference between the two max-pooled attribute description representations. The new vector representation, P, is sent

Table 2. An example entry from the OMAP dataset.

CDM schema	Source schema	CDM description (Des 1)	Source description (Des 2)	Label
person-person_id	beneficiary summary-desynpuf_id	the person domain contains records that uniquely identify each patient in the source data who is time at-risk to have clinical observations recorded within the source systems.a unique identifier for each person	beneficiarysummary pertains to a synthetic medicare beneficiary. beneficiary code	1

to the final classification layer which consists of several fully-connected layers and a softmax layer to predict whether or not two sentences are related.

3.5 Data Augmentation and Controlled Batch Sample Ratio

As attribute-to-attribute mapping generally results in a skewed distribution, SMAT uses data augmentation and controlled batch sample ratio (CBSR) to achieve better predictive performance. Data augmentation occurs on two levels. First is to generate new positive samples using synonyms for different words in the descriptors. For example, an augmented sample may replace the word "uniquely" with "unambiguously" and "identify" with "describe". However, since the number of synonyms is limited, we utilize a second technique to improve the attribute name description. We use the part-of-speech (POS) tags for the descriptions and concatenate the identified nouns to enlarge the dataset safely.

Since SMAT uses batch SGD to learn the parameters, a batch can contain no positive samples and thus only properly learn the representation for negative samples. Thus, we controlled the ratio of positive samples in each batch size to ensure that our model learns from a few positive examples for each batch [12]. Note that since the positive samples are small, they are likely to be chosen repeatedly, while there is diversity in the negative samples.

4 OMAP: A New Benchmark Dataset

Since existing matching datasets only spans purchase orders, web forms, and bibliographic references, we created OMAP, a new benchmark schema-level matching dataset that annotates several source-to-target mappings in the healthcare domain. Healthcare data is collected worldwide using a wide variety of coding systems. To draw conclusions with statistical power and avoid systematic biases, a large number of samples should be analyzed across disparate data sources and patient populations. Such broad analyses requires data harmonization to a common data standard (e.g., the Observational Medical Outcomes Partnership (OMOP) Common Data Model (CDM) standard) to facilitate evidence gathering and informed decision making [31]. Since patient data cannot be queried due

Table 3. Summary statistics of each conversion captured in OMAP.

Data source	# elements	# attributes	# Positive labels	# sentence pairs
MIMIC	25	240	129	64080
Synthea	12	111	105	29637
CMS	5	96	196	25632

Table 4. Summary statistics of the additional benchmark datasets used.

Data source	# elements	# related	# pairs	# Domains
Purchase order [11]	50–400	659	63933	1
OAEI[a]	80–100	9494	825021	1
Web-forms [16]	10–30	5548	201769	18

[a]The OAEI competitions can be found at http://oaei.ontologymatching.org/2011/benchmarks/

to privacy concerns, schema-level matching is of great importance. OMAP maps between three different healthcare databases and the OMOP CDM standard.

1. MIMIC-III [22]: A publicly available intensive care unit (ICU) relational database from the Beth Israel Deaconess Medical Center.
2. Synthea [37]: An open-source dataset that captures the medical history of over one million Massachusetts synthetic patients.
3. CMS DE-SynPUF [7]: A set of realistic claims data generated from 5% of Medicare beneficiaries in 2008.

For each dataset, the element table name with its descriptions and attribute column name with its descriptions are used to construct a sentence. The label is based on the final ETL design. If the table-column in the source schema was mapped to a table-column in the OMOP CDM the label is 1, otherwise it is 0. Table 2 provides one example from the OMAP dataset.

OMAP currently contains 121,689 matching pairs from three different datasets and is available publicly on Github[1]. The summary statistics for each of the three conversions are captured in Table 3.

Note that the dataset does not contain any patient information, only attributes and their descriptions.

5   Experiments

We designed the experiments to answer three key questions: (1) How *accurate* is SMAT in automating the schema matching? (2) How sensitive is SMAT to the training size? (3) How important are the different components of SMAT?

---

[1] https://github.com/JZCS2018/SMAT.

5.1   Dataset

We use the `OMAP` dataset to evaluate our proposed model (see Table 3 and Sect. 4). We also used three popular schema matching benchmark datasets as shown in Table 4. Reference matches in these datasets were manually constructed by domain experts and considered as ground truth for our purposes. Experiments are performed per dataset consistent with existing schema matching papers [17,30,36]. For each dataset, 80% was used to train the initial prediction model, the 10% used to further tune the weights, and the remaining 10% used to evaluate the experiments.

5.2   Baseline Models

`SMAT` is evaluated against five baseline models. For data sensitivity purposes, we focused only on schema-level matching. The entity matching solutions that involve semantic relatedness technique are chosen to represent the existing schema matching or entity matching work.

- **ADnEV** [35]. A schema matching model that utilizes DNN to post-process results from state-of-the-art (SOTA) matchers in an iterative manner.
- **InferSent** [8]. A SOTA sentence embedding model that classifies the sentiment between two sentences. The last layer is modified to tackle a binary classification task. GloVe embeddings [32] are used for the input sentences.
- **DeepMatcher** [29]. An entity matching solution that customizes the Recurrent Neural Network (RNN) architecture to aggregate the attribute values then compares the aggregated representations of attribute values.
- **DITTO** [26]. A SOTA entity matching model that cast the problem as a sequence-pair classification and fine-tunes RoBERTa [27], a pre-trained Transformer-based language model.
- **BERT** [10]. Bidirectional Encoder Representations from Transformers (BERT) has achieved SOTA results in many natural language understanding tasks. We fine-tuned the pre-trained BERT-base-uncased model on our datasets.

5.3   Experimental Setup

We implemented `SMAT` and the baseline models in Python 3.6 using PyTorch. Our code is made publicly available on Github[2]. Performances were measured on the Google Cloud Platform with Intel Xeon E5 v3 CPU @ 2.30 Ghz, and a Nvidia Tesla K80 with 12 GB Video Memory.

For experiments in this paper, the embedding dimension is 300. The number of hidden units of BiLSTM is 1024 for InferSent and 300 for `SMAT`. For the classification model, we apply a fully connected layer with one hidden layer of 512 hidden units. Stochastic gradient descent is chosen as the optimize algorithm with a batch size of 64. The learning rate and weight decay are 0.1 and 0.99 for

---

[2] https://github.com/JZCS2018/SMAT.

Table 5. Comparison of precision (P), recall (R), and F1 (F) on the datasets.

Dataset	ADnEV			InferSent			DeepMatcher			DITTO			BERT			SMAT		
	P	R	F	P	R	F	P	R	F	P	R	F	P	R	F	P	R	F
MIMIC	0.08	34	0.16	9.8	76.9	17.4	0.04	38.1	0.09	0.3	46.2	0.6	0.4	84.6	0.7	**11.5**	**84.6**	**20.2**
CMS	0.49	44	0.97	20.8	80.0	32.9	0.31	60.7	0.62	2.4	40	4.5	2.4	55.0	4.5	**33.9**	**95.0**	**50.0**
Synthea	0.14	21	0.28	19.2	90.9	31.7	0.06	48.8	0.13	0.7	63.6	1.3	0.9	**100**	1.8	**24.4**	90.9	**38.5**
Purchase order	**80**	77	**78**	14.3	59.6	23.1	48.9	80.2	60.8	54.5	98.6	70.2	54.0	98.2	69.7	57.9	**99.5**	73.2
OAEI	78	76	76	84.5	99.9	91.5	56.1	62.9	59.3	80.5	99.9	89.2	78.3	99.8	87.8	**87.8**	**99.9**	**93.5**
Web-forms	81	69	72	68.4	**90.8**	81.2	48.2	74.5	58.5	68.8	95.5	80	63.5	96.3	76.5	79.1	99.3	**88.1**
Average	34.3	49.9	32.5	33.6	78.2	43.3	22.0	56.8	25.8	29.7	69.4	35.4	28.6	**88.8**	34.7	**45.7**	87.0	**56.3**

InferSent and 0.001 and 0.99 for SMAT. For AdnEV, DeepMatcher, DITTO, and fine-tuning BERT model, Adam is chosen as the optimization algorithm with a learning rate of 0.001, 0.001, 3e–5, 2e–5, respectively, and the batch size as 64, 64, 64, and 32 respectively. These parameters were obtained from initial experiments on a subset of the training data as they provided the most robust performance across multiple runs.

6 Results

6.1 Predictive Performance

Evaluation of SMAT with Existing Baseline Models. Table 5 summarizes the results of the six models tested on the six datasets. We observe that the precision and recall varies depending on the dataset suggesting differences in the semantic content of their attribute names and descriptions. The results demonstrate that SMAT does not require additional hand-coding due to the overall strong performance. It achieves the best performance across all three metrics in 3 of the datasets (OAEI, MIMIC, CMS). It also yields the best F1 score for all but the Purchase Order dataset. Thus, our proposed model is fairly versatile.

ADnEV achieves a higher precision on Purchase Orders and Webforms and a better F1 score on Purchase Orders than others. Yet, SMAT outperforms the ADnEV model on OAEI and Web-forms in terms of F1 score by 12.4% and 16.1% respectively. Moreover, the results on the OMAP datasets illustrate the pitfall of ADnEV. Since ADnEV leverages other matchers, it is limited by the capability of the matchers. Thus, ADnEV may not be suitable for all domains. Furthermore, comparisons of the DNN-based models (InferSent, Fine-tuned BERT, and SMAT) and ADnEV in terms of F1 and recall also illustrate the power of end-to-end training without requiring additional feature engineering.

For the OMAP dataset, SMAT achieves a higher precision and recall score suggesting that the prediction capability of SMAT is better than the other models. However the precision across these four datasets are noticeably lower than those of Purchase Order, OAEI and Web-forms. This may be a result of the more complex textual information in the healthcare domain. Moreover, there are many abbreviations which can prevent the general model from achieving a higher score. This highlights the importance of benchmarking the models across various applications and supports the development of OMAP.

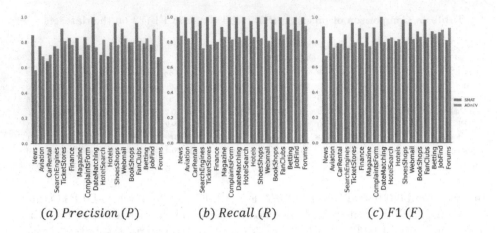

(a) *Precision (P)*   (b) *Recall (R)*   (c) *F1 (F)*

Fig. 2. Comparison by domain between ADnEV and SMAT

The results also capture the difference that arises from schema-level matching. Even though DITTO and DeepMatcher perform well in the entity matching task, they do not offer comparable performance across the different datasets. This may be due to the inconsistencies across the datasets present in the textual information. Moreover, InferSent seems to provide better F1 scores compared to the more complex transformer models outside of the Purchase Dataset. This suggests that the Bi-LSTM based sentence modeling approach shared by InferSent and SMAT may offer better predictive power compared to the more complex transformer-based models. In comparing InferSent and SMAT, the results suggest that SMAT's attention mechanism and representation can help capture the elements and attributes in source schema and target schema differences better than the other models regardless of whether the textual information is rich (OMAP) or not (Purchase Order, OAEI and Web forms).

Analysis on Web-form, A Cross-domain Schema Matching. The Web-forms dataset contains 18 domains to represent the cross-domain matching task. Figure 2 analyzes the match quality per domain and compares the results between SMAT and ADnEV since ADnEV achieves the best precision. From the results, we observe that SMAT outperforms ADnEV across all the domains in terms of recall. Moreover, for the majority of the domains, SMAT offers better precision and F1 score over ADnEV. For example, the Webmail, Finance, and News domains are difficult for the ADnEV model. For example, existing matchers fail to identify the mappings *Measures the price performance of a stock in comparison to all other stocks (12 month Relative Strength)* ↔ *YTD total return* and *Mailbox* ↔ *@gmail.com (Email)*. However, SMAT can capture the semantic meaning of these pairs. The results also demonstrate that ADnEV performs better on the domain Forums and Hotels than SMAT. This is because SMAT excludes the number and type constraints in the element and attribute.

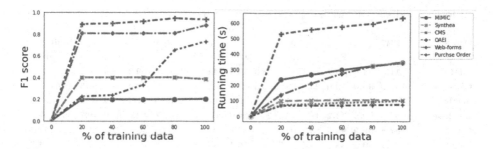

Fig. 3. F1 score (left) and running time (right) per epoch when varying (%) of training data

6.2 Training Size Sensitivity and Scalability

We assessed the robustness of SMAT to the size of the training data. We varied the amount of data used to fit SMAT and evaluate its impact on the test dataset performance. Figure 3 illustrates the results on the six different datasets in terms of F1 score and running time. From the results, we notice that SMAT achieves a decent F1 score with only about 20% training data (the lone exception is Purchase Orders) and can save 30% of the training time. We also notice that the running time per epoch is fairly linear suggesting that SMAT is scalable.

6.3 Ablation Study

To gain further insights of the various components in SMAT, we examined the effectiveness and contributions of the attribute name input, the AOA module, and the two different class imbalance approaches.

- *SMAT w/o AOA*: The AOA module is removed and instead the outputs of the attribute name BiLSTM and description BiLSTM are max-pooled together and concatenated with the difference of the two descriptions.
- *SMAT w/o column*: The attribute name is omitted and only the description is fed into the AOA module to calculate the mutual information with itself.
- *SMAT w/o DA*: The data augmentation with additional positive samples and concatenation of nouns to the column name is omitted.
- *SMAT w/o CBSR*: The batch size is randomly sampled without ensuring positive samples are present in each batch.

The results of the ablation study are shown in Table 6. It can be seen that the SMAT model outperforms the rest of four models on F1 and most precision. In particular, comparing the result with *SMAT w/o AOA* illustrates the importance of the AOA module. The module captures the interaction between the attribute description and the correlated attribute name better than max-pooling the outputs from BiLSTM. The same conclusion can also be drawn by comparing *SMAT w/o AOA* and *SMAT w/o column*, the precision of the former is lower

Table 6. Results for ablation experiments on Precision (P), Recall (R), and F1 (F).

Dataset	SMAT			w/o AOA			w/o column			w/o DA			w/o CBSR		
	P	R	F	P	R	F	P	R	F	P	R	F	P	R	F
MIMIC	**11.5**	**84.6**	**20.2**	10.3	84.6	18.3	10.2	84.6	18.2	10.7	69.2	18.6	0	0	0
CMS	**33.9**	**95.0**	**50.0**	23.5	80.0	36.3	25.4	80.0	38.6	25.8	80.0	39.0	0.13	15.6	0.25
Synthea	24.4	90.9	**38.5**	15.3	90.0	26.1	20.0	100	33.3	**36.4**	36.4	36.4	0	0	0
Purchase order	**57.9**	**99.5**	**73.2**	17.7	50.0	26.2	26.9	30.3	28.5	42.1	98.2	58.9	10.7	38.2	16.7
OAEI	**87.8**	**99.9**	**93.5**	83.0	99.9	90.7	83.8	99.9	91.2	85.9	99.9	92.4	35.9	72.5	48.0
Web-forms	**79.1**	**99.3**	**88.1**	75.7	96.7	84.9	76.4	93.5	84.1	70.0	99.8	82.3	32.5	68.4	44.1

than the latter. Even without the attribute name feature and the associated data augmentation, the AOA module can still generate more useful features.

The ablation results also highlights two benefits of the model. First, the attribute name is important as there is a noticeable drop in precision across all the datasets when comparing *SMAT w/o column* with SMAT and *SMAT w/o D/A*. Second, the two techniques for dealing with class imbalance play a crucial role towards improving the predictive power of the model. The results of *SMAT w/o DA* and *SMAT w/o CBSR* shows that CBSR is more effective toward combating the skewed data than data augmentation method due to the higher precision values of the former model.

7   Conclusion

This paper proposes an automated schema-level matching model based on the semantic meaning of the descriptions. This is particularly beneficial for schema integration involving sensitive data, such as healthcare domain. The extensive experiments on a variety of datasets illustrate that SMAT serves as the SOTA solution for the schema-level matching task. This paper also introduces a new benchmark dataset, OMAP, that captures three different dataset conversions from the healthcare domain. As shown in the experiments, OMAP can help assess the generalizability of schema-level matching models.

Although the empirical results of SMAT are not yet high enough to be put into practice, this work illustrate the potential of automating schema matching. Future directions include collecting more data to improve the sentence embedding quality, exploring other DNN architectures to tackle the class imbalance problem, and incorporating instance-level features to obtain a robust hybrid schema-level and instance-level model.

Acknowledgements. This work was supported by the National Science Foundation award IIS-#1838200, National Institute of Health award 1K01LM012924, and Google Cloud Platform research credits.

References

1. Alexe, B., Hernández, M., Popa, L., Tan, W.C.: Mapmerge: correlating independent schema mappings. Proc. VLDB Endow. **3**(1–2), 81–92 (2010)
2. Arenas, M., Barceló, P., Libkin, L., Murlak, F.: Foundations of Data Exchange. Cambridge University Press, Cambridge (2014)
3. Atzeni, P., Bellomarini, L., Papotti, P., Torlone, R.: Meta-mappings for schema mapping reuse. Proc. VLDB Endow. **12**(5), 557–569 (2019). https://doi.org/10.14778/3303753.3303761
4. Cappuzzo, R., Papotti, P., Thirumuruganathan, S.: Creating embeddings of heterogeneous relational datasets for data integration tasks. In: Proceedings of SIGMOD, pp. 1335–1349 (2020)
5. Ten Cate, B., Kolaitis, P.G., Qian, K., Tan, W.C.: Active learning of GAV schema mappings. In: Proceedings of SIGMOD/PODS, pp. 355–368 (2018)
6. Chen, C., Golshan, B., Halevy, A.Y., Tan, W.C., Doan, A.: Biggorilla: an opensource ecosystem for data preparation and integration. IEEE Data Eng. Bull. **41**(2), 10–22 (2018)
7. Centers for medicare & medicaid services (cms). https://www.cms.gov/OpenPayments/Explore-the-Data/Data-Overview.html
8. Conneau, A., Kiela, D., Schwenk, H., Barrault, L., Bordes, A.: Supervised learning of universal sentence representations from natural language inference data. In: Proceedings of EMNLP, pp. 670–680 (2017)
9. Cui, Y., Chen, Z., Wei, S., Wang, S., Liu, T., Hu, G.: Attention-over-attention neural networks for reading comprehension. In: Proceedings of ACL (2017)
10. Devlin, J., Chang, M.W., Lee, K., Toutanova, K.: Bert: pre-training of deep bidirectional transformers for language understanding. In: Proceedings of of NAACL-HLT, pp. 4171–4186 (2019)
11. Do, H.H., Rahm, E.: Coma-a system for flexible combination of schema matching approaches. In: Proceedings of VLDB, pp. 610–621 (2002)
12. Dong, Q., Gong, S., Zhu, X.: Imbalanced deep learning by minority class incremental rectification. IEEE Trans. Pattern Analy. Mach. Intell. **41**(6), 1367–1381 (2019). https://doi.org/10.1109/TPAMI.2018.2832629
13. Fagin, R., Haas, L.M., Hernández, M., Miller, R.J., Popa, L., Velegrakis, Y.: Clio: schema mapping creation and data exchange. In: Borgida, A.T., Chaudhri, V.K., Giorgini, P., Yu, E.S. (eds.) Conceptual Modeling: Foundations and Applications. LNCS, vol. 5600, pp. 198–236. Springer, Heidelberg (2009). https://doi.org/10.1007/978-3-642-02463-4_12
14. Fagin, R., Kolaitis, P.G., Popa, L., Tan, W.C.: Schema mapping evolution through composition and inversion. In: Schema Matching and Mapping, pp. 191–222. Springer (2011)
15. Fernandez, R.C., et al.: Seeping semantics: linking datasets using word embeddings for data discovery. In: Proceedings of ICDE, pp. 989–1000 (2018)
16. Gal, A.: Uncertain schema matching. Synth. Lect. Data Manag. **3**(1), 1–97 (2011)
17. Gal, A., Roitman, H., Shraga, R.: Learning to rerank schema matches. IEEE Trans. Knowl. Data Eng. (2019)
18. Halevy, A., Nemes, E., Dong, X., Madhavan, J., Zhang, J.: Similarity search for web services. In: Proceedings of the 30th VLDB Conference, pp. 372–383 (2004)
19. Han, L., Kashyap, A.L., Finin, T., Mayfield, J., Weese, J.: Umbc_ebiquity-core: semantic textual similarity systems. In: Second Joint Conference on Lexical and Computational Semantics (* SEM), Volume 1: Proceedings of the Main Conference and the Shared Task: Semantic Textual Similarity, pp. 44–52 (2013)

20. He, B., Chang, K.C.C.: Statistical schema matching across web query interfaces. In: Proceedings of SIGMOD, pp. 217–228 (2003)

21. Hernandez, M., Ho, H., Naumann, F., Popa, L.: Clio: a schema mapping tool for information integration. In: 8th International Symposium on Parallel Architectures, Algorithms and Networks (ISPAN 2005), p. 1. IEEE (2005)

22. Johnson, A.E., et al.: Mimic-iii, a freely accessible critical care database. Sci. Data **3**, 160035 (2016)

23. Kettouch, M.S., Luca, C., Hobbs, M., Dascalu, S.: Using semantic similarity for schema matching of semi-structured and linked data. In: 2017 Internet Technologies and Applications (ITA), pp. 128–133. IEEE (2017)

24. Kolyvakis, P., Kalousis, A., Kiritsis, D.: Deepalignment: unsupervised ontology matching with refined word vectors. In: Proceedings of NAACL-HLT, pp. 787–798 (2018)

25. Koutras, C., Fragkoulis, M., Katsifodimos, A., Lofi, C.: Rema: graph embeddings-based relational schema matching. In: EDBT/ICDT Workshops (2020)

26. Li, Y., Li, J., Suhara, Y., Doan, A., Tan, W.C.: Deep entity matching with pre-trained language models. arXiv preprint arXiv:2004.00584 (2020)

27. Liu, Y., et al.: Roberta: A robustly optimized bert pretraining approach. arXiv preprint arXiv:1907.11692 (2019)

28. Mecca, G., Papotti, P., Santoro, D.: Schema mappings: from data translation to data cleaning. In: Flesca, S., Greco, S., Masciari, E., Saccà, D. (eds.) A Comprehensive Guide Through the Italian Database Research Over the Last 25 Years. SBD, vol. 31, pp. 203–217. Springer, Cham (2018). https://doi.org/10.1007/978-3-319-61893-7_12

29. Mudgal, S., Kumar, S.: Deep learning for entity matching: A design space exploration. Tech. rep. (2018)

30. Nguyen, Q.V.H., Weidlich, M., Nguyen, T.T., Miklós, Z., Aberer, K., Gal, A.: Reconciling matching networks of conceptual models. Tech. rep. (2019)

31. Observational Health Data Sciences and Informatics: The book of OHDSI. Independently published (2019)

32. Pennington, J., Socher, R., Manning, C.: Glove: global vectors for word representation. In: Proceedings of EMNLP, pp. 1532–1543 (2014)

33. Rahm, E., Bernstein, P.A.: A survey of approaches to automatic schema matching. VLDB J. **10**(4), 334–350 (2001)

34. Sennrich, R., Haddow, B., Birch, A.: Neural machine translation of rare words with subword units. arXiv preprint arXiv:1508.07909 (2015)

35. Shraga, R., Gal, A., Roitman, H.: Adnev: cross-domain schema matching using deep similarity matrix adjustment and evaluation. Proc. VLDB **13**(9), 1401–1415 (2020)

36. Toan, N.T., Cong, P.T., Thang, D.C., Hung, N.Q.V., Stantic, B.: Bootstrapping uncertainty in schema covering. In: Wang, J., Cong, G., Chen, J., Qi, J. (eds.) ADC 2018. LNCS, vol. 10837, pp. 336–342. Springer, Cham (2018). https://doi.org/10.1007/978-3-319-92013-9_29

37. Walonoski, J., et al.: Synthea: An approach, method, and software mechanism for generating synthetic patients and the synthetic electronic health care record. J. Am. Med. Inform. Assoc. **25**(3), 230–238 (2017)

38. Wu, W., Yu, C., Doan, A., Meng, W.: An interactive clustering-based approach to integrating source query interfaces on the deep web. In: Proceedings of SIGMOD, pp. 95–106 (2004)

Towards a Cloud-WSDL Metamodel: A New Extension of WSDL for Cloud Service Description

Souad Ghazouani[1], Anis Tissaoui[2(✉)], and Richard Chbeir[3]

[1] LISI Laboratory of Computer Science for Industrial Systems, Carthage University, Tunis, Tunisia
[2] VPNC Laboratory, FSJEG, University of Jendouba, Avenue Union Maghreb Arabe, 8189 Jendouba, Tunisia
anis.tissaoui@fsjegj.rnu.tn
[3] Univ. Pau & Pays Adour, E2S UPPA, LIUPPA, 64600 Anglet, France
rchbeir@acm.org

Abstract. Several approaches have been proposed to describe services in a rich and generic manner (such as WSDL, OWL-S, WSMO, and SAWSDL). However, current approaches remain inappropriate for cloud computing since: 1) they lack in a way or another semantic or business aspect, 2) they cannot fully cope with non-functional properties and cloud characteristics, 3) they are unable to cover all kinds of services (such as SaaS, PaaS, IaaS). Despite the existence of several attempts which have tried to extent existing studies, the problem remains open. In this paper, we propose Cloud-WSDL, a new description model aligned with WSDL language, the most popular language, to make it more suitable for describing cloud services. The idea is to enhance WSDL description with our ontological *Generic Cloud Service Description* called GCSD to cope with many aspects (technical, operational, business, semantic and contextual) to ensure a high interoperability between services belonging to multiple heterogeneous clouds, and to support all the kinds of cloud services (SaaS, PaaS, and IaaS).

Keywords: Cloud service · Generic Cloud Service Description · WSDL · OWL-S ontology · Cloud computing

1 Introduction

Service description consists in defining an interface describing the operations carried out by the service and linking each operation to its realization. It ensures the communication between the consumer and the provider.

The service description should be defined in a readable and interpretable language for both humans and machines in order to enhance the service discovery and composition. Although commonly adopted, *Web Services Description Language* or WSDL cannot ensure this since it is syntactic oriented. Semantic

© Springer Nature Switzerland AG 2021
L. Bellatreche et al. (Eds.): ADBIS 2021, LNCS 12843, pp. 275–288, 2021.
https://doi.org/10.1007/978-3-030-82472-3_20

oriented service description is needed to ensure that, where the capabilities of each service are associated with semantic concepts to enhance both discovery and selection processes.

In this context, several semantic oriented approaches [1–8] have been proposed in the literature to offer a detailed service description and overcome WSDL limitations. However, the major limitations of these approaches are related to the fact that they don't cover the semantic level, the non-functional properties and the contextual information.

In cloud computing, most of services are described as Web services using different languages such as WSDL, OWL-S, and WSMO. However, the existing languages are destined to the Web and not for cloud computing domain. That is why, several attempts [11–14] have emerged recently to provide a richer service description to support SaaS, PaaS, and IaaS services.

The proposed approaches to describe cloud services have, also, some limitations. They are intended to be used for specific tasks only (service description task, service discovery task, service composition task, etc.). Also, they do not cover all cloud concepts (pricing, legal, SLA, etc.). Besides, they focus on specifying some dedicated aspects (for example the technical aspect only) and they fail to cover all aspects (technical, operational, business, and semantic). For instance, WSDL covers only technical aspect and does not cover business and semantic ones.

Furthermore, service providers have used various techniques such as models [10,21], taxonomy [22], languages [13,23–25], ontologies [26–28], and template [29,30] to describe their cloud services. The diversity of techniques leads to the vendor lock-in problem and thus the interoperability issue.

Several challenges are to be met when describing cloud services, mainly:

- How to represent the functional properties of cloud services?
- How to specify the non-functional properties of cloud services?
- How to specify the cloud characteristics?
- How to describe all cloud services (SaaS, PaaS, IaaS)?

In a previous work [9], we proposed a *Generic Cloud Service Description* (GCSD) and showed its expressive power and genericity. In essence, GCSD covers functional, non-functional, business, and contextual properties unlike existing alternatives. In this paper, we provide Cloud-WSDL, an extension of WSDL using GCSD.

Hence, Cloud-WSDL is a description devoted to cloud computing and derived from the famous language WSDL. It makes WSDL able to cover several aspects: technical (functional properties), operational (functional properties), business (non-functional properties) and semantic. Besides, Cloud-WSDL takes into account the contextual aspect to support the context adaptation.

The rest of this paper is structured as follows. In Sect. 2, we give an overview of WSDL and its extensions by citing several research works. Section 3 presents our new Cloud-WSDL metamodel based on WSDL and GCSD. In Sect. 4, we compare the proposed extension with the existing services descriptions (WSDL,

OWL-S, WSMO, etc.). Section 5 concludes this study and provides several perspectives.

2 Background and Related Work

In this section, we give an overview on WSDL and present the main alternatives for its extensions.

2.1 WSDL

WSDL language is a W3C standard that describes a service through an interface presenting a set of operations and their respective input and output parameters in the form of an XML document. The WSDL interface describes the functionality accomplished by the service (what the service does), but it does not describe how to accomplish this functionality (how the service does it). As shown in Fig. 1, the WSDL document contains 5 kinds of XML elements: *<types>*, *<message>*, *<portType>*, *<binding>* and *<service>*.

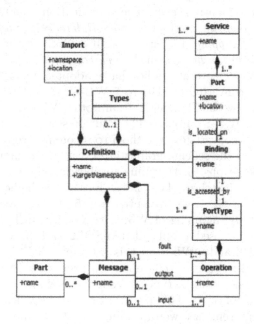

Fig. 1. Metamodel of WSDL

The information contained in WSDL essentially corresponds to the description of the functional profile of the service. With WSDL, the client can invoke the service by referring to the information in its WSDL file, providing information on its abstract description (available methods, input and output parameters, etc.) and its concrete description (description of communication protocols, service access points, etc.). The main problem with WSDL is its limitation to characterize the semantics of the functionality accomplished by the service. To overcome the lack of semantics of WSDL, several approaches have been proposed to add a layer on top of WSDL supplementing the syntactic description by semantic precision. We detail the best known approaches and show their limitations.

2.2 Semantic Extensions

To overcome the semantic limitation of WSDL, several researchers have been provided in the literature.

On one hand, some of them adopted *semantic annotations*. These consist in enriching and completing the description of a service by establishing correspondences between elements of the WSDL description and concepts of a set of reference ontologies (OWL-S [19], WSMO [20], etc.). In [1], the authors have proposed WSDL-S. It consists in annotating the WSDL specification by ontological concepts. Its meta-model allows the addition of 3 elements: $<category>$, $<precondition>$, $<effect>$ and 2 attributes *modelReference* and *schemaMapping*. In [2], the authors have proposed SAWSDL, which is also an extension of WSDL to cover the semantic aspect. The specification annotates a WSDL 2.0 document with the following attributes: *modelReference, liftingSchemaMapping*, and *loweringSchemaMapping*. In particular, it annotates the elements: *operations, input, output, type schemas*, and *interfaces*.

On the other hand, several studies have adopted OWL-S language. The authors of [3] have converted WSDL to OWL-S. They have proposed a service annotation framework. The idea is to annotate WSDL service descriptions with metadata from OWL-S ontology. The solution starts by aligning concepts of WSDL with OWL. It converts each of them to a common representation (called schema Graph). After the schema graphs are created, the matching algorithms are executed on the graphs to determine similarities. So, once the concepts of the schema graph are matched, the concept having the highest matching score is chosen. Likewise for the work presented in [15]. Other researchers aimed at proposing an automatic mapping of WSDL to OWL-S such as [7,8,18]. In [7], Paolucci et al. have proposed a tool called WSDL2OWL-S, which allows a transition between WSDL and OWL-S. In this attempt, all XSD complex types of WSDL are converted to generate concepts and properties for each type. In this approach, the conversion of XSD types to concepts is done without any relationships between these concepts. This manner of conversion leads to use a lot of concepts and missing semantic web meaning. Another interesting work is presented in [8] where a mapping tool called ASSAM (*Automated Semantic Service Annotation with Machine Learning*) is proposed. ASSAM helps to convert the WSDL file into OWL-S file. It suffers from some limitations: ASSAM cannot provide an organization for the used ontologies, which provides a great number of returned concepts. The list of concepts is found based on the text search and not on the meaning. Also, the concepts provided to users are not ranked by importance. Sagayara et al. [18] have worked on the automatic transformation of complex type WSDL to OWL-S. They have proposed an WO framework which helps to extract the elements from WSDL document and place them, by using OWL-parser, in OWL-S. However, the proposed framework does not modify the concepts after their conversion.

2.3   Non-functional Properties Extensions

Other attempts to enrich WSDL files not only by considering the semantic level in the description of services but also by taking into account the non-functional aspect, like WS-Policy standard [4]. In [5], D'Ambrogio et al. have proposed an extension called P-WSDL (*Performance-enabled WSDL*) which enriches WSDL with several performance properties of Web services. They have followed MDA principle and proposed a metamodel transformation. El Bitar et al. [6] have proposed a semantic description model aligned with standards for the automatic discovery of Web services. They rely on WSDL 2.0 standard and WS-Policy. Also, the work of [16] has proposed an extension, called Q-WSDL, to describe QoS characteristics of a Web service. The authors have followed the principle of MDA for Q-WSDL according to a meta-model transformation. Chabeb et al. [17] have proposed YASA4WSDL (*Yet Another Semantic Annotation for WSDL*) which is an extension of SAWSDL that uses two types of ontologies: (i) *Technical Ontology* which contains concepts defining semantics of services, their QoS.; and, (ii) *Domain Ontology* which contains the concepts defining the semantics of the business domain. However, these approaches have addressed, most of the time, some non-functional properties namely response time, availability, cost and they dismiss the other ones (reputations, risk evaluation, actors, usage license, etc.) which help users to select the suitable service.

2.4   Discussion

As mentioned previously, various extensions of WSDL have been proposed. As depicted in Table 1, most of them have tried to enhance the description from the technical and operational aspects (functional properties) [1–3, 5–8, 15–18]. While, others have added the non-functional properties [4–6, 16, 17] and the semantic aspect [1–3, 6–8, 15, 17, 18]. However, all these approaches are still inappropriate to cloud computing domain. Indeed, they don't cover cloud characteristics such as: delivery model (SaaS, PaaS, IaaS), deployment model (public, private, hybrid, and community), cloud provider, used resources (RAM size, CPU brand, virtual machine type, etc.), etc. Besides, they don't take into account the contextual information.

Therefore, we aim to enhance WSDL in order to propose a new service description suitable for cloud computing and which is able to support technical, operational, business, semantic and contextual aspects.

Table 1. Comparison between studied approaches.

Approaches	(1)	(2)	(3)	(4)	(5)
[1]	✓			✓	
[2]	✓			✓	
[3]	✓			✓	
[4]		✓			
[5]	✓	✓			
[6]	✓	✓		✓	
[7]	✓			✓	
[8]	✓			✓	
[15]	✓			✓	
[16]	✓	✓			
[17]	✓	✓		✓	
[18]	✓			✓	

(1) Functional properties / (2) Non-functional properties / (3) Cloud characteristics / (4) Semantic aspect / (5) Contextual information

3   Our Proposal: Cloud-WSDL Metamodel

In this section, we will present Cloud-WSDL, our extension for WSDL to cope with Cloud Service Description. We will start by giving an overview of GCSD, the core of Cloud-WSDL before detailing our proposal.

3.1   Overview of GCSD

We have proposed in a previous work [9] GCSD, a *Generic Cloud Service Description*, which is based on USDL language [10]. The proposed description has been designed in the form of an OWL ontology to cover the semantic aspect. Besides, it supports the technical, operational and business properties, which offer more expressiveness compared to WSDL, OWL-S and WSMO languages. Thus, this universal description resolves the interoperability problem.

We recall, in Fig. 2, the metamodel of GCSD in the form of UML class diagram. This metamodel shows the characteristics related to cloud computing such as *delivery model, deployment model, etc.*, etc. Besides, it includes information about the context of service usage (time of service availability, service location, agents participating in the service lifecycle, resources used to create and consume the service, etc.). Furthermore, it covers multiple non-functional properties (*PricePlan, reputation, risk, security*, etc.).

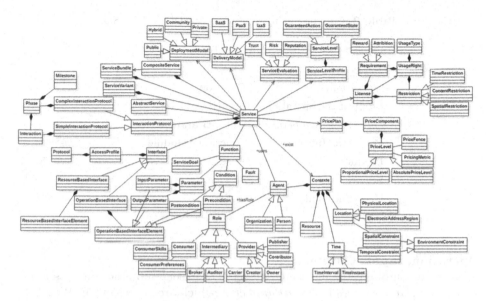

Fig. 2. Metamodel of GCSD [9].

3.2 Adopted Methodology

As mentioned previously, WSDL provides information on how to interact with a service in a functional and technical manner such as operations, inputs, outputs and default parameters. However, it cannot support the semantics nor describe the non-functional properties (service QoS). Besides, WSDL cannot allow the notation of goals, precondition and postcondition. To cope with these issues, we propose a new extension of WSDL that enriches it with the OWL cloud ontology. We rely on SAWSDL (*Semantic Annotations for WSDL*), which annotates a WSDL 2.0 document by using three attributes *modelReference*, *liftingSchemaMapping* and *loweringSchemaMapping*. *modelReference* allows to annotate interface, operation, fault elements of WSDL 2.0. The annotation is in the form: *sawsdl:modelReference = "OntologyNameConcept"*.

In this work, we follow two steps to enhance WSDL with GCSD: (i) Step 1: annotating the elements of WSDL by concepts of the cloud ontology GCSD when a matching exists between them; and, (ii) Step 2: adding new elements to WSDL with concepts and attributes of the cloud ontology.

Step 1: Annotating WSDL Document by GCSD

The idea, here, is to find and align the WSDL elements corresponding to the GCSD concepts according to Table 2. GCSD is in the form of an OWL ontology.

Table 2. Correspondences between WSDL and GCSD.

WSDL	Cloud ontology (GCSD)
Types	–
Operation	Function
Input of the operation	InputParameter
Output of the operation	OutputParameter
PortType/Interface	FunctionalModule
Binding	AccessProfile
Service	Service
Port/Endpoint	urlService

Operation, Input, Output

In the cloud ontology, the functional aspect is represented by the concepts *Function, InputParameter* and *OutputParameter*, which are equivalent in WSDL to *Operation, input, output* elements. Therefore, we annotate:

- *Operation* element with *Function concept* (see Fig. 3, line 24),
- *input* element by *InputParameter* concept (see Fig. 3, line 25), and
- *output* element by *OutputParameter* concept (see Fig. 3, line 26).

```
23    <interface name="" sawsdl:modelReference="CloudOntology#FunctionalModule">
24        <operation name="" sawsdl:modelReference="CloudOntology#Function">
25            <input message="" sawsdl:modelReference="CloudOntology#InputParameter"/>
26            <output message="" sawsdl:modelReference="CloudOntology#OutputParameter"/>
27            <preconditon name="" sawsdl:modelReference="CloudOntology#PreCondition"/>
28            <postconditon name="" sawsdl:modelReference="CloudOntology#PostCondition"/>
29            <goal name="" sawsdl:modelReference="CloudOntology#UserGoal"/>
30        </operation>
31    </interface>
32    <binding name="" type="" sawsdl:modelReference="CloudOntology#AccessProfil">
33        <soap:binding style="rpc" transport="http://schemas.xmlsoap.org/soap/http" />
34        <operation name="">
35            <soap:operation soapAction="" />
36            <input>
37                <soap:body encodingStyle="" namespace="" use="" />
38            </input>
39            <output>
40                <soap:body encodingStyle="" namespace="" use="" />
41            </output>
42        </operation>
43    </binding>
```

Fig. 3. Annotation of WSDL document by the cloud ontology (GCSD).

Interface/PortType

The functionalities of a service are defined through a set of operations which are regrouped into an element named "Interface" or "PortType" without specifying the means (the protocol) for exchanging messages. That is why, we consider the concept FunctionalModule of the GCSD ontology equivalent to "Interface/PortType". Thus, we annotate the element Interface/PortType by the concept *FunctionalModule* (see Fig. 3, line 23).

Binding

The concept *Protocol* covers information about technologies used in the communication with the service (transport protocols, messaging protocols, etc.), which is equivalent to *Binding* element of WSDL. So, we annotate the element *Binding* by the concept *AccessProfile* (see Fig. 3, line 32).

Step 2: Adding New Elements to WSDL Document

Figure 4 shows the metamodel of WSDL after extension where all the important concepts have been added: actors (blue color), contextual information (pink color), pricing information (green color), legal aspect (orange color), SLA (purple color), cloud-specific information (delivery models (red color), deployment models (red color), service evaluation (yellow color), etc.).

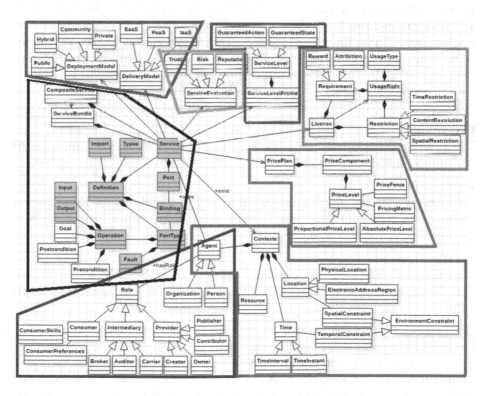

Fig. 4. New metamodel of WSDL after enhancement.

We can categorize the new WSDL metamodel, introduced in Fig. 4, into:

- **Functional properties:** *Service, Definition, Import, Types, Operation, Input, Output, Precondition, Postconditon, Goal, Port, Binding, PortType, Fault, CompositeService, ServiceBundle, Resource.*
- **Non-functional properties:**
  - *DeploymentModel* (Public, Private, Hybrid, Community),
  - *DeliveryModel* (SaaS, PaaS, IaaS),
  - *PricePlan* (PriceComponent, PriceLevel, ProportionalPriceLevel, AbsolutePriceLevel, PriceFence, PriceMetric),
  - *ServiceLevelProfile* (ServiceLevel, GuaranteedAction, GuaranteedState),
  - *License* (Requirement, Reward, Attribution, UsageRight, Restriction, TimeRestriction, ContentRestriction, SpatialRestriction),
  - *ServiceEvaluation* (Trust, Risk, Reputation),
- **Contextual properties:** *Context, Agent, Resource, Location, Time, etc.*

Resource is considered also as a functional property, because, in the case of an IaaS service, a user looks for a service which has storage size equal to "500 GB", RAM equal to "4 GB" and CPU kind is "Intel Xeon".

In the following, we explain each new added element.

A. Functional Properties

The goal, precondition and postcondition elements deemed essential for the service discovery. These three elements complete the description of each operation, while remaining compliant with the WSDL standard. Thus, we add to Operation element of WSDL some sub-elements "precondition", "postcondition", "Goal" and we annotate them by the concepts "PreCondition", "PostCondition" and "UserGoal" from the cloud ontology (see Fig. 3 lines 27, 28 and 29 and Fig. 4).

Precondition

The concept *Precondition* indicates the conditions to be checked in order to execute the operation as expected.

Postcondition

The concept *Postcondition* allows users to define conditions on the expected results of the requested operation. Its value must be true after the execution of an operation of the service description.

Goal

Goal represents the consumer purpose which enhances the discovery process to find the appropriate service whenever two services have the same inputs and outputs.

B. Non-functional Properties

Since WSDL cannot describe the non-functional properties (price, evaluation, legal aspect, SLA, etc.), we added to WSDL metamodel information about consumption pricing, legal aspect, SLA, reputation, trust, risk, etc. The new information enhances the service discovery process, and thus, meets the user request easily. All these properties are explained in a detailed manner in our previous work [9].

Pricing: *PricePlan* includes one or more *PriceComponent* associated with different capabilities related to various pricing aspects. *PriceComponent* has monetary value specified via *PriceLevel* which can be fixed per measure (*AbsolutePriceLevel*) or proportional to a some base (*RelativePriceLevel*). *PriceLevel* has *PriceMetric* as a measurement on which pricing is defined. The dynamic variations of Pricing (such as rewards statutes of consumer, bundled deals, and other accepted negotiations with consumer) are supported through *PriceFence*.

Service Evaluation: *ServiceEvaluation* includes *Reputation*, *Trust* and *Risk*. *Reputation* helps to measure the reputation after service usage from the feedback of users. *Risk* helps to measure the risk produced by the service.

Legal: Each service should be licensed (*License*). The license includes *UsageRight* which is composed of *UsageType*. This latter puts a well-defined manner of how to use a service (such as the right to distribute). All these properties help users to easily select the suitable services.

C. Contextual Information

A service exists in a context (*Context*). For that, a connection between *Service* and *Context* should be established. However, the context includes *services, agents, resources, location,* and *time.*

Resource concept represents different real-world objects types such as application, system, tool used to perform a service. These resources may be, in cloud computing, storage, CPU, RAM, etc. *Location* covers both physical and virtual addresses (for example, a location of service availability or a valid area for a specific price). *Time* provides means to express (for example, a service availability or a period of prices validity, etc.). The precision of time of service usage or the service location helps to precise the research space of services. Thus, we can say that the contextual information enhances the result of the service discovery.

WSDL is poor from information about context. Therefore, we add these missing information to WSDL metamodel in a detailed manner as depicted in Fig. 4.

4   Comparison Between Cloud-WSDL and Other Description Languages

Based on the literature, we present in Table 3 a comparison between WSDL, OWL-S, WSMO and our proposed extension Cloud-WSDL according to some criteria (functional properties, non-functional properties, semantic aspect, cloud computing, contextual information, etc.).

We notice that Cloud-WSDL can handle in a better way cloud computing. Unlike the other existing descriptions languages (WSDL, OWL-S and WSMO), it takes into consideration several criteria: (i) functional and non-functional properties such as input, output, precondition, postcondition, effect, assumption, actor; (iii) cloud characteristics (deployment model, delivery model, SLA, license, etc.); (iii) semantic aspect; and, (iv) contextual aspect.

Table 3. Comparison between WSDL, OWL-s, WSMO and Cloud-WSDL.

Criteria	WSDL	OWL-S	WSMO	Cloud-WSDL
(1)	Operation	AtomicProcess	Choreogaphy	Function
	Input	Input		InputParameter
	Output	Output		OutputParameter
		Precondition	Precondition	Precondition
			PostCondition	PostCondition
		Result	Effect	Effect
			Assumption	Assumption
		CompositeService	Orchestration	CompositeService
	Fault	Fault		Fault
(2)		Participant, Provider, Consumer, physicalAddress, email, phone, fax, WebURL	Owner, Creator	Provider, Creator, Owner, Consumer, Role, Agent, Person, Organization, PricePlan, ServiceLevelProfile, License, ServiceEvaluation
(3)				*Resource* (OS, CPU, RAM, Storage), *DeploymentModel* (Public, Private, Hybrid, Community), *DeliveryModel* (SaaS, PaaS, IaaS)
(4)				Context, Agent, Resource, Location, Time, etc.
(5)		✓	✓	✓

(1) Functional properties / (2) Non-functional properties / (3) Cloud characteristics / (4) Contextual information / (5) Semantic aspect

5 Conclusion

WSDL is the popular language used to describe Web services. However, it covers only the functional properties of services and lacks semantic aspect. Also, it can't cover the non-functional properties and the contextual information. Furthermore, WSDL isn't dedicated to cloud computing not support its characteristics. To overcome these shortages, we enhance, in this paper, WSDL with our Generic Cloud Service Description (GCSD). The new extension supports functional and non-functional properties, contextual information, cloud characteristics and the semantic aspect. The proposed WSDL extension ensures a high interoperability and improves the result of service discovery. In our future work, we aim to propose a transformation rules based on our current work. Also, we aim to propose, based on our generic cloud services description, two new extensions by enhancing OWL-S and WSMO and make them appropriate for cloud computing domain.

References

1. Akkiraju, R., Farrell, J., Miller, J.: Web Service Semantics - WSDL-S. A joint UGA-IBM Technical Note, version 1.0, Technical report, UGA-IBM, April 2005

2. Farrell, J., Lausen, H.: Semantic Annotations for WSDL and XML Schema, W3C recommendation (2007). http://www.w3.org/TR/sawsdl/
3. Patil, A.A., Oundhakar, S.A., Sheth, A.P.: Meteor-s web service annotation framework. In: 13th International Conference on World Wide Web, pp. 553–562 (2004)
4. Vedamuthu, A., Orchard, D., Hirsch, F.: Web Services policy 1.5 - Framework, W3C recommendation (2007). http://www.w3.org/TR/ws-policy/
5. D'Ambrogio, A.: A WSDL extension for performance-enabled description of web services. In: Yolum, I., Güngör, T., Gürgen, F., Özturan, C. (eds.) ISCIS 2005. LNCS, vol. 3733, pp. 371–381. Springer, Heidelberg (2005). https://doi.org/10.1007/11569596_40
6. El Bitar, I., Belouadha, F-Z, Roudies, O.: Towards a semantic description model aligned with W3C standards for WS automatic discovery. In: 2014 International Conference on Multimedia Computing and Systems (ICMCS), 14–16 April 2014, Marrakech, Morocco. IEEE (2014)
7. Paolucci, M., Srinivasan, N., Sycara, K.: Towards a semantic choreography of web services: from WSDL to DAML-S. In: The International Conference on Web Services, pp. 22–26. IEEE (2003)
8. Heß, A., Johnston, E., Kushmerick, N.: ASSAM: a tool for semi-automatically annotating semantic web services. In: The 12th International Conference of Web Technologies, pp. 470–475 (2008)
9. Ghazouani, S., Slimani, Y.: Towards a standardized cloud service description based on USDL. J. Syst. Softw. **132**, 1–20 (2017)
10. Barros, A., Oberle, D.: Handbook of Service Description: USDL and Its Methods. Springer, New York (2012). https://doi.org/10.1007/978-1-4614-1864-1
11. Liu, D., Zic, J.: Cloud#: a specification language for modeling cloud. In: 2011 IEEE International Conference on Cloud Computing (CLOUD), Washington, DC, 4–9 July, pp. 533–540. IEEE (2011)
12. Hamdaqa, M., Livogiannis, T., Tahvildari, L.: A reference model for developing cloud applications. In: 1st International Conference on Cloud Computing and Services Science, pp. 98–103. SciTePress (2011)
13. Sun, L., Ma, J., Wang, H.: Cloud service description model: an extension of USDL for cloud services. IEEE Trans. Serv. Comput. **11**(2), 354–368 (2015)
14. Galan, F., Sampaio, A., Rodero-Merino, L.: Service specification in Cloud environments based on extensions to open standards. In: 4th International ICST Conference on COMmunication System softWAre and middlewaRE (COMSWARE 2009), New York, USA, no. 19, pp. 1–12. ACM (2009)
15. Le, D., Nguyen, V., Goh, A.: Matching WSDL and OWL-S web services. In: IEEE International Conference on Semantic Computing, Berkeley, CA, pp. 197–202 (2009)
16. D'Ambrogio, A.: A model-driven WSDL extension for describing the QoS of web services. In: IEEE International Conference on Web Services, pp. 789–796 (2006)
17. Chabeb, Y., Tata, S.: Yet another semantic annotation for WSDL. In: IADIS International Conference, Freiburg, Germany, pp. 437–441 (2008)
18. Sagayaraj, S., Santhoshkumar, M.: Transformation of complex type WSDL into OWL-S for facilitating SWS discovery. Int. J. Inf. Technol. **11**(1), 5–12 (2018). https://doi.org/10.1007/s41870-018-0249-2
19. Martin, D., et al.: Bringing semantics to web services: the OWL-S approach. In: Cardoso, Jorge, Sheth, Amit (eds.) SWSWPC 2004. LNCS, vol. 3387, pp. 26–42. Springer, Heidelberg (2005). https://doi.org/10.1007/978-3-540-30581-1_4

20. Roman, D., et al.: WWW: WSMO, WSML, and WSMX in a nutshell. In: Mizoguchi, Riichiro, Shi, Zhongzhi, Giunchiglia, Fausto (eds.) ASWC 2006. LNCS, vol. 4185, pp. 516–522. Springer, Heidelberg (2006). https://doi.org/10.1007/11836025_49

21. Gudenkauf, S., Josefiok, M., Göring, A.: A reference architecture for Cloud service offers. In: 2013 17th IEEE International Enterprise Distributed Object Computing Conference (EDOC), 9–13 September, Vancouver, BC, pp. 227–236. IEEE (2013)

22. Hoefer, C.N., Karagiannis, G.: Taxonomy of cloud computing services. In: 2010 IEEE Globecom Workshops, 6–10 December 2010, pp. 1345–1350. IEEE (2010)

23. Hoberg, P., Wollersheim, J., Krcmar, H.: Service descriptions for cloud services-the customers perspective. In: ConLife Academic Conference (2012)

24. Charfi, A., Schmeling, B., Novelli, F.: An overview of the unified service description language. In: 2010 IEEE 8th European Conference on Web Services (ECOWS), Ayia Napa, 1–3 December, pp. 173–180. IEEE (2010)

25. Shetty, J., D'Mello, D.A.: An XML based data representation model to discover infrastructure services. 2015 International Conference on Smart Technologies and Management for Computing, Communication, Controls, Energy and Materials (ICSTM), Chennai, India, 6–8 May, pp. 119–125. IEEE (2015)

26. Nagireddi, V.S.K., Mishra, S.: An ontology based cloud service generic search engine. In: 2013 8th International Conference on Computer Science & Education (ICCSE), Colombo, 26–28 April, pp. 335–340. IEEE (2013)

27. Tahamtan, A., Beheshti, S.A., Anjomshoaa, A.: A cloud repository and discovery framework based on a unified business and cloud service ontology. In: 2012 IEEE 8th World Congress on Services, Honolulu, Hawaï, 24–29 June, pp. 203–210. IEEE (2012)

28. Alfazi, A., Sheng, Q.Z., Qin, Y.: Ontology-based automatic cloud service categorization for enhancing cloud service discovery. In: 2015 IEEE 19th International on Enterprise Distributed Object Computing Conference (EDOC), Adelaide, Australia, 21–25 September, pp. 151–158. IEEE (2015)

29. Nguyen, D.K., Lelli, F., Papazoglou, M.P.: Blueprinting approach in support of cloud computing. In: Future Internet 2012, 21 March 2012, vol. 4, no. 1, pp. 322–346. Molecular Diversity Preservation International (2012)

30. Nguyen, D.K., Lelli, F., Taher, Y., Parkin, M., Papazoglou, M.P., van den Heuvel, W.-J.: Blueprint template support for engineering cloud-based services. In: Abramowicz, W., Llorente, I.M., Surridge, M., Zisman, A., Vayssière, J. (eds.) ServiceWave 2011. LNCS, vol. 6994, pp. 26–37. Springer, Heidelberg (2011). https://doi.org/10.1007/978-3-642-24755-2_3

Author Index

rinted in the United States
Baker & Taylor Publisher Services